STRUCTURAL CHANGE
IN CENTRAL

This b   ailab.

before the last date st

Edit

Georg

and

Guy Standing

ORGANISATION FOR ECONOMIC CO-OPERATION AND DEVELOPMENT

ORGANISATION FOR ECONOMIC CO-OPERATION AND DEVELOPMENT

Pursuant to Article 1 of the Convention signed in Paris on 14th December 1960, and which came into force on 30th September 1961, the Organisation for Economic Co-operation and Development (OECD) shall promote policies designed:

— to achieve the highest sustainable economic growth and employment and a rising standard of living in Member countries, while maintaining financial stability, and thus to contribute to the development of the world economy;

— to contribute to sound economic expansion in Member as well as non-member countries in the process of economic development; and

— to contribute to the expansion of world trade on a multilateral, non-discriminatory basis in accordance with international obligations.

The original Member countries of the OECD are Austria, Belgium, Canada, Denmark, France, Germany, Greece, Iceland, Ireland, Italy, Luxembourg, the Netherlands, Norway, Portugal, Spain, Sweden, Switzerland, Turkey, the United Kingdom and the United States. The following countries became Members subsequently through accession at the dates indicated hereafter: Japan (28th April 1964), Finland (28th January 1969), Australia (7th June 1971) and New Zealand (29th May 1973). The Commission of the European Communities takes part in the work of the OECD (Article 13 of the OECD Convention).

The Czech Republic, Hungary, Poland and the Slovak Republic participate in the OECD Programme "Partners in Transition", which is managed by the Centre for Co-operation with Economies in Transition.

FOREWORD

The International Labour Organisation (ILO), with its unique tripartite structure and 165 member States, brings together worker, employer and government representatives to improve labour standards and to promote employment, social justice and better living conditions world-wide. The ILO has launched a broad range of activities to assist Central and Eastern European countries in coping with unemployment and other social problems created by drastic economic change and to help build and strengthen new social institutions that sustain democracy.

The Centre for Co-operation with Economies in Transition (CCET), created in March 1990, is a focal point for co-operation between the Organisation for Economic Co-operation and Development (OECD) and Central and Eastern European countries and the former Soviet Union. Its major responsibility is to design and manage a programme of policy advice, technical assistance and training which puts the expertise of the Secretariat and Member countries at the disposal of countries engaged in economic reform.

In the framework of the CCET's work programme, the OECD's Directorate for Education, Employment, Labour and Social Affairs and the ILO jointly organised a High-Level Conference on Labour and Social Implications of Structural Change in Central and Eastern Europe in September 1991. The Conference was attended by government officials, experts from the social partners and labour market analysts from Bulgaria, the former Czech and Slovak Federal Republic, Hungary, Poland, Romania and the former Soviet Union.

One of the Conference's main messages was that human resource policies should be given high priority as they have a threefold role to play in the transition process. First, by developing the human capital and establishing industrial relations that promote co-operation between the economic agents, they can improve the longer-term economic performance of Central and Eastern European countries. Secondly, they have a crucial role to play in the strengthening of pluralistic democracy, by allowing democratically elected governments to transform the requests of their people into policies and by improving the forms of representation of the interests of the social partners. Thirdly and most urgently, in the absence of a quick and effective policy response to the emergence of major social and labour market problems at the beginning of transition, there is a risk that the ongoing economic reform process may be impeded, delayed or some steps even reversed.

This book, edited by Georg Fischer of the OECD and Guy Standing of the ILO, is a selection of papers presented at the conference. It is published on the responsibility of the Secretary-General of the OECD.

Heribert Maier   Salvatore Zecchini
Deputy Director-General ILO   Assistant Secretary-General OECD
                                                        Director of the CCET

Publications in the CCEET Series

Employment and Unemployment in Economies in Transition:
Conceptual and Measurement Issues Format 16X23 (1993)
(14 93 05 1) ISBN 92-64-13910-9   FF110   US$26.00   DM45

Bulgaria - An Economic Assessment
1992 Format 16X23
(14 92 05 1) ISBN 92-64-13753-X   FF90   US$23.00   DM37

Romania - An Economic Assessment
1993 Format 16X23
(14 93 08 1) ISBN 92-64-13939-7   FF110   US$26.00   DM40

OECD Economic Surveys/CCEET. 1991-1992 Series: Poland
(1992) Format 16X23
(09 92 03 1) ISBN 92-64-13723-8   FF90   US$20.00   DM37

Hungary (1991) Format 16X23
(09 92 01 1) ISBN 92-64-13554-5   FF90   US$20.00   DM37

Czech and Slovak Federal Republic (1991) Format 16X23
(09 92 02 1) ISBN 92-64-13607-X   FF90   US$20.00   DM37

Price for the three surveys: Hungary, Poland,
Czech and Slovak Federal Republic   FF230   US$52.00   DM95

Short-Term Economic Indicators Central and Eastern Europe. No.2
(1993) (Bilingual) Format 16X23.
(07 93 02 3) ISBN 92-64-03867-1   FF 40   US$ 9.00   DM16

Prices charged at the OECD Bookshop. THE OECD CATALOGUE OF PUBLICATIONS and
supplements will be sent free of charge on request addressed either to the OECD Publications Service
or to the Distributor in your country.

TABLE OF CONTENTS

CHAPTER 8

Women's employment in central and eastern Europe: Status and prospects

CHAPTER 9

Labour market developments and policies in central and eastern Europe:
A comparative analysis

Rapporteurs' Reports:

Annex:

Chapter 1

Policy Issues of the Emerging Labour Markets of central and eastern Europe

by
Guy Standing and Georg Fischer

I. Introduction

After the exhilarating days of 1989 and 1990, a more sombre mood of consolidation spread across central and eastern Europe in 1991, as the enormity of the structural challenge facing a new generation of political leaders and policy-makers was realised. The break-up of the Soviet Union may well bring long-term economic regeneration, but in the immediate future the deep decline in national income and in living standards will almost certainly continue. The economic woes have been made worse by regional and subregional social tensions that have made the prospect of an economic upturn in 1992 hard to predict with confidence.

Across central and eastern Europe, 1989-91 was undoubtedly a period of learning and experimentation. With the slow emergence of new institutions and independent organisations of employers and workers, this learning process has had to compress into as short a time as possible a vast array of policy changes that took the Western industrialised countries four decades or more to develop. But, whereas in the first flush of the transition it was understandable that in some countries policy-makers were inclined to do little more than copy systems and laws from specific western European and North American countries, it could be expected that there would be a growing desire to adopt reforms more in tune with their own cultures and social structures. No country has the perfect set of laws and social institutions that may simply be transposed to another country.

The transition strategy has often been characterised in terms of a "big bang" versus a gradual approach. No doubt this characterisation is simplistic, yet it might serve to depict two polar tendencies in competition, from which a wide range of compromise structures could emerge. The underlying debate is between the "decentralised market" and "regulated market" approaches. The exact role of the State continues to be at the heart of the debate. It is surely not good enough to talk of a "market economy" ; the issue is what type of market, presuming that everybody in the policy mainstream recognises

7

the virtue of market mechanisms. But by what type of institutions and regulations will labour market mechanisms be mediated? All western industrialised countries have introduced institutional, legislative and legal forms of regulation, including provisions for collective bargaining, and legislation on labour contracts, working time, occupational health and social security.

The labour market dilemma can be seen in the context of, for example, the United Nations Universal Declaration of Human Rights and the ILO's Declaration of Philadelphia of 1944, in which it is stated unequivocally that "labour is not a commodity". It is intriguing that these principles were established at a time in the 1940s when the western countries were in a somewhat analogous phase of rekindling and strengthening democracy. Such principles imply that protective regulations and institutional safeguards should modify pure market forces, by limiting labour market insecurities and by promoting a spirit of social consensus and negotiations, rather than one of unbridled reliance on pure market forces. At the same time, the new regulatory frameworks and institutional structures will have to be flexible and promote economic growth, productivity and international competitiveness. This tension has preoccupied labour analysts in the industrialised market economies over the past decade and is now at the heart of the pro-market reforms in central and eastern Europe. This is the background against which debates over labour market and social policy can be interpreted.

The following sections are intended to review the main issues in the spheres of the labour market, industrial relations and social policy in the near future. Any such exercise risks the twin threat of appearing little more than a "shopping list" and of superficiality coupled with excessive generalisation. The following focuses on the major issues in the restructuring period, rather than on longer-term reforms and the type of labour market and social structure beyond it.

II. Recent labour market developments in central and eastern Europe

In 1990-91, the central and eastern European economies were hit by a cruel combination of economic factors that made structural adjustment much harder to achieve. The enormous declines in gross domestic product (GDP) in 1990 and 1991 have to be seen in the context of the collapse of trade among these countries themselves, the inflationary and recessionary impact of energy price rises as a result of the Gulf war and the adverse effects of the recession in the industrialised market economies. At the end of the 1980s, GDP per capita in central and eastern Europe overall was probably no more than one-eighth of the average in the rest of Europe. Yet in 1990 real GDP in the whole region fell by over 7 %, and in 1991 it almost certainly fell by well over 10 %.[1] In Bulgaria, it fell by as much as 20 %, in the former German Democratic Republic output probably shrank by over 25 % while in the ex-USSR the fall was probably much higher. In no country in the region did real GDP rise in 1991, and for much of 1992 the declines are likely to continue.

These stark realities would have caused severe labour market problems in any country, whatever the structural adjustment strategy. Yet despite the enormous declines in aggregate economic output, the overall decline in employment in 1990-91 was *relatively* modest. Although there would also have been a lag in the fall in employment, had such declines in national income occurred in industrialised market economies, the cutback in jobs and the rise in unemployment would have long since raised the spectre of the Great Depression. *By the end of 1991*, that had not happened in central and eastern

8

Europe. However, with the gathering pace of privatisation and the decline of the famous "soft budget" constraint, a spate of redundancies from state enterprises in all countries of the region was beginning to push unemployment remorselessly upwards.

In one sense, massive labour shedding is essential. Without it, productivity levels will remain dismally low, economic growth will be curtailed and the expansion of new industries oriented to consumer goods and services will be unduly constrained. In 1989 and 1990, the rise in unemployment came mainly from a combination of a slow decline in employment and an influx of new labour force entrants. In 1991-92, dis-employment became the dominant factor. Thus, for example, Alexander Shokhin, the Russian Minister of Labour appointed in August 1991, forecast in November 1991 that in the ex-USSR about 30 million workers would lose their jobs in the next year or so and that up to 15 million people would become *long-term* unemployed.

Since the late 1980s, structural changes in central and eastern European economies have taken several forms, each of which accelerated in 1991. The state sector, although still the overriding source of production, income and employment, has shrunk, while — however haltingly — the private economy has been growing. *Privatisation* initially occurred more as a result of internal restructuring of industrial enterprises and the emergence of small-scale enterprises, co-operatives (in some countries) or joint ventures than by explicit privatisation of state enterprises through direct legislation. The latter form accelerated in 1991, as evidenced by legislation in Romania, Czechoslovakia and elsewhere. Thus, for instance, over 900 state enterprises were privatised in Poland during the year. However, by the end of 1991 the shift from state to private sector production and employment had come primarily from new sources of jobs outside the economically stagnant or sharply declining state sectors. The employment cuts in the latter sphere had greatly outweighed the absolute growth of jobs in the former.

Privatisation has also taken the form of conversion of state enterprises into joint ventures with foreign firms; this has established an intriguing pluralism of competing employment practices and industrial relations at the enterprise level. It has also been seen in the growth of small-scale firms, most in the retail trade sector. One of the biggest questions in late 1991 was : What should be done with the large state enterprises that have dominated the industrial landscape of central and eastern Europe over the past 40 years ? Clearly, alternative approaches were being pursued in the different countries of the region. For instance, in Hungary it was likely that many of these would be transferred into joint ventures with foreign capital ; in Czechoslovakia, Poland and Romania it was more likely that ownership rights would to some extent be distributed to the population through ESOPS (Employee Share Ownership Plans), voucher schemes and other forms of employee capital. Without making any judgement on the respective merits of the various forms of privatisation, it is important to consider whether the choice will have different labour market implications, or require distinctive labour and social policies.

Other aspects of the economic restructuring will also shape labour market developments. For some years, there will be mass labour mobility out of agriculture, which was a labour reservoir for years, absorbing much larger proportions of the labour force than was typical in industrialised market economies. There has also been a start made in the considerable shift needed from heavy industries — "material production" — to consumer goods and services. There has also been the beginning of a move within manufacturing away from the military industrial complex towards high-technology light industry.

The difficulty is that by the end of 1991 new investment in the *potential* growth sectors in most of the countries had been sluggish, as had the adoption of more up-to-date technology and production structures. Many of the new jobs in the 1990s will probably be in new small-scale firms and in self-employment, as has been the case in Hungary, perhaps the country most advanced in its restructuring. Although earnings may be relatively high in the new small-scale concerns compared with the old state sector, employment in them under conditions of wage labour or self-employment will mostly be precarious, posing further problems for labour and social policy-makers. Some jobs in small-scale businesses will offer very good incomes and benefits, but most will not.

One issue has received insufficient attention, although it is by no means unique to the region. In all countries, much of the new economic activity has taken place outside the "formal" sphere. "Parallel", "black" or "second" economy work has long supplemented work in state enterprises, and while in some countries there has been a legitimisation of many of these activities with growing pluralism, in others there are signs that such illegal activities have grown dramatically. Although we make little further reference to this, it does have implications for some types of labour market and social protection policy. It is also, of course, related to the problem of rising unemployment.

Unemployment

Although it might have been expected to rise even more, a major labour market development of 1991 was the growth of *unemployment*. The situation will become much worse before it begins to improve, and unemployment will be boosted not just by the stabilisation and privatisation measures, which lead to labour shedding from moribund state enterprises, but by trade liberalisation, which has led to a rapid rise in imports.

As the following chapters show, in most central and eastern European countries (CEECs) for most of 1991 unemployment remained fairly low by the standards of western Europe in the 1980s and 1990s, but it was the rate of increase that was alarming. Most of the six economies will experience double digit rates of unemployment in 1992, and the levels will rise to well above 10 % in areas affected by industrial restructuring, for which in 1991 there were already reports of unemployment rates up to 40 %. In eastern Germany, the unemployment rate was over 14 %, by the end of 1991 while a further 15 % of the labour force were working short time.[2] In Poland, the official registered unemployment rate had risen to well over 10 % by the end of 1991, and was close to that in Bulgaria, Czechoslovakia and Hungary. In Poland, the number of registered unemployed passed the two million mark in November 1991, representing 11.1 % of the active population. In the ex-USSR, official fears of up to 30 million unemployed in 1992, mentioned earlier, represented both a daunting prospect and an indication of the uncertainty among officials tackling the new realities.

Responding to unemployment will be a high priority in 1992. It is probable that the period of high unemployment will not be short and transitional, but will last many years, probably at rates over 15 %. Can that be prevented ? And if the period is lengthy, what will be the labour market and social effects ? The double digit unemployment rates over some five to ten years in certain western European countries which pursued economic restructuring in the 1980s, and where labour market mechanisms are relatively well developed must be worrying for policy-makers facing a period of restructuring without such well-established mechanisms to facilitate necessary labour mobility and employment regeneration.

In tracking what is happening to unemployment, it must be stressed that the *statistical information* available is very patchy. The main reason is that as unemployment was scarcely recognised as legitimate in the old "full employment" system, there was little perceived need to measure its level or incidence. Moreover, networks of employment exchanges did not exist, so that jobseekers could not "register" as looking for work. In 1990-91, statistical offices throughout central and eastern Europe came to terms with conceptualising and measuring unemployment, and the sample surveys being launched should become a valuable means of generating labour market information with which to formulate policies for dealing with emerging unemployment. Besides chronicling the immediate labour market outcomes of the restructuring process, such data are essential for *monitoring* and *evaluating* the direct and indirect effects of new labour market policies, vital if such policies are to be efficient.

Labour market-related poverty

The fears associated with rising unemployment would be soothed somewhat if there were a reasonable prospect that those on the margins of the labour market were not going to experience severe financial hardship. This is the crux of the problem. The extent of poverty in most of the region has grown alarmingly. For instance, the number of households in poverty has risen sharply in Bulgaria, Poland, Romania and Czechoslovakia; the real situation is probably much worse than that implied by the official statistics, a point made by Alena Nesporova in relation to Czechoslovakia (Chapter 3). In Bulgaria, by early 1991 over 70 % of all households had incomes below the official social minimum, up from 41 % two years earlier (Chapter 2). In Poland, in 1991 over 40 % of all households were classified as living in poverty, again up sharply from two years earlier (Chapter 5). In the countries of the ex-USSR, prominent economists claimed that by the end of 1991 about 100 million people were living below the official poverty line, with real family incomes in some countries being some 26 % below their level at the beginning of the year.[3] These figures may be approximations, but are alarming, as well as more in line with developing country statistics than to industrialised market economies.

Whatever the criteria for measuring poverty, it is the rate of increase and the lack of effective forms of social protection in the new labour market that are most alarming. One issue is the possibility that the incidence of poverty has become much more related to labour market status and experience. Many people suffering precipitous declines in living standards have been those cut off from the labour force, such as pensioners, but many others have been impoverished as a result of their position in the labour force, in some cases because of their precarious employment, in others because minimum wages have not been applied or because enterprises have been unable to pay even the minimum wages (as in Bulgaria, where the real level of the minimum wage fell by half in the 12 months ending in April 1991).

As the following papers indicate, there is much to be learned about the links between labour market developments, poverty and inequalities. It is essential to identify those links if cost-effective and equitable labour market and social policies are to be formulated.

Regional imbalances

A related labour market aspect of the transition process is the intensification of regional imbalances, particularly with the decline in heavy industries and the accelerating process of industrial conversion. Once again, there are analogies with what happened in parts of western Europe and North America in the early 1980s, where such industries as coalmining, steel, shipbuilding and certain "smokestack" industries went into sharp decline, leading to a cumulative deterioration in the local economy and labour market. Thus, the economic decline of some east European industrial regions may be compounded by the emigration of young, relatively qualified workers, leaving the regions even less attractive for investors and thus intensifying their stagnation. This has already been seen in eastern Germany, where the number employed fell by over two million between late 1989 and mid-1991, in which time over 300,000 workers moved to work in western Germany. In some countries, distress migration may only take on major proportions in 1992, when the shrinking of major smokestack industries and the release of currently subsidised workers become substantial.

As employment falls in the industrial districts it may be the outlying rural areas that most experience the rise in unemployment, since workers previously commuting will stay in their residential rural areas, where the number of agricultural jobs is unlikely to increase.

Labour market segmentation : Marginalisation

As unemployment rises and economic pluralism spreads, labour market stratification and segmentation could become acute, as specific groups face *labour market marginalisation,* pushed into low-income, precarious jobs or out of the labour force altogether. This is a perennial problem of open labour markets in all market economies, and in many parts of central and eastern Europe the fear is that ethnic minorities and non-local residents in areas hit by restructuring could face severe difficulties, particularly if there is a resurgence of nationalism. For instance, the unemployment rate of Gypsies in Slovakia reached 27 % by May 1991, probably four times the rate of other groups in the population.

The following country chapters suggest that various forms of discrimination and segmentation have been developing or are likely to develop. In any market economy, employers use certain rules in their recruitment, training, promotion and retrenchment practices and preferences. This invariably results in different opportunities and forms of labour market disadvantage.

In CEECs, there is extensive anecdotal evidence of the deteriorating experience of minorities, but more detailed data are needed to enable policy-makers to monitor developments adequately. This should help in identifying mechanisms to limit or reverse practices that are leading to the labour segmentation and the marginalisation of particular groups. The industrialised countries have tried a wide range of approaches, including anti-discrimination legislation, positive incentives to hire specific groups, selective wage subsidies and targeted training programmes. No single approach presents a panacea, but the immediate challenge in central and eastern Europe is to identify measures with the best chance of preventing rigid social differentiation from emerging through the operation of market forces. It cannot be presumed that left to itself, the labour market will produce a socially integrated labour force.

Which groups, besides ethnic minorities, are most vulnerable to marginalisation ? We know that, although their position in industrialised market economies may have improved in recent years, *women workers* internationally still face difficulties. In central and eastern Europe, under the old system, women were relatively integrated into the labour force, having high participation rates by international standards, even if opportunities for occupational mobility were far from equitable. There was also concern over women's "double burden", i.e., full-time wage employment and domestic work. A fear now is that women will lose as labour force participants by being converted into "secondary workers", suffering disproportionately from dis-employment and unemployment, being pushed out of the labour force or having their wages and benefits lowered relative to men. In eastern Germany, for instance, women made up 60 % of all the registered unemployed in 1991, and many other women had been eased out of the labour force. The following chapters assess the evidence on similar trends throughout the region, and highlight the need for more information on a deteriorating situation.

As in western Europe, another group hard hit by restructuring and rising unemployment is *older workers,* i.e., those in their fifties and sixties. A long-standing tradition has been for extensive employment of "pensioner workers", to compensate for low pensions. In most CEECs, this has given way to displacement of such workers and more consideration of early retirement schemes. Perhaps the main labour market problem is that older workers may be pushed to the margins of the labour force because of discrimination in hiring and firing, for which there is no justification on efficiency grounds. One way or another though, older workers may find it hard to remain in the economic mainstream or to avoid severe declines in living standards.

The third group of concern is *young people*. There has been a rapid growth of youth unemployment as new employment opportunities have dried up. Because those entering the labour force must possess the skills and aptitudes needed for economic regeneration, it is worrying that a vast number of teenagers could drift into a debilitating period of long-term unemployment, making it hard for them to acquire the necessary abilities to make the transition a success.

Another labour force trend of immediate policy concern is the growth or threat of mass *labour migration.* Data on this are very poor. What is clear is that with rising unemployment and worsening poverty, many workers will move out of old industrial areas, just as millions may wish to cross into western Europe; this will further intensify social tensions and labour market difficulties. This volume is not a forum for discussion of migration *per se.* It is worth recalling that migration was the subject matter of a number of technical and ministerial conferences in the first half of 1991, such as those held in Prague, Rome and Vienna. There are fears that large areas will be depleted of their relatively young and skilled workforce, making it harder to regenerate local economies hit by much higher rates of unemployment than elsewhere. However, migration also brings individual and social benefits that are easily underestimated, in both sending and receiving regions not the least of which are those associated with return migration by those gaining skills and experience.

In the 1990s, labour migration may become the serious phenomenon most analysts expect, given the inadequate employment services, underdeveloped housing markets and the steep decline in incomes. It will be vital to ensure that migrants and potential migrants are not treated as scapegoats or as threats to society, and to recognise that labour mobility is essential for a more flexible labour market and for structural adjustment. It is appropriate to be fearful, in order to be vigilant, since the ethnic character of the probable migration may create a fertile basis for prejudicial and hasty reactions. Prominent among the migrant population will be groups such as the Romanian gypsies, Bulgarian Turks and other ethnic minorities. Many observers predict that international migration will be the most explosive issue in Europe in the 1990s. The fears aroused make it even more important to analyse the labour market implications objectively and extensively.

III. Labour market policies for labour market restructuring

Labour market policies will figure prominently in central and eastern Europe in the next few years, as they have in western Europe over the past decade.[4] They will be expected to (i) cut unemployment, (ii) reduce labour market segmentation and the disadvantaged position of various groups in society, (iii) promote geographical, occupational and industrial mobility, and (iv) raise labour productivity. Underlying everything, they will be expected to move the labour market from overfull, low productivity employment to low unemployment, high productivity employment. The trouble is that so far there has been a wide gap between the rhetoric of government pronouncements and laws, and the reality of limited progress.

In the initial stages of the reform process, the striking feature of government responses has been the passage of comprehensive "framework" employment laws. An early example was the USSR's *Fundamentals of Employment Legislation of the USSR and the Union Republics,* adopted in January 1991, which was intended to come into effect in July 1991 ; individual Republics soon introduced their own versions of an employment law. In Czechoslovakia, the *Law on Employment* was introduced in 1990, and in Hungary the strands of earlier partial reforms were integrated in a comprehensive law on employment introduced in February 1991. Such laws have created the basis for a wide array of labour market policies, ranging from income transfers to public works and labour market retraining schemes. They represent the first steps to a *regulated labour market.*

An initial set of questions to which responses would be valuable for the new authorities concerns the identification of the most appropriate administrative structure. Which level of government should be responsible for the design and implementation of the labour market policies that such framework laws presage ? And should the government alone be responsible or should these policies be determined by some tripartite mechanism, such as those operating in the Nordic countries, for instance ?

The wide range of measures contained in the new employment laws of various CEECs have attempted to match recent policy developments in western Europe, where governments have recognised the importance of a balanced combination of policy measures. Often, labour market policies have been classified as either "passive" or "active", where the former term is taken to imply income transfers and the latter training, job creation and so on. Although the concept of "active" labour market policies has figured prominently in a number of European economies, any rigid classification of active and passive oversimplifies the objectives and implications of most policies. The basic issue is how to develop a policy framework which combines income protection with opportunities for reintegrating the unemployed into productive employment, without contravening the principles of freedom in the labour market. Experience with labour market policy elsewhere suggests that reintegration should start as soon as possible, since difficulties increase disproportionately with the duration of unemployment.

To function adequately, all labour market policies depend crucially on an adequate network of employment exchanges and support services. Nowhere in central and eastern

Europe has such a network existed. Great efforts — and in some cases considerable international financial assistance — have been devoted to developing employment services. The biggest programmes so far have been in eastern Germany and Poland, where a huge project funded by the World Bank is to be launched in 1992. Until employment services have taken shape — and perhaps not even then — it will be hard to estimate accurately the extent of unemployment or to operate conditional unemployment benefits with even reasonable efficiency or equity.

Unemployment benefits as labour market policy

Once governments legitimised unemployment, they were bound to introduce *unemployment benefits,* often through the adoption of benefit systems believed to operate in specific industrialised market economies.

Whether unemployment benefit systems based on social insurance can provide social protection for those most hit by industrial and socioeconomic restructuring, they are part of the armoury of labour market policy. Yet all forms of transfer play multiple roles in the labour market, and may have features designed to increase, reduce or redirect labour supply, or regulate certain forms of economic activity. Unemployment benefits are a typical case of a mechanism with potentially conflicting social and labour market objectives, and as such raise issues for policy-makers in central and eastern Europe that are not as easy to resolve as some statements would suggest. Among these issues are the following :

1. To what extent should unemployment benefits (or other transfers) be conditional on labour market behaviour, such as past work record, reasons for leaving past employment, job-seeking activity, employment exchange registration and wage-job aspirations?

2. Should benefits be paid for a short period only, to induce a quick acceptance of some sort of job? Or for a long period, provided that the unemployed person satisfies specified labour market criteria? Or, as in the United States, for a period that depends in part on the overall level of unemployment?

3. Should there be some "workfare" elements, i.e., an obligation on the unemployed person to perform some work-related activity as a condition for benefit receipt? Would that help to reintegrate the unemployed person into the mainstream labour force? As noted later, we have serious reservations about this approach.

4. Should benefits be provided on a different basis for different groups, on the grounds that, supposedly, they face different opportunities, or have different needs, or could be expected to satisfy labour market behavioural criteria to a different extent from other groups?

The questions are posed starkly, and the theoretical and empirical research on them in the industrialised market countries is extensive and controversial. How such questions are answered will determine the type of labour market that evolves. While most transfers are anything but passive, they *may* be as efficient and equitable as other policies designed to regulate labour force behaviour. Mobility grants, for example, combine income transfers with the possibility of improving labour market efficiency. Whatever the virtues of other types of policy, benefit systems will remain the core of labour market policy.

Besides what have been increasingly conditional ("targeted") unemployment benefits, most countries have been slow to develop income support schemes for vulnerable groups. These schemes require a well-developed employment exchange system, operated by well-qualified staff. Minorities, young people, women with small children, older workers and those physically challenged all face additional employment difficulties likely to require extra financial and direct assistance. This underdevelopment of social welfare is one reason for preferring systems of basic income support that demand few behavioural conditions for entitlement. Complex systems will simply not reach those in need.

Throughout the region, the development of *employment services* will be a major policy priority for some years. Not only were the old employment offices expected to fulfil a different role from the one which employment services are expected to achieve in a well-functioning labour market, but the number of offices and staff were minimal.

It will take many years to implement an effective and equitable network of employment services. However, in the context of labour market policy, it is suggested that the following are the main issues :

1. Fundamentally, what should be the main functions pursued by the employment services?

2. Should the functions of labour market information and career guidance be separated in some clear way from the functions of labour market regulation and, in particular, administration of unemployment benefits?

3. To what extent, and how, should employment services be selective in their treatment of different groups, as they try to reduce labour market segmentation and stratification?

In central and eastern Europe, not only will the nature of the employment services have to change, but it will also take time for them to overcome the stigma associated with having had a peripheral, directional role in the command system. It will be essential to develop employment services in tune with the more flexible, informal labour markets that are likely in the 1990s.

Labour market and on-the-job training

There are great expectations of three forms of government-assisted "skill" formation in order to curb unemployment, raise productivity, increase labour mobility and help to integrate or reintegrate disadvantaged groups in the labour force.

First, there is general and vocational education. In forging economically viable societies, effective "human resource development" strategies will need to be based on broad and flexible educational policies, rather than on systems that direct students to currently available jobs.

The second and third forms are labour market training schemes and on-the-job training and retraining schemes intended to keep workers in employment or to change jobs without a period of unemployment. Much may be said in favour of variants of these policies that have sprung up in recent years in industrialised countries. However, training is not an all-purpose recipe for labour market adjustment.

One difficulty is identifying the type of training needed. Thus, in central and eastern Europe it is widely believed that the level of skills is inadequate for the new types of

16

employment, thereby implying an enormous need for major new training schemes. However, how are the training needs to be identified? If they are not identified, should large amounts of scarce resources be devoted to training programmes?

Certainly, vacancy data are not appropriate guides to training needs or even particularly useful in designing training programmes. In the transition to more open labour markets, training that is oriented to a broad range of qualifications useful in the market economy, and the use of new technologies, will surely yield higher social and individual returns than training oriented to current vacancies.

Experience outside the region suggests that the relatively successful economies have developed training schemes with a view towards long-term technological and industrial restructuring. The question is how to translate this into viable schemes for the unemployed in need of immediate, practical skills.

It is essential to monitor and evaluate labour market training schemes as part of labour market policy, especially as much is expected of the careful allocation of scarce resources. Even in western Europe, proper evaluation of training schemes has been rare. The main reason for caution in advocating massive programmes is the likelihood of extensive "deadweight" and "substitution" effects. Thus, if a government subsidises labour market training, it *may* be unnecessary because the training would have been carried out in any case. It is a deadweight because the resources could have been used in a more productive manner. A substitution or displacement effect arises to the extent that the (unemployed) person who receives the training may merely take the place of someone who was employed or who could have done the job perfectly adequately.

These notes of caution should not be interpreted as "anti-training", merely as a statement that the issue is more open than is often recognised. The reality in the countries under review is that many large industrial enterprises have cut training considerably in response to financial pressures ; some have shut down their training facilities altogether.

In such circumstances, how should governments react? One option would be to detach training institutions from industrial enterprises and to run them directly. The German authorities in 1991 began to use their privatisation agency, the Treuhandanstalt, for this purpose. This may be an appropriate route for other countries to follow, because huge centralised training institutions are out of tune with the more flexible labour markets of the 1990s. Another option is to provide subsidies to encourage enterprises to maintain or initiate training. This could help new small-scale firms, in particular ; assisting skill formation of these may be among the major labour market policy challenges of the next few years.

Public works

Another policy on which — perhaps excessive — hopes are placed is direct job creation through short-term public works. These have figured prominently in legislative reforms, as in the USSR's 1991 Employment Law. Usually the main objective is to cut unemployment directly, saving unemployment benefits in the process. Certainly, there is ample scope for social and physical infrastructural improvements in all countries of the region. However, public works schemes are often criticised for being costly and for failing to provide the unemployed with ways of reintegration into the economic mainstream. Usually involving relatively low-paid, unskilled jobs with little long-term potential, they easily attract a stigma, thereby undermining rather than strengthening worker motivation and morale. Such schemes open up the prospect of a recurrent cycle of short-term jobs interspersed with periods of unemployment. Schemes that combine training with work experience, although more costly in the short term, may be more successful, but only if participation in them is voluntary.

Finally, deadweight and substitution effects may be greater than in the case of training schemes. Also, if a government organises a public works scheme it *may* "crowd out" a non-government project — or even another government scheme — so having little or no net effect on unemployment.

Employment subsidies

Another policy much used during periods of high unemployment, and one being utilised implicitly as well as explicitly in CEECs during the stabilisation and adjustment period, is the provision of wage subsidies to keep workers in employment. These have become increasingly popular as unemployment has started to accelerate. For instance, Poland has introduced an incomes policy that among other matters encouraged the preservation of low-paid employment; Bulgaria has considered giving subsidies to state enterprises provided that they maintain some previous level of employment. In some of the countries, workers have accepted pay cuts or paid or unpaid leave in return for keeping their jobs. This is attractive to workers, since they retain entitlement to enterprise benefits and a niche in the event that employment prospects improve.

Wage subsidies as a transitional measure might slow down the massive spate of redundancies that restructuring requires, while making foreign investment in the region more attractive and possibly making the products of the region more competitive in both domestic and foreign markets. Wage subsidies might also slow down the predicted mass emigration from many parts of central and eastern Europe, by narrowing the gap between labour productivity and wages. To the extent that unemployment benefits would actually be paid, their direct cost to governments would be less than the outlay. The direct costs would also be reduced if the employed workers earned enough to pay income taxes or social insurance contributions. If the subsidies also enabled the government to sell state enterprises for higher prices, then the direct cost of the subsidies would be further reduced.

In this regard, analysis of the Kurzarbeit (short-time work) programme in eastern Germany should be a high priority. Many industrialised countries have used similar schemes in an attempt to achieve a socially acceptable adjustment process and to preserve skills. A well-known case is the *cassa integrazione* scheme in Italy, which utilises unemployment insurance during temporary lay-offs. All such schemes have the advantage that they provide income support for *de facto* redundant workers, and avoid open unemployment without disguising the fact that adjustment is needed. Particularly promising are schemes that combine subsidies with retraining or measures to create enterprises.

Yet there are drawbacks with all wage and employment subsidy schemes, including a tendency for widespread deadweight and substitution effects. Critics would contend that they are a form of market distortion which impedes essential changes. Less tendentiously, it is widely accepted that they may also weaken the discipline over wage bargaining, which leads to consideration of various sorts of incomes policy. (We will return to this question later).

Start-up measures and mobility incentives

While there should not be excessive expectation of the employment impact of direct job creation and training schemes, is there scope for speeding up the process of job creation? As it seems that in the near future most new jobs will be in new *small-scale enterprises,* including self-employment, this issue is linked to that of enterprise creation. Major obstacles to the spread of new productive enterprises include lack of credit, marketing skills and entrepreneurial experience. The rhetorical commitment is likely to run ahead of reality. The difficulty is made worse by the precipitous decline in living standards, cutting consumer demand for products and services provided by small businesses. As one east German plumber put it in May 1991:

"I know a lot of small tradesmen like myself who boomed under the old system and are sinking fast now. If you think it over, it's ironic, isn't it?"

Overcoming the difficulties will require a comprehensive approach which integrates packages of policies, and this raises an awkward question. To what extent, if any, should financial resources devoted to other labour market policies and income protection be redirected to try to stimulate small-scale enterprises? Most of the new employment laws include provisions which commit governments to support such enterprises, but an integrated approach is a major undertaking that will take years to refine.

Meanwhile, *mobility grants* are a means of enabling workers to move to where there are opportunities to start businesses or obtain wage jobs. In western Europe there have been debates on whether "jobs should be taken to the workers, or workers taken to the jobs". Besides the obvious answer that both are desirable, an advantage of mobility grants is that they should help to reduce regional disparities in unemployment, wages and benefits, particularly important in a period of industrial restructuring. Here too, it is advisable to recognise potential deadweight and substitution effects.

Labour policies for vulnerable groups

Recalling the emerging patterns of disadvantage and labour market segmentation, and the fact that these are endemic to open labour markets, it is clear that labour market policies have responded in different ways to those groups regarded as vulnerable in the labour market. Although there are others, such as minorities and those with work-constraining handicaps, we will focus on the three demographic groups that have received most consideration.

Older workers

Because they are often the first and most seriously hit by industrial restructuring, it is perhaps appropriate to start with workers aged in their fifties and sixties. *Early retirement schemes* adopted in many west European countries in the 1980s to reduce labour supply of older workers hit or likely to be hit by mass redundancies have been controversial. Though for different reasons, similar schemes were introduced in CEECs. A criticism is that such schemes easily lead to discrimination against older workers, both by employers and by the employment services, impoverishing many of those denied jobs and worsening their social marginalisation.

19

In any case, it would be hard to resort to that policy now. The average age of retirement in central and eastern Europe has long been much lower than in the rest of Europe, nearly five years lower for men (60 compared to 64.4) and up to eight years in the case of women (55 compared to 63).[5] There are grounds both for raising the pensionable age and for raising pensions, which have been abysmally low. Although it might be claimed that this would fuel unemployment when the primary concern is to reduce it, this assumes that older and younger workers are substitutes, and this is uncertain.

The widespread displacement of employed pensioners can be interpreted as another policy for reducing labour supply and should be a cause for anxiety. In some countries, pensioners have accounted for a significant share of total employment: in Hungary in 1990 the figure was 8 per cent. While many have remained in jobs because of inadequate pensions, as unemployment rises there will probably be discrimination against older workers in general, and this would worsen their already poor standard of living. However, are the types of jobs that such older workers perform really those that would be taken by young workers wanting full-time employment?

By contrast, policy-makers could try to increase the labour supply and employment prospects of older workers. As in western industrialised countries, this will be essential in the longer-term, given the "greying" of the labour force, if not the fiscal imperative of reducing a rising dependency ratio.

Policies to reintegrate older workers displaced by industrial restructuring or threatened by redundancy include measures reserving certain jobs for older workers, retraining schemes and subsidies to employers prepared to hire or keep them. Perhaps the most promising are policies to encourage work-sharing, at least until decent pensions are feasible, after which the State *might* become more neutral to such economic activities. In sum, older workers should not be seen as the "easy option" for labour market marginalisation. Rather, they should be considered as active participants in the transition process.

Young people

Policy-makers faced by rising youth unemployment may be inclined to reduce their labour supply, boost their employment directly and/or improve their competitive position in the labour market. All three approaches have been pursued intensively in the industrialised market economies over the past two decades.

The first set of issues concerns the scope for reducing the *short-term* labour supply, usually with a view to improving its quality in the longer term. The most direct way would be to increase the age of compulsory schooling, which might also have other advantages. Other possible mechanisms include job-sharing schemes or partial wage subsidies, so as to permit skill training at the same time.

One popular way of boosting youth employment has been through special public works schemes. This could be seen as a form of "workfare", critics of which believe that it is inconsistent with a free labour market to oblige young workers to perform set activities as a condition for receipt of benefits. There is also the fear, and likelihood, that public works schemes tend to involve "dead end" or low productivity jobs that, rather than improve the long-term commitment of young workers to labour market activity, impede that development.

Policy-makers will no doubt try to improve the employment prospects of young workers. They could encourage that by extending labour market training, vocational schooling or subsidised on-the-job training. Or they could provide wage subsidies and special grants to encourage entrepreneurship. With high unemployment, it would be unrealistic to expect rapid or substantial short-term results from any of those measures. Nevertheless, their potential needs to be explored.

Women workers

Labour market policies can reduce the likelihood that, with growing reliance on market mechanisms and with high unemployment, women workers may be turned into a "secondary" labour force. One much debated issue in market economies is whether policies should discriminate in favour of women and other groups likely to be disadvantaged in the labour market. In most periods of rising unemployment, there are those who argue that women should be given fewer opportunities because that would open up more for male bread-winners and therefore improve family welfare. This reasoning is unacceptable, since — even if the fact that many women are their household's primary earner — a basic principle is that labour market policies should promote equality of opportunity.

One issue likely to figure more prominently in policy debates is whether the promotion of *part-time employment* for women (and others) is appropriate or feasible. In most market economies in recent years the number of part-time jobs has grown relative to the number of full-time jobs. This source of employment has been little developed in the formal economy of CEECs.

In sum, labour market policies are crucial for improving the labour adjustment process and for reducing the level and inequitable distribution of unemployment. Most have their limitations, however. The possibilities of substantial deadweight, substitution and "crowding out" effects in the current circumstances are considerable, and represent the most important reason for careful evaluation of all labour market policies, including income protection measures, training and public works.

Whereas all such schemes may have the virtue of enabling the unemployed, particularly the long-term unemployed, to have opportunities to be reintegrated into the labour force, if the work is "dead end" or if there are no job opportunities after the training, disillusion may soon undermine the positive potential of such policies. It is vital to remember that active labour market policies work best when the level of aggregate demand for labour is *close* to full employment.

IV. Labour market issues of social protection

With rising unemployment, price liberalisation, drastic cuts in consumer subsidies, industrial restructuring and dramatic falls in GDP, governments in all CEECs have been forced to give high priority to reforming their systems of social protection. Unless the resultant system of social protection is equitable and effective, the transitional reforms are likely to flounder, eroded by a loss of social legitimacy. In 1991, disillusion with the reforms endangered emerging democracy. For example, in Poland a survey in mid-1991 reported that 86 % of the adult population were pessimistic about their personal situation and prospects. Partly in response to public discontent, Parliament voted to increase social benefits, but did so against a background of a growing budget deficit. Comparable situations existed in all the other countries.

Under the old regimes, social policy was highly centralised, closely linked to employment in state enterprises and with little or no "incentive" function. In 1990-91, there was a consensus that the old system was inappropriate for the new challenges, but much less agreement on what the new system should look like.

There were three contextual issues that should be borne in mind. It has been widely argued that under the old regimes, total expenditure on social policy relative to GDP per capita was excessive. That may be true, if social policy is defined in its widest sense, taking account of its regulatory and administrative aspects. It has also been argued that social policy was actually less redistributive than in many industrialised market economies. The latter may be dubious as a generalisation, but both arguments raise familiar questions about what levels of social policy expenditure would be appropriate and the extent to which the new policies should be redistributive. International experience suggests that there is no ideal level or extent either within or across generations.[6]

A second contextual issue concerns the role that the various levels of government should play. The type of market economy will depend in part on the role allocated to the various levels of state administration and of non-state institutions, particularly in the provision of social protection during restructuring, given that market insurance-based schemes scarcely exist. A more "federal" network must be created as soon as possible, since local government must play a much greater administrative role if an effective and equitable system of social assistance or basic income transfers is to be established.

The third issue is tantalising. Should a distinction be made between income protection policy during a presumably short period of transition, and the system of social protection desirable for the longer term, when a market economy has been created?

Social safety nets and targeting

Some analysts have indeed distinguished between transitional social policy and long-term social security reform. There are precedents for special measures for a limited period of major restructuring. In the post-war reconstruction period in western Europe, measures such as the rationing of basic consumer goods and selective price controls were used. Now, in central and eastern Europe, the idea of a social "safety net" directed at the poor has been widely canvassed as a response to the immediate difficulties. It is not as simple as it seems.

Two arguments in favour of a safety net are that the rapid economic changes are putting certain identifiable groups into acute poverty and that a more universal scheme of social protection would have severe funding difficulties. However, a highly targeted approach to transfers, based on complex conditions and means tests, may not be consistent with an effective safety net. Targeting has become the euphemism for providing benefits only to those deemed by the authorities to deserve and need them. It is not clear that targeting is feasible in circumstances of high and unpredictable inflation without serious administrative difficulties and adverse consequences in terms of social equity.

At the outset of the reform process, most new governments were tempted to introduce *relatively* generous unemployment benefits. However, financial constraints led to a reshaping of the schemes and a tightening of the conditions for receipt of benefits . It is debatable whether more selective, targeted benefits, paid to recipients for a shorter period than the expected period of job-seeking, are justified in the circumstances faced by CEECs. Whether justified or not, there will certainly be agonising debates over the labour market and social equity effects of the more conditional benefits that were being proposed in 1991.

Another principle worth stressing is that the less developed the local employment and social security services, the simpler the system of basic income transfers should be. If social assistance is applied through strict conditionality tests, many of those in need will fall through the safety net. The strengthening of the role of local authorities in social protection will be a major task in the next few years, but in the meantime it is questionable whether complex conditionality and targeting should be applied to poverty-reducing transfers as if they were already functioning well.

Incentives and distribution

Social policy under the old system had no incentive function. Yet should social protection policy have an incentive objective as a primary feature, and if so, how? What are the distributional and labour market efficiency implications of adopting this approach?

Under the old regimes, the highly centralised social policy was linked to employment in state enterprises and organisations. As privatisation proceeds, and unemployment and intermittent labour force participation become more common, how will the old unified enterprise-based social protection become differentiated without some groups being seriously disadvantaged? Developing a lasting system of equitable welfare with efficient incentive properties has been an unresolved issue of social policy in industrialised market economies. The situation will be much worse in the less affluent countries of central and eastern Europe.

Flat-rate and earnings-related benefits

To what extent should social protection policy rely on flat-rate or earnings-related benefits? *If* there are only small wage differentials, an earnings-related system of income transfers is little different from a flat-rate benefit system. However, if wage differentials grow, as expected, during the period of restructuring, should there be moves in the direction of flat-rate benefits? If so, should the benefit-earned income ratio (the income replacement ratio) decline for successively higher-income groups, or should income differentiation be reduced by taxation ? And what would be the implications of moving towards earnings-related benefits for social solidarity during the transition process?

Most international organisations have advocated flat-rate benefits. Yet all the countries in the region have felt obliged to introduce earnings-related schemes — Hungary in 1989, Bulgaria and Poland in 1990, Czechoslovakia, Romania and the ex-USSR in 1991. Some countries, such as Bulgaria, have started to reduce the earnings-related component, but it is unclear which tendency will predominate.

The merits of flat-rate schemes are that they are simple, efficient, transparent, easy to administer — both to set up and operate — and more likely to be fair because they involve fewer or no income or means tests. Although the distinction between flat-rate and earnings-related schemes may diminish in a period of high inflation and partial indexation, a drawback of earnings-related schemes is that the long-term unemployed are left to fall back on inadequate, means-tested social assistance.

Price liberalisation and compensation policies

The alacrity with which governments have cut consumer subsidies and liberalised prices not only had the predicted inflationary consequences but left many millions of people in the region exposed to poverty or income insecurity. Perhaps a more gradual liberalisation of prices would have been preferable from a social viewpoint, but it was felt that rapid liberalisation was needed to increase incentives and remove supply constraints to production.

Governments have tried to cushion the blow by compensation schemes, but these have had mixed success, partly because it has been hard to compensate all groups with equal success or to identify the best form of compensation. Should payments be flat rate or graduated according to income, labour force status or perceived need determined by socio-demographic status ? Another difficulty has been in deciding who should pay the direct costs. If employers are expected to pay, they may be induced to cut employment at a time when unemployment is rising. If the social security system is expected to pay, through increased pensions, family allowances, supplements to unemployment benefits, etc., that will almost certainly require budgetary transfers from central or local government, and will probably lead to a reduction in ordinary benefits or to more narrow targeting, thereby intensifying problems of social exclusion. This issue has particularly exercised policy-makers in Czechoslovakia, although all countries have had to explore alternative options.

Pensions, sickness benefits and family assistance reform

Pension reform has demanded a high priority throughout central and eastern Europe. The situation was complicated by the rapidly deteriorating labour market position of older workers, many of whom were pushed into unemployment, premature retirement or dependence on meagre pensions that under the old system had been linked to a continuation in low-paid wage labour. Perhaps paradoxically, despite low life expectancy compared with western Europe, the old-age dependency ratio was high under the old regimes. Although workers were entitled to pensions at a relatively early age, they suffered from being inadequately linked to labour force behaviour. If workers retired at an early age they could still obtain approximately the same pension as those who did not, because the number of years of pensionable work needed to qualify for full pension was small, and because there were only small increments for later retirement, less than what workers could earn from post-retirement work. Reforms have to rectify such anomalies. Perhaps most crucially, for those in their early fifties in particular, there should be incentives to remain in the labour force, and for all workers there should be a reasonable prospect of a decent pension at a reasonable retirement age.

Another aspect of social policy that required urgent reform was *sickness pay*. Although it has also been widespread in some industrialised market economies, *work absence* due to sickness has been extensive and costly in most CEECs. In the 1980s, Hungary, for instance, had one of the highest sickness absence rates in the world. Much of this absence was surely caused by the system of *sickness pay*, which allowed workers to take time off easily (perhaps to work in second jobs, many of which were created by the artificial labour shortage). There is little doubt though about the high levels of morbidity in the region, resulting from the nature of the main industries, extensive pollution and poor working conditions.

Workers and managers must have more incentives to reduce sickness-related absence and outlays on sick pay. In state enterprises operating with a "soft budget constraint", management (except in periods of intense activity) had little incentive to reduce such absence, since compensation came from the government's general budget, rather than from the wage fund. With privatisation, if that system persisted, employers would have a strong incentive to put surplus workers on sick pay rather than pay them wages or lay them off, while workers would prefer that to unemployment, because they would keep their job and receive a higher income replacement rate.

The alternatives would be to make employers wholly or partially responsible for sickness benefits, or to oblige workers to forfeit pay for a few days before they start receiving sick pay. In 1991, Bulgaria, Hungary and Czechoslovakia all moved in this latter direction.

The next element of social policy needing reform was *family benefits*. These have been high as a percentage of GDP in CEECs compared with other European countries, although less so if tax credits are taken into account in the latter. In the former, family benefits were supplemented by indirect benefits, such as preferential housing for families, all of which were intended to accompany low wages, and were sometimes rationalised by reference to a pro-natalist policy. The low-wage, high-benefits policy was a long-term trend reflecting the official view that under communism, wages would eventually disappear. Now, perhaps the most controversial issue for social policy is whether family benefits should be targeted, via means tests and work availability tests, or made into a universal form of income transfer. As with other benefits, policy-makers will have to decide whether family benefits should be related to the average wage or to some measure of subsistence income.

Wages and incomes policy

As real wages were always low in central and eastern Europe, the fall experienced by many workers during the economic decline of 1989-91 was extremely painful. Real wages fell by 40 % in Poland between December 1989 and December 1990; in 1991 other countries experienced comparable declines. Whereas in the 1980s, real wages in CEECs declined while full employment was maintained, in the early 1990s both fell. Admittedly, real wages in terms of purchasing power may not have declined by as much as the data suggest. More research will have to clarify the position. The country papers provide a wealth of information on recent trends, but one difficulty has been that the statistical base for assessing these trends and their implications has been patchy ; the data must be interpreted with caution, particularly when making international comparisons on wage structures and differentials.

Real wages must sooner or later rise in all the countries of the region to above what they were before 1990, because unless they do the undervaluation of labour will continue, productivity growth will be impaired and workers' living standards will continue to decline precipitously, given the shrinking role of the State in the direct provision of goods and services. This raises the issue of the appropriate mechanisms for wage determination. There has been a debate in industrialised market economies about the relative merits and demerits of centralised and decentralised pay bargaining, the consensus being that for macroeconomic and labour market performance both very centralised and very decentralised systems perform better than the intermediate case.

Besides the level and rate of change of wage levels, in many respects both wage structures and wage differentials in CEECs were similar to those found in the industrialised market countries. Yet many economists and politicians have claimed that *wage differentials* have been too narrow, that there has been excessive "levelling" through administrative meddling and that labour utilisation and mobility have been impaired by narrow and rigid wage differentials.

Yet in aggregate, wage differentials have been similar to those found in the industrialised market economies, though in some countries they may have been somewhat narrower and in all of them they were distorted in favour of heavy industry. Yet it has not been demonstrated that massively widening differentials is a necessary, efficient or desirable means of securing labour reallocation and higher labour productivity. In any case, as long as most employment remains in large state enterprises, it is difficult to see how systems of state regulated wage scales can be abandoned, although in the longer term wage differentials should surely change to reflect skill, work performance and relative productivity. The feasibility of determining relative wages by reference to job classification schemes has been explored as an option in such circumstances. However, it remains difficult to define wage scales to reflect relative productivity and labour scarcity.

Traditional bonus systems based on material production targets were inadequate in CEECs, but the use of productivity incentive schemes has run into objections, primarily connected with fears of wage inflation and the growth of massive wage inequality (as some workers raise their productivity significantly).

As the old administrative mechanisms for pay determination fade, there will be a general widening of wage differentials and an erosion of incomes at the bottom. In this context, policies will be needed to protect the lowest earners. This raises unresolved debates over the effectiveness of *statutory minimum wages* and the desirability of *wage indexation*. The main argument in favour of both has been that vulnerable groups should be protected against declines in living standards caused by price increases and against cuts in wages resulting from unemployment or other labour market factors that put them in weak bargaining positions.

Most market-oriented countries maintain some sort of minimum wage protection. Some economists however, claim that (i) they price vulnerable workers out of jobs, thereby pushing up their unemployment ; (ii) they only protect a small minority of workers; and (iii) they discourage labour-intensive industries, thus hindering job generation.

Among the counter-arguments are that minimum wages help to raise productivity, both by inducing workers to work more effectively and by encouraging firms to value and train workers more diligently, rather than treat them as "cheap labour". Although the debate is unresolved, it may be better to provide basic income security by means other than statutory minimum wages, in part because experience suggests that they can only be partially successful in protecting the wages of vulnerable groups.

While wage protection has preoccupied many economists concerned with the lower end of the labour market, others have been concerned about the almost unprecedented increases in nominal wages in 1990-91. This was due in part to price liberalisation and the erosion of old systems of centralised administrative control over wages, and to the opening up of the region's economies to international market forces. Whatever the factors involved, the wage pressures led to a desire for some form of *incomes policy*.

Since the 1970s, most governments in industrialised market economies have moved away from incomes policies because of disillusionment with statutory forms of them. The conventional view is that they cannot work for very long, since they bottle up inflationary pressures that sooner or later produce a wage-price explosion and in the interim intensify labour market rigidities. However, certain forms of incomes policy have worked quite well in past periods of reconstruction, notably after the Second World War. Additionally, some countries continued to operate and refine incomes policy during the 1980s, notably Finland, with some success. The scope for negotiated incomes policy is best left to the next section, on industrial relations.

As far as central and eastern Europe is concerned, the main form adopted so far has been some variant of a *tax-based incomes policy* (TIP). This has been advocated for the region by several international organisations, but has not been introduced in industrialised market economies.

The basic idea is that to limit the growth of nominal wages, any increase in wages above some stipulated level should be taxed at a punitive and possibly progressive rate. The tax threat is meant to deter wage increases so as to reduce the chances of hyper-inflation. The rationale is simple. Since large state enterprises still predominate, management does not act as the representative of owners, so that they are too easily persuaded to grant excessive wages unjustified by productivity growth, or if justified by enterprise productivity are inflationary because they raise nominal incomes in circumstances in which there is no increase in the supply of consumer goods and services. Where state enterprises are still domestic monopolies, the likelihood of such wage concessions is all the greater. Only if a "hard budget" constraint exists, i.e., if there are adverse consequences for managers if wages or other labour costs are allowed to rise unjustifiably, resulting in lower market shares, declining sales or profitability, will there be effective control over wage increases at the enterprise or industry level. This has been the main justification for a tax-based incomes policy.

However, there are serious drawbacks to this line of reasoning. The standard model of a TIP is for enterprises to be allowed to raise wage bills up to a threshold level to compensate for price increases or for some percentage of past or anticipated price increases. Among the criticisms is that this does not focus on individual wage rates, so that it does not link to inflation at an individual level. Perhaps most significantly, a TIP can penalise or discourage the growth of production or productivity.

Such a rigid tax rule would also lead to a shift in relative wages in favour of "insiders" at the expense of groups in a weaker bargaining position. A tax on the total wage bill also encourages labour shedding, which may not be desirable at a time of steeply rising unemployment. That seems to have been a reason that the Polish authorities modified the policy to one of a tax on the average wage. Unfortunately, that

27

too has drawbacks, including a tendency to encourage use of low-wage, low-skill labour rather than a policy of upgrading. It also discourages enterprise-level bargaining between unions and employers, by limiting the scope for productivity-enhancing wage deals.

Some governments have contemplated abandoning the idea of a TIP, and have sought to find other ways of limiting the inflationary consequences of higher wages. Others, notably the Government of Romania, have considered coupling a TIP with steps towards a negotiated incomes policy, which depends — crucially — on the existence of effective, representative bargainers.

The old centralised system left little scope for bargaining between managers and workers ; formally, conflicts of interest between workers and managers were not recognised, while unions were more a part of management than bargainers with it. Since then, there has been a slow emergence of organisations representing employers and new forms of trade unions more detached from the organs of government.

It is too early to say which institutional form of industrial relations will predominate. The early 1990s will be seen as a period of experimentation, in which the *fragmentation of institutions* will probably precede consolidation and multi-layered bargaining at the national, industrial and enterprise levels. In some countries, something like a unified trade union movement has been preserved so far, in others such as Romania and Bulgaria fragmentation has occurred. Although one might anticipate some reconsolidation, the final outcome is hard to predict. Will the learning process in collective bargaining make such fragmentation endemic and even undermine the long-term legitimacy of trade unionism?

A major fear is that whatever level of wage bargaining develops, it will contribute to inflation and unemployment, particularly in the transition period during which new unions and union leaders have to secure legitimacy with their actual and potential members, and employers have to demonstrate their right to manage by demonstrating bargaining prowess. Those factors, coupled with a lack of mutually shared information about what each side has to offer and about the likely consequences of their actions, will impede identification of points on which to compromise.

The fear of accelerating inflation and unemployment during the evolution of free collective bargaining is perceived by some as an argument for tax-based incomes policy, and for it to be maintained for a rather long time. However, surely this would limit the scope for, and meaningfulness of, collective bargaining? It would also confuse rather than clarify the respective roles and interests of workers and trade unions, employers, management and government. As long as regulatory and administrative mechanisms are used to determine wages, including taxes, there will be a tendency for workers and management to coalesce to circumvent government policies.

Some governments have been attracted by the policy of statutory control over wages and benefits in essential industries and services, notably the energy-related industries. Workers in these are perceived to have a powerful bargaining position, making it relatively easy for them to obtain higher wages. Is it appropriate to introduce compulsory arbitration and mediation procedures, as some governments have done? And would it be reasonable, as some believe, to declare strikes illegal in certain sectors ? Even if these policies are only meant for the transition period, one should surely reflect on their possible effects on the longer-term development of tripartism and collective bargaining before rushing to introduce them.

In the search for the appropriate system of labour relations, some form of tripartism will emerge, probably with the government playing an active role in the search for new forms of social consensus. Yet it would be very surprising if the final institutional structures were to be similar either among the different CEECs themselves or to any structure in western Europe.

A crucial task in the early 1990s will be determining which bargaining levels — national, regional, industrial, local — are most appropriate for specific issues — wages, benefits, working conditions and job structures. During the restructuring period, it may be appropriate as part of a process of social bargaining for the State to take over functions previously left largely to the trade unions, most notably the provision of non-wage benefits.

It is also possible that widespread *de-unionisation* will accompany the shift to a more decentralised labour market system, partly because unions may find it hard to establish legitimacy among workers, partly because of labour market trends that have contributed to the dramatic de-unionisation in many market economies in recent years. Undoubtedly, the proportion of the working population belonging to trade unions will decline from the artificial figures of over 90 % that have been typical. If that enfeebles worker representation, there will be profound implications for labour legislation and regulations, for income distribution and institutional mechanisms for social protection and for many other aspects of the labour market. That is why it will be important to create a legislative framework for genuine collective bargaining and representative organisations to flourish. Would political democracy be able to gather strength in the absence of industrial democracy and collective negotiation over a wide range of labour and social affairs?

A final issue is the feasibility of negotiated incomes policy, pursued through centralised collective bargaining by representative organisations of employers and workers, with the government indirectly involved. The prospects would depend on the existence of suitable organisations, and on their credibility and capacity to bargain. Although in the transition period at least, those conditions may not exist, it is encouraging that in 1990-91 some governments began the potentially valuable task of helping them into existence.

Even if they did exist, some economists argue that this form of incomes policy is undesirable, and claim that they introduce wage and labour market rigidities, and are ultimately inflationary. Only a few countries have succeeded in implementing a consensual incomes policy for any substantial period. However, seen from the perspective of changing attitudes in the industrialised countries, perhaps they will be considered more favourably in the 1990s than they were in the 1980s.

A few derivative questions arise. If it is claimed that such a policy would not work because the respective bargaining organisations that are expected to pursue social consensus in the labour market would not be representative, what could governments do? The provision of a framework for industrial relations to evolve in will have to include regulations setting standards of internal democracy within both workers' and employers' organisations, so that, for instance, more vulnerable groups of workers are adequately represented and small-scale businesses are represented as much as the large enterprises.

The extent to which governments involve employers' and trade union organisations in the design and implementation of the reform process will vary among the countries of central and eastern Europe. There is surely much to be learned from the variety of approaches taken in other European countries in this respect. One hopes that no particular model will be held up as an ideal or that initial problems do not give way to a spirit of intolerance.

Finally, there is the key issue of reforming industrial relations in the public sector, which will probably remain large for years, despite the upsurge of privatisation. There is perhaps much to be learned from the experience of neighbouring countries, where many major firms have long been in public ownership.

VI. Concluding remarks

As stated at the outset, this paper is necessarily somewhat selective on points of emphasis. In general, labour and social policy problems have been emphasised. This should not be interpreted as reflecting a view that all is gloomy. There are many reasons for believing that, if effective social and labour market policies are introduced, an efficient and equitable regulated labour market can evolve, in tune with the more flexible, high-tech society that will emerge in the 1990s.

Notes

1. According to the Vienna Institute for Comparative Studies, industrial output in eastern Europe was 13 % lower at the end of the first quarter of 1991 than in the corresponding period in 1990. More worrying still, investment fell by about 20 %.

2. Nearly 2 million workers in the former German Democratic Republic were kept out of unemployment in 1991, through early retirement, job creation and retraining programmes, at a cost of over 20 billion Deutschemarks (US$ 12 billion). By late 1991, leading politicians were expressing alarm at the rising amount needed for social transfers and were calling for cuts in planned expenditure in 1992.

3. *Trud* (Moscow), Nov. 21, 1991.

4. Both the ILO and the OECD have co-ordinated much research on active labour market policies in industrialised market economies, as have other international organisations, such as the European Commission.

5. In practice, "early retirement" for special categories of workers in CEECs meant age 50-55 for men and 50 for women. In some countries, up to 20 % of the working-age population were in early retirement for "hardship" reasons.

6. Social policy has always been an instrument of stratification to some extent in all countries. See, e.g., G.Esping-Andersen, *The three worlds of welfare capitalism* (Princeton, Princeton University Press, 1990); Z.Ferge, The "crisis and the welfare state" in Eastern Europe, with a focus on Hungary", in *European Economic Review*, Vol.31, 1987, pp.212-19.

Chapter 2

Bulgaria: Labour market trends and policies

by

Iskra Beleva*, Daniela Bobeva, Silvia Dilova, Asen Mitchkovski

Prior to the political, economic and social changes of recent years, labour use in Bulgaria reflected the peculiarities of the centrally planned economic system. The right to work was guaranteed by the constitution but was expressed as a duty and realised in practice through economic and administrative coercion. Predominantly labour-intensive economic development was accompanied by an artificial shortage of labour and considerable hidden unemployment. Centrally administered management of labour prevented the emergence of a market and the free movement of labour. An equalising, centralised wage system ensured that wages were independent of the quantity and quality of labour, which in turn led to low levels of productivity as employees aimed for stable jobs rather than better qualifications. Inflationary pressures were masked by fixed prices. Finally, the employment system led to equal but low living standards. These problems have been highlighted in the political and economic changes that have occurred since November 1989.

Bulgaria's transition to democracy and a market economy is taking place in an unstable political situation. The economic reform itself began in very unfavourable conditions. The Bulgarian economy was badly affected by the collapse of the Council for Mutual Economic Assistance (CMEA) and ruptured trade relations with the former USSR; the Gulf crisis created additional difficulties. Moreover, unlike most of the former socialist countries, economic reform began without foreign financial assistance, while the state's previous monopoly of ownership meant there was no tradition or experience of the free market. As a result of all these factors, the creation of a labour market and new social and industrial relations policies exacted a high price in both social and economic terms.

* Iskra Beleva is at the Economics Institute of the Bulgarian Academy of Sciences, Daniela Bobeva works in the Institute for Social Trade Union Studies, Silvia Dilova is at the Sociology Institute of the Bulgarian Academy of Sciences and Asen Mitchkovski is with the Confederation of Labour (Podkrepa).

Labour market developments

Economic reform began in early 1990 at a time of deep economic crisis (table 2.1). The primary objectives were to stabilise the budget deficit and the currency, curb expansion of the black market and tackle the problem of a severe shortage of goods. High interest rates and taxes were introduced which succeeded in bringing inflation down, but at the cost of steadily falling output.

Table 2.1. **Macro-economic indicators, Bulgaria, 1981-1991 (per cent)**

	Average annual 1981-85	Growth rate 1986-90	1990 1991[1]
Gross output	3.90	0.40	-27.1
National income	3.70	0.10	-29.5
Per capita national income	3.50	-0.10	-
Gross industrial output	4.30	-0.45	-28.9
Gross agricultural output	-0.60	-0.50	-11.7
Capital investment	3.83	9.81	41.6[2]
Foreign trade turnover (imports and exports combined)	6.60	-5.30	438.0[3]

1. Percentage change over 1990.
2. Current prices.
3. Current prices.
Source: Central Statistical Office (CSO), *Statistical Yearbook*, 1991 (Sofia), p. 40.

Gross output fell by 11.7 per cent between 1989 and 1990. In the first five months of 1991 it dropped by 21.7 per cent compared to the same period in 1990, with the decrease most marked in industry (22 per cent), construction (11.4 per cent) and transport (10 per cent). Communications, distribution and other branches of material production also showed a decline. Most of the drop in industrial output — over 75 per cent — was due to lower production in electrical engineering and electronics, chemicals and oil refining, food, wine and tobacco, and machine building.

Output in all basic agricultural activities fell in the year to end May 1991, including land under cultivation, harvested produce, greenhouse production, and animal husbandry.

As indicators of value are unreliable because of price changes, indicators of physical output will be used for estimating changes in output. In the first quarter of 1991, 97.3 per cent of the 500 or so physical indicators of the main items of production were below their level of a year earlier, and 47 per cent had fallen to about half the previous year's level. By the end of May 1991 the latter proportion had increased, with some estimates of output changes — based on physical indicators for 160 basic products — showing an average drop of 45.6 per cent.[1]

The main reasons for the fall in production were a shortage of raw materials, lack of equipment and lower sales: together these accounted for 68 per cent of the fall.

Lower sales reflected the ever-larger number of insolvencies among domestic customers caused by high prices and unfulfilled contracts. Debts owed by enterprises to banks and the Government in 1991 were estimated at about 40 billion leva.

Before the transition to a market economy, Bulgaria had strong links to the other former socialist economies and especially to the ex-Soviet Union. Payment difficulties meant that a considerable proportion of Bulgarian production could not be sold in the Soviet market; a large number of enterprises faced closure.[2]

The shut-down of enterprises, or lower production, became an increasingly important factor in the drop in overall production: their output fell by 1.5 billion leva between January and May 1991. Only 44.2 per cent of enterprises were producing as much as one year earlier; 21 per cent were producing 40 per cent less.

Investment did not fall as sharply as output, although the share of construction work in progress was very high, at about 17 billion leva. Figures for exports and imports worsened. In the first quarter of 1991 exports were 56 per cent lower than in the same period of 1990, and foreign trade turnover was almost halved. Inflation stood at about 4 per cent a month according to government estimates, and 5-6 per cent according to certain independent estimates. State debt was high, estimated at about 173 billion leva.

Shrinking output reduced the demand for labour and total employment began to fall; unemployment rose to about 5.4 per cent in May 1991. However, no major changes in employment have yet been observed, because no basic changes have been made to the laws of ownership; the government retains its dominance over the economic structure.

In 1980 the share of state ownership in gross output was 92 per cent; in 1989 this share was 90.7 per cent. In 1980 3.5 per cent of gross output was produced by co-operatives; in 1989 this share was 3.1 per cent. The share of private firms in gross output was 5.8 per cent in 1980[3] and 4.9 per cent in 1989.

The process of privatisation is still at the preparatory stage, but demonopolisation is already taking place. Seven large monopolies were broken up at the end of May 1991, and replaced by 536 new enterprises.

In June 1991, 50 firms in the construction industry were demonopolised and 343 new firms created. The first public auctions to sell state-owned businesses (for example, petrol stations) to private entrepreneurs were also held in June 1991.

By mid-1991, although decrees and laws underpinning the transition to a market economy are almost ready, there have been no fundamental changes to the employment system. At present, the demand for labour is at a considerable variance from the supply of labour in terms of industrial structure, educational and skill levels, and in possibilities for retraining.

Labour demand

Sectoral employment structure

Official data show contradictory trends in employment during the period 1980-90. Employment has been falling since 1987 but it dipped below its 1980 level only in 1990, at which point it was 6.3 per cent lower than ten years earlier. The decline in employment was most marked in construction, science, forestry and industry. Figures do not show this (table 2.2).

Table 2.2. **Employment trends by sector, Bulgaria, 1980-91**

Industry	Average annual growth rate (%)				
	1980-90	1980-85	1985-89	1989-90	1990-91
Total employment in non-production sector	-1.0	0.2	-0.9	-7.1	-14.6
of which:					
Industry	-0.1	1.6	-0.2	-7.7	-19.1
Construction	-0.8	1.0	-0.8	-8.8	-26.4
Agriculture	-3.4	-2.6	-3.5	-7.2	-10.1
Forestry	2.6	1.2	11.8	-12.0	-20.1
Transport	-0.8	-0.3	-0.8	-3.6	-10.2
Communications	2.0	2.1	1.2	4.6	-0.5
Trade	0.4	1.5	1.5	4.8	-14.2
Other material production	-0.7	3.4	-6.0	0.0	-20.7
Total employment in non-production sector,	0.9	1.4	1.2	-2.5	-7.3
of which:					
Housing, communal and consumer services	0.0	1.0	-0.2	-4.1	-11.2
Science	2.8	4.2	4.6	-10.3	-20.4
Education	1.3	2.1	0.8	0.7	-1.0
Culture and arts	-0.2	0.9	0.0	-2.2	-15.1
Health, social security, sports and tourism	1.5	1.6	1.4	1.4	5.2
Financial services, credit and insurance	1.8	1.9	3.2	-4.0	-0.0
Administration	-1.6	-1.9	0.4	-8.3	-7.9
Other non-productive branches	-4.8	-1.1	-3.0	-26.6	-33.9

Source: CSO: *The Economy of Bulgaria: Statistical Yearbook,* 1990 (Sofia), p. 27.

The distribution of employment reveals the predominance of the material sphere and the underdevelopment of the service sector, in spite of a slight increase in the numbers employed in services over the last few years. Material production is characterised by a high consumption of labour, capital, energy and materials. The non-production sector has not created the necessary infrastructure either to expand nor to meet the populations needs for services.

This employment structure represents a major obstacle to economic development. Future restructuring of the economy will be impossible without a big shift of employment out of the material sphere, and without investment and job creation in the non-production sector. However, these imperatives do not accord with the characteristics of the existing workforce.

Labour productivity and labour hoarding

Although total employment has fallen since 1987, it has fallen much more slowly than output. Consequently, labour productivity dropped by about 22 per cent in the two years to mid-1991. Indeed, labour productivity declined throughout the period 1980-89, especially in metal casting and some branches of light industry (table 2.3).

Table 2.3. **Labour productivity in industry [1], Bulgaria, 1980-90**

	1985[2]	1986	1987	1988	1989	1990
	% change from previous year					
All industry	12.3	4.9	4.6	3.4	0.6	-7.2
Electricity	6.1	42.0	-32.6	5.2	-3.4	35.1
Metal casting	40.7	16.0	-31.9	-33.9	-48.9	-74.1
Non-ferrous metallurgy	-15.9	-26.4	8.0	-33.8	7.9	-
Chemicals	49.3	-14.7	-8.0	33.8	35.5	-20.2
Machine building	50.6	7.0	15.0	12.3	-5.7	-11.4
Building materials	4.3	30.4	0.0	-20.3	-15.2	-40.0
Timber and wood-working	20.2	2.0	6.2	-3.2	-6.4	-48.0
Pulp and paper	-2.4	8.1	-3.4	-7.1	-21.5	-33.6
Glass	19.7	-1.9	7.7	8.8	16.5	-50.8
Textiles and knitwear	24.0	10.6	21.2	3.8	10.6	-31.8
Clothing	16.4	7.3	10.3	12.5	-4.6	-37.0
Leather	14.6	10.4	-0.8	4.3	-32.8	-14.6
Food	-63.6	6.2	5.3	2.8	-1.0	-10.6

1. Labour productivity is estimated as the value added per employee.
2. Percentage change from 1980.

Source: CSO: *Statistical Yearbook,* 1991 (Sofia), p. 143, pp. 150-151.

The trend continued into 1990 and the first five months of 1991. In 1980-89, days actually worked in material production, especially in industry, declined by about 15 per cent (figure 2.1).

Figure 2.1. **Days actually worked in the material production sector**

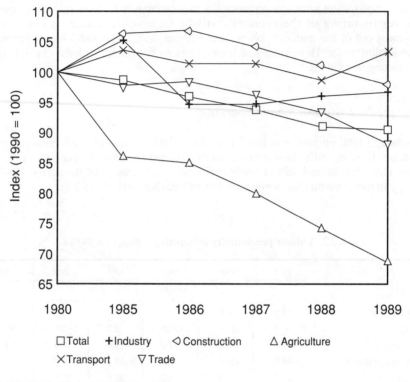

Source: CSO, *Statistical Yearbook 1990* (Sofia), p. 108.

There are no complete or systematic data on labour hoarding, or estimations based on modelling, because of a lack of appropriate information. However, an analysis of changes in labour productivity, time actually worked and numbers of people employed suggests considerable labour hoarding in the economy. This is borne out by a number of indirect indicators, for example, those concerning the efficiency of labour use.

Labour economists in Bulgaria are generally of the opinion that the centrally planned system encouraged inefficient labour use and that, consequently, full employment was an illusion, with an employee working, on average, only six hours of an eight-hour working day. According to official statistics, workers are idle for 15 per cent of their working time; some sociological studies put the figure as high as 30 per cent.[4]

Other information shows that certain categories of worker, such as engineering workers, spend about 60 per cent of their time on additional and unproductive activities. Utilisation rates for machinery and equipment range from 50 to 80 per cent.

Within total working time, the proportion of time not worked as a result of seasonal employment is 6 per cent, absences with leave 9 per cent, absences without leave nearly 3 per cent and free time 2 per cent.

Under the policy of full employment implemented by a centralised command economy, there was no link between work and economic work results. A consequence of this was the potential for considerable wastage of working time. The whole system engendered little interest in efficient labour use and initiative. Labour morale and labour discipline were low, while labour management practices were poor owing to a lack of interest and experience in that field.

There is still a high level of employment among the working-age population, but with significant hidden unemployment. At the end of April 1991, among those in employment, about 18 per cent were taking compulsory holidays (with or without pay); some 50 per cent were receiving the minimum wage.

Employment structure by industry[5]

The employment structure in material production during the period 1980-90 shows that some industries did not follow the overall trend towards lower employment. For example, employment in communications increased by 9,000 and in trade by 17,000. However, employment fell by 17,000 in industry, 27,000 in construction, 21,000 in agriculture and 21,000 in transport.

Changes in employment in material production have to be understood in the context of the centrally administered allocation of labour which operated beyond the scope of market forces. Thus these changes cannot be attributed to developments in the economic circumstances of the industries concerned but have to be treated as a consequence of government employment policy. The basic aim of this policy was a reduction in employment, implemented through administrative measures that compulsorily restricted employment growth, especially in industrial production.

Attempts were made to limit the bureaucracy and the number of administrative and managerial personnel, and to raise the efficiency of labour use; they did not, however, achieve the results expected. Problems of labour inefficiency remained. For example, the reduction in the number of people employed in construction was not the result of lower demand for labour — in fact, such demand remained unsatisfied — but was, primarily, the result of workers' reluctance to take jobs because of the sector's poor working conditions. This was despite special incentives including wage supplements and housing privileges. The chronic labour shortage was partly covered by the use of special brigades of workers, or members of the armed forces.

The agricultural sector also suffered from a serious labour shortage for a long time; this was partially covered, as in construction, by brigades. These brigades, the use of which became widespread, were recruited on a compulsory basis from among schoolchildren and students, workers from nearby enterprises, and army personnel. An additional problem in agriculture is the high average age of the agricultural population, the low degree of mechanisation and the lack of versatility and motivation among the labour force.

Now that private land ownership is permitted, agriculture may show a demand for labour. Some landowners are likely to return to their villages and become involved in agricultural production while others will hire labour. A survey in April 1991 showed that about 60 per cent of the economically active population would be ready to start a private agricultural business if they were to lose their present job.[6] Employment among those holding leases in agriculture, tourism, trade, catering and restaurants, and other services, as well as seasonal employment in these sectors, will expand.

Estimates of inter-industry shifts in employment in the period 1980-89 show little structural change overall. The coefficients of rank correlation characterising changes in employment structure are estimated at 0.988 for the period 1980-85 and 0.966 for 1985-89. However, the lower coefficient in the second period points to greater structural change than before.[7]

Taking 1980 as the base, the mean deviations in employment are greatest in machine building and the manufacture of fabricated metal products (2.80), the electrical and electronic industry (2.45), textiles and knitwear (1.05) and food, wine and tobacco (1.25). These industries, with an artificially high level of employment are likely to be responsible for the majority of job losses during economic restructuring.

Regional structure of employment[8]

The regional distribution of employment shows a high share of the employed population in the cities and in some big towns. In 1989 this share was 14.2 per cent in the capital, Sofia, 13.8 per cent in Plovdiv and 12.1 per cent in the Sofia region. This urban concentration of labour is the result of a long-term policy to transform Bulgaria into an industrialised country. Such a policy has been followed with widespread disregard for traditional, national, regional, social and environmental considerations.

Employment by size of enterprise

In 1989, nearly a third (31.5 per cent) of Bulgaria's employment was in enterprises with 1,000 to 3,000 production employees; 28.2 per cent was in enterprises with under 500 people; and 22.3 per cent was in enterprises with 501 to 1,000 people (table 2.4).

Table 2.4 **Employment by size of enterprise, Bulgaria, 1980-90**

Size of enterprise	Average annual growth rates (%)			Share of employment		
	1980-89	1980-85	1985-89	1980	1989	1990
Total	1.2	0.5	2.4	100.0	100.0	100.0
Up to 500	1.6	0.5	3.4	27.3	28.2	30.1
501 - 1 000	1.5	0.5	3.1	21.8	22.3	22.9
1 001 - 3 000	-0.2	0.3	-0.8	36.3	31.5	33.0
3 001 - 5 000	3.9	1.8	7.7	5.3	6.8	5.8
5 001 - 10 000	-1.0	-1.1	-1.1	7.1	5.6	4.8
More than 10 000	11.4	9.2	17.4	1.9	5.2	2.3

Source: CSO: *Statistical Yearbook,* 1990, (Sofia), p. 141. Data concern only state enterprises and the size distribution is calculated according to the number of production staff employed.

Employment changes in 1980-89 show the highest rates of growth in very large enterprises — i.e. those with more than 10,000 production employees. This raised their employment share from 1.9 per cent in 1980 to 5.2 per cent in 1989 (although it fell to 2.3 % in 1990). The next largest increase was among enterprises with 3,001 to 5,000 employees. The very large enterprises were highly inefficient and heavily subsidised. Under the imminent economic restructuring measures, their employment levels will fall sharply, as they will be the most difficult to privatise and will undergo more radical restructuring than smaller ones.

Employment by type of ownership

The public sector was the main source of jobs (table 2.5).

Table 2.5. **Employment by type of ownership, Bulgaria, 1980-90**

	% share			
	1980	1985	1989	1990
Material production				
Total employment	100.0	100.0	100.0	100.0
of which:				
Public sector	87.2	88.8	87.4	87.5
Co-operative enterprises	6.7	6.2	6.2	6.1
Renters (leaseholders)	-	-	0.6	0.5
Private firms and enterprises	0.6	0.5	1.6	1.9
Non-production sector				
Total employment	100.0	100.0	100.0	100.0
of which:				
Public sector	97.8	97.9	97.7	97.3
Co-operative enterprises	0.4	0.5	0.3	0.4
Renters (leaseholders)	-	-	0.2	0.5
Private firms and enterprises	5.6	1.3	1.5	1.6

Source: CSO: *The Economy of Bulgaria* (Sofia), 1981, p. 203; 1986, p. 173;1990, p. 159.

Even in the last few years of the old system, when the need for other types of ownership became clear, ownership by the state remained the only form that was officially sanctioned. The shares of different forms of ownership differ very little among the various sectors, with the state dominant almost everywhere: 100 per cent in forestry, science, communications, 90 per cent in industry, and 79 per cent in agriculture. The largest share of co-operative ownership is seen in the distributive trades (22.9 per cent), while the largest share of tenants (leaseholders) is in agriculture (16 per cent). The proportion of private enterprises is greatest in the non-production sphere, at 19.1 per cent, followed by trade at 2.6 per cent, transport at 1.6 per cent and industry at 1.4 per cent.

Employment in the parallel economy

It is difficult to estimate employment in the "parallel" economy as no detailed official information exists. About 140,000 private firms were registered in Bulgaria at the end of June 1991, but the number was increasing rapidly and may have reached 200,000 a few months later. In the public sector, social insurance taxes were being paid for 3,700,000 employees in mid-1991. There were approximately 200,000 unemployed people at this date. These figures suggest that a very small number of people — 200,000 — were working outside the public sector (compared to 4,090,000 employed in the national economy in 1991). Obviously, this is not correct; some of those employed in the public sector have also taken steps towards the private sector by registering private firms.

Parallel and official employment have always existed in Bulgaria and a sizeable proportion of the economically active population has more than one job. (This can be seen by looking at the expenditure-income structure of certain strata of the population).

Labour supply

At the end of 1990, Bulgaria's population was 8,989,000, of which 4,432,000 were male and 4,557 000 female.[9] Table 2.6 shows certain characteristics of the population during the period 1980-1990. The most notable feature is the increase in the proportion of the population over working age. This tendency is more marked in rural than in urban areas.

Table 2.6. **Population below, at and above working age, Bulgaria, 1980-90**

	1980	1985	1989	1990
	(thousands)			
Population below working age[1]	2084	2057	1997	1958
Male	1071	1056	1024	1004
Female	1013	1001	973	954
Of working age[2]	5089	5012	4996	5011
Male	2704	2656	2647	2652
Female	2385	2356	2349	2359
Over working age[3]	1704	1881	1999	2020
Male	647	722	767	777
Female	1057	1159	1232	1243
Share of population over working age (%)	19.2	21.0	22.2	22.5

1. Under 15 years.
2. Men 16 - 59 years ; women 16 - 54 years.
3. 60-plus for men and 55-plus for women.
Source: CSO : *Statistical Yearbook, 1991* (Sofia), p. 43.

According to the 1985 census the economic activity rate of the population was 53.7 per cent. Activity rates had risen in all age groups, except among those aged between 16 and 20. Economic activity has always been, and still is, higher among men: in 1985, 56.8 per cent of men and 50.6 per cent of women were economically active. The share of economically active women has continued to grow faster than that for men.[10]

There has been a steady growth in the numbers of better educated groups. However, in 1985, those with primary education only represented the largest share of the population (table 2.7).

Table 2.7. **Educational level of the population, Bulgaria, 1985**
(Youth and adult population only)

	Number	%
Total	7 184 320	100.00
Higher education	472 505	6.58
College education	209 524	2.92
Specialised education	837 422	11.66
Secondary	1 134 705	15.78
Basic (8 classes)	2 292 790	31.91
Elementary	1 481 929	20.63
Unfinished elementary	755 445	10.52

Source: Census, 1985.

There are currently no data on the labour supply among different ethnic groups. A sociological study of the Rhodopes region[11] found substantial differences between the three examined ethnic groups of Bulgarians, Turks and Muslims. Four-fifths of workers from the two latter groups were doing jobs involving hard physical labour, as opposed to only half of Bulgarian workers. The main reason was the lower level of qualifications among Turks and Muslims.

Women's employment in the 1980s as a share of the total was broadly constant. About fifty per cent of all employees (blue-collar and white-collar workers) are women (table 2.8). Women account for 45.8 per cent of workers in material production and 67.5 per cent in the non-material sphere (table 2.9).[12]

Certain branches may be characterised as feminine, such as education (over 70 per cent of all employees), public health (over 70 per cent), and financial services (over 90 per cent)[13] (table 2.9). As a rule, women outnumber men in lower-paid jobs with less paid annual leave, and in repetitive manual work.

Women's employment reflects the lack of variety and inflexibility of working time arrangements. Under the old system, a working day of eight and a half hours five days a week was the norm. The Communist system did not make any distinction between male and female workers or between married and single women, with or without children, etc. Women do not therefore show any preference for different types of employment.

41

Table 2.8. Workers in the national economy by occupation, Bulgaria, 1988-89

Occupation	1988 Total	of which: Women	1989 Total	of which: Women	% Women
Total	4 101 874	2 048 403	3 957 053	1 887 802	47.7
of which:					
Workers	3 059 835	1 427 737	2 908 198	1 358 754	46.7
of which:					
Specialists	732 993	495 142	739 383	502 634	68.0
of which:					
General	395 807	246 280	402 523	253 775	63.0
Economy	175 299	144 181	176 875	146 942	83.1
Agriculture	22 932	8 708	22 464	8 762	39.0
Juridical	4 574	2 095	4 777	2 189	45.8
Other	27 330	18 059	28 589	19 128	66.9
Teaching	163 286	122 910	161 436	121 061	75.0
Medical	112 619	94 459	112 967	95 498	84.5
Culture and arts	31 398	19 459	31 665	19 728	62.3
Sport and tourism	6 763	1 684	7 012	1 933	27.6
Social and political org.	4 603	2 570	4 871	2 688	55.2
Management	180 851	54 237	179 987	55 413	30.8
Services	83 489	68 894	82 543	68 341	82.8
Security guards	44 706	2 393	46 942	2 600	5.5

Source: CSO: *Statistical Yearbook, 1991* (Sofia).

Table 2.9. Sectoral structure of employment by sex, Bulgaria, 1980-90

Sector and branch	1980 Men	1980 Women	1985 Men	1985 Women	1990 Men	1990 Women
	% share					
Material production						
Total employment	55.0	45.0	54.3	45.7	54.2	45.8
of which:						
Industry	51.7	48.5	51.0	49.0	51.9	49.1
Construction	79.8	20.2	79.0	21.0	77.9	22.1
Agriculture	51.5	48.5	51.3	48.7	52.9	47.1
Forestry	50.8	49.2	55.7	44.3	60.3	39.7
Transport	81.2	18.8	79.2	20.8	77.2	22.8
Communications	41.5	58.5	38.8	61.2	37.2	62.8
Trade	36.9	63.1	35.3	64.7	34.7	65.2
Other	49.0	51.0	48.0	52.0	43.5	56.5
Non-production sector						
Total employment	33.5	66.5	32.2	67.9	32.5	67.5
of which:						
Housing, communal and consumer services	51.4	48.6	51.3	48.7	55.5	44.5
Science	48.5	51.5	47.2	52.8	46.6	53.4
Education	26.0	74.5	23.7	76.3	24.6	75.4
Culture and arts	45.0	55.0	43.3	56.7	40.7	59.3
Health, social security, sport and tourism	34.9	75.1	25.2	74.8	25.9	74.1
Finances, credit and insurance	20.2	79.8	18.3	81.7	16.4	93.6
Administration	49.6	51.4	44.9	55.1	42.2	57.8
Other	60.2	39.8	53.1	46.9	52.1	47.9

Source: Estimates on the basis of data from CSO: *The Economy of Bulgaria: Statistical Yearbook, 1990* (Sofia), p. 31.

A recent survey of working women[14] suggests a lack of enthusiasm to move jobs or become entrepreneurs. Only 13 per cent work flexible hours, and only 10 per cent would consider starting a private business. At the same time, 10 per cent think it is wrong for women to work and 30 per cent would accept being a housewife only, provided their husband's income was sufficient to support the family.

Table 2.10 shows the age structure of employment in different branches of the economy. In most branches the average age of people employed is close to the national average, with the exception of agriculture and forestry where they are older. A large number of people over working age — about 88,000 — have jobs in the public sector, as well as in private activity (often private farms).

Table 2.10. **Employment by industry and age, Bulgaria, 1987 (percentage of total)**

Industry	Total	Years					Average age
		16-24	25-34	35-44	45-54	55-60	
Total	100.0	9.0	24.1	27.9	24.1	18.8	40.8
Industry	100.0	13.1	26.5	28.5	21.9	12.9	38.5
Construction	100.0	7.4	25.3	29.8	23.3	18.0	40.7
Agriculture	100.0	5.3	15.7	22.3	28.2	36.5	45.6
Forestry	100.0	5.1	16.5	21.5	24.5	42.6	46.0
Transport	100.0	8.0	27.2	31.0	23.8	11.9	39.6
Communications	100.0	10.3	25.7	28.9	22.2	16.5	39.7
Trade	100.0	8.2	29.5	31.5	19.4	14.4	39.2
Housing etc.	100.0	8.6	24.4	28.0	22.6	20.9	41.0
Science	100.0	6.7	28.5	31.8	22.1	13.8	39.8
Education	100.0	4.9	25.6	31.0	27.7	13.3	41.0
Culture, arts	100.0	7.0	29.2	31.0	21.4	14.4	39.6
Health, social security, sports	100.0	5.5	26.8	30.1	25.2	15.6	40.8
Finances, credit, insurance	100.0	10.0	29.4	31.8	20.7	9.9	38.4
Administration	100.0	5.4	34.3	25.6	22.9	13.8	38.4

Source: Workers and staff, Statistical Book, 1988, p. 115.

The implementation of measures to provide training for young workers has been hindered by lack of finance and by the established system by which the *nomenclatura* protect their jobs. Some 600,000 young people enter the labour market every year. The educational structure of the workforce shows a substantial difference between the material and non-material sectors. The ratio of workers with no secondary education in these sectors is 2.25:1. According to a sociological study in 1985,[15] 27.5 per cent of the active population have low qualifications, 43.3 per cent have medium-level qualifications and 29.2 per cent are highly qualified. A weak point of Bulgaria's system of labour supply is that the middle and upper echelons in administration and management have been recruited from among workers with a low level of education.

Labour mobility

Labour mobility involves both labour turnover — dismissals and recruitment — and changes of profession and social status. Data collected by the Central Statistical Office show that 588,902 people left their jobs in 1988; 5.6 per cent of them left as a result of the liquidation of their enterprise or redundancy. Over the same period 436,841 people were recruited, of whom 7,907 entered newly created jobs.

According to the most recent population census, only 12 per cent of the employed changed their working status in the five years 1980-85. At present labour turnover is limited by the fear of unemployment, and many of those who have set up and registered private firms still continue to work at their old jobs, usually in the state sector.

The most common migratory movements are between towns and from villages to towns. The main reason is a change of workplace; over the past two years the number of daily commuters has also grown. Education is an important factor. Younger and better qualified workers make up the bulk of potential and actual migrants.

In terms of emigration abroad, there is no defined emigrant status. Emigrants are simply those who have not returned to Bulgaria in the time expected. Data on emigration are collected as a by-product of travel statistics which suggest that, during January to September 1990, nearly 24,000 people (one quarter of them women) went abroad permanently ; 52,000 went abroad for private employment (including 9,000 women) ; and 200,000 went abroad for official employment (one eighth of them women)[16]. Emigration is politically a very sensitive issue, mainly because of the long-standing restrictions on travel abroad and the policy of alienation towards those who have left the country. However, migrant status needs to be defined soon, and in accordance with existing international conventions.

There have been two recent waves of emigration. In 1989, due to special factors, 300,000 Bulgarian Turks left Bulgaria, of whom almost 100,000 later returned.

A second wave occurred after the elections in July 1990, when about 240,000 people left the country. Some 70 per cent of those who applied for a visa quoted the political situation as the main reason for their interest in migration. Over three-quarters (78.2 per cent) of the migrants were men, 67 per cent were aged between 15 and 39, and the majority were highly qualified engineers, technicians, doctors and other specialists.

The more qualified migrants tend to go to western Europe, Canada and the United States, while the unskilled go to Turkey and to Greece. About 30,000 unskilled Bulgarians are employed in Greece, most of them illegally. A considerable number of Bulgarians also work in casual or seasonal employment in Turkey.

Public opinion polls have frequently sounded out interest in migration. There is great interest in working abroad, especially among qualified workers, with highly skilled specialists and academics showing the most likely to migrate. Public opinion on migration is negative, and usually sees it as an economic and social problem. Against this background the Government has abstained from preventing emigration but aims to ensure that migration takes place legally, through bilateral agreements with receiving countries.

Unemployment

An "unemployed" worker in Bulgaria is considered to be someone of working age who has not signed a work contract, who does not exercise any kind of paid activity, and is registered with an employment office (LEO) as seeking a job. There are two types of registered unemployed. The first, defined by government decrees, covers unemployment due to enterprise closures or redundancies. The second covers all other registered jobseekers. The first group receives unemployment benefit and monthly allowances for children under 16, for a period that depends on length of service and age. Young people, specialists and skilled workers are treated in a similar way. If they agree to take part in retraining courses they receive the national minimum wage for six months.

The second group of unemployed, though registered, are not entitled to unemployment benefits, and include:

- individuals who have left their jobs voluntarily and by mutual agreement;
- persons dismissed against their will for breach of discipline, e.g. for misconduct;
- persons whose temporary labour contract has expired. However, if they are dismissed during the period of their contract they are treated like other dismissed workers and are entitled to unemployment benefit and other allowances;
- persons who refuse employment. Whereas in the past they were usually forced to work, they can now register for employment at the LEO in the hope of receiving social security benefits.

Surveys show that 25 per cent of all the unemployed have not tried to find work. Among those who left their jobs voluntarily the figure is 31.5 per cent, and among those who have just completed their education, 31.6 per cent. There is also evidence that many unemployed, particularly young persons, are not registered, but numbers can only be guessed at.

Registered unemployment increased from 31,030 in July 1990 to 205,950 at the end of May 1991, to account for 5.4 per cent of the active population (table 2.11), even though structural change in the economy had hardly begun. Public sector productivity fell by almost 20 per cent, which suggests increases in unemployment in the future.

Table 2.11. **Unemployment, Bulgaria, 1990-91**

	Number	Monthly increase %
1990		
July	31 630	-
August	32 792	3.6
September	38 992	18.9
October	48 399	24.1
November	59 149	22.2
December	65 079	10.0
1991		
January	74 134	13.9
February	103 186	39.1
March	104 184	0.9
April	176 939	69.8
May	205 950	16.4
June	233 724	13.5
July	280 075	19.8
August	316 277	12.9
September	343 345	8.6
October	375 922	9.5
November	400 812	6.6
December	419 123	4.6

Source: Data published by the National Labour Exchange.

Those dismissed from the material production sector accounted for 83 per cent of all those entitled to unemployment benefits, of whom 54 per cent came from industry, 14 per cent from construction, 11 per cent from agriculture and 21 per cent from other branches.

The share of women in total unemployment is about 55 per cent. The share of women registered as unemployed due to enterprise closure or redundancy is greater than in the group which is not entitled to unemployment benefits, whose numbers are increasing. About 44 per cent of the unemployed are under 30 — a proportion that has been increasing — although the age group most affected is that between 30 and 50 years. In all age groups except those over 50, women predominate.

Manual workers, and those with only basic or primary education, represent the largest unemployed groups from the material production sector. In the non-material production sector, the worst affected groups are specialists and people with secondary education. An ever greater number of ordinary workers are being dismissed, and a high proportion of unemployed people have no particular occupation. Women account for more than 60 per cent of this group.

The majority of unemployed people live in urban areas. (Similarly, before 1989, 56 per cent of the economically inactive lived in towns). Today, the largest number of unemployed people live in Bulgaria's biggest cities, namely Plovdiv and Sofia districts. Combating local unemployment is not, however, a consequence of the numbers involved. Individual areas have different potentials for creating new jobs, based on local economic and industrial factors, human and natural resources, and local traditions. For example, the relatively high level of industrialisation of towns such as Sofia, Plovdiv and Gabrovo will enable them to offer a greater number of job opportunities than other towns with lower levels of unemployment but narrower industrial specialisations.

The short-term outlook for unemployment will reflect the following:

- the State will remain the main regulator of employment and will also be responsible for labour force allocation in the short term;
- the number of new jobs will lag behind the number of unemployed despite a wide range of incentives for employers and for enterprise development;
- the share of unemployed people with higher education began to shrink in early 1991. This group is more mobile and dynamic and can be expected to adjust to change more easily;
- the majority of unemployed people are women, but this proportion has been constant. Rising unemployment in the future will be mainly due to redundancies among the male workforce;
- emigration will increase, especially among younger and more qualified workers.

Official forecasts have predicted a doubling of the unemployment rate to 10 per cent or more by the end of 1991, depending on economic and social developments and the pace of privatisation.

Labour market policy

General policy

The main labour policy objective for the early period of transition has been to establish the legislative basis for well-functioning labour markets. The main thrust of the changes is to abolish administrative regulation in favour of a movement to a free labour market. Because this legislative basis is still in a preparatory stage, current problems in this area have been tackled by separate government decrees. Draft legislation — including the new employment law, the labour code and several decrees — was under discussion in mid-1991, but had not yet been adopted by the National Assembly.

In the job market itself, Bulgaria experienced lay-offs and a labour surplus at the begining of 1991, following the introduction of a new wage system and as a result of the deepening economic crisis. The Government could no longer guarantee full employment but did not initially acknowledge that unemployment had become a regular feature of the economy, using instead euphemisms such as "temporarily unoccupied" and "temporarily without employment".

In late 1989 the Government officially abandoned the full employment guarantee and in December 1989 it introduced certain income protection measures for the unemployed and a special fund for labour market measures. In 1990 a draft employment law was drawn up.

At first, workers laid off by enterprises received benefits for six months, equivalent initially to 100 per cent of earnings, falling to 50 per cent over time. After six months those still without jobs could receive unemployment assistance at a level equal to the minimum wage for a further three months. Workers who voluntarily left their jobs were not entitled to benefits.

The benefit system was changed in June 1991 as part of the process towards more final employment law. The level of benefit is now based on the minimum wage plus an earnings-related supplement of 20 per cent of the difference between the previous actual wage and the minimum wage. The duration of benefits depends on age and length of service. Benefits may be suspended or terminated if an unemployed person refuses to accept suitable employment or training.

In June 1991 the Government (in power since the general strike of late 1990) issued a decree which contained the major elements of the draft law as a result of discussions with unions and employers' organisations. In addition, the Government and the social partners accepted the general principles of the next stage of economic reform, thereby confirming the decree as a step towards legislation on labour market policies. Subsequently, the draft law was agreed upon in a tripartite commission. This tripartite agreement also requested the Government to expand training activities in 1991, discourage pensioners from working and prepare regional employment programmes. It called for the establishment of national and regional tripartite labour market commissions to supervise labour market administration; the regional bodies would be consulted on any major redundancy plans.

In terms of employment creation, the tripartite agreement emphasised the importance of the private sector and requested privatisation and demonopolisation programmes.

Finally, it asked for provisions, including early retirement, to protect workers at bankrupt enterprises.

At a more fundamental level, the tripartite accord stipulated an 8 per cent unemployment rate as a socially acceptable maximum. If unemployment rises above this level, the Government is required to take emergency measures.

The draft law, as well as the decree of June 1991, regulates the unemployment benefit system and the financing of income protection and active labour market measures; it contains provisions on the employment services, on assistance for job mobility, on the promotion of training and employment for new labour market entrants, on retraining, on wage subsidies for the disabled and on support for the unemployed who would like to set up small businesses. The decree introduces mobility grants to cover a proportion of moving expenses. Employers receive a subsidy equal to six months' minimum wage for employing young specialists and equal to three months' minimum wage for employing young workers with qualifications. The draft employment law requires employers to inform employment offices within three days of job vacancies, filled vacancies, workers hired through employment offices, job offers rejected and employers' rejections of candidates sent by employment offices.

Employment services

There are 121 employment offices in the country with almost 700 employees, against the 1,300 employees originally thought necessary by the Ministry of Labour for the present situation. These offices are organised on a regional basis under the aegis of the National Labour Exchange, supervised by the Ministry of Labour and Social Protection. These employment offices replace the former labour departments within the local people's councils. Their main functions include registering the unemployed, providing information about vacancies, paying out unemployment benefits and giving financial assistance for retraining courses. The offices have recently started to offer other services, such as assistance for setting up a business and active help for young specialists to find employment.

One survey found that only 5.2 per cent of unemployed people relied entirely on employment offices when looking for work, while 37.9 per cent had no confidence in them.[17] Employment offices evidently fall short of what an efficient labour exchange should offer. The professional level of staff is not high and there are few sociologists, psychologists and expert advisers. The staff also lack technical equipment and experience. In addition, the command economy mentality of the old labour departments is still prevalent and is impeding any successful development of services to the unemployed.

Private employment bureaux were established in 1990, but were declared illegal in early 1991. The draft employment law however, permits their existence under the supervision of the Ministry of Labour.

Labour restructuring and upgrading policies

To attend a retraining course a worker must normally be employed under a contract of labour . If there is no such contract, the worker must meet his or her own retraining expenses. The Ministry of Labour and Social Protection has announced that the professional and training centres for labour reskilling will be maintained as they are.

Official data show that only a tiny number of the unemployed attend retraining courses: 2,201 at the end of 1990 (0.9 per cent of those registered), and 4,068 in May 1991 (3.9 per cent). Most attend short courses of one to three months.[18] Surveys show that only 17.4 per cent of workers say they are ready to retrain, 35 per cent do not wish to retrain while 47 per cent have not considered the matter.

The system of professional qualifications has disintegrated. Under the previous economic regime, one-quarter of all workers had to attend training courses each year. The old standards and training methods were subsequently abandoned, and training centres were deprived of resources for retraining with funds directed elsewhere. However, no new qualification and retraining system has yet been established. The tripartite agreement requested the Government to allocate 135 million leva for the modernisation of the training and retraining system and set a target of 30,000 unemployed to be trained under the new system by the end of 1991.

In 1991 regional employment programmes, seen as the route to accelerating the implementation of future employment and unemployment measures, were still in the course of preparation.

The development of small and medium-sized businesses offers one avenue for providing jobs and reducing unemployment. There were 140,000 registered private firms in spring 1991; registrations will soon reach 200,000. Data from the National Public Opinion Research Centre show that about 5 per cent of the total population is engaged in private business — equivalent to 425,000 people or 10 per cent of the economically active population. However, nearly 30 per cent of registered firms are not trading owing to the general economic crisis.

The new procedure of public auctions for selling smaller trading and service enterprises may give an impetus to the development of private businesses. In June 1991, the first petrol stations were sold to private individuals. However, most Bulgarian citizens do not have the financial means to take part in the auctions; consequently, the level of foreign investment is causing concern in some quarters.

Policies to reduce labour supply

Measures have been taken to limit the number of working pensioners, estimated at 88,000, equivalent to 42 per cent of the current unemployment figures. Employers who use pensioners at work have to pay contributions to a "qualification and upgrading" fund at the rate of 30 per cent of the wages fund — that is nearly ten times the present rate of 3.75 per cent. In response to significant numbers of redundancies, early retirement is also being encouraged.

An option frequently discussed for the reduction in the number of workers seeking employment is the repopulation of rural areas. The rapid industrialisation in the 1950s and 1960s led to large numbers of agricultural workers leaving their villages for urban areas — but many of them maintained their links with the villages and with farming. One great advantage of a return to the rural areas is the stock of vacant housing. However, while there is some interest among workers to return as small, independent farmers, it is difficult to see how a large number of those who moved to the urban centres could go back.

Migration could be an important aspect of the supply side of the employment question, given the great interest among certain parts of the Bulgarian population for work abroad. The government aim is to negotiate official state contracts for those working abroad. The first contract for 4,000 construction workers has been concluded with Germany; another contract was to be signed with Greece in June 1991.

Labour market budget

The financing of labour market measures comes mainly from the "qualification and upgrading" fund, financed by enterprises and the State through a tax on the wages fund. Originally set at 0.5 per cent, the tax was raised to 3.75 per cent and may, depending on predicted unemployment levels, reach 5 per cent. The fund's current resources, at about 0.2 per cent of national income, are completely inadequate.

Policies for income support

Growth of poverty

The number of people living in poverty in Bulgaria has grown since the transition towards a market economy was begun at the end of 1989, with steep falls in real incomes, including income in kind (table 2.12). One effect of poverty has been the rising proportion of income in kind in total household income. Its share rose from 5.9 per cent of total income in January 1990 to 16.4 per cent in February 1991 and 12.9 per cent in March 1991. During summer 1991, this share will have been larger, given the seasonal character of agricultural production that makes up the bulk of income in kind.

Table 2.12. **Growth of nominal and real incomes[1], Bulgaria, 1990-91**

	Nominal incomes	Consumer prices	Real incomes
	May 1990 = 100		
1990			
May	100.0	100.0	100.0
June	109.5	104.1	105.1
July	106.8	107.8	99.0
August	116.9	119.5	97.8
September	129.9	124.9	104.0
October	124.8	130.0	96.0
November	116.1	136.4	85.0
December	121.8	150.6	80.9
1991			
January	109.5	170.1	64.3
February	156.3	379.2	41.2
March	200.9	570.7	35.2

1. Total income comprises cash and income in kind.
Source: Monthly data from *Household Budget Survey,* Central Statistical Office.

The growth of poverty has not been confined to the period of the price shocks and the first steps towards reform. As table 2.12 shows, real incomes fell steadily after May 1990, when the new consumer price index was introduced. The monthly drop was 11 per cent in November 1990, 5 per cent in December, 21 per cent in January 1991, 36 per cent in February and 15 per cent in March. It is obvious that, whatever the definitions and methods for estimating incomes, the decline has been dramatic.

The price of transition for the Bulgarian population has therefore been extremely high. Since 1989, the proportion of households and individuals on or below the social minimum income has increased significantly. According to official data, in 1989, 40.9 per cent of households had incomes below the social minimum level and 17.9 per cent had incomes below subsistence levels. Over 70 per cent of households and individuals fell below the social minimum in March 1991 of 715.67 leva (table 2.13). Falling consumption also shows a significant proportion of the population at or below the social minimum.

Table 2.13. **Per capita income distribution of households, Bulgaria, 1991**

Leva per month	January %	February %	March %
Up to 220	45.0	16.0	4.5
221-260	13.2	7.7	3.1
261-300	10.6	9.8	4.1
301-340	7.8	10.7	7.1
341-380	6.5	14.6	12.6
381-420	4.0	9.5	12.5
421-460	3.8	6.8	10.1
461-500	1.8	5.0	8.2
501-540	1.8	3.5	6.8
Over 540	5.5	16.9	30.9

Note : Percentages may not add up exactly owing to rounding.
Source: Central Statistical Office.

As table 2.14 shows, sales of many basic consumer goods fell sharply in the year to early 1991. For some goods — such as sugar, coffee and soap — the drop in sales reflected the existence of household stocks. For other goods though, lower sales were a direct indication of lower consumption — about 30 per cent for milk, 63 per cent for meat and 78 per cent for fish. Purchases of clothes, textiles and shoes fell by about half.

Table 2.14. **Sales of selected consumer goods, Bulgaria, 1990-91**

	(Q1-1991 / Q1-1990) %
Sugar	19.8
Milk	70.7
Coffee	55.5
Cheese	59.3
Eggs	51.3
Wine	69.8
Soap	70.5
Bread	106.1
Meat	37.3
Fish	21.6
Cigarettes	98.9
Shoes	49.4
Woollen material	49.4
Cotton	38.9

Source: Central Statistical Office, Consumer basket of 32 goods, in *Fax*, No. 61, 13 June 1991.

The drop in consumption was reflected in a major restructuring of household budgets. As a result of higher food prices, spending on food increased from 33.8 per cent of household income in March 1990 to 53.3 per cent in February 1991 and 46.1 per cent in March. Spending on clothes, shoes and furniture fell by half, as did spending on transport. Impoverishment and falling consumption have resulted in a lack of essential vitamins and proteins for the Bulgarian population — especially detrimental for children — with unpredictable consequences for the country.

The national economic crisis has also been a household economic crisis (table 2.15). The deficit between current income and expenditure in the family budget increased from 36 leva in January 1990 (5.1 per cent of income) to 143 leva in March 1991 (7.6 per cent of income). This shortfall may have been bridged by previous savings, goods in kind or loans from relatives and friends.

Table 2.15. **Total incomes and total household expenditure, Bulgaria, 1990-91 (leva per capita)**

	1990			1991		
	Jan.	Feb.	March	Jan.	Feb.	March
Total income	708	748	860	1 119	1 434	1 888
Total expenditure	744	757	876	1 210	1 586	2 031
Deficit	36	9	16	91	152	143
Deficit as % of income	5.1	1.2	1.9	8.1	10.6	7.6

Source: Central Statistical Office.

The share of income from loans and savings rose sharply in 1990-91 as a result of high interest rates that encouraged both the repayment of loans and an increase in deposits (table 2.16). This policy may stimulate households to save and invest more; at present, investment in profitable activities is insignificant in family budgets (they are included in the "other" category in table 2.17). After the price shock has subsided household investment may gradually improve and play a significant role.

Table 2.16. **Household savings, Bulgaria, 1990-91 (leva per capita)**

	1990			1991		
	Jan.	Feb.	Mar.	Jan.	Feb.	Mar.
Withdrawals	49.0	79.0	124.0	137.0	174.0	201.0
Deposits	54.0	66.0	83.0	59.0	79.0	92.0

Source: Central Statistical Office.

Table 2.17. **Structure of household expenditure, Bulgaria, 1990-91 (percentage shares)**

	1990			1991		
	Jan.	Feb.	Mar.	Jan.	Feb.	Mar.
Total	100.0	100.0	100.0	100.0	100.0	100.0
Food	36.7	35.4	33.8	35.1	53.3	46.1
Spirits	3.0	2.9	3.1	4.3	3.3	3.1
Tobacco	2.5	2.4	2.0	3.2	3.3	3.0
Clothing	12.7	11.9	12.1	15.1	8.1	8.3
Housing	6.7	6.9	8.0	6.8	5.8	8.4
Furniture	3.3	4.0	4.6	5.1	2.8	2.3
Culture	4.5	5.9	4.2	4.2	2.8	3.8
Health	2.5	2.4	2.2	2.0	1.9	1.8
Transport	10.3	11.0	8.4	4.2	4.8	5.6
Taxes	8.6	8.2	7.2	6.5	4.5	5.0
Other	10.2	9.0	14.4	13.5	9.4	12.6

Note : Percentages may not add up exactly owing to rounding.
Source: Central Statistical Office.

Growth of inequality

The income structure of society was transformed in the first three months of 1991, with a shift towards higher income groups (table 2.13). In January 1991 about 7 per cent of households had incomes of 501 leva or above, in February 20 per cent, and in March 38 per cent.

The traditional advantage in living standards of urban centres over the countryside also disappeared. In February 1991 incomes of rural workers exceeded those of urban workers by 12 per cent (table 2.18). The immediate costs of the reform have been higher for the urban population, not only because of higher prices in the cities, but also because rural households have more reserves in terms of cash and goods in kind.

The growth of unemployment increased income differentiation between households with different numbers of people employed (table 2.18). Between January and February 1991, the biggest nominal increase in income was for households with no working members. Their income more than doubled while that of families with three working members rose by just 25 per cent. This did not materially alter the huge gap between them: households with no working members had incomes of less than half of those with three workers. Consequently because the burden of the crisis is evidently much greater for non-working households, more people are likely to want jobs, thereby increasing the labour supply and exacerbating unemployment.

The economic crisis has transformed income stratification by social group (table 2.18). The most significant changes were experienced by families of workers, who slipped from second to last place in the income ranking between February and March 1991. By contrast, "other" households (mostly entrepreneurs) had the lowest incomes in January but the highest ones in February and March. The incomes of rural households increased faster than those of workers and staff.

54

Table 2.18. **Household income by group, Bulgaria, 1991 (leva per month)**

	January	February	March
Household income by employment status			
With one employed	703.5	1 022.6	1 303.9
With two employed	1 104.9	1 464.8	1 954.5
With three employed	1 477.3	1 834.6	2 560.9
None employed	369.2	804.9	860.2
Coefficient of variation (v)	45.6	31.1	38.6
Income of rural household	868.7	1 134.5	1 512.8
Income of urban household	842.5	1 402.7	1 699.2
Household income by social status			
Workers	843.9	1 180.4	1 532.8
Staff (incl. managers)	946.7	1 249.6	1 617.6
Agricultural workers	742.1	1 319.5	1 583.6
Others	651.3	1 676.2	2 304.3
Coefficient of variation (v)	13.9	14.1	17.9

Source: Central Statistical Office.

Social policy

Social policy in the transition towards a market economy in Bulgaria faces four basic constraints.

First, the economic crisis and stagnation limit the funds available to implement social policy measures. Consequently, measures to implement social policy will not be very ambitious or effective.

Second, an unexpectedly high rate of impoverishment of the population, with many falling below the social minimum income in February and March 1991, has been confronted by the problem of a treasury left almost empty by the last socialist government. High levels of social protection would have increased inflationary pressures in the whole economy. This situation has defined the basic approach of social policy, namely, higher protection for non-working and low-income groups to guarantee their survival in recession. Middle and high-income groups received little protection and suffered relatively more with a significant proportion of them joining the ranks of the poor.

Third, trade unions exerted heavy pressure on the Government from the end of 1989 up to the present. Thus state institutions were to a great extent forced to create a social policy that accorded with the demands of the trade unions.

Fourth, as with economic reform, the Government's social policy is influenced by the International Monetary Fund (IMF) and the World Bank, because of the aid they have promised. The implementation of some of these institutions' proposals may restrict social spending.

All these constraints resulted in a very narrow range of social policy measures over the period. The ever greater hardships suffered by the population were emphasised by the country's negotiators during the second stage of the reform discussions with the IMF in May 1991. Such hardships not only have social, psychological and physiological effects, but also an adverse economic impact: the dramatic downturn of consumer demand contributed to the economic decline and further recession is in prospect.

Changes in social policy since the end of 1989 reflect agreements reached with the trade unions. With no law on social security and related legislation to define social policy during the transition, the agreements later issued as government decrees, served as the basis for social policy.

Up to the second stage of economic reform, social policy was hampered by the lack of legislation and the proliferation of decrees, agreements and so on. Social funds were not maintained separately but remained part of the state budget managed under the old regulations. This budget had to absorb the additional social benefits. Nevertheless, several important steps were made towards changes in social policy.

A new system of income tax was introduced in January 1991. Its main features are: raising the threshold for tax-free income to above the minimum wage level; second, treating all incomes equally (wages, fees, private activities, etc.). Under the previous system incomes from private activities were taxed at 85 per cent; third, raising the thresholds for higher rates of tax and lowering the rates (e.g., 40 per cent at 20,000 leva) thereby allowing for significant increases in income; fourth, exempting agricultural incomes from taxation for five years.

Pension policy also underwent a profound change. From January 1990 the maximum pension was substantially reduced, which hit hard the extremely high pensions of those known as "active anti-fascists" and former political and economic leaders. The minimum pension was also raised, beginning a process of redistribution that will sever the link between pensions and an individual's previous employment record. As pensioners were regarded as a "socially weak" group, they received the maximum compensation and indexation — equal to the minimum wage compensation and indexation — throughout the period. This resulted in rapid growth of the share of pensions in the income structure. In November 1990 three types of minimum pension were introduced - a retirement pension (75 per cent of the minimum wage), a disability pension (70 per cent of the minimum wage) and "other pensions" (60 per cent of the minimum wage). According to the tripartite agreement on the second stage of economic reform, the consolidation of the minimum wage (including compensation) will result in higher pension levels.

A similar policy was implemented for child allowances, student grants, unemployment benefits, etc., with payments out of the state budget. The aubersoul and inflexible system of social security benefits was largely responsible for the insignificant role played by the benefits themselves in the previous social protection mechanism.

Socially weak groups were helped to some extent by foreign charities, as well as by charities and mutual aid at home, which distributed free meals, clothes for the poor, etc. Many political, trade union, public and other organisations took part in such activities.

The second stage of economic reform required a greater pace in adapting social policy to market conditions. As outlined in the June 1991 tripartite agreement, the main objectives of the new social policy were as follows.

First, a second social safety net for the poorest levels of society was to be established, with a differentiated approach to each. The social minimum would be determined according to age, health, number of household members, etc., and not averaged across the whole country. In this way an attempt was thus being made to reverse the levelling effects of previous social measures and to target allowances on needy groups.

Second, child allowances were to be paid from the budget as a fixed amount for each child, but varied according to family needs.

Third, social policy was to be implemented at national and regional levels, with initiatives subject to discussion by the tripartite commission. The planned adoption of the two principal laws on social security benefits gave an impetus to the development of the legislative basis of social policy.

Fourth, the social insurance funds were to become independent of the State. The main problem related to their initial size as they could not be funded entirely from the budget. The Confederation of Labour, *Podkrepa* suggested using the proceeds of property confiscated from the various organisations of the former regime. All Bulgarian investments and firms abroad are to be subject to an inventory.

Fifth, credits are to be given to students to help them pay for education, and a new student grant system will also be established.

As of mid-1991, all these resolutions contained in the tripartite agreement are due to be implemented in the near future.

Wages, incomes policy and industrial relations

Wage differentials

When at the end of 1989, social and economic reforms began in Bulgaria, there was a relatively closed and stable industry wage structure (table 2.19). Over the ten years 1980-90, the average nominal wage increased by 78.3 per cent.[19] The rise was largest in public health (97.6 per cent), agriculture (93.1 per cent) and finance (91.2 per cent). Much of the increase took place in 1990; in 1989-90 the average wage jumped by 27.6 per cent, with a bigger rise in the non-production sector (37.4 per cent) than in material production (25.6 per cent). One factor for the rapid wage changes in 1990 was the introduction of the "new system of basic wages"; this preserved centrally planned wage regulation but allowed management of enterprises some freedom in fixing individual wages, contributing in turn to a reduction in employment and wider wage differentials. Another factor was the wave of strikes, aimed mainly at raising wages, which led to pay rises in transport, public health and education.

Table 2.19. **Monthly nominal average wages by industry, Bulgaria, 1980-90**

| | Average wage (leva) | | | % increase | |
	1980	1985	1990	1980-90	1989-90
Total	189	223	337	78.3	27.6
Industry	202	243	346	71.3	19.5
Construction	214	258	379	77.1	27.6
Agriculture	175	208	338	93.1	35.0
Forestry	140	160	265	89.3	19.0
Transport	213	246	391	83.6	29.0
Communications	167	199	332	98.8	32.0
Trade	166	189	283	70.5	31.7
Other branches of material production	185	224	325	75.7	17.5
Housing	166	185	294	77.1	28.1
Science	208	241	349	67.8	19.4
Education, culture, arts	172	193	288	67.4	30.0
Health, social security, sport	170	200	336	97.6	54.5
Finance, credit, insurance	170	203	325	91.2	37.7
Administration	214	241	368	72.0	38.1
Other non-production branches	206	232	352	70.9	27.2
Wage dispersion (σ)	22.8	28.3	35.4		
Coefficient of variation between industries (v)	12.6	12.7	10.5		

Source: CSO: *Rabotna zaplata na personala za July 1990* (Employees' incomes in July 1990) (Sofia, 1991), p. 5.

In the second half of 1990 the main determinant of wage changes was the collapse of the economy as pent-up inflation and economic imbalances came into the open once the Zhivkov regime fell. The severing of economic relations between Bulgaria and the former Soviet Union led to a shortage of raw and secondary materials and a lack of markets for Bulgaria's output. The resulting loss of sales caused a shortage of funds with which to pay wages (see below).

From 1980 to 1990 inter-industry wage differentials narrowed slightly. The coefficient of variation fell from 12.6 in 1980 and 12.7 in 1985 to 10.5 in 1990. This levelling became more marked after the introduction of anti-inflationary policies in 1990.

In 1990 occupational wage differentiation was considerable (table 2.20). Managers were the best paid. On average, "specialists" (with development and supervisory responsibilities) earned only a little more than workers. Relatively, the worst paid were specialists in material production, where average wages were higher than elsewhere (table 2.21).

The biggest gap between the salaries of specialists and managers was in public health, followed by education. A tendency to undervalue the work of specialists and their low status in society is seen in the fact that drivers and mechanics in the transport industry earned an average wage of about 395 leva a month, miners 509 leva, metallurgists 448 leva and specialists with higher education and qualifications in public health (doctors, pharmacists, dentists) 381 leva. Scientists earned on average 358 leva.[20]

Table 2.20. **Wage differentiation by occupation, Bulgaria, 1990**

Occupation	Average monthly wage (leva)	Proportion of average wage
Total (average wage)	337	1.00
Workers	331	0.98
Specialists	346	1.02
Managers	446	1.32
Auxiliary and service personnel	260	0.77
Security guards	218	0.64
Wage dispersion (σ)	80.1	
Coefficient of variation (v)	23.7	

Note: Workers: employed directly in production.
Specialists: with development and supervisory responsibilities.
Auxiliary and service personnel: in production and management.
Source: CSO: Rabotna zaplata na personala za July 1990, (Sofia, 1991), pp. 16-17.

Table 2.21. **Wage differentiation by occupation and industry, Bulgaria, 1990**

| | Proportion of average wage in relevant industry | | |
	Workers	Specialists	Managers
Average wage	1.00	1.00	1.00
Industry	0.98	0.99	1.24
Construction	1.01	0.98	1.16
Agriculture	1.01	0.91	1.28
Transport	1.01	1.02	1.18
Science	0.87	1.11	1.39
Education	0.71	1.05	1.45
Public health	0.75	1.13	1.68

Source: CSO: *Rabotna zaplata na personala za July 1990*, (Sofia, 1991).

Regional differentials were small, ranging from 96 per cent to 106 per cent of the average wage. This was due to the administrative division of the country in 1985, designed to create regions that covered developed and economically weak areas to disguise regional inequalities. The highest wages were in Sofia, a feature of the once strong position of large towns (especially the capital) in terms of wages, incomes, living standards and so on. This changed rapidly with the start of reform; urban areas suffered not only higher consumer prices but also more redundancies and higher unemployment.

In general, women receive lower wages than men (table 2.22). In 1990, the difference in average nominal wages was about 25 per cent. There were no sectors where women's wages were equal to or higher than men's. They worked not only in lower-paid sectors, but in lower-paid jobs and occupations within them. Labour safety standards meant that fewer women than men worked in poor conditions, but work in such conditions is often better paid.

The main reason, however, for women's lower average wages is their absence from highly-paid managerial positions. A correlation also exists between women's share of employment in an industry and the wage level. Feminised industries (public health, education, finance) have lower wages, which cannot be explained by lower levels of education or skills.

Uneven nominal wage growth in 1990 led to widening inequality (table 2.23). In 1980 and 1985, the share of employees receiving wages below the minimum was about 3 per cent. In 1990, 11.6 per cent of employees earned 200 leva or less a month which — bearing in mind mounting inflation — were poverty wages.[21] Meanwhile, the number earning higher wages also increased.

Table 2.22. **Wage differentials by sex and industry, Bulgaria, 1990**

	Average monthly wage (in leva)		Ratio (2) to (1)
	Men (1)	Women (2)	(3)
Total	383	291	75.9
Industry	397	295	74.3
Construction	452	306	67.6
Agriculture	400	276	69.0
Forestry	298	232	77.8
Transport	476	306	64.3
Communications	349	315	90.2
Trade	298	268	89.9
Other branches of material production	346	304	87.8
Housing	330	258	78.2
Science	384	314	81.7
Education, culture, arts	307	285	92.8
Health, social security, sport	299	259	86.6
Finance, credit, insurance	347	325	93.6
Administration	339	311	91.7
Other non-production branches	394	310	78.6

Source: CSO: *Rabotna zaplata na personala za July 1990*, (Sofia,1991).

Table 2.23. **Employment by nominal wage level, Bulgaria, 1980-90**

Monthly wage (leva)	1980		1985		1990	
	Number	%	Number	%	Number	%
Up to 100	105 924	3.0	85 299	2.5	-	-
101-200	2 227 872	63.2	1 616 221	46.5	358 225	11.6
201-260	645 610	18.4	775 908	22.4	595 374	19.4
261-350	543 428[1]	15.4	733 252	21.1	1 003 130	32.8
351-450			259 743[2]	7.5	633 888	20.6
451-500					165 997	5.4
501-600					167 529	5.5
601 and over					139 537	4.7

1. 261 leva and over.
2. 351 leva and over.
Source: The Economy of Bulgaria, (Sofia, 1991), p. 118.

Wages, incomes and prices

The second half of 1990 and the first quarter of 1991 saw a fall in employment (about 12 per cent) and a squeeze on real wages as a result of indexation and compensation policy (table 2.24). Between the last quarter of 1990 and the first quarter of 1991, the nominal wage fund dropped by about 7 per cent while nominal wages increased by only 4 per cent. The tripartite agreement provided for wage compensation for sharp price increases, which enterprises had to pay out of their reserves. According to the agreement, compensation of 520 leva per worker should have been paid for February and March alone. In the first quarter of 1991, 1,320 million leva was paid as compensation, equivalent to only 388 leva per person employed.

Nevertheless, as table 2.24 shows, the nominal wage fund would have fallen by 32 per cent in the first quarter of 1991 and the nominal wage fund per employed person by 23 per cent if compensation had been paid. Thus, nominal wage changes in early 1991 were largely due to compensation, with basic wages practically frozen.

Table 2.24. **Quarterly change in nominal wages, Bulgaria, 1990-91 with compensation (without compensation in brackets)**

	1990				1991
	Q1	Q2	Q3	Q4	Q1
Employed:					
(thousands)	3 381	3 855	3 851	3 819	3 404
% change from previous quarter	..	0.6	-0.1	-0.8	-10.9
Wage fund:					
(million leva)	3 157	3 596	3 909	5 370	4 986
					(3 666)
(% change from previous quarter)	..	13.9	8.7	37.4	-7.2
					(-31.7)
Wages per employed person:					
(leva)	824	933	1 015	1 406	1 465
					(1 077)
% change from previous quarter	..	13.2	8.8	38.5	4.2
					(-23.4)

Source: Preliminary data from Labour Department of Central Statistical Office.

These developments in nominal wages are similar to those in nominal cash incomes (table 2.25). Both increased at a slower rate in the first quarter of 1991 than in the last quarter of 1990. The unusual increase in wages and incomes at the end of 1990 reflects the fact that indexation payments for the previous five months were all received in this period. In addition, under the existing wage system, profit-sharing bonuses are paid at the end of the year. Another reason for the fall in enterprises' wage funds in the first quarter of 1991 was the economic crisis.

Table 2.25. **Growth and structure of cash income by source, Bulgaria, 1990-91**

| | 1990 | | | | | | | | 1991 | |
| | Q1 | | Q2 | | Q3 | | Q4 | | Q1 | |
	%	Index[1]	%	Index	%	Index	%	Index	%	Index
Cash incomes	100.0	1.00	100.0	1.17	100.0	1.19	100.0	1.64	100.0	1.81
Wages	54.6	1.00	52.8	1.11	57.2	1.24	56.9	1.71	47.1	1.56
Sales of farm produce	5.1	1.00	4.9	1.14	4.5	1.07	9.7	3.09	9.2	1.15
Pensions	14.1	1.00	13.0	1.08	13.2	1.10	13.0	2.72	18.7	2.51
Social benefits	5.8	1.00	4.7	0.96	5.1	1.04	6.8	1.88	6.1	1.91
Grants	0.3	1.00	0.0	0.50	0.4	3.00	0.4	1.33	0.4	1.96
Insurance compensations	1.7	1.00	2.1	1.47	0.8	0.61	2.1	2.06	0.9	1.03
Loans	6.1	1.00	10.8	2.12	9.5	1.85	7.4	1.98	2.3	0.67
Interest receipts	0.8	1.00	0.9	0.23	-	0.33	0.6	0.45	7.0	15.60
Others	11.5	1.00	10.8	1.07	9.3	0.88	3.7	0.50	14.6	1.18

1. 1st quarter of 1990 = 1.00
Note : Percentages may not add up exactly owing to rounding.
Source: Preliminary data from the Central Statistical Office.

The beginning of 1991 saw enterprises in a very difficult situation. With production slowing, they were spending their wage funds on the indexation costs for the last five months of 1990. As a result, by the end of April 1991, 37 per cent of enterprises had workers on compulsory unpaid leave. (These workers were not entitled to any indexation or compensation payments according to Decree No. 8 of 1991).[22] About 8 per cent of enterprises were on short-time working and 12 per cent had given notice of lay-offs. According to data from the Central Statistical Office, in the first quarter of 1991 nearly 2 million working days were lost as a result of unpaid leave.[23]

Table 2.29 shows that different sources of income have played different roles in income changes over time. Wages were quite important until the end of 1990, after which wages grew more slowly than other incomes. The relative share of wages in total incomes slipped from 54.6 per cent in the first quarter of 1990 to 47.1 per cent in the first quarter of 1991.

The steady growth of pensions, resulting from government policy to protect pensioners' incomes, accounts for their increasing share in cash incomes, from 14.1 per cent to 18.7 per cent over the year to the first quarter of 1991.

Revenue from sales of agricultural products surged in the last quarter of 1990, but then fell back. The reason was not only the seasonal character of this income source but also the dramatic shortage of foodstuffs which meant that people ate their own produce rather than selling it. The importance of private smallholdings for income and employment can be shown using household budget data (see the section on policies for income support), and they played a vital role in coping with the unexpectedly strong price shock, given an ineffective compensation policy.

The most variable elements of income were loans and interest receipts, the result of the Government's successful monetary policy. Between the fourth quarter of 1990 and the first quarter of 1991, the share of interest receipts increased from 0.8 per cent to 7 per cent of incomes. There was a rush to repay loans after price liberalisation, prompted by the announced rise in interest rates on savings. About one-third of cash held by the public was withdrawn from circulation as high interest rates encouraged people to deposit their money with the banks.

A new consumer price index (based on a representative basket of consumer goods for households with incomes around the social minimum) was introduced in May 1990 by the Central Statistical Office. Table 2.26 shows the first big price rises in August 1990 with the liberalisation of fruit and vegetable prices and the second in February and March 1991 when all prices (excluding electricity, gas and coal) were freed. The delayed liberalisation detonated a price explosion. In April 1991 prices were nearly six times their level of May 1990. The Government forecast a post-liberalisation rise in the price level of 225 per cent, but the actual increase over December 1990 was 379 per cent to March 1991 and 388 per cent to April. Since then consumer prices have risen more slowly, though the prices of foodstuffs have increased faster than those of other goods.

With nominal wages and incomes growing sluggishly, real wages and incomes slumped in the first quarter of 1991 (table 2.27).[24] Real wages fell to 41.1 per cent and real incomes to 36.5 per cent of their level in the last quarter of 1990. The real minimum wage also declined sharply to 51.6 per cent of its May 1990 level in April 1991 (table 2.26).

Table 2.26. **Changes in nominal and real minimum wages, Bulgaria, 1990-91**

	Consumer prices	Nominal monthly minimum wage	Nominal minimum wage	Real minimum wage
	(May 1990 = 100)	(leva)	(May 1990 = 100)	
1990				
May	100.0	165	100.0	100.0
June	104.1	165	100.0	96.1
July	107.8	165	100.0	92.8
August	119.5	165	100.0	83.7
September	124.9	191	115.7	93.3
October	130.0	191	115.7	89.0
November	136.4	191	115.7	85.0
December	150.6	210	127.3	84.3
1991				
January	170.1	229	138.3	81.6
February	379.2	435	263.6	69.5
March	570.7	435	263.6	46.2
April	585.0	518	313.9	51.6
May		505		
June		620		

Source: Department for Statistical Study of Prices, Central Statistical Office.

Table 2.27. **Quarterly change in nominal and real wages and incomes, Bulgaria, 1990-91**

| | % change from previous quarter in: | | | | |
	Nominal wages	Real wages	Nominal cash incomes	Real cash incomes	Consumer price index
1990					
Q1	-	-	-	-	-
Q2	12.6	8.1	13.7	9.2	4.1
Q3	9.5	-8.7	9.0	-3.4	12.8
Q4	40.7	18.8	37.5	23.5	11.3
1991					
Q1	2.5	-58.9	-8.9	-63.5	149.3

Source: Computed from data available in Labour and Balance Departments, Central Statistical Office.

The reason why reform has been so costly for the population is the collapse of the economy. According to government figures, production was about 22 per cent lower in April 1991 than in December 1990. According to the trade unions, the drop was as much as 40 per cent and, according to the leader of the Union of Owner Initiative, it was 38 per cent. This collapse was caused by a number of factors, including: the damaging consequences of the Gulf War for the Bulgarian economy (Iraq's debt to Bulgaria was the State's biggest outstanding foreign loan); delayed credits from international institutions; the severing of economic relations with the former Soviet Union; the unstable domestic political situation; and inefficient and inadequate management of enterprises.

With output declining and markets shrinking, most enterprises could pay wage increases only by reducing employment. According to the Institute for Social and Trade Union Research, in mid-1991 nearly 46 per cent of enterprises could not afford to pay a minimum wage of 670 leva (the minimum wage for July 1991 was fixed by the Government and the social partners at 652 leva).[25] Under these circumstances, the depressed economy needed active structural, privatisation and investment policies, the foundations of which were laid by the tripartite agreement of June 1991.

Wage policy

Centralised wage regulation was modified in 1989-90 by the "new system of basic wages", which granted some freedom to enterprises in distributing the wage fund. The State made an attempt to regulate the total wage fund and relax control over individual wages, but without much success.

The tripartite system established at the beginning of 1990 had a strong impact on wage regulation. Under trade union pressure the Government was compelled to increase the minimum wage in spring 1990. The centralised approach was maintained, with the agreement of the social partners. Wage bargaining was implemented at national level and covered only price compensation, indexation and minimum wages. Decree No. 103 of October 1990 introduced an automatic indexation mechanism with the aim of protecting wages against inflation. For wages more than 1.7 times higher than the minimum, less than full indexation was applied. This put average and high-wage groups at a disadvantage and restored the levelling of incomes.

Another feature of the indexation mechanism was the delay in implementation. Index-linked rises were paid three months after the tripartite agreement was signed. However, the rise in inflation and the decline of production made further operation of the indexation mechanism impossible.

The choice of mechanism for compensating wage earners against inflation was influenced at the start of the economic reform by the IMF. The social partners negotiated a 30 per cent decline in living standards, but prices far exceeded government forecasts. Output dropped drastically and in this situation the social safety net could not operate effectively. Wage levelling increased still further. The shortage of funds at enterprise level made conditions in the material production sector yet more difficult. Compensation per person employed during the first quarter of 1991 amounted to 418 leva in the non-production sector and 408 leva in the material sector. An important reason for the low efficiency of the compensation system was the decision that wage indexation should cover only people working under a basic labour contract. Since employees in the private sector do not have such contracts they were deprived of compensation.

These problems and the deep recession necessitated the introduction of a new wages policy for the second stage of the economic reform. The new policy abandoned compensation and indexation, and introduced wage bargaining at branch, regional and enterprise levels parallel with national bargaining. The role of national wage bargaining is to fix the minimum wage and to give some "advisory" coefficients for wages based on education and skill levels. The State has given up management of individual wages and concentrated its efforts on the regulation of wage funds so as to control inflationary pressures resulting from the growth in wages.

To soften the effect of the abandonment of compensation and indexation, and taking into account the excessive impoverishment of the population, the Government raised the threshold below which wage fund growth is untaxed. Under the previous system, growth below 3 per cent was tax free; above this percentage wage increases were heavily taxed. Under the new system the level has been increased to 34 per cent.

The trade unions believe that the implementation of wage bargaining will remove the last obstacle to the establishment of a labour market and may enable them to play a bigger role in enterprises. However, it may also increase competition between the big trade union organisations; according to the amended Labour Code it will be possible to have several collective agreements in the same enterprise. Wage bargaining in conditions of stagnation might also revive still-latent ethnic, social, political and other conflicts. If the economy does not pick up, the distribution of a reduced wage fund in enterprises will only serve to exacerbate these tensions. Another possible consequence of wage bargaining could be a further decline in employment as enterprises choose to pay higher wages rather than maintain employment levels.

Industrial relations

Trends in unionism

In early 1990 the socialist system of industrial relations began to disintegrate. Political and economic changes required the formation of a new system of industrial relations, including the establishment of independent unions and organisations of employers and employees. These involved new types of inter-relation between the social partners; the need to regulate these new labour relations required significant changes in legislation. Because of the slow pace of parliamentary activity, legislation lagged well behind the rapid changes in industrial relations practices. As of mid-1991, no law on trade unions nor the Employment Law nor the Social Insurance Law, had yet been passed. The Labour Code — although repeatedly amended — was criticised as unsuitable by all three partners. Economic and social life was still ruled by governement decree and not by parliamentary approved legislation.

Until the beginning of the reforms, Bulgaria had a single trade union confederation (Bulgarian Trade Unions) with a highly centralised structure based on regions and sectors. The BTU was dominated by the Communist Party and was an organ of the State. After the collapse of the Zhivkov regime, the Confederation of Independent Trade Unions in Bulgaria (CITUB) was founded out of the former trade unions. CITUB rejected the BTU's functions — assuring the holidays of working people and their families, controlling labour conditions, and so on — declared its independence from the State and all political parties and movements, and stated its intention to move towards real trade unionism. A considerable part of its property was given to different state and public organisations.

At the end of May 1991, CITUB published a list of its assets and stated that they were financed entirely from membership fees. This issue is still, though, being discussed with the Bulgarian Socialist Party and with the Confederation of Labour, Podkrepa. CITUB was a participant in the national strike at the end of 1990, which brought down the Socialist government. At the end of April 1991, it claimed 2.2 million members; 1.8 million of them (about 60 per cent of those in employment) paid their membership fee in May.

A new alternative trade union, closely connected with the emerging opposition movement, was established in the spring of 1989. Podkrepa has a vote in the Co-ordination Council of the Union of Democratic Forces, but has stressed its independence from all political parties. It is built on occupational and territorial organisations and has a steadily increasing membership. According to its own figures, membership reached 500,000 by the end of May 1991.

Many claim that a third recently founded trade union, Edinstvo, is connected to the Bulgarian Socialist Party (formerly the Communist Party). It was established in January 1991 after CITUB joined the strike against the socialist government and when some of the trade union federations left CITUB. According to Edinstvo's leader, some 250,000 people (about 8.7 per cent of the employed population) are members.

Besides the centralised trade union confederations, a number of small independent unions exist, mainly at sectoral level. Some of them have links with one or other of the big confederations — CITUB or Podkrepa. After the initial period when many trade unions were set up, there is now a certain process of consolidation. This process has been reinforced by the establishment of the tripartite system and new plans for wage bargaining. Competition for members among the big trade unions has generated sometimes intense conflicts, though Podkrepa and CITUB co-operate in negotiations with the Government.

More than 78 per cent of those employed are members of a trade union. This is one reason for the crucial role that the unions play in industrial relations and socio-economic developments in the transition towards a market economy. Another reason is the formation of a real trade union policy to defend members' interests. Trade unions took the lead in all labour conflicts during 1990, achieving, through the two big strike waves, early retirement for workers enduring poor working conditions, and wage rises. As a result of these mass strikes, the Law on Labour Conflicts was passed in the spring of 1990.

Seven employers' organisations have also been established, with six in the private sector and one in the state sector.

The specific socio-political situation in Bulgaria makes industrial relations highly sensitive to changes in the political situation. The strike by Podkrepa and CITUB led to the resignation of the socialist government at the end of 1990. Under the tripartite agreement, from February 1991 trade unions must refrain from strike activity. According to CITUB data, there were only 72 labour conflicts in the first three months of 1991 against 300 for the same period of 1990. This fact, together with dramatic impoverishment and infringement of the agreement limiting the drop in real incomes to 30 per cent, demonstrates the key role of trade unions and the patience of the population. Most people supported reform even in February 1991, the most difficult month, according to a public opinion poll at the time.

However, after the serious economic shock in April 1991, a new wave of strikes spread across the country, prompted by the inertia of employers who took no measures to revive production; enterprises' turnover remained at an estimated 14 billion leva. In February 1991, the value of fixed assets remaining idle was over 7 billion leva, according to Mr. Ivan Kostov, Minister of Finance.

The strikes had a considerable political and psychological impact, and revealed the resentment felt towards the *nomenclatura* of the old regime who had remained relatively unaffected by the difficult economic situation. The attack on enterprise directors antagonised both the private and the public employers' organisations, and put the spotlight on the issue of contracts for directors of state-owned enterprises (i.e., those 50 per cent or more state-owned) in the February 1991 agreement between the social partners. This is, in effect, a return to the election of managers by workers in the enterprise.

Tripartism in the regulation of industrial relations

The absence of laws to drive market reform, the problems in parliament and the difficult political situation were the main factors that turned the tripartite system into the only mechanism that was capable, both of guaranteeing civil peace and securing the implementation of reform. Tripartism came into being as a result of the numerous and powerful trade unions. The role of trade unions is in many ways non-traditional, for example, in activities related to privatisation, incentives for private businesses, and deregulation of the economy. The specific socio-political situation has, however, turned them into the most important champions of reform.

The tripartite system was founded on the initiative of CITUB with the signing of the "General Agreement" between CITUB, the Government and the National Union of Employers in February 1990. Podkrepa did not sign the agreement as it considered that the then Government was "not a serious partner". The main aims of the General Agreement included the establishment of new relations between the social partners, wage increases and limits on strike activity. The Agreement also covered improvement of working conditions, and earlier retirement and wage bonuses for those employed in poor working conditions. The monthly minimum wage was raised from 140 to 165 leva; about one million workers were classified as employed in poor working conditions. However, with nearly half the promises in the agreement not fulfilled by the Government, trade union popularity rose at the Government's expense.

Tripartism developed in two directions: an increase in the number of institutions represented in policy debates, and an expansion of the range of issues discussed. In this way tripartism turned into a mechanism for regulating the economic and — to a certain extent — social life of the country.

The second Agreement was signed in August 1990, with the addition of Podkrepa and the two main private employers' organisations. Its principal goal was to protect the incomes of the population against inflation.

The third tripartite Agreement was signed in February 1991, at the beginning of economic reform, with the aim of guaranteeing civil peace and the conditions appropriate for continuing reform. In addition to establishing an enhanced Social Protection Net it fixed targets for a certain number of basic macro-economic indicators (interest rates, the exchange rate, the state budget deficit, investment) and requested the Government to prepare legislation on dismissals, lock-outs, recruitment, and the environment. The issue of privatisation was also discussed. The two main trade union confederations wished to participate actively in this process, and it was agreed that employees could buy up to 20 per cent of the shares in an enterprise.

The tripartite system has been established at national level only. Local agreements on a tripartite basis have been concluded in about a third of municipalities but they have not been successful. Local authorities — known as "temporary authorities" — are not functioning normally because of divisive tensions; in any event, they have few powers or financial resources. Though regional structures have been established mainly on a tripartite basis, comprising the employers' organisations, local authorities and the trade unions, there are exceptions.

Uncertainty about privatisation and the terms on which it will be conducted was a major contributor to economic recession. The passage of the Law on Land and the need for additional regulations to implement it demonstrated the potential problems facing privatisation. There was uncertainty also over the roles of the social partners, political parties and foreign businesses in the privatisation process.

Two months after price liberalisation in February 1991, at the time of the drop in living standards below the agreed 30 per cent, the slump in production and large-scale redundancies (nearly 20,000 a month) acute political conflicts arose. This made a new agreement necessary but it was extremely difficult to negotiate one against a backdrop of increased political activity, growing support for restoration of the monarchy and problems in parliament. With trade union pressure, the tripartite agreement was concluded.

The depressed economy needed an active economic policy, as envisaged in the second stage of the reform process. Consensus on this issue was reached in the tripartite agreement of June 1991, despite problems: during the negotiations, the employers' organisations from the state and private sectors left the tripartite commission, claiming that they were not satisfied with the slow pace of privatisation, the lack of government professionalism, inadequate tax incentives, etc. In addition, the Government and the two big trade union confederations did not allow the participation of the trade union Edinstvo.

It should be seen that the central concerns of the June 1991 agreement on the second stage of economic reform were related to employment, implementation of wage bargaining and economic restructuring. The link between pay rises and employment reduction in conditions of economic stagnation is obvious. The agreement includes guarantees for IMF proposals for economic restructuring. Major credits have been granted by the IMF and the World Bank and it is hoped that these will provide a basis for a successful continuation of Bulgarias' reform process.

Notes

1. The index used is a geometrical mean of changes in output.

2. This was the case, for example, of 20 enterprises in Bulgaria's second biggest town, Plovdiv. In total they employ about 30,000 people.

3. Central Statistical Office (CSO): *The Economy of Bulgaria: Statistical Yearbook, 1990* (Sofia), p.47.

4. Data from *Statistical Yearbook 1990*, CSO, p. 108.

5. This chapter uses the industrial classification of the Council for Mutual Economic Assistance (CMEA).

6. The results of the inquiry were published in *168 Hours LTD.* (newspaper) April 16, 1991.

7. Estimated as $\quad X = \displaystyle\sum_{i=1}^{n} \dfrac{\left(X_i^{(t)} - X_i^{(to)} \right)}{n}$

8. The territorial division of the country comprises nine regions and 30 municipalities and communes.

9. CSO: *Statistical Yearbook,1991*, (Sofia) p.41. This is the permanent population including those who are temporarily absent.

10. *Analytical Materials,* 1986.

11. *Lifestyle of people living in the Rhodopes region*, 1984. The author was a member of the research team.

12. CSO: *The Economy of Bulgaria: Statistical Yearbook*, p.31.

13. *Blue-collar and White-collar Workers, 1989*, pp. 14-15.

14. *Problems and Prospects in Women's Employment*, March 1991. The author is a member of the research team.

15. "Labour opportunities and their achievement by the employed population", carried out during the 1985 census, in *Analytical Materials*, 1986, pp.26-31.

16. CSO : *Statistical Yearbook, 1990,* (Sofia), pp. 12-24.

17. Centre of Management Study, carried out in June 1991, published in the press (June 1991).

18. Information from the National Labour Exchange.

19. The average nominal wage of workers and employees in the state and co-operative sector (i.e., excluding the private sector).

20. Central Statistical Office, *Rabotna zaplata na personala za july 1990* (Employees' incomes in July 1990), (Sofia) 1991, pp. 22-24.

21. The minimum wage in July 1990 was 165 leva a month.

22. According to unpublished data of CITUB.

23. Data from the Labour Department of the Central Statistical Office.

24. The indices of nominal average wages are computed from the data for table 2.28. The indices of nominal cash incomes are computed from the data for table 2.29.

25. *Democratia* (Sofia), May 23, 1991 ; *Troud* (Sofia), May 27, 1991.

26. "Financial Motivation of the Firm", in *Democratia* (Sofia), May 28, 1991.

Chapter 3

The Czech and Slovak Federal Republic: Labour market trends and policies

by
Alena Nesporova
Institute for Forecasting
Czechoslovak Academy of Sciences

Introduction

In the 1980s the Czechoslovak economy stagnated and showed an underlying deterioration in key aspects of economic performance. The growth of real gross domestic product (GDP) averaged 2.2 per cent a year in constant official prices but, after accounting for hidden inflation of an estimated 2-3 per cent, growth was close to zero. Labour productivity grew by just 1.5 per cent a year while capital productivity declined by 2.1 per cent annually. The long-term trend was clearly downwards and, at the end of the 1980s, the Czechoslovak economy faced crisis. Clearly, the "Velvet revolution" of November 1989 must be seen not only in a political, but also an economic, context.

In 1990, a plan for the transition to a market economy was adopted by the Government and parliament, and was accompanied by a social reform programme. In January 1990, the final reform of the Communist regime gave enterprises more economic freedom (though with insufficient budget constraints) while subsidies to enterprises were reduced. Before the scheduled price liberalisation expectations of inflation encouraged enterprises to divert resources into capital goods and stocks of raw material and other supplies. The investment ratio reached a long-term peak of over 30 per cent of GDP, in spite of uncertain production prospects. The inflationary expectations gave rise to panic buying which destabilised the consumer market. The declines of 3.2 per cent in industrial production and 3.1 per cent in GDP were therefore primarily connected with the supply side: problems with input deliveries from abroad due to the breakdown of the Council for Mutual Economic Assistance (CMEA) and from the domestic market due to shrinking supplies from enterprises. In spite of two devaluations of the Czechoslovak crown, in real terms exports fell by 11.6 per cent and imports by 3.8 per cent in 1990. A considerable shift in trade away from the CMEA market and developing countries, and towards the developed Western economies, occurred.

Post-Communist economic reform began with the elimination of food price subsidies in July 1990 and continued with price liberalisation, the third devaluation of the Czechoslovak crown, and the introduction of internal convertibility in January 1991. The price shock cut consumer demand, while sales abroad also fell sharply. Exports to non-market economies dropped by more than 20 per cent, and to market economies by 23 per cent, in the first three months of 1991. This dampened investment activity and, together with strict monetary and fiscal policies, produced a deepening economic recession. Net material product declined by 9.5 per cent in the first quarter of 1991, industrial production by 14.8 per cent in the first five months and construction activity by 36.8 per cent. The economic recession continued for the rest of 1991 and, without any change in economic policy, the economy could sink into long-term depression.

Labour market developments

Labour supply

Demographic indicators from 1980 are given in tables 3.1 and 3.2. The size and share of the population of working age[1] is forecast to increase between 1985 and 2000, growing fastest in the period 1989-95 as the children of the baby boom of the early 1970s reach adulthood. The shares of both dependent groups of the population (children aged up to 15 years and the elderly) are falling — even absolute numbers drop between 1989 and 2000 — and dependency ratios are relatively advantageous for the economy (table 3.3).

Table 3.1. **Demographic structure of Czechoslovakia, 1985-2000**

	1985		1989		1995		2000	
	(000s)	(%)	(000s)	(%)	(000s)	(%)	(000s)	(%)
Children aged up to 15 years	3 781	24.4	3 599	23.0	3 231	20.9	3 225	20.7
Population of working age[1]	8 746	56.3	9 022	57.6	9 494	61.4	9 635	62.0
Population above working age	2 994	19.3	3 029	19.4	2 728	17.7	2 695	17.3

1. 15-60 for men, 15-54/57 for women.
Source: Statistical Yearbook of CSFR (CSSR), various years; Demographic prognosis of the Federal Statistical Office, 1987.

Table 3.2. **Demographic indicators, Czechoslovakia, 1980-1989**

Indicator	1980	1985	1989
Birth rate[1]	16.3	14.6	13.3
Death rate[1]	12.2	11.9	11.6
Mortality rate[1]	12.2	11.9	11.6
Infant mortality rate[2]	18.4	14.0	11.3
Life expectancy at birth			
men	66.8	67.2	67.8[3]
women	74.0	74.7	75.3[3]

1. Per 1,000 inhabitants.
2. Deaths of children in first year per 1000 live births.
3. 1988.
Source: Statistical Yearbook of CSFR (CSSR), various years.

Table 3.3. **Dependency ratios[1], Czechoslovakia, 1985-2000**

	1985	1989	1995	2000
Children up to 15 years	0.43	0.40	0.34	0.33
Population above working age	0.34	0.34	0.29	0.28

1. Calculated in relation to the population of working age.
Source: Statistical Yearbook of CSFR (CSSR), various years. Demographic prognosis of the Federal Statistical Ofice, 1987.

The distribution of labour resources in 1985 and 1989 is given in table 3.4. The increase in full-time employment slowed in the second half of the 1980s, in spite of the baby boom, and in 1989 full-time employment actually fell. This decline was, however, more than offset by the rise in part-time employment due to an expansion of private businesses. In 1990 and 1991, labour resources grew by over 1 per cent.

Table 3.4. **Labour resources and their distribution, Czechoslovakia, 1985 and 1989**
(numbers at December 31, in thousands)

	1985	1989
Labour resources	9 488	9 778
of which:		
Population of working age	8 747	9 023
Workers of retirement age	705	721
Working foreign citizens	37	35
Labour resource distribution		
of which:		
Workers in main occupation	7 468	7 558
Women on maternity leave	351	376
Students and apprentices of working age	717	808
Disabled	266	270
Others of working age	686	766
Workers in second jobs	181	310
Total employment	7 649	7 868

Source: Statistical Yearbook of CSFR (CSSR), various years.

In 1989, the proportion of the working-age population economically active (excluding women on maternity leave) was 83.5 per cent for men and 72.2 per cent for women.[2] These participation rates are high by international standards, and reflect the very high full-time employment of women (only 12 per cent of women work part-time), in which economic factors play a significant role. Although falling, the activity rate of post-working age groups was also very high at 24.3 per cent (representing 9.2 per cent of total employment). This too was probably due mainly to economic factors, primarily the large drop in income after retirement.

The high labour force participation rate was stimulated by a social policy predicated on a model of a two-income family and the collective upbringing of children. The involvement in paid employment of previously inactive labour was necessitated by the policy of heavy industrialisation, reinforced by a strategy of low wages coupled with price subsidies for food and services.

The occupational structure of employment reflects the low technical level of production, the industrial structure of the economy and the undervaluation of the contribution of qualified and motivated workers. As shown in table 3.5, two-thirds of employees in 1989 were in manual production or service jobs. Even this hides an important feature of work content resulting from the central administrative system of management: a high degree of "bureaucratisation" of all activities.

Table 3.5. **Occupational structure of employment, Czechoslovakia, 1989**
(shares in per cent)

Blue-collar workers (labourers)	52.2
of which:	
Agriculture	2.9
Mining, metalworking and energy	4.3
Manufacturing	25.4
Construction	6.4
Transport and services	13.3
Operational and service workers	15.4
White-collar workers	32.4
of which:	
Technical	11.0
Managerial and administrative	10.3
Education, culture and health care	9.7
Research and development	1.3

Source: Statistical Yearbook of CSFR, 1990.

Skilled workers and mid-level technicians constitute the basic workforce in most sectors. Commercial professions, experts in finance and law, highly qualified designers, and specialists in construction and technology, are inadequately represented. There is also a shortage of specialist employees in services. In spite of the fact that employees with university education represented only 9.2 per cent of total employees in 1989 (employees with secondary education accounted for 18.7 per cent and skilled workers 38.1 per cent),[3] their qualification, and abilities were often utilised in a purely formal way.

Labour demand

Aggregate labour demand weakened in the second half of the 1980s, as a result of the stagnation of the Czechoslovak economy. The slow-down in employment growth was the first sign of this trend, although the number of vacancies remained high and no unemployment appeared.

Employment in 1990 fell by nearly 0.8 per cent, main jobs by 2.4 per cent. In the state and co-operative sectors the number employed decreased by 2.5 per cent, but over the year the decline accelerated; in the fourth quarter, these sectors employed 5 per cent fewer people than in the same period in 1989.

Falling employment in both sectors was linked to pressure for saving labour and for organisational change. The Government's restrictive fiscal policy, enterprises' uncertain future prospects and their current economic problems discouraged the creation of new jobs. Employment growth was seen registered only in services.

In contrast to the state and co-operative sectors, private sector employment rose; in 1990 the number of registered private entrepreneurs increased from nearly 100,000 to 488,000, though only 20 per cent ran their private businesses full-time and only a small proportion employed others. Three-quarters of private firms employed fewer than five people and 90 per cent no more than 10. However, many enterprises preferred to hire self-employed workers to avoid paying social security contributions and to avoid complying with labour laws.

At the start of 1991, workers in the state and co-operative sectors still accounted for about 97 per cent of total employment, although, during the year the private sector share increased to between 5 and 8 per cent.

This trend continued in 1991. The economic recession and cuts in government expenditure reduced the demand for labour in the state and co-operative sectors. Although production in industry and construction fell, employment decreased comparatively less because the extra profits from price increases after price liberalisation, and from exports after currency devaluation, enabled enterprises to continue to pay redundant workers. However, since these profits were only temporary, employment was set for a sharp cutback later in the year.

The number of private entrepreneurs rose in the first quarter of 1991, to 655,000, although the economic recession discouraged them from fully committing themselves to private business. They operated mainly in construction, services and light industry, the sectors most affected by falling aggregate demand.

Labour productivity grew very slowly in the 1980s, peaking at 1.8 per cent in 1985-88, owing to the poor management of labour, enterprises' low wages and other labour costs, poor work discipline and worker motivation, as well as unsatisfactory technical conditions for production.[4] Czechoslovakia lagged behind developed industrial countries in output per employee, especially in terms of hourly labour productivity. The latter fell more steeply than economic performance measured by gross domestic product per capita, reflecting high labour input from over-employment and long working hours. While the length of the normal working week was comparable with that in industrial countries, the most decisive differences were shorter and fewer holidays in Czechoslovakia and more overtime work (4.6 per cent of total working hours in industry in 1989, 6.6 per cent in rail transport, 14.4 per cent in bus and truck transport). A worker's average working hours per year were 15 to 20 per cent higher than in industrially advanced countries.

Estimates of labour hoarding, based on comparing non-technologically based differences in labour productivity between Czechoslovakia and comparable economies,[5] range between 12 and 20 per cent of total employment, equivalent to up to 1.6 million employees. Over-employment thus had universal as well as structural dimensions.

The production fall in 1990 led to a drop in labour productivity; the estimated decline in productivity for the whole economy was 2.3 per cent. This trend continued in 1991, as enterprises continued to hoard labour. Preliminary estimates show a fall in labour productivity in industry of 6.8 per cent between January and May (in May alone 18.2 per cent) and in construction of 25.9 per cent (in May 52.8 per cent) by comparison with the same period of 1990, with a clear deterioration over time. As the financial situation worsens, enterprises will inevitably be forced to dismiss larger numbers of employees.

Structural over-employment was linked to the distorted industrial structure, typified by over-sized industry and heavy industry in particular. The industrial structure of employment in 1980 and 1989 is shown in table 3.6. Industry accounted for 38 per cent of total employment in 1989 and agriculture for 12 per cent (though this includes employment in associated industrial and service production). By contrast, practically all services, especially producer services, personal services and trade, faced significant labour shortages.

Table 3.6. **Industrial structure of employment, Czechoslovakia, 1980 and 1989**
(% share)

	1980	1989
Total employment	100.0	100.0
of which:		
Agriculture and forestry	13.5	11.6
Industry[1]	38.1	38.0
Construction	8.9	8.9
Trade	10.5	10.6
Transport	5.3	5.1
Communications	1.4	1.4
Research and development	2.3	2.3
Education	5.4	6.1
Health and social care	4.5	5.2
Financial and business services	2.4	2.7
Housing administration, personal services	3.0	3.3
Other	4.7	4.8

1. Including mining and energy production.
Source: Statistical Yearbook of CSFR, 1990.

This situation improved only slightly in 1990. Employment in agriculture, industry and construction, where there had been most hoarding, fell by 5 per cent, 3.4 per cent and 6.2 per cent respectively. Meanwhile, some growth of employment was registered in education, health care, housing administration and financial services. A modest employment increase in trade, repair services, transport and tourist services was a purely private sector phenomenon.

The 1991 economic recession impacted primarily on employment in industry and construction, which declined by 8.6 per cent and 14.7 per cent respectively in the first five months of the year. It also affected agriculture and transport, as well as most services. The only expanding branches were tourist services, financial services and public administration connected with the market system.

The structure of employment by size of firms for 1989 is given in table 3.7. In 1990, and more notably since the beginning of 1991, many large enterprises — mainly in light industry and construction — were split into smaller ones, although no data are yet available on this process.

Table 3.7. **Structure of employment by size of firm in the state and co-operative sectors, Czechoslovakia, 1989**

Size of firm (number of employees)	Share in total employment %
Total	100.0
Up to 100	1.2
101 - 500	11.2
501 - 1000	12.8
1 001 - 2 500	17.0
2 501 - 5 000	12.8
5 001 - 10 000	13.8
10 001 - 20 000	10.2
20 001 - 30 000	4.1
30 001 - 50 000	7.0
50 001 and over	9.9

Source: Statistical Yearbook of CSFR, 1990.

Internal labour migration was relatively stable in the 1980s. The latest data for 1988 show a net flow of 27,000 workers commuting from the Slovak Republic to jobs in the Czech Republic. The number of Czechoslovak citizens working abroad before 1990 was small. In 1990 about 25,000 people worked legally abroad, while another 8,000-10,000 worked illegally. By contrast, the number of foreign workers in Czechoslovakia declined during 1990 from 46,100 to 35,000.

Unemployment

In 1990, open unemployment appeared for the first time in 40 years; the registered unemployment rate reached 1 per cent by the end of the year. The increase since then has been dramatic; the figure for May 1991 was 3.2 per cent, with the rate in the Czech Republic being 2.2 per cent and that in the Slovak Republic 5.4 per cent. The forecast for the rest of the year was for an acceleration of this trend, suggesting a rate of unemployment between 7.5 and 13 per cent by the end of December. The level will depend, among other things, on the development of economic policy and sales opportunities on domestic and foreign markets.

Unemployment has affected women more than men, and disabled workers and Gypsies more than other groups. Their shares in unemployment are significantly higher than their shares in employment. The share of women in unemployment is 49.5 per cent and in employment 45.9 per cent. The rate of unemployment for Gypsies is available only for the Slovak Republic where in May 1991 it reached 27 per cent. Unemployment has also affected younger age groups more especially school-leavers; the proportion of university graduates unemployed was 9.8 per cent and of secondary school-leavers 5.8 per cent in May. Shares of educated people in registered unemployment are, however, lower than their shares in employment. In December 1990, those with university education accounted for 7.9 per cent of total unemployment compared with 9.2 per cent of total employment; those having secondary education without apprenticeship accounted for 17.4 per cent compared with 18.7 per cent; and skilled workers represented 28.5 per cent of total unemployment compared with 38.1 per cent of total employment.

Unemployment-vacancy ratios are given in table 3.8. The number of vacancies has decreased since 1990 and the unemployment-vacancy ratio has risen very quickly. In May 1991 it reached 5.9 for the whole country: although a modest 3.2 for the Czech Republic, it stood at 22.0 for the Slovak republic.

Table 3.8. **Unemployment to vacancy ratio[1], Czech and Slovak Republic, 1990-1991**

End of month	Czech and Slovak Rep.	Czech Rep.	Slovak Rep.
October 1990	0.66	0.45	1.32
December 1990	1.07	0.68	2.58
January 1991	2.05	1.21	6.22
March 1991	4.14	2.41	10.65
May 1991	5.89	3.19	21.95

1. Number of registered unemployed to number of vacancies.
Source: Federal Ministry of Labour and Social Affairs.

Data on the duration of unemployment are available for the Czech Republic only (table 3.9). These show that, in March 1991, a fifth of unemployed people had been out of work for between three and six months, 11.8 per cent for between 6 and 12 months, and 0.5 per cent for over a year. The data for women only show no appreciable differences from this pattern.

Table 3.9. **Unemployment duration in the Czech Republic(as at March 31, 1991)**

Duration in months	All unemployed	Unemployed women
	% share of unemployment	
0 - 3	65.8	66.0
3 - 6	22.0	21.0
6 - 9	9.7	9.9
9 - 12	2.1	1.9
Over 12	0.5	0.3

Source: Czech Ministry of Labour and Social Affairs.

Labour market policies

During 1990 legislative provisions were drafted to allow the labour market to function properly in market conditions. The Federal Assembly adopted a Law on Employment that with the Labour Code, Law on Social Security and Law on Collective Bargaining, created a legal framework which covered the right to employment, areas of responsibility for the adoption and implementation of state employment policy, and labour relations between employers and employees.

Czechoslovak employment policy identifies one of its main aims to be the achievement of full, productive and freely chosen employment. The right to work is taken to be the right of a citizen to receive help in finding a suitable job and to obtain retraining and assistance before entering or after losing employment. A "suitable job" must take account of the person's state of health, and take into consideration age, qualifications and abilities, duration of previous employment and housing possibilities. In practice, an unemployed person may be required to accept a job for which he or she is overqualified.

The Law on Employment stipulates that state labour institutions are responsible for implementing state employment policy, and specifies their tasks and responsibilities. Besides the Federal Ministry of Labour and Social Affairs, a ministry for each republic has been created. A nation-wide network of employment offices was created during the second half of 1990; at the end of the year there were 124 offices and 1.920 employees. These offices provide information, advice and assistance in finding employment, provide retraining, help create jobs — including support for small enterprises — and if necessary organise public works. The offices are responsible for implementing employment policy in their region, but may co-operate in, for example, creating employment programmes. Special consideration is given to certain social groups, including young people, school-leavers, the long-term unemployed, disabled people and Gypsies).

Jobseekers who are not given a suitable job or retraining within seven days of registration are provided with unemployment assistance for up to one year. If a worker is unemployed for more than a year, he is given social assistance. If redundancy is due to organisational and structural changes, workers are paid compensation.

Job placement can also be provided by non-state or private individuals and organisations on a non-profit-making basis if they have a licence from either the Czech or Slovak Ministry of Labour and Social Affairs.

The Law on Employment gives employers full rights to hire whom ever they want in the numbers they desire, but requires them to inform the local employment office of vacancies, and to inform trade unions and employment offices within specified time limits about intended structural and organisational changes or rationalisation measures involving dismissals. The employer is also obliged to create suitable jobs for disabled people.

Since 1991, schemes to create "socially efficient" jobs have been set up by employment offices. The aim is to decrease social tensions arising from redundancies. When considering such schemes, employment offices must take into account their effectiveness, usefulness and the time necessary to create jobs. It is assumed that job creation agreements will be concluded between employment offices and employers, with the former offering financial inducements for job creation, such as subsidies, loans, or interest-free credits. Jobseekers will be given financial support to set up small businesses. Public works will be organised as a short-term solution to unemployment, mainly providing low-skilled employment in services.

In the event of bigger structural changes initiated and regulated by the State, special government measures to solve employment problems will be an integral part of any measures undertaken.

The greatest difficulties faced by the employment offices have been a lack of technical equipment, especially in the Slovak Republic, inadequate training of staff, and insufficient co-operation with firms. The first two problems are now being tackled with the installation of new equipment and retraining courses. With unemployment expected to grow rapidly, it is planned to double staff in the employment offices by the end of 1991, with each office having its own local computer network. The activity of employment offices has been confined to giving information, placing people in jobs and providing unemployment assistance. Support for new job creation has been minimal, and attempts to organise public works and training have not been very successful. Labour policies can therefore be seen to be "passive" rather than "active" in character.

Active state labour policies are focused on two areas. A programme of support and development of small enterprises and self-employment was devised by the Federal Ministry of Labour and Social Affairs, in co-operation with other organisations. Institutional and financial support for the programme is intended to come from employment offices and local authorities as well as from foreign sources (especially the European Communities' Phare programme). Unemployed people who wish to become entrepreneurs can receive financial support up to the amount of their yearly unemployment assistance, and the same amount again when creating a new vacancy. A project to help women set up private businesses, which would prevent their excessive unemployment, is also being undertaken in co-operation with the ILO.

A second programme that has been proposed to the Government aims to facilitate the employment of school-leavers through wage subsidies and tax relief for employers, education and retraining courses, public works and other measures. In 1991 about 200,000 school-leavers are due to enter the labour market and enterprises are unlikely to employ more than a small proportion of them.

Several further principles of active labour policy are expressed in the tripartite General Agreement for 1991, among them, the preparation and financing of state and enterprise employment programmes. Special employment programmes are being prepared for those industries and areas likely to be particularly affected by future cutbacks. In addition, the General Agreement determines support to regional programmes of enterprise activities within an active employment policy, including the provision of financial assistance (e.g., subsidies, payment of interest charges) to jobseekers who wish to set up their own businesses.

Despite these activities dealing with labour demand, it is clear that to reduce imbalances on the labour market, policy must also be directed towards reducing labour supply. The following possibilities are open:

- Reducing labour force participation of certain groups whose living standards are not wholly dependent on labour incomes, such as old-age pensioners. The system inherited from the past enables some categories of workers to collect an old-age pension and earn wages. This no longer reflects the needs of the country when there is a shortage of jobs for young people. A principle of "either a wage or a pension" has been proposed. This should not be seen as discriminatory because it would enable those over retirement age to keep their jobs, but not receive a pension while they work.

- Indirectly influencing opportunities for and interest in labour participation. The maternity allowance has been changed to a parental allowance, raised (fees in creches and kindergartens are rising rapidly) and extended to cover three years from birth. It is also proposed that compulsory schooling be extended by one year.

- Controlling labour immigration from abroad.

- Reducing working time, for instance by increasing the length of holidays and by creating suitable conditions for part-time work.

Introducing early retirement up to two years before the normal retirement age on full pension when workers are dismissed for structural and organisational reasons.

The enterprises' uncertain future and the economic recession have resulted in low demand for both on-the-job and off-the-job retraining. The proportion of unemployed people attending retraining courses was only 0.4 per cent in May 1991. Although stipulated in the Law on Employment, no retraining system or policy has yet been implemented, and this could significantly delay the needed restructuring and revitalisation of the economy.

A special fund has been created within the state budgets of the Czech and Slovak Republics, primarily for the employment offices. The purpose of the fund is to cover expenses connected with: the employment-related consequences of government-inspired structural changes; the creation of socially efficient jobs and public works schemes; retraining; support for small businesses; and the provision of unemployment assistance. On the basis of the tripartite General Agreement, at least 25 per cent of this reserve fund must be allocated to active labour market policies. For 1991 this reserve amounted to 9.9 billion crowns, that is, 1.2 per cent of 1990 GDP. In future, an independent employment fund will be financed from contributions by employers and employees paid mainly in the form of taxes.

Policies for income support

Social protection and unemployment

In Czechoslovakia a deliberate equalisation policy in respect of wages, incomes and retirement pensions implemented by the Communist regime led to relatively small income differences among different strata of the population. Only 6 per cent of the population — mainly old-age pensioners and large families — lived below the social minimum level in 1988, though living standards in the 1980s stagnated. Personal consumption grew by 1.9 per cent annually but, after eliminating hidden inflation in retail prices, growth was close to zero.

In 1990 there was a rapid increase in living costs, caused by rising retail prices of goods and services. This reflected the removal of subsidies, changes in availability of consumer goods and, in the fourth quarter of the year, increased production costs connected with the steep devaluation of the Czechoslovak crown. The index of living costs rose by 10 per cent year on year, but in the fourth quarter it was nearly 19 per cent above the level a year earlier. Money incomes also grew very rapidly in 1990, by 8.7 per cent, as a result of the increase in social incomes, the indexation of old-age pensions, bank credits — mainly heavily subsidised credits for individual housing construction, etc. — and state compensation payments. These held the fall in real incomes to 1.1 per cent over the year. However, the drop in real incomes accelerated during the year: in the last quarter of 1990 they were nearly 5 per cent lower than in the same period in 1989.

Price liberalisation in a monopolistic structure of production and trade caused prices to jump in January 1991. Although inflation weakened in the subsequent months, other measures such as the increase in energy prices from May and higher telephone charges, together with knock-on effects of currency devaluation, contributed to continuing inflationary tendencies. The prospective steep rise in food prices after the 1991 harvest, delayed rent increases and the impact of wage rises will have further pushed up prices in the year. In the first five months of 1991 living costs increased by 55 to 58 per cent (for different social groups) in comparison with the same period of 1990. A moderate wage rise due to restrictive wage regulation and the financial problems of many enterprises and organisations financed from the state budget led to a fall in the real purchasing power of incomes by 27 per cent between the first quarters of 1990 and 1991. Indexation of old-age pensions in October 1990 and in March 1991 limited their drop in purchasing power to 15 per cent over the same period.

The lowest level of pensions, which represent the only source of income, rose by nearly 60 per cent (including the state compensation payment) in the year to the first quarter of 1991. These pensions are now worth 80 per cent of the average old-age pension. Higher "poverty thresholds" have been proposed, based on calculations of minimum living costs, i.e., the minimum monthly income that allows satisfaction of all basic human needs and costs of the household (table 3.11). The lowest pensions are currently above these "poverty thresholds".

The increase in living costs raised the proportion of the population living in poverty to 9.2 per cent in March 1991. However, this proportion is not comparable with the 6 per cent mentioned earlier for 1988; the real purchasing power, both of a minimum pension and the minimum costs of living (whether actual or forecast) in 1991, is lower than the real value of the "poverty thresholds" applicable in 1988. On the 1988 basis about 15 per cent of the population would have been living in poverty at the end of March 1991, and this share will increase still further as prices continue to rise. Compensation for these price rises is yet to be implemented through the newly established social assistance scheme.

Social policy

The new social policy currently in preparation is crucial for maintaining a social consensus in favour of reforming measures and thus the smooth functioning of the future market economy. This policy based on three main principles:

- i) Social justice — the creation of equal opportunities for all. This includes guaranteeing the right to education, health (of the individual and the nation) as well as the right to employment.
- ii) Social solidarity — the guarantee of a certain level of income security in old age, disability, illness, maternity, unemployment and temporary hardship, etc.
- iii) Social guarantees — against inflation and excessive increases in living costs over the transition period to prevent large numbers falling into poverty. This is the concept of the "social safety net" as used in Czechoslovakia.

Based on these principles, transition policy measures are being gradually introduced; a new social security system is being prepared for implementation at a later stage of the transition process.

As a first step, amendments to the Law on Social Security have been introduced. They abolished personal pensions (special old-age pensions for prominent Communists) and transferred the administration of sickness insurance from trade unions to the new social security bodies. Social assistance is the responsibility of the new local and district authorities. In May 1990, social security for the self-employed, members of their families and for employees in private firms was introduced.

In October 1990 the tripartite Council for Economic and Social Agreement was established to discuss and approve all the important economic measures, their anticipated social consequences and social security benefits. After the tripartite negotiations, in February 1991 the Government adopted the Social Safety Net as the State's guarantee of minimum assistance for citizens suffering hardship. The Social Safety Net covers unemployment assistance; family assistance; guarantees against poverty (i.e., a minimum pension for the elderly and for the disabled, a minimum family income and minimum wage); assistance with housing problems; and the indexation of wages, pensions, social security benefits and allowances against rising living costs.

At an early stage income protection for the unemployed was established. The first law provided comparatively high benefit levels (up to 90 per cent for workers laid off because of industrial restructuring) and fairly wide coverage. In early 1991, when unemployment started to rise, the law was significantly revised. Under the modified law, unemployment assistance is primarily to encourage re-employment by active measures for the creation of jobs, private businesses and self-employment, and for retraining. Unemployment assistance is granted to all registered jobseekers if they are not offered any suitable job or retraining within seven days of registration at the employment office, provided that they have not received unemployment assistance within the previous six months (unless dismissed for structural and organisational

83

reasons). If the dismissed workers receive redundancy compensation (by law it must equal at least two months' salary but it can be increased in collective agreements to a maximum of five months' salary) they are entitled to unemployment assistance only after the period of redundancy compensation has ended. School-leavers currently receive benefits — but it is proposed to link payments to participation in education or work. The Law on Employment sets the lower limit of assistance at 60 per cent of the previous wage for the first six months of unemployment and 50 per cent for the next six months, provided that this is not lower than the minimum income. The General Agreement between the social partners for 1991 increased the lower limits to 65 and 60 per cent respectively; assistance during retraining amounted to 70 per cent of the previous year's salary.

One of the social measures adopted in 1990 and 1991 was the replacement of maternity allowance by a parental allowance, a higher allowance of Czechoslovak crowns (CSK) per month and its extension to the child's first three years (or first seven years if the child is seriously ill). The "nursing" benefit has been extended to seven working days for each instance of child illness; childbirth grants have been increased from 2,000 to 3,000 CSK. The increase in the maximum daily wage for the calculation of sickness benefit was accompanied by an increase in maternity benefits.

Along with the introduction of the Social Safety Net, a system of social assistance has been developed, and a review and reform of the previous family-related benefits instigated. The new system of family assistance comprises social care benefits for families with dependent children. Child allowances will be updated. The present pre-natal allowances that increase progressively up to the fourth child will be replaced by benefits based on the child's age. Other benefits to be replaced by the new family assistance schemes will be the above-mentioned parental allowances, childbirth grants, other maternity grants, benefits for soldiers' families, foster-parent benefits, widow and widower benefits, benefits for handicapped children, and certain other benefits from the old system.

When family incomes drop below minimum living costs (see table 3.10) families will be entitled to additional social benefits. These minimum living costs will be set by the Law on Minimum Living Costs in the second half of 1991.

Table 3.10. **Proposed minimum living costs, Czechoslovakia, 1991**

	Czechoslovak crowns per month
A child aged up to 6 years	900
A child aged 6 to 10 years	1000
A child aged 10 to 15 years	1200
A person aged 15 to 26 years	1600
Others	1200
Additional benefits for the household:	
A single person	500
A couple or a parents with one child	650
A family with more than two persons	800
Additional benefit for a person with a special diet	500

Source: Federal Ministry of Labour and Social Affairs.

It is not yet feasible to pay these social benefits through social security offices. Huge administrative demands are placed on the system when the number of claimants increases rapidly, as now. The offices lack the necessary technical equipment for simplified administration, and have too few well-qualified staff. It is estimated that local social security offices currently provide social benefits to only 15 to 25 per cent of children in families whose income is below the poverty threshold. In the near future these offices will mainly provide assistance to children from families which seem most threatened by poverty. The proportion of these families will rise.

Minimum pensions were raised in October 1990 and March 1991 to 1,440 CSK for an individual, and to 2,400 CSK for a couple (with the state compensation payment, these figures were 1,580 CSK and 2,680 CSK, respectively). Another increase of 220 CSK is proposed from July 1991.

Virtually all social benefits are to be increased during 1991 in line with the inflation rate. The principles of indexation are as follows:

— benefits related to wages are upgraded when average wages rise by 5 per cent;

— benefits related to living costs are upgraded when these rise by 10 per cent.

However, by summer 1991 indexation had been applied only to wages (not the minimum wage), pensions, childbirth grants and sickness insurance benefits. The rise of energy prices had also been accompanied by an increase of 80 CSK in the state compensation payment for pensioners and dependent children.

At present all costs connected with unemployment are covered fully by the state budget, as are the social assistance schemes. An amount of 10.9 billion CSK from the state budget was earmarked for the costs of indexation; virtually all of this will be taken up by the increase in old-age pensions in March and July 1991.

The new social security system is now in preparation. It will combine two principles: universality with aid for individuals in difficult circumstances; and personal responsibility for one's own standard of living. The State will guarantee all citizens an income to meet minimum living costs, and retain the decisive role in setting the amount of state benefits and services for families with children. In the proposed new system of social and sickness insurance, basic security in sickness and old-age for all citizens will be provided from funds independent of the state budget and financed by compulsory contributions from employers, employees and the self-employed. Such a fund, to which employers will contribute two-thirds and insured persons one-third, presumes public and transparent administration of resources. This universal system will be supplemented by the voluntary additional insurance paid by enterprises or individuals. Unemployment assistance as well as the costs of active labour policy measures will be covered by a separate employment fund, financed equally by employers and employees. The self-employed will pay contributions fixed by law; the proposed rate is 2.4 per cent of wages. The family assistance scheme will be financed from the state budget and other social care benefits will be administered and financed by municipalities.

The introduction of the new social security system is scheduled for 1993. Implementation depends, however, on two elements: a fundamental tax reform which is seen as a precondition for the introduction of social security contributions; and, what is probably more important, the general economic situation. The decision will have to be made whether the economy is stable enough to sustain the replacement of the Social Safety Net by a fully developed social security system.

Wages, incomes policy and industrial relations

Wages

The low level of wages in Czechoslovakia and in other central and eastern European countries is well known. It was historically conditioned by the undervaluation of the contribution of labour to the quality and efficiency of production (and by the overvaluation of the importance of investment) and by a mistaken concept of social justice.

The wage structure was built on the central tariff system that gave priority to heavy industry, hard physical work, the employee's age and number of years in the job, and his or her formal education. The scope for wage supplements that exceeded the tariff system was very limited and was tied more to the formal performance of an enterprise in terms of plan targets than to its real efficiency or the capabilities and achievements of the employees themselves. The fact that in 1989 a full two-thirds of monthly wages fell within the narrow range of 2,000 - 4,000 Czechoslovak crowns is indicative of the high rate of wage equalisation.

Table 3.11 shows the level of average wages in individual branches of production in 1989. The ratio between the branch with the highest average wages (mining) and the lowest (housing administration and personal services) is only two to one, and wages in industries demanding skilled workers barely reach the average levels of capital goods industries, chemicals and engineering.

Table 3.11. **Average monthly wages by industry, Czechoslovakia, 1989**
(excluding agricultural co-operatives)

	CSK
Total economy	3 161
Agriculture	3 258
Industry	3 277
of which:	
Mining	4 641
Metallurgy	3 824
Chemicals	3 445
Engineering	3 330
Electrical engineering and electronics	2 987
Wood-processing	2 887
Paper and pulp	3 022
Glass and china	2 917
Leather and shoes	3 004
Textiles	2 747
Clothing	2 541
Food	3 055
Construction	3 478
Transport	3 544
Communications	2 729
Distributive trades	2 638
Research and development	3 497
Education	2 876
Health care	2 885
Social care	2 424
Financial and business services	3 312
Housing administration and personal services	2 347

Source: Statistical Yearbook of CSFR, 1990.

This undervaluation of creative and skilled work can be seen even more clearly when average incomes in selected occupations are compared (table 3.12). The differences in evaluation of work in individual industries also reflects the ratio of male to female employees: strongly feminised branches of light industry, health care, education and services paid much lower average wages than typically male-dominated industries. In general, women's wages were some 32 per cent below men's; and in occupations requiring low skills the differential was greater than in highly qualified occupations where it was, as it were, "only" 21 per cent.

Table 3.12. **Average monthly income in selected occupations, Czechoslovakia, 1989**

Profession	CSK	Profession	CSK
Domestic cleaner	1 732	Metalworker	3 713
Postal delivery worker	2 330	Brewer	3 720
Salesman, foodshops	2 363	Woodcutter	3 751
Cook	2 395	Carpenter	3 779
Worker in storeroom	2 431	Setter of numerical by	
Secretary	2 535	controlled machines	3 811
Salesman,		Tractor driver	3 811
industrial goods	2 539	Worker in research and development	
Agricultural worker		with university degree	3 860
(in plant prod.)	2 557	Cattle herder	3 871
Dressmaker	2 673	Electronic or mechanical engineer	
Machine knitter	2 681	in research and development	3 924
Book-keeper	2 895	Lorry driver	3 996
Nurse	2 961	Secondary-school teacher	3 997
Fitter, telecom.	3 130	Journalist, editor	4 001
Mechanic, electrical-engineering equip.	3 263	Head of computer centre	4 032
Programmer	3 405	Hardener (forging)	4 043
Car mechanic	3 458	Blacksmith	4 103
Mason	3 576	Designer	4 148
Tool maker	3 590	Rolling mill operator	4 349
Plumber	3 626	Foundry worker	4 572
Geologist	3 663	Metal worker	4 992
Machine fitter	3 692	Doctor	5 062
Teacher, elementary school	3 698	Head of scientific department	5 647
		Head of scientific dept. with doctorate	6 188
		Manager in industry	7 083
		Miner	7 199
		University professor	
		with science doctorate	7 911

Source: Statistical Yearbook of CSFR, 1990.

Wage differences according to age and educational level are shown in table 3.13. The wage system has a strong component of seniority even for less skilled workers.

In the 1980s, wage increases continued to be strongly regulated by the State for fear of inflationary pressures. Wages grew in nominal terms by 2 per cent a year in the 1980s and so officially did real wages, although after accounting for hidden inflation they stagnated. Consequently, wage developments did not create inflationary tendencies in the Czechoslovak economy, in contrast with other east European countries, and there was an overall balance between supply and demand in the consumer market (with the exception of short periods of panic buying, usually provoked by non-economic factors).

Table 3.13. **Average monthly wages by age and education, Czechoslovakia, June 1988 (sample survey, in Czeckslovak crowns)**

Age groups	Total	Educational level			
		Basic	Skilled worker	Secondary	University
Total	3 196	2 660	3 275	3 273	4 213
Up to 19 years	2 135	1 857	2 247	2 074	n.a.[1]
20 - 24	2 676	2 469	2 824	2 585	2 612
25 - 29	3 019	2 634	3 199	2 909	3 133
30 - 34	3 193	2 675	3 343	3 140	3 741
35 - 39	3 350	2 792	3 462	3 369	4 210
40 - 44	3 477	2 798	3 531	3 574	4 598
45 - 49	3 508	2 850	3 594	3 788	4 880
50 - 54	3 496	2 812	3 585	3 964	5 051
55 - 59	3 462	2 711	3 479	4 106	5 138
60 and over	2 596	2 100	2 640	3 157	4 345

1. not applicable.
Source: Statistical Yearbook of CSSR, 1989.

Modification of the wage system from January 1990, proposed by the last Communist government, transferred many decisions on wages policy to enterprises and organisations and simplified the income system. A relatively tight regulation of wage funds has nevertheless been retained to prevent uncontrolled spiralling of wages and prices, because the first period of transition to the market system is clearly vulnerable to high cost-driven inflationary tendencies. Enterprises use a two-tier system for determining the permitted increase in total wages and other benefits — with payments out of the wage fund and out of the compensation fund. Four methods for controlling the wage fund's increase are used, based either on net production, growth of tariff wages, the fixed maximum share of wages and other benefits in the wage fund, or a special method (stipulation of the permitted percentage change in wages and other benefits or of its limit). The wage fund in organisations financed from the state budget is controlled by limiting its size directly. As far as compensation funds are concerned, enterprises can create them from their profits, while organisations funded by the state budget can create them independently of their fixed wage limits by allocating a certain share of savings from wages and benefits.

A decree governing the total incomes of private sector workers was of great importance for the development of private business. It determined the remuneration of employees on the basis of an agreed wage, the lower limit of which was fixed by wage tariffs.

As a consequence of a relatively big reduction in the labour force, the total wage bill in the state and co-operative sectors increased by only 1.1 per cent in 1990 compared with the previous year. Average wages rose by 3.8 per cent to 3,380 CSK over the same period. The pressure for larger wage increases, strong at the beginning of the year, abated subsequently, but began to regain momentum by the end of the year owing to rising inflation. In the fourth quarter of 1990, nominal wages were 6.3 per cent higher than a year earlier.

Wages in 1990 grew by 3.7 per cent in enterprises and 5.1 per cent in organisations funded by the state budget owing to the effect of certain central wage rises in health care and other public services.

Wages grew most rapidly in those branches where incomes are below average — in internal trade, health care, communications and housing administration. High wage growth was also seen in agriculture, where wages are above average (in contrast to developed countries). Wage rises in the private sector were higher, especially after the ending of wage regulation in enterprises with fewer than 25 employees.

Wage rises and the consequent increase in living costs were, however, so fast (and accelerating over time) that real wages fell on average by 5.6 per cent in 1990 compared with 1989, and by 10.6 per cent in the year to the fourth quarter of 1990. These figures exclude monthly government allowances of 140 crowns per capita or person as compensation for the withdrawing of state subsidies on foods. Including these allowances, the drop in real wages was 3.1 per cent year on year and 6.5 per cent in the year to the fourth quarter.

Incomes policy

The establishment of the Council for Economic and Social Agreement in October 1990 represented an important institutional measure towards establishing a wage policy based on tripartite talks and agreements between the social partners and the State.

After the first round of negotiations, measures to regulate the growth in average money wages and in wage adjustments to rising living costs, and in the level of the minimum wage, were accepted and included in the General Agreement for 1991.

The maximum permitted growth rate of average wages for the year to the first quarter of 1991 was set at 5 per cent for enterprises and 6 per cent for organisations funded by the state budget. This growth rate should have been increased in March to ensure that real wages in the first quarter would not have fallen by more than 12 per cent from their level of December 1990. The permitted growth rate in wages was in fact adjusted to an annual 16 per cent in March, equivalent to 9 per cent between December 1990 and the first quarter of 1991. As living costs rose by 31 per cent in this latter period the permitted fall in real wages will have been about 10 per cent steeper than that agreed. The permitted growth rate in wages for the rest of 1991 was to be set at a level that ensured that the drop in real wages would not at any time be greater than 10 per cent over December 1990. For the second quarter, however, it was recently accepted that real wages could fall to 22 per cent lower than a year earlier. Changes in permitted wage growth will be reflected in taxation of wages for both enterprises and state funded organisations.

The wages of individual workers are adjusted for increased living costs in line with the permitted growth rate of average nominal wages during the year. The procedures for this adjustment are stated in collective contracts or agreements between employers and employees, and in the wage regulations. It is implemented through a percentage increase either in the wage that is included in production costs, or in one of its components, or through a special bonus which is included in production costs.

If the permitted growth in wages is exceeded, regulatory taxation is implemented in two ways, which reflects the still-existing division of wage payments by enterprises into a part included in production costs and a part taken from profits. The first form of taxation is used when the growth rate of production cost wages exceeds that allowed by more than 3 per cent. It is set at 2 CSK for an excess of 3 to 5 per cent and 7.50 CSK for an excess above 5 per cent, for every 1 CSK overpaid. The second form of regulatory taxation deals with excessive growth of total wage payments — including wages taken from profit — and is set at 7.50 CSK for every 1 CSK overpaid. Clearly, this strongly limits wages growth. In the case of state funded organisations, wage increases are controlled either through the permitted growth rate in wages, or through a direct limit on wage funds. The sources of their compensation funds are either savings made on current spending or income from operations.

Minimum wage

In February 1991, minimum wage was introduced in Czechoslovakia for the first time. The tripartite General Agreement set the rate at 10.80 CSK per hour for a 42.5-hour working week and 2,000 CSK per month for workers paid under the monthly wage tariff system. Workers with shorter working hours, and workers who do not work all the working days in a month, are paid in proportion to the time worked. The minimum wage is lower for fully and partially disabled people and for disabled workers aged under 18 years, as fully disabled people are socially protected if they do not work. The minimum wage for workers aged under 16 years is lower, to reflect lower productivity.

If a worker earns less than the minimum wage, the employer has to pay the difference, irrespective of the economic situation of the enterprise or organisation. All components of the wage, including bonuses, etc., but excluding wage refunds, are taken into account in deciding whether a supplement is required. About 8 per cent of employees receive such supplements .

The minimum wage now stands at 60 per cent of the average wage and is leading to a further equalisation of wages in the national economy. The original intention of fully protecting the minimum wage against inflation would have strengthened this tendency, weakened motivation at work and had an unfavourable effect on employment, especially among groups such as youths, women with small children, and Gypsies. So far though, no such indexation has been implemented and negotiations among the social partners are likely to moderate its extent.

The actual growth rate of nominal wages was lower than the permitted level, at 6.1 per cent in the year to the first quarter of 1991. For the private sector the increase was 6.3 per cent. Real wages fell by 30 per cent over this period (with state compensation the drop was 27 per cent) or by 20 per cent from December 1990. There were large differences in wage developments between different social groups (nominal wages of agricultural workers fell by 3.3 per cent and their real wages by 36.9 per cent between the first quarter of 1990 and the first quarter of 1991) and especially between sectors. Most heavy industrial enterprises increased their wages to at least the permitted level, while many light industrial enterprises and state-financed organisations kept their wages unchanged or even let them fall.

In spite of the moderate increase in nominal wages, the gap between the growth in wages and in labour productivity has widened. In industry the difference between the two growth rates over the year to the first quarter of 1991 was nearly 11 per cent; for construction it was 25 per cent.

Wage reform

Wage reform, the principles of which were approved in December 1990 by the federal Government, aims to eliminate detailed state regulation of wage levels and increases, in favour of a system of collective bargaining by the social partners and agreements on basic employment conditions between them and Government. Wage tariffs will again form the basis of the new wage system in enterprises, and will reflect the complexity, responsibility and intensity of the job. They will also provide a social guarantee and protection for the worker against exploitation, and will serve as the lower limit for collective bargaining on wage tariffs at the industry and enterprise level. Basic wage tariffs will have a maximum of 12 steps, seven covering blue-collar workers. The tariff system in small enterprises will have six steps at the most. It will be possible to fix wages on an individual basis for specialists of outstanding abilities. The basic wage tariffs will be set so that differentials between one tariff level and the next will widen with each move up the scale. They will be the same for all industries apart from mining. Typical work activities in all industries will be classified using an objective and uniform system of scoring, and form the basis of a schedule covering some 450 occupations (positions) with about 3,500 listed basic work activities. This schedule can then be used by enterprises for drawing up their own schedule of work activities.

After discussions with the trade unions, an enterprise will make its own decision about wage forms and levels. Workers will be guaranteed tariff wages and bonuses stipulated in the wage rules or in a collective agreement. A new system of remuneration is being introduced for directors of enterprises, and will be extended to certain other managers at enterprises if collective agreements allow for it. Their salaries will be fixed by agreement.

The wage system in state-financed organisations will be based on a unified classification of typical work activities and positions, on work organisation and on the creation of compensation funds within their budgets. Tariff wages of individual work activities (positions) will vary according to the duration of the worker's employment and his or her ability to hold a higher position. Basically, there will be a uniform wage scale irrespective of the type, position and size of the institution or organisation. Differences in the activity of these institutions or organisations will be reflected in the internal structure of occupations and work positions. As in enterprises, employees will be provided with bonuses.

Industrial relations

The reconstruction of trade unions in Czechoslovakia began at the end of 1989. Trade unions, independent of political parties and the state, were established at extraordinary congresses. All levels of unions were established, i.e., from grass-roots bodies to central organisations. The monopolistic Revolutionary Trade Union Movement terminated its existence at a congress held in March 1990. New trade unions joined the Czech and Slovak Confederation of Trade Unions (CSKOS), which comprises 60 unions — 21 state-wide, 19 Czech and Czech-Moravian, and 20 Slovak. The supreme body of CSKOS is the General Council, with representatives from every member trade union. In the Czech Republic the majority of trade unions belong to the Czech-Moravian Chamber of CSKOS, and in the Slovak Republic the Slovak Confederation of Trade Unions. Both these bodies represent their members in negotiations with the national Government, state authorities and employers. The most active trade unions are those representing miners and metalworkers; by contrast, trade unions in services (especially in the private sector) are weak.

The great majority of trade unions, with almost 7 million members, belong to CSKOS. In addition, there is a Confederation of Arts and Culture, with about 80,000 members, and other smaller independent trade unions and organisations which are not associated in confederations, and which are not represented in central tripartite negotiations. These are held at the federal and republican levels within the framework of the Councils of Economic and Social Agreement of Czechoslovakia and of the Czech and Slovak Republics. Despite their considerable difficulties and misunderstandings in the past, all three parties signed the compromise General Agreement in January 1991, which outlined the economic and social conditions of the reform process for the year for employees, employers and the general population.

The weakest of the parties in the central tripartite negotiations are the employers, represented by the delegates of special associations that are gradually emerging. Employers' organisations had no place in the centralised administrative system, and with the market system not yet developed they have only limited scope for activity. The most important employers' organisations are the Union of State Enterprises and the Union of Private Entrepreneurs, and in each of the Czech and Slovak Republics, the Union of Industry and the Union of Construction. The Unions of Industry are the most active. In the current transition period it is significant that, as a hangover of a long era of paternalistic government, their main partners in the negotiations (or, more precisely, dialogue) are state authorities, as is the case for trade unions at the top level.

The new role of trade unions and their relations with employers have been incorporated into legislation, principally in an amendment to the Labour Code and the Law on Collective Bargaining, both of which came into force in February 1991.

The amendment to the Labour Code provides for the participation of trade unions in many types of social and legal relations. In contrast to former practice when — according to the Labour Code — a trade union was a co-partner in decision-making, decisions on many issues are now made by enterprises and organisations after negotiations with a trade union body. The previous partnership in decision-making was in effect purely formal because the important decisions were made by a Communist Party committee, whose resolutions were binding on all party members in a trade union body. According to the amended Labour Code, trade unions must be consulted on proposed redundancies or measures for creating new jobs for workers, mothers, young people and the disabled, on major problems of workers' welfare, on measures for improving working conditions and the working environment, as well as on other measures that affect large numbers of workers. There was a lengthy argument over the extent of trade union participation in decision-making on basic development guide-lines, plans, economic problems and allocation of profits. The new rule in the Labour Code, which requires an enterprise or organisation to inform a trade union in these cases only, is unsatisfactory. This is because real participation in decision-making can help to motivate workers, which is crucial if economies in transition are to improve economic efficiency.

By law, trade unions are involved in social and legal activities such as the transfer of workers to other jobs, termination of work contracts, and wage setting. In all cases the trade union represents the interests of all workers in the enterprise or organisation, including those who are not trade union members. More explicitly, this principle is contained within the Law on Collective Bargaining where the right to conclude a collective agreement is given only to trade unions. Collective agreements are concluded at the enterprise level, and at higher levels between the appropriate higher trade union body and an organisation (or organisations) of employers. Collective agreements are not regulated by the state.

In 1991, collective agreements were made on the basis of the General Agreement, the Labour Code and other legislation. They dealt with problems that, in the opinion of employers and employees, required a legal solution and regulation. Certain provisions appeared in some higher-level agreements which conflicted with the law. Similarly, certain aspects of collective agreements concluded within enterprises were not valid because they covered fewer (or more) employees' demands than the relevant higher-level agreement. These shortcomings, caused by the social partners' inexperience in concluding the new type of collective agreement, are gradually being overcome.

The Law on Collective Bargaining states the provisions for solving collective disputes on collective agreements and for meeting the obligations of a collective agreement. The right to strike is allowed as an extreme measure in such disputes. A strike is illegal both before mediation (which must be the first step) and after unsuccessful mediation before arbitration has been asked for. (At the same time, certain conditions determined by law must be fulfilled). Solidarity strikes, which involve workers striking over a collective agreement that does not concern them (under the above-mentioned conditions) are also illegal.

It is not yet known whether there have been any strikes under the Law on Collective Bargaining. A short-term interruption of work or a declaration of intent to strike in some enterprises or factories may stem not from a dispute between the employer and employees, but from workers' support for the employer against the state authorities, for example over problems of sales, non-payment of subsidies or the future security of the enterprise. Basic data on strikes will be given each month in official statistics, but as yet they are unavailable.

The Law on Collective Bargaining also covers partial or full lock-outs by an employer. The law gives detailed examples of lock-outs and the instances in which they are illegal. No lock-outs have yet been notified.

It is evident that, at all levels, collective bargaining is characterised by a lack of experience and often by insufficient knowledge of the problems and of the relevant laws. However, there is no doubt that collective bargaining will be further developed and improved as an important instrument in managing socio-economic processes and safeguarding social peace.

Notes:

1. Retirement age for men is 60, for women 54-57 years (varying with the number of children). Statistics usually take 55 years as the median retirement age for women.

2. The share of employed people in the total number of men and women of working age, excluding women on maternity leave, and self-employed or family workers, whose numbers were insignificant.

3. Education indicators for the whole population are available only from the census (the last was in 1980). In 1989, out of all primary - school leavers, 37 per cent went on to secondary schools and 58.4 per cent to apprentice schools.

4. *Statistical Yearbook of CSFR (CSSR)*, various years.

5. The calculation was based on a comparison of the number of workers per 1,000 inhabitants in different industrial sectors in Czechoslovakia, Austria and Belgium (i.e., countries which once had a similar industrial structure) for years when their economic product was roughly the same (Czechoslovakia = 1988, Austria = 1980, Belgium = 1975).

Chapter 4

Hungary: Labour market trends and policies

by
Gyorgy Sziraczki *
International Labour Office

Introduction

It is not easy to say precisely when Hungary began its move from classical "socialism" to a market-regulated socio-economic system because there was a lengthy and gradual process of erosion even under the old order. This process was due essentially to the peculiarities of the post-1956 phase of socialism in Hungary, which led to significant moves towards the market economy and private ownership within a socialist setting. This erosion gathered pace in the 1980s as the symptoms of an overall crisis in the economy became apparent. The traditional sources of growth based on ever-increasing labour inputs, cheap raw materials and capital-saving investment were exhausted, and additional external resources from foreign borrowing proved inadequate to finance the economy in its unchanged form.

The new economic policy adopted by the Communist Party (HSWP) in 1978, which aimed to promote foreign trade, required more market-oriented reforms. These included gradual liberalisation of prices and of imports, freer labour movement based on demand and supply rather than administrative direction and, from 1982, some private enterprise. These moves were reflected in a more tolerant social and political system. Another feature of liberation was the widespread participation in the second or parallel economy, which was far larger in Hungary than elsewhere in the region. By the mid-1980s three-quarters of all households had additional income from informal activities.

---

* With contributions from Maria Lado of the Institute of Labour Research and Julia Szalai of the Institute of Sociology, Budapest.

Recent economic trends[1]

The political changes of 1989-90 dramatically accelerated the move towards a market economy: there was a rapid shift in trade away from eastern Europe and the former Soviet Union to industrialised market economies; privatisation gained momentum; inefficient industries were forced to cut back production severely; large state enterprises were broken up; and thousands of small firms started trading. The Government's economic programme made priorities of privatisation, and of the control of inflation through the removal of subsidies and the imposition of a tight monetary policy.

These changes had to be implemented at a time when the long-term deterioration in the economy produced severe crisis (table 4.1). In 1990, falling domestic demand, aggravated by drought, and trade disruptions with the CMEA economies led to a deep recession, with GDP dropping by 4.3 per cent. The production of industrial enterprises, with 50 or more employees, declined by as much as 8.5 per cent, and all branches of industry except power generation cut output. The decline was particularly steep in iron and steel (19 per cent), engineering (13.7 per cent) and mining (11.8 per cent). This trend reflects the beginning of a fundamental restructuring of the economy away from energy-intensive and often loss-making products produced for eastern European markets towards the production of higher value-added goods for more competitive markets. The expansion of small firms, employing fewer than 20 people, partly offset the drop in output attributable to large enterprises, which represented about 94 per cent of total production. Taking into account the growth of output in the small-firm sector, total industrial production fell by 5 per cent.

Table 4.1. **Macroeconomic indicators, Hungary, 1986-90**
(annual percentage change)

	1986	1987	1988	1989	1990
GDP	1.5	4.1	-0.1	0.2	-4.3
Gross industrial output	1.9	3.8	0.1	-1.0	-5.0
Gross agricultural output	2.4	-2.0	4.3	-1.3	-6.4
Gross investment	2.3	7.6	-7.7	4.5	-6.3
Consumer price inflation	5.3	8.6	15.7	17.0	28.9
Hard currency account US $bn	-1.49	-0.88	-0.80	-1.44	0.13

Source: KSH (Central Statistical Office), Budapest.

There has been a spectacular growth in the number of enterprises, up by 50 per cent in 1989 and doubling in 1990, mainly due to the establishment of thousands of limited liability companies (table 4.2). There has also been a massive shift away from large companies towards small ones (table 4.3), a process encouraged by the introduction of a new Company Law in 1989, changes in the corporation tax system and incomes policy.[2]

In the absence of reliable statistics, it is not possible to say to what extent the growth of the small-firm sector is due to organic development, the transfer of businesses from the parallel to the legal economy, or the break-up of large companies. An analysis[3] by the Central Statistical Office has shown that the dismemberment of large enterprises tends to create a significant number of medium-sized enterprises; the vast majority of small firms, however, have been set up as a result of private initiative. The trend towards small firms may create a more competitive economic environment, which in turn may be an important factor in generating a more dynamic economy. However, the share of small firms in the economy was still modest in 1990, and did not exceed 10 per cent of total output in the material sector.

Table 4.2. **Number of companies: Hungary, 1985-90 (end of period)**

	1985	1986	1987	1988	1989	1990
Total	7 816	8 488	9 507	10 745	15 619	29 470
of which:						
State-owned enterprises or trusts	1 910	1 940	1 955	1 986	2 001	2 004
Agricultural co-operatives	1 350	1 340	1 337	1 333	1 333	1 348
Other co-operatives	2 735	2 719	2 658	2 439	2 510	2 629
Small co-operatives	762	1 258	2 154	3 108	3 233	3 155
Joint-stock companies	62	74	137	116	307	646
Limited companies	-	-	-	451	4 485	18 317

Source: KSH: *Statisztikai Havi Kozlemenyek* (Monthly Statistical Information), various issues, (Budapest).

Table 4.3. **Distribution of companies by size of workforce[1], Hungary 1989-90**

Workforce	Jan. 1989 %	Dec. 1989 %	June 1990 %	Dec. 1990 %
Up to 20	22.7	37.6	45.1	59.5
21-50	17.2	17.6	15.8	19.9
51-30	32.9	25.5	23.6	16.2
301 and over	27.2	19.3	15.5	9.4
Total	100.0	100.0	100.0	100.0
Number	9 737	13 568	16 661	27 662

1. In material production.
Source: KSH: *Az anyagi ágak munkaügyi jellemzöi 1990-ben*
(Employment in the field of material production in 1990) (Budapest, 1991).

Labour market developments

Labour demand and labour supply[4]

Full employment was a primary objective and a characteristic feature of the socialist economy in Hungary, as in other east European countries. It was achieved by a combination of low wages, high fixed investment, centrally initiated output growth and an incentive structure encouraging high demand for labour. Open unemployment was virtually non-existent during the 1970s and the first part of the 1980s. However, labour hoarding (disguised unemployment) was widespread and labour productivity was very low by international standards.

Excess demand for labour disappeared as the economy moved into deep recession and the transition to a market system accelerated. Declining investment and domestic demand, cuts in public spending, and privatisation have all contributed to a falling demand for labour, as seen in the number of registered vacancies which dropped from an average of 70,000 in 1988 to 15,000 in December 1990.

The sharp deterioration in trade with eastern Europe and the former Soviet Union severely affected many industries, and the survival of many firms depends on finding new markets in the West. Enterprises that are accustomed to producing for low quality CMEA markets are facing great difficulties in successfully reorienting production for more demanding customers.

Jobs are being lost through: restructuring, with a scaling-down of production and employment; the break-up of large companies or the closure of units; and the closure of small and medium-sized firms. Mass redundancies have begun, involving all types of labour. Firms not yet affected await future developments, hoping they can survive, and meanwhile reduce the number of shifts, introduce short-time work or temporarily dose production lines.

In January 1990, total employment, including employed pensioners, was 5.2 million, 4.4 per cent less than a decade before (table 4.4). This drop was caused by a fall in labour supply throughout the decade and by a decline in labour demand in the late 1980s. Labour supply was significantly influenced by demographic trends. The birth rate fell from an average of 16 per 1,000 in the 1970s to 12 per 1,000 in the 1980s, resulting in an older and smaller population. The working-age population fell from 6.2 million in 1980 to 5.9 million in 1990, while a rising level of education and improved child-care leave also contributed to a reduction in labour supply.

The number of employed persons over working age fell slowly until 1987, a process that accelerated as the demand for labour declined and many enterprises began to cut employment (table 4.4). Enterprise managers systematically targeted elderly employees and working pensioners to shed labour easily.[5] Thus, the high labour force participation rate of the working-age population was maintained at the expense of older workers in the late 1980s. About 79 per cent of the total working-age population was employed during the 1980s and, in January 1990, the participation rate was 84 per cent for men and 75 per cent for women.

Table 4.4. **Employment: Hungary, 1980-90 (beginning of year)**

| | Total employment[1] | | Of which | | | |
| | | | of working age | | over working age | |
	(000s)	1980=100	(000s)	1980=100	(000s)	1980=100
1980	5 469.6	100.0	4 845.1	100.0	624.5	100.0
1981	5 446.5	99.6	4 819.4	99.5	627.1	100.4
1982	5 436.9	99.4	4 837.0	99.8	599.9	96.1
1983	5 413.9	99.0	4 822.3	99.5	590.8	94.6
1984	5 392.0	98.6	4 797.7	99.0	594.3	95.2
1985	5 372.9	98.2	4 477.8	98.6	595.1	95.3
1986	5 360.5	98.0	4 762.2	98.3	598.3	95.8
1987	5 364.2	98.1	4 755.9	98.2	608.3	97.4
1988	5 317.8	97.2	4 719.5	97.5	598.3	95.8
1989	5 263.7	96.2	4 704.1	97.1	559.6	89.6
1990	5 227.2	95.6	4 684.8	96.7	542.4	86.9

1. Including employed pensioners.
Source: KSH: *A nemzetgazdaság munkaerőhelyzete a 80-as években* (Employment situation in the 1980s) (Budapest, 1991).

The expulsion of pensioners from employment, which has a devastating impact on their living standards, is likely to continue. Another means of maintaining employment for those of working age may be part-time work, but this avenue has been little used: apart from employed pensioners, only about 3 per cent of the employed worked part-time in 1989. The Government thus needs to implement measures to mitigate the impoverishment of pensioners who lose their jobs and to encourage the spread of part-time work.

Further reductions in the labour supply seem unlikely for several reasons. First, the working-age population is expected to increase because large numbers of school-leavers will enter the labour force in the coming years. Second, immigration has increased, with an inflow of about 36,000 in 1989 and 1990, mostly Romanians of Hungarian descent.[6] Third, the Government intends to reduce the size of the army and the police. Finally, an intensifying deterioration in living standards may push many of those outside the labour force to enter the labour market. A confrontation between declining labour demand and growing labour supply thus looks unavoidable in the first half of the 1990s, leading to a fall in the participation rate and a growth in unemployment.

Employment structure

During the 1980s, falling employment was accompanied by noticeable changes in the structure of employment by sector, industry, enterprise size and ownership. The employment share of agriculture declined from 21 per cent in 1980 to 17.4 per cent in 1990, and that of industry from 41.3 per cent to 36.1 per cent. Meanwhile, the employment share of services rose from 37.7 per cent to 46.1 per cent - a level comparable to that in southern European countries. The shift towards services became more pronounced in 1990; employment fell by 3.2 per cent in industry and by 12.5 per cent in agriculture, while remaining unchanged in services.

Employment declined in all industrial branches, except electricity, in 1990 (table 4.5). Given past over-expansion of heavy industry, it is not surprising that the largest reductions were in iron and steel (down 17.9 per cent) and mining (down 17.3 per cent). However, most branches of industry cut employment in line with production. This indicates that labour hoarding in state-owned enterprises remains pervasive, although it is hard to estimate its extent.

Table 4.5. **Employment in industry[1], Hungary, 1987-90**

	1987	1988	1989	1990	1990
	Change in per cent		over previous year		Workforce (000s)
Mining	-2.8	-5.1	-8.0	-17.3	78
Electricity	3.3	2.1	-1.1	4.7	44
Iron and steel	-4.7	-4.9	-8.1	-17.9	62
Engineering	-2.0	-2.2	-1.4	- 9.9	380
Building materials	-3.4	-2.7	-1.8	-4.9	57
Chemicals	-1.0	0.5	2.3	-4.1	103
Light industry	-3.9	-3.8	-0.3	-10.3	267
Others	-3.7	-7.3	-10.8	-21.3	23
Food industry	-1.7	-1.3	0.2	-3.3	195
Total	-2.5	-2.6	-1.7	-9.1	1 209

1. Industrial enterprises with more than 50 employees.
Source: KSH: *Statisztikai Havi Közlemények,* (Monthly Statistical Information), various issues (Budapest).

Employment in firms with more than 300 employees dropped by 406,000 (down 13.0 per cent), while employment in medium-sized enterprises, with 50 to 300 employees, increased by 36,000 (up 9 per cent). Small firms (fewer than 50 employees) also created thousands of jobs, though the exact number is not known since many jobs simply shifted from big to small enterprises or from the parallel to the registered private economy. (The data also refer only to material production, which covers about 80 per cent of total employment.) On balance, however, total employment fell by 170,000 (3.7 per cent) in the economy as a whole. The small-firm sector is still relatively weak, representing about 10 per cent of total employment, but is playing a part in increasing labour flexibility by spreading flexible contracting and working-time patterns, including part-time work, and flexible wage systems.

The growth of the legal private sector, which began in the early 1980s, speeded up towards the end of the decade. The employment share of the legal private sector, including independent entrepreneurs (craftsmen, retail traders, leaseholders, farmers) and their employees, and various forms of small-scale undertaking, increased from 4.9 per cent in 1983 to about 11 per cent in January 1990.[7]

In addition, joint stock companies and limited liability companies accounted for about 20 per cent of total employment at the end of 1991, although it is not known how many were in private ownership. There were about 5,000 joint ventures registered in early 1991, but employment data for them are not available.[8]

A feature of the Hungarian economy during the past two decades has been the huge expansion of the parallel economy. In 1985, the number of participants approached the 5.4 million employed in the entire socialist sector, with an estimated 3.3 to 4.8 million people involved.[9] Workers and employees "moonlighted" in the evening, at weekends and during holidays, even on sick leave. Some became "unemployed" in order to take a well-paid temporary job in the parallel economy. In addition, large numbers of "statistically inactive people" (pensioners, housewives, students) regularly or occasionally worked in this sector. Estimates suggest a ratio of 1 to 2 between working time in the parallel and the official economies in the mid-1980s.[10]

With recent reforms, the character and role of the parallel economy is changing. Some market-oriented businesses are moving to the legal private sector, while other traditional, parallel activities (eg., farming on private plots) survive and even flourish. However, there are troubling signs that the growth of poverty and unemployment may bring about a new underground economy.

Unemployment

The registration of the unemployed began in January 1986. Since then the unemployment rate has been rising continual (table 4.6), slowly between 1986 and 1989 and rapidly since. In January 1990, the unemployment rate was 0.6 per cent; by November 1991 it was 7.3 per cent, affecting 350,000 people. By early 1992 unemployment is expected to rise to at least 450,000 (or 10 per cent), and may climb even further depending on the drop in trade with the former Soviet Union, the speed of removal of subsidies, and the pace at which enterprises are closed.

Unemployment figures, based on registration with local employment offices, should be viewed with caution. Lack of unemployment compensation and underdeveloped employment services may discourage the unemployed from registering. For example, at the end of 1988, when employment offices recorded about 15,000 unemployed, the real number was estimated to be up to 12 times as high.[11] The introduction of comprehensive unemployment benefits in 1989 narrowed this gap. In January 1990, a national population census found 110,000 unemployed people actively looking for work, "only" five times as many as the number of registered unemployed.

The new Employment Law, passed by parliament in February 1991, decentralised the labour market budget. Because the distribution of central resources between regions is largely influenced by local unemployment, employment offices all over the country launched a "registration campaign" — a factor which certainly contributed to the rapid increase in official unemployment in the first quarter of 1991.

Regional unemployment varies greatly and the differences appear to be widening.[12] In November 1991, regional unemployment rates ranged from 2.4 to 14.0 per cent. The ten counties with the lowest rates of unemployment are located primarily in the industrial western part of the country, including Budapest and surrounding areas. They are close to Austria and to Germany — Germany especially an increasingly dominant economic force in Hungary. The worst-hit counties are mostly in the eastern and northern parts of Hungary, including traditionally underdeveloped regions, agricultural areas, regions dominated by "crisis" industries and areas with a high concentration of subsidiaries of enterprises with headquarters elsewhere. It is likely that the move to a market economy will further widen this division between western, eastern and northern parts of the country.

Table 4.6. **Unemployment and vacancies, Hungary, 1986-91**

Year	Quarter/ month	Number of registered unemployed	Number of vacancies	Vacancies per unemployed person	Unemployment rate (%)
1986	1	1 442	61 468	42.6	
	2	4 613	75 434	16.4	
	3	7 595	81 654	10.8	
	4	6 387	63 888	10.0	0.1
1987	1	10 381	56 652	5.5	
	2	9 188	60 877	6.6	
	3	10 465	55 473	5.3	
	4	10 809	46 795	4.3	0.2
1988	1	16 845	43 762	2.6	
	2	11 462	54 127	4.7	
	3	15 254	70 129	4.6	
	4	14 163	72 637	5.1	0.4
1989	1	22 678	68 131	3.1	
	2	23 488	66 748	2.1	
	3	22 146	60 236	2.7	
	4	28 484	46 609	1.6	0.7
1990	January	23 426	37 711	1.6	
	February	30 055	38 335	1.2	
	March	32 498	34 048	1.1	
	April	32 146	35 191	1.1	
	May	38 155	37 938	1.0	
	June	41 754	37 859	0.9	
	July	45 055	36 222	0.8	
	August	45 518	33 732	0.7	
	September	56 115	26 969	0.5	
	October	60 997	22 763	0.4	
	November	69 982	17 150	0.3	
	December	79 521	14 815	0.2	1.7
1991	January	100 526	12 949	0.1	2.1
	February	128 383	14 721	0.1	2.7
	March	144 840	13 583	0.1	3.0
	April	167 407	16 478	0.1	3.4
	May	165 022	14 919	0.1	3.4
	June	185 554	18 860	0.1	3.9
	July	216 568	15 168	0.1	4.5
	August	251 084	14 124	0.1	5.2
	September	292 756	15 351	0.05	6.1
	October	317 000			6.6
	November	351 000			7.3

Source: National Labour Market Centre, Budapest.

Flows into unemployment comprise those already in the labour force, school-leavers and other new labour market entrants. The overwhelming majority of the registered unemployed have lost their jobs. However, jobless school-leavers, who do not qualify for benefits, are certainly under-represented in registered unemployment figures. Table 4.7, based on preliminary results of the population census of January 1990, shows that the highest unemployment rates are among those aged 15 to 19 and 20 to 24.

Table 4.7. **Unemployment rates by age, Hungary, January 1990**

Age	Men (%)	Women (%)	Total (%)
15 - 19	8.9	7.0	8.1
20 - 24	4.1	2.9	3.5
25 - 29	3.4	2.3	2.8
30 - 39	2.5	1.3	1.9
40 - 49	2.1	0.9	1.5
50 - 54	1.7	0.7	1.2
55 - 59	1.1	-	0.9
15 - 59	2.9	-	
15 - 54	-	1.7	
Total		-	2.4

Source: KSH *Preliminary results of the census of 1990* (Budapest, 1991).

Men are more likely to be unemployed than women. They make up 54 per cent of the workforce but account for 60 to 62 per cent of the registered unemployed — a share which has remained unchanged in recent years. The January 1990 census shows an unemployment rate of 2.9 per cent for men and 1.7 per cent for women. The male-female differences in unemployment can be explained by the fact that heavy job losses have primarily hit male-dominated industries.

Unemployment tends to affect particularly unskilled and less educated groups. In February 1991, the unemployment rate for non-manual workers was 1.5 per cent, and for semi-skilled and skilled workers, 2.5 and 2.6 per cent, while the unemployment rate for unskilled workers stood at 10 per cent. In all occupational groups those seeking work outnumber registered vacancies.

Statistics on flows in and out of unemployment refer to benefit recipients only. Furthermore, the available data on the duration of unemployment refer to the average length of time a person receives unemployment compensation. Although this group represents only a part of total unemployment, data suggest that the recent rise in the jobless figure has resulted from a large inflow of unemployed people and from a significant increase in the duration of unemployment.

In 1990 the inflow amounted to about 81,000 people. Of the total unemployment stock, only 30.9 per cent left the register over the year (17.5 per cent found work, 11.6

per cent on maternity leave, retired or died, while 1.9 per cent were denied further benefits for various reasons). Between February and December 1990, the average length of time for which benefits were paid increased from 3.3 months to almost 5.1 months.[13]

Clearly, with employment falling steeply, the chances of the unemployed rejoining the workforce are declining. Jobs have been cut, and there is no sign of emerging sunrise industries. Meanwhile, the small-firm sector, though expanding, is still small and absorbs mainly skilled and well-educated workers. An analysis of flows onto and out of the unemployment register has forecast that the average unemployment spell could approach one year.[14] If current employment trends continue, the country will quickly face large-scale, long-term unemployment.

Labour market policies[15]

The Hungarian Government introduced a number of employment measures in the second half of the 1980s to respond to labour market changes. Active measures such as employment services, retraining programmes and job-creation schemes were the first to be implemented. Passive measures followed, including unemployment compensation and early retirement schemes, and a programme-package designed to manage local crises. All these measures were designed to deal with low unemployment that was considered transitory and frictional. Labour market policies were redesigned in early 1991 to cope with the changed employment situation.

Programmes in action

The establishment of a nation-wide network of *employment offices* started in 1985. Initially, they focused on job placement but were gradually given additional responsibilities such as finding work for hard-to-place labour, organising public work programmes and retraining courses, and administering the unemployment benefit system. As the pace of labour market change accelerated, employment offices found it increasingly difficult to perform their functions efficiently. There were 47 unemployed jobseekers for each employment office employee in January 1990, 62 in December 1990 and 104 in March 1991. The increasing workload has undermined the quality of basic services delivered by the offices. In addition, the staff do not have the necessary training and expertise to adjust services to needs, for example, in offering special support programmes for disadvantaged groups.

Programmes designed to provide *retraining assistance* began in 1983. Originally, these were designed to facilitate the retraining of workers already in employment. In 1987, the scope of the retraining scheme was extended to include programmes and assistance for those at risk of losing their job and for the unemployed. The number of participants in supported programmes grew rapidly, from 2,800 in 1984 to almost 23,000 in 1990.

Recently, efforts have shifted further towards those threatened by lay-offs — especially in connection with restructuring, and the unemployed. However, retraining activities appear to be constrained by falling vacancies. In the second half of 1990, only 3,500 — 20.5 per cent — of the 17,000 people participating in retraining programmes were unemployed, representing less than 6 per cent of all jobless. Another problem is that many of the subsidised training programmes focus on firm-specific skills or skill shortages in the existing industrial structure, and they rarely attempt to match services with the future needs of the workforce.

In the second half of the 1980s the Government set up four programmes to promote employment: subsidised public works for hard-to-place labour, support for the unemployed who set up private enterprises, assistance for enterprise investment to create jobs in depressed regions, and subsidised employment for school-leavers.

The *public works* scheme was introduced in four counties as an experiment in 1987, and then extended to the whole country the following year. Since then the programme has provided the unemployed people with low-paid temporary work. The average number of participants increased from about 800 a month in 1987 to 4,500 in 1990. The programme is useful in offering earning opportunities for unemployed people who are not eligible for benefits, and may help reduce the risk that some of the long-term unemployed become alienated from working life. However, the type of work involved (clearing away unauthorised dumps, drainage, forestation projects, gardening and small maintenance jobs in public places and buildings) does not help improve the future job chances of participants. The public works scheme is rarely combined with training programmes.

Assistance for enterprise investment to promote employment, introduced in 1988, offers enterprises preferential loans or, in some cases, grants for job-creating investment in regions with a surplus of labour. According to official figures, the number of jobs created by this programme was 10,463 in 1988-89, and 2,694 in the first three quarters of 1990. However, the reliability of available data and the effectiveness of the programme have frequently been questioned. First, enterprises often used investment subsidies to fund jobs already created.[16] In practice, these subsidies served only to improve the enterprise's financial position. Second, many enterprises benefiting from the scheme created low-skill jobs using obsolete technology, preserving an already outdated industrial structure. Third, shortly after receiving financial assistance, some enterprises went into bankruptcy, so that jobs were lost and programme money wasted.[17]

One of the most controversial measures, the *"start-up" loan scheme,* also introduced in 1988, offered the unemployed assistance in creating their own private businesses. Financial support included a bank loan of up to 400,000 HUF[18] ($5,700), with no interest to pay for the first four years. Interest was paid instead by the Employment Fund (see below). The four-year interest-free period made the programme very popular among the unemployed. Almost anyone who could show that he had no work had access to a loan, so that sometimes people left their jobs or were deliberately fired in order to qualify. In addition, a number of already established entrepreneurs, who were often not well served by the underdeveloped banking system and capital market, also benefited from the programme. The number of participants increased rapidly, from about 8,000 in 1988 to 21,400 in the first half of 1990. Soaring expenditure on this scheme exhausted a large part of the labour market budget, and the programme was dropped in mid-1990.

In 1989 the Government launched a programme of *subsidised employment* designed to assist job placement of university graduates. Wage subsidies for up to 18 months were offered to enterprises which recruited an unemployed graduate. However, the scheme was little used by employers.

An *early retirement* scheme introduced in 1987 covers redundancies arising from enterprise reorganisation, large-scale employment reduction or plant closure. Employees must be within five years of normal retirement age (60 for men and 55 for women), with 25-30 years' employment including at least five years with their present employer. In 1988, 2,604 workers took early retirement, a figure which grew to 9,000 in 1990. Of these, 5,600 were partly or fully subsidised from the Employment Fund.

In late 1989, faced with large-scale redundancies and their impact on local labour markets, the Government set up a *programme for crisis regions*. In practice, it offered financial support not to a region but to a few big enterprises to facilitate mass lay-offs or plant closures. Redundant workers of these enterprises were entitled to severance payments, resettlement assistance and special support to start private businesses. The enterprises concerned could receive assistance to cover most of the costs associated with early retirement. Furthermore, the programme provided wage subsidies for those employers who recruited redundant workers. In 1990 the programme was implemented in five regions, dominated by the mining, steel and electronics industries. As table 4.8 shows, efforts were concentrated on income maintenance (early retirement and severance pay). It might therefore be said that the scheme served mainly to "buy off" redundant workers rather than to help them find new jobs.

Table 4.8. **Participants in programmes for crisis regions, Hungary, 1990**

Crisis regions	Active measures		Passive measures			Total
	Wage subsidies to regular employment	Subsid. to unemployment starting enterprises	Resettlement assistance	Severance payments	Early retirement	
Baranya (mining)[1]	1	-	5	557	189	772
Ozd (steel)	107	1	-	142	1 317	1 567
Recsk and Egercsehi (mining)[1]	-	37	4	236	34	311
Fejer (electronics)[1]	-	-	-	863	236	1 099
Nograd (mining)[1]	10	16	-	48	380	454
Total participants	118	54	9	1 866	2 156	4 203
(per cent)	(2.8)	(1.3)	(0.2)	(44.5)	(51.3)	(100.0)

1. Dominant industry.
Source: Lado, M. and Toth F.: *Létszámleépités felszámolás, munkahelyek megszüntetése* (Employment reduction, closures, job losses), Budapest, Labour Institute, 1991 (manuscript).

Labour market budget and programme priorities

Until the end of 1987, employment programmes were directly financed from the state budget. In 1988, although funding still came from state resources, the government set up a separate Employment Fund for labour market policy. The resources available for employment measures were increased from 0.24 billion HUF in 1987 to 1.2 billion HUF (0.07 per cent of GDP) in 1988 and 2.4 billion HUF (0.15 per cent of GDP) in 1989. In 1990 the Government initially allocated 5.5 billion HUF for labour market policy, almost twice as much as the year before, but this proved inadequate. The surge in expenditure on labour market programmes was caused primarily by unexpected growth in unemployment (and the resulting cost of unemployment benefits) and spending on the start-up loan scheme. Some programmes were cut, suspended or dropped during the year to keep spending down. Even so, total spending on labour market programmes in 1990 amounted to 7.5 billion HUF (0.4 per cent of GDP).

Table 4.9 shows expenditures for the main programme categories as a percentage of the total labour market budget between 1988 and 1990. In the latter part of the 1980s, the Government believed that what it saw as small-scale regional unemployment could adequately be addressed by job creation. In 1988, 86 per cent of the total employment budget was spent on job creation, overwhelmingly through investment subsidies. These programmes were not concerned with the efficiency of the labour market but tried rather to absorb unemployment or hide it through public works. In 1989, job-creation programmes still accounted for 55 per cent of the budget. However, with the dramatic changes in labour market conditions, there has been a marked shift away from job creation towards income protection. Unemployment compensation became the largest single item of expenditure in 1990, and its share in the budget was set to increase further in 1991.

Table 4.9. **Distribution of public expenditure on labour market programmes, Hungary, 1988-90**

Programme category	1988 (%)	1989 (%)	1990 (%)
1. Employment services and administration	-	15.4	3.5
2. Labour market training	9.1	15.3	11.1
3. Youth measures	-	0.2	0.0
4. Start-up loan	-	4.9	25.4
5. Public works	10.5	11.1	5.1
6. Investment subsidies for job creation	75.6	39.0	13.9
7. Special measures for crisis regions	-	-	5.3
8. Early retirement	0.4	0.3	1.3
9. Unemployment benefits	4.4	13.8	34.4
Total expenditure (%)	100.0	100.0	100.0
(HUF billion)	1.14	2.13	7.55

Source: Ministry of Labour, Budapest.

Recent changes in labour market policy

In February 1991, the parliament adopted a new Employment Law which introduced changes in both labour market policy and its financing. Some programmes have been discontinued, others redesigned, and some new schemes have been implemented.

The start-up loan scheme was replaced with a new programme to provide support for the unemployed who start enterprises. Unemployment benefits were extended for an additional six months, and the programme now offers up to 50 per cent reimbursement for special counselling and training for starting a business.

Investment subsidies have been dropped, in favour of two forms of subsidy for regular employment. The first promotes employment for jobless people, especially for school-leavers and the long-term unemployed. The scheme offers up to 50 per cent reimbursement of wage costs for each unemployed person taken on, for a period of one year, on condition that other workers employed by the enterprise are not dismissed. The second subsidy aims to prevent lay-offs by encouraging short-time working. It provides benefits (up to 50 per cent) to participating workers for a period of one year. A number of other programmes are currently under consideration, including measures for crisis regions, the long-term unemployed, unemployed youth, the disabled and refugees. As past experience indicates, the success of these programmes depends largely on improvements in the labour market information system, programme management and the employment services.

The Employment Law separates income protection programmes from the budget. It has created an unemployment insurance fund (the Solidarity Fund) based on compulsory contributions from employees and employers; a separate Employment Fund is financed from the state budget and revenues from privatisation. The Solidarity Fund will be used for unemployment compensation, expenditure associated with the employment services and administration, and part of the training programmes and the early retirement scheme. The Employment Fund will finance active labour market programmes. Total spending for labour market policy in 1991 is expected to amount to 28 billion HUF (1.6 per cent of GDP), almost four times as much as in 1990. However, there are two trends which cause concern. First, only about 13 per cent of the total budget will be available for financing new active measures, which sets considerable limits on efforts to improve labour market efficiency. Second, unless the current rate of increase in unemployment slows, spending on unemployment benefits will soon exhaust the Solidarity Fund.

Policies for income support

by
Julia Szalai*
Institute of Sociology
Budapest

Introduction

Trends in macroeconomic aggregates hide a crucial aspect of the transition to a market economy, namely, the significant increase in social inequalities of all kinds. True, the majority of people with access to private resources, and/or a protective (extended) family network behind them, could cope and even prosper. But those who, for one reason or another, remained outside this informal safety net have suffered the adverse consequences of economic transformation.

Poverty during transition

Our present knowledge about the extent and composition of poverty is limited. Until recently no data were collected on the number of people living below the minimum subsistence level. The acknowledgement of the existence of poverty was one of the strongest taboos of socialist ideology and politics. The first "official" minima were computed by the Central Statistical Office as late as 1984, and published data have been available only since 1988. Table 4.10 presents some calculations on the numbers and incidence of those living below the poverty line as defined by the subsistence minima. The total number of those in poverty seems to have fluctuated between 1.1 million and 1.8 million, representing 10 to 17 per cent of the population.

There were significant differences in poverty rates and their change over the decade 1977-87 between the two major groups of households, i.e., those with active earners and those of pensioners. The risk of poverty was markedly higher in the latter group in the first half of the period, but this situation was reversed in the early 1980s. Between 1977 and 1987 there was a 3 per cent increase in the number of poor living in active households, while the risk of poverty dropped by some 10 per cent in pensioner households. This reflected a significant change in the structure of the pensioner population over the period, improvements in pension levels and the expansion of the parallel economy.

* With contributions from Gyorgy Sziraczki, International Labour Office, Geneva.

Table 4.10. **Persons living below subsistence level, Hungary, 1977-87**

Year	Number of persons living below the minimum, living in:			Percentage of those living below the minimum, as a percentage of total population, living in:		
	Households with active earner(s)	Households without active earner(s) (000s)	All households	Households with active earner(s)	Households without active earner(s)	All households
From income surveys:						
1977 [1]	963.7	274.2	1 237.9	10.7	18.0	11.7
1982	906.7	195.7	1 102.4	10.0	11.9	10.9
1987	1 191.2	152.8	1 344.0	13.5	8.5	12.7
From household surveys:						
1978 [1]	1 314.8	322.8	1 637.6	14.4	21.1	15.4
1980 [1]	1 179.9	247.4	1 427.3	13.2	17.2	13.8
1982	1 360.0	218.7	1 578.7	15.0	13.3	14.8
1983	1 476.8	414.9	1 791.7	16.5	18.0	16.7
1985	1 426.3	247.4	1 673.7	16.0	14.2	15.7
1987	1 279.5	188.8	1 468.3	14.5	10.5	13.8

1. Subsistence minima were retrospectively calculated by KSH only back to 1982. The values for 1977, 1978 and 1980 are estimated, on the assumption that the ratio of the national subsistence minimum to the average monthly per capita income was the same for those years as for 1982. Average monthly per capita income data are drawn from the household surveys for 1978 and 1980, and from the (more accurate) data of the income survey for 1977.

Source: KSH: *Statistical Yearbooks,* Budapest (various years).

The social composition of the poor is shown in tables 4.11 and 4.12. While income differences according to the occupation of the head of the houseold, and/or other household members, seem to have diminished, other factors which generate inequalities have become more important, such as access to and participation in the informal economy, and family support. The most marked inequalities reflect the ratio of earners to dependants in the household — an important characteristic of the income distribution of the state-dominated society of recent decades.

The past ten years have seen an increasing proportion of active earners among urban families living in poverty. While the poor of the 1960s typically lived in rural areas, alone or with their spouses on pensions or on welfare, the poor of the 1980s typically lived in urban families with active earners, were relatively young, and had (often several) children. Table 4.11 shows that while there was only a slight decline in the proportion of active earners in the total population between 1977 and 1987, there was a marked increase in their proportion among the poor. The opposite is true for pensioners and adult dependants (mainly elderly housewives who do not work).

The most worrying development is the rapid growth in the number of children living in poverty. In the late 1980s two out of five individuals living in poverty were children, and of these roughly one-third were under 6 years old.

Table 4.11. **Social composition of poor households, Hungary, 1977-87**

Composition of households	Lowest income decile[1] (%)	All households (%)
1977		
Active earners	18.6	47.0
Those receiving child-care benefits[2]	3.3	2.5
Pensioners	25.5	18.6
Children under 6 years old	15.0	9.0
Children in education	19.4	15.4
(All children)	(34.4)	(24.4)
Other dependants	18.2	7.5
Total	100.0	100.0
1982		
Active earners	23.7	45.7
Receiving child-care benefits[2]	4.8	2.2
Pensioners	17.3	20.3
Children under 6 years old	18.9	9.0
Children in education	21.9	17.2
(All children)	(40.8)	(26.2)
Other dependants	13.4	5.6
Total	100.0	100.0
1987		
Active earners	27.0	45.8
Those receiving child-care benefits[2]	4.2	2.0
Pensioners	16.4	22.4
Children under 6 years old	15.7	7.2
Children in education	24.8	18.2
(All children)	(40.5)	(25.4)
Other dependants	11.7	4.4
Total	100.0	100.0

1. According to per capita income, based on income surveys.
2. Child-care fee, an earnings-related cash benefit for the first two years after childbirth, or child-care grant, a lower flat-rate benefit for the third year after childbirth.
Source : Calculators are based on the income survey for the year (KSH, Budapest).

Table 4.12. **Risk of falling below subsistence minimum, Hungary, 1985 and 1987**

	Those living below subsistence level, as percentage of total population in given group	
	1985	1987
Urban, active earners	13.9	13.4
Rural, active earners	9.6	6.8
Urban, receiving child-care benefits	42.1	40.3
Rural, receiving child-care benefits	25.3	18.6
Urban, pensioners	8.7	7.5
Rural, pensioners	6.6	4.4
Urban, children	28.2	27.8
Rural, children	21.0	18.2
Other dependants (urban and rural)	28.0	27.6
Total	15.7	13.8

Source : KSH : Household survey, 1985 and 1987, CSO, (Budapest, 1986, 1988).

Traditionally, families with more children than average were over-represented among the poor. During the decade from 1977 to 1987, however, for all households the number of single-child families decreased while the opposite occurred among poor families. The number of children in small families increased among the poor from 24 to 25 per cent, while for all households with children, the share of small families decreased from 34 to 17 per cent.

Poverty has increased among young urban families with children for several reasons. First, there is the emergence of unemployment. Unemployment has been highest among men aged 20-25, many of whom may have started a family. Since their spouses are usually at home receiving child-care benefits, they cannot compensate for the loss of income. Young families, when losing their main source of income through unemployment of the principal earner, face serious absolute poverty.

Second, recent price rises have hit young families with children particularly hard. For the period between 1987 and 1990, prices increased by 211 per cent for households with only adult members, but the increase was 225 per cent for families with three or more children.

Third, cuts and restrictions on state spending have adversely affected social security schemes: child-care allowances, pensions, sickness benefits and so on have not kept pace with inflation. This has become an important factor in the rapid impoverishment of those whose primary source of income is these cash benefits. Thus the number of children on regular monthly welfare increased from 30,656 in 1986 to 79,728 by 1989. Over that time, average monthly assistance grew by only 14 per cent, while the increase in consumer prices was 46 per cent.[19]

Social security and income protection

The social security system is undergoing a fundamental change. To understand present developments and constraints, the main characteristics and problems of the previous social security system have to be outlined.

Between 1968 and 1988, total spending on social services and social security remained almost unchanged at roughly one-third of the state budget. Priority was given to the "productive" spheres through redistribution of over-centralised resources. The outcome was a relatively (later even absolutely) decreasing share of expenditure for public services such as health care, education and public transport. The victims have been the users of these services, who have suffered increasing inequalities of access, deterioration in the standards and quality of services, permanent overcrowding and chronic shortages of basic services and facilities.

Although the social security system operated under tight budget limits, the different social security schemes were frequently misused. For example, social security programmes, especially sick pay and disability pension schemes, gave state-run enterprises scope to gain a greater measure of independence from rigid wage regulation and to build "wage buffers" into their normal systems. Central wage regulations did not take into account the social security income of those on sick leave or applying for a disability pension. Thus managers could "save" a considerable sum by classifying these workers as employees. The savings remained with the firm and could be used to increase workers' earnings without breaching aggregate limits on wage expenditures.[20]

This use of social security benefits increased the number of applicants, straining limited budget resources, and led to a re-emergence of "targeted" policies designed to concentrate scarce resources on those most in need. The result has been significant cuts in public spending and an increase in income inequalities, with many of the poor dropping out of income-producing activities (table 4.13).

Table 4.13. **Composition of personal disposable incomes for poor and above average active households, Hungary, 1987**

Percentage of income derived from:	Households with per capita monthly income:	
	Below subsistence minimum (poor)	Above average
Formal economy		
1982	58.6	70.7
1987	57.4	63.0
Parallel economy		
1982	9.3	16.5
1987	10.7	24.7
Cash benefits		
1982	31.0	12.2
1987	30.6	11.4
Family transfers		
1982	1.1	0.9
1987	1.3	0.6
Total income		
1982	100.0	100.0
1987	100.0	100.0

Increase in monthly incomes between 1982 and 1987 (1982 = 100), derived from:

	Formal economy	Parallel economy	Cash benefits	Family transfers	Total income
Poor households	132	155	133	160	135
Above average households	149	250	156	251	167

Monthly earnings of above average households

	Formal economy	Parallel economy	Cash benefits	Family transfers	Total income
1982	207	305	68	93	172
1987	233	491	79	146	313

Source: Author's calculations based on the 1982 and 1987 income surveys of KSH, Budapest.

These cut-backs have led to the creation of a "second society", mainly of people whose lives and aspirations were conditioned by the incentives, attitudes and rules of the past 40 years. In response to industrialisation, they moved to large housing estates in urban settings, educated their children according to "socialist" precepts, and gave up their peasant roots and traditions. They are now facing a high risk of unemployment. The risk of the emergence of a marginalised "underclass" may be increased by the high incidence of poverty among children.

As can be seen from table 4.13, many poor families have tried to protect their income by undertaking more work in the parallel economy (often the worst jobs) and by mobilising informal family networks. However, without a simultaneous strengthening of the society-wide safety net, Hungarian society risks falling apart. Serious symptoms of social disintegration are already apparent.

Towards a new social policy

The direction of social policy in the future is still being debated. There are in essence three main sets of proposals. Several interest groups have argued that comprehensive and compulsory social security should be replaced by a regulated network of enterprise-based insurance schemes, on the grounds that the present system is expensive and wasteful, discourages capital investment and adversely affects the new entrepreneurs.[21] Enterprise-based insurance schemes would be cheaper and reflect the mutual interests of employers and workers. With regard to the non-employed, proponents argue for "targeted" welfare assistance and services for the poor, financed from taxation and administered by the State.[22]

Another set of proposals is the conversion of the present state-dominated social security scheme to public ownership, administered and controlled by a tripartite body representing employers, workers and the State. These proposals entail a more equal share of contributions, and envisage that in future the social security system would be a Western-style public investment fund, in part financed by society's immobilised wealth which will be released by means of privatisation.

The main interest of the present "owner" — the Government — is to reduce state expenditure and to divest itself of state responsibilities. It has proposed separating the "classical", contribution-based tasks from "social policy", the former being handled by national pension and health insurance funds, and all the other services (i.e., support for families with children, aid for the handicapped and disabled, services for the elderly, etc.) being provided through decentralised, community-based schemes. These would be financed from local and central taxation, and complemented by the activities of charity organisations, voluntary non-profit agencies and other associations, including the state-subsidised services of the Church.

Unemployment compensation

The first attempt to provide income maintenance for redundant workers was made as early as 1986. The "re-employment benefit" introduced at that time was available only to those dismissed in lay-offs involving 10 or more workers. This condition was relaxed in 1988, although an unemployed person could not receive benefits unless formally laid off by his employer. Between January 1989 and February 1991, unemployment benefit was paid for up to two years to all jobless with an employment record, though still with conditions i.e., lack of a suitable vacancy, last employment within the previous 12 months, and at least 18 months' employment in the previous three years. Benefits ranged from 60 to 70 per cent of previous average monthly earnings depending on the reason for unemployment: redundancy 70 per cent, resignation with notice by the employee 65 per cent, and resignation without notice 60 per cent. After six months benefit was reduced by 10 per cent, and after another 12 months by 25 per cent. The level of benefit varied between 80 and 300 per cent of the minimum wage. Since the introduction of this system the share of benefit recipients among the registered unemployed has increased steadily, reaching 78 per cent in February 1991.

However, income protection for the jobless was insufficient, for two reasons. First, those without an employment record of at least 18 months — such as unemployed school-leavers and many other young workers — did not qualify. Consequently, young people who experienced the higher unemployment rates often suffered from income insecurity as well. Second, the level of benefits was very low. In the first quarter of 1990, for example, about 60 per cent of the unemployed received benefits below the minimum wage level. In the case of the long-term unemployed, 90 per cent received benefits below the minimum wage. In addition, high inflation coupled with an increase in the duration of unemployment tended to erode the purchasing power of benefits. Inevitably, the unemployed and their families suffered from a significant deterioration in living standards.

To improve financial assistance to the unemployed and to stabilise the financing of the Employment Fund, changes were made to the unemployment benefit scheme in February 1991 within the framework of the new Employment Law. Eligibility was extended to secondary-school-leavers or university graduates and the criteria of employment suitability was relaxed. The benefit system was rebased on insurance principles, with unemployment benefit paid from the compulsory contributions of employers and workers. According to the new Employment Law, unemployment benefit is paid to those who have been in work for 360 days within the past four years. Unemployment benefit is paid for a period of 180 to 720 days depending on the duration of employment over the past four years. During the first half of this period benefit is equal to 70 per cent of previous income, in the second half, 50 per cent; the amount cannot exceed three times the minimum wage. Those who leave their job voluntarily do not receive benefit for 90 days.

Despite these improvements, problems remain. The current contributions from employers and employees to the Solidarity Fund may not be sufficient to finance benefits for the rapidly growing number of unemployed. However, an increase in contributions is likely to run into strong opposition from the social partners. In addition, the present insurance scheme provides a low level of income maintenance; the earnings which are used as a basis for calculating benefit are not indexed, nor is there any indexation for unemployment benefit itself. At times of rapid inflation, average earnings are relatively low, and the benefit calculated from them quickly loses its purchasing power. The unemployed are therefore facing not simply a drop in living standards but a serious risk of poverty.

Another problem is how to guarantee a minimum income for those whose unemployment benefit expires. The unemployment insurance scheme has not yet been synchronised with social security provisions. The growing number of the long-term unemployed and deepening recession make it increasingly likely that those receiving unemployment benefit may later have to rely on social security.

Wages, incomes policy and industrial relations

by
Maria Lado*
Institute of Labour Research, Budapest

Wages and incomes policy

Wages and incomes policy in Hungary has been made irrelevant to a large extent by the massive participation in the informal economy from the early 1980s; this has considerably altered income distribution (table 4.14). The proportion of income originating from the state-controlled economy has been gradually declining, so that wage controls have had only limited results and affected workers less severely than planned. Also, income generated in the parallel economy has prevented sharp declines in real wages from cutting real incomes.

Table 4.14. **Net income of the population, Hungary, 1980-90**

Source	1980	1986	1989	1990[1]
Income from work in socialist sector	61.5	54.1	49.0	47.0
Income from the parallel (private) economy	6.5	11.9	12.3	14.0
Social transfers	32.0	34.0	38.7	39.0
Total	100.0	100.0	100.0	100.0

1. Estimates.
Source: Cukor, E. - Kővári, Gy.: "Wage trends in Hungary", in International Labour Review (Geneva, ILO), No 2, 1991, pp. 177-189.

Trends in wages and wage differentials

Between 1980 and 1989 real wages declined by 6.5 per cent, and in recent years this decline has accelerated. Real wages fell by 5.1 per cent in 1990 and by 7 per cent in the first half of 1991.

* With contributions from Julia Szalai, Institute of Sociology, Budapest.

Wage differentials in Hungary have never been as compressed as might be supposed in a socialist country that stressed equality. There were significant industrial and occupational wage differentials, though differentials by sex and age were less marked.[23]

There has been no significant change in industrial differentials in recent years. Among the branches of material production, earnings are highest in construction (table 4.15). Within industry it is still the traditional, socialist branches (such as mining and chemicals) where earnings are highest (table 4.16). These privileged branches have been able to keep their favoured wage status during the transition despite major redundancies and closures.

Table 4.15. **Gross earnings in material branches, Hungary, 1988-90 (Average = 100)**

Branches	1988	Rank	1989	Rank	1990	Rank
Construction	113.1	1	116.3	1	108.6	1
Water	105.7	2	107.2	2	104.7	3
Industry	105.5	3	104.8	3	103.0	4
Other material activity	102.1	4	99.6	4	99.8	2
Transport, post and telecommunications	97.5	5	96.6	5	100.1	5
Trade	89.1	6	94.1	6	103.7	7
Agriculture and forestry	88.4	7	88.2	7	87.6	6

Sources: Based on data in: KSH: *Statisztikai havi közlemények, 1989/2-3* (1989), *1990/2-3* (1990), *1991/2-3* (1991), Budapest.

Table 4.16. **Gross earnings in industry, Hungary, 1988-90 (Average = 100)**

Branches	1988	Rank	1989	Rank	1990	Rank
Mining	150.4	1	142.1	1	140.2	1
Chemicals	121.8	2	123.8	2	123.2	3
Metal manufacturing	114.2	3	118.4	3	119.2	4
Electricity generation	110.3	4	114.1	4	125.9	2
Food	99.9	5	100.0	5	100.7	5
Machine engineering	95.1	6	95.1	6	93.9	7
Construction materials	90.4	7	92.1	7	96.9	6
Other industries	81.2	8	82.3	8	77.7	9
Light industry	79.2	9	79.4	9	79.3	8

Sources: Based on data in: KSH: *Statisztikai havi közlemények, 1989/1* (1991), *1990/1* (1990), *1991/1* (1991), Budapest.

Since the early 1980s, a decline in real wages has been accompanied by widening wage differentials. In 1990, gross and net earnings of non-manual workers exceeded those of manual workers by 71.4 per cent and 53.5 per cent respectively. There has been a continual deterioration in the relative earnings position of manual workers, and a widening of earnings differentials among non-manual workers.[24]

Two new factors have recently had a growing impact on trends in wage differentials — company size and form of ownership. Smaller ventures (with fewer than 50 employees) offer greater possibilities for higher earnings compared with medium-sized and large firms. Small companies pay better wages to both manual and non-manual workers, although this is less marked for manual workers and most marked for female non-manual workers (table 4.17).

Table 4.17. **Gross earnings in material branches, Hungary, 1990[1]**

	Small companies (less than 50 employees) HUF/month	Larger companies (more than 50 employees) HUF/month	Earnings differential in favour of small companies (%)
Manual workers			
Male	14 364	13 007	9.8
Female	9 632	9 342	3.1
Total	13 338	11 708	13.9
Non-manual workers			
Male	27 272	24 315	12.2
Female	18 378	15 000	22.5
Total	22 720	18 719	21.4
All workers	16 960	13 362	26.9

1. Data are from the annual earnings survey conducted each September. It covered small companies for the first time in 1990.
Source: KSH: *A kereseti arányok alakulása a gazdaságban, 1990,* (Budapest, 1991).

The growing private sector has also contributed considerably to the increasing wage differentials since the mid-1980s, though this is difficult to quantify since earnings statistics do not distinguish by type of ownership. According to one of the few comparative studies, depending on type of ownership sharp income differences already existed in 1986 between firms involved in the same activity.[25]

Wage differentials are likely to widen further due to privatisation and the increasing share of foreign capital. The experience of joint ventures established so far in Hungary strongly supports this assumption.[26] In 1989 the profitability of these ventures was almost double that of Hungarian companies. They were able to pay wages 30 to 40 per cent higher, attract and retain the best workers and, at the same time, set high standards for employment. However, the most striking contrast between joint ventures and Hungarian companies is their remuneration policy.

In joint ventures a strong link is usually created between wages and productivity at shop-floor level through various forms of performance-related bonuses. This is almost unknown in state-owned companies. At hiring, joint ventures stipulate a probationary period of (generally) three months, after which they raise basic wages by 30 to 35 per cent. When determining wages, managers take into consideration the requirements of the job and not the characteristics of the person (age, qualification, experience, etc.). To motivate workers, they pay performance-related bonuses and often rewards based on profit achieved, usually by offering 13th and 14th months' wages. Bonuses for managers are strictly profit-oriented, and they may exceed basic salaries. Nevertheless, if the given target is not reached, the whole bonus is lost. Joint ventures often provide social benefits rarely found in other enterprises. The basic difference is not in the content of the benefits but in the fact that they are performance-related. For example, joint ventures organise holidays in the period of compulsory leave and thereby provide "a performance-based contribution to recreational expenses". This contribution may, in some cases, be equal to a month's salary. In this way social benefits also serve to motivate workers.

Changes in forms of remuneration also occur in state-owned enterprises when they undergo reorganisation. The new managers tend to prefer time rates (with bonuses) to piece rates or other payment-by-results schemes. Prospering companies have introduced time rates with special bonuses to increase performance and ensure their workers' direct interest in efficiency, as in joint ventures.

For companies in an unfavourable and uncertain market situation, time rates ease the problems associated with lack of demand, caused, for example, by the collapse of east European and former Soviet markets. Managers expecting an upturn did not want to reduce the workforce, and piece-rate schemes proved unsuitable. By changing to time-rate payments, management could shift the responsibility for dealing with the lack of orders to shop-floor managers.

Developments in wage determination

Developments in wage determination illustrate Hungary's gradual steps towards a market economy over the past decades. Before 1968, wage determination was one of the most rigid elements of the centrally planned economy. From 1968 to 1988 the Government gave enterprises greater autonomy in wage determination, but still exerted strict central control over wages growth. In 1989, the wage determination system was partially transformed and integrated into the profit taxation system. Wage control did not apply to two important spheres of the economy: organisations where the annual wage bill did not exceed 20 million HUF; and joint ventures where the firm's fixed assets were worth more than 5 million HUF or the share of foreign investment exceeded 20 per cent. Gaining exemption from the central wage regulations was one of the basic forces behind the dismemberment of huge, state-owned enterprises. In 1991, almost 70 per cent of firms were exempt from wage regulation, though they accounted for only 20 per cent of all employees.

At the end of 1988, the first step towards collective wage bargaining at the national level was taken with the creation of the National Council for the Reconciliation of Interests (NCRI).[27] Its main function was to reconcile the different interests on labour issues, especially wages. Its structure was not clearly tripartite, though it claimed to function as a tripartite institution. The National Council of Hungarian Trade Unions (SZOT) was the only representative of workers' interests, while the Hungarian Chamber of Commerce represented employers, and three other organisations represented co-operatives and the Government.

Between December 1988 and June 1989, the NCRI dealt with several wage policy issues, including the functioning of the wage mechanism. One of its first decisions, taken by consensus, was to increase minimum wages. The NCRI also issued proposals to influence wage setting, primarily to persuade employers to limit wage increases to between 3 and 10 per cent — but wages actually rose by 5 to 45 per cent in the period.

In August 1990, the NCRI was replaced by the Council for the Reconciliation of Interests (CRI). This is a tripartite institution, with employers and employees represented by several autonomous organisations; the third party is the Government.

Wage determination and minimum wages were again the key issues for the CRI. Full liberalisation of wage determination was jointly, but not unanimously, demanded by representatives of the employers and workers, while the Government insisted on maintaining the existing regulations. In the absence of a consensus, the Government on its own responsibility extended the validity of previous wage mechanisms, but promised that wage liberalisation would be examined with a view to its introduction in 1992.

Policy dilemmas remain the same: how to halt the price-wage spiral; how to restrain wages and incomes when financial constraints on enterprises are still weak and the market is not yet strong enough to exert downward pressure of its own; and how to lower wage increases when inflationary expectations are raising pay demands. These dilemmas are difficult to resolve at any time, but especially so when the legacy of a distorted wage structure considerably limits room for manoeuvre.

Since January 1989 minimum wages have been a subject of bargaining between employers, workers and the Government, in the framework of the NCRI and the CRI. Minimum wages were raised by 233 per cent between January 1989 and April 1991, considerably more than the increase in average nominal wages over the period.

As wages and earnings are rather low, agreements on minimum wages affect a wide range of employees. The increase in minimum wages in April 1991 (from 5,800 HUF to 7,000 HUF) improved the wages of 22.1 per cent of all employees. This poses an awkward policy dilemma: on the one hand, is it acceptable that the minimum wage is lower than the official subsistence minimum (table 4.18) but, on the other, would it be acceptable if hundreds of thousands of employees lost their jobs because of an alignment of minimum wages with the subsistence minimum?

Table 4.18. **Minimum wages and subsistence minimum, Hungary, 1985-91**

Year	Official subsistence minimum[1]	Subsistence minimum (UJCSAKO)[2]	Minimum wages (average for the year)	Minimum wages as percentage of official subsistence minimum	Social minimum	Minimum wages as percentage of social minimum
1985	2 510	-	2 000	0.79	3 050	0.66
1986	2 620	-	2 000	0.76	3 200	0.63
1987	2 850	-	2 000	0.70	3 480	0.57
1988	3 310	-	3 000	0.91	4 040	0.74
1989	3 940	4 527	3 658	0.93	4 730	0.77
1990	5 050[3]	6 497	5 017	0.99	6 060[3]	0.83
1991	-	8 058	6 700[4]	0.83	-	-

1. Official subsistence minimum covers only the very modest necessities conventionally considered to be essential.
2. Subsistence minimum is based on a typical basket of consumer goods and services for a couple with two children.
3. Estimated.
4. Assuming no further increase in minimum wages during the year.
Sources: KSH: Statisztikai évkönyv (Budapest, 1989), p. 224. Javaslat a minimálbér emelésére (Proposal on the increase in minimum wages). Érdekegyezetetö Tanács elé került elöterjesztés (Proposal for discussion on representation in the council). Munkaügyi Minisztérium, (Ministry of Labour), January, 1991.

Branch-level collective bargaining has not become widespread in Hungary.[28] The main obstacle is identifying the potential bargaining partners, especially on the employers' side. As a result, enterprise-level problems tend to become national issues for negotiation by the CRI.

Enterprise-level collective bargaining has become much freer in recent years, mainly due to the increase in the number and strength of local worker organisations. However, co-operation among the different trade unions (and in some places co-operation with workers' councils[29] is full of tensions: the various employee representatives frequently cast doubt on the legitimacy of the others and carry out separate negotiations with the employer. The long-standing self-contradiction of employer representation (confusion of the roles of owner and employer) also causes serious problems, as do legal regulations governing enterprise-level bargaining.

Very limited information is available on enterprise-level bargaining, but empirical studies have outlined two trends. First, at many companies, collective agreements have been renegotiated, enabling the new workers' representatives to modify the agreements concluded by their predecessors. Second, the content of agreements has broadened and guarantees of employment security have become as important as wage-related issues. Despite this progress in collective bargaining, these developments have not replaced the traditional system of informal individual (and group) bargaining.

The role of the parallel economy

A striking aspect of the economic crisis of the 1980s was that the steady decline in real wages was not accompanied by a parallel decrease in the aggregate indicators of income and consumption. While the level of real wages in the "official" economy never regained 1980's levels in the second half of the decade, indices of per capita real incomes and aggregate consumption showed a modest (though fluctuating) increase in the same period (table 4.19).

Table 4.19. **Indices of (net) real wages, real incomes and consumption, Hungary, 1980-1990**
(1980 = 100)

Year	Real wages per capita		Real incomes per capita	Real value of
	Workers and employers	Agricultural workers	Total population	yearly consumption Total population
1980	100.0	100.0	100.0	100.0
1985	96.1	96.2	108.8	108.4
1986	97.9	98.6	111.6	111.1
1987	97.5	96.8	112.7	115.8
1988	92.7	94.5	111.6	111.4
1989	93.5	90.4	114.4	114.1
1990	88.7	81.5	112.6	109.3

Source: KSH: *Magyar Statistikei tsebköhyr 1990*, (Budapest, 1991).

The growth of the parallel economy was stimulated by government attempts to limit the domestic use of production with measures to restrict investment and consumer demand, and stricter taxation of wage increases. This policy led to a gradual shrinking of the official economy and to unexpected growth in consumer prices. People responded with a remarkable expansion of participation in the parallel economy. Time-budget surveys revealed that between 1977 and 1988 "the work-fund of the economy as a whole has not decreased, though the number of economically active has significantly decreased. This leads to the conclusion that there has been a substantial increase in workloads among certain social groups. Furthermore, the share of activities in the parallel economy has increased significantly in relation to the whole economy: the proportion of working time spent on them was 28.9 per cent in 1977 and 35.5 per cent in 1986.[30]

The most important activities of the informal economy have been small-scale agricultural production and house building, but it has also embraced services, traditional small-scale repair work and industrial labour. A relatively new, expanding area comprises various white-collar activities including typing at home, counselling and telephone services. Time-budget surveys give information on the importance of some of these activities.[31]

Table 4.20 gives estimated annual working time in the official and parallel economies, while table 4.21 shows how both participation in, and duration of, activities in the parallel economy increased in the 10 years 1977-87. This expansion was based principally on a big rise in participation of the "inactive" population (mostly pensioners), especially outside agriculture. Analysed by sex, agriculture has become increasingly the domain of men, while women have intensified their work in white-collar services. Families have begun to diversify the work and participation of their members, following optimal combinations of gainful employment and self-initiated flexible and adaptive production, adjusted to existing skills, other family commitments and aspirations of family members.

Table 4.20. **Total annual hours worked, Hungary, 1977-86**

	1977 million hours	1986 million hours	Percentage change 1977-86
Working time in formal economy	9 984.5	9 296.3	- 7
Small-scale agricultural production of			
Active earners	1 737.5 1	1 896.6	+ 9
Inactive population	632.0	1 137.0	+ 80
Dependants	384.8	375.7	- 2
House-building activities (in the informal economy)			
Active earners	266.9	374.7	+ 40
Inactive population	33.7	79.6	+136
Dependants	21.0	17.2	- 18
Total	13 060.4	13 177.1	+ 1

Source: See "Time Budget: Changes in the Way of Life of Hungarian Society According to the Time-Budget Surveys" of spring 1977 and spring 1986, (Budapest, KSH, 1987).

Table 4.21. **Participation rates and time devoted to given activities by all aged between 15-69 on an average day, by sex, Hungary, 1977, 1987**

	Participation rate %		Percentage increase/ (decrease)	Average time devoted to activity by participants (minutes)		Percentage increase/ (decrease)
	1977	1987	1977	1977	1987	1987
Men						
Work at official (main) workplace	55.7	47.6	(15)	498	480	(4)
Additional[1] white-collar work	0.5	1.3	160	134	215	60
Additional non-agricultural manual work	1.1	5.0	355	234	286	22
Small-scale agricultural production	35.9	40.0	11	174	198	14
Women						
Work at official (main) workplace	37.6	33.5	(11)	456	445	(2)
Additional white-collar work	0.4	0.8	100	139	244	76
Additional non-agricultural manual work	0.4	2.8	600	190	256	35
Small-scale agricultural production	35.2	34.2	(3)	147	142	3

1. "Additional" refers to parallel economy activities. A given activity is included in the formal economy if it is a main job and/or is in the institutionalised formal sphere, and in the parallel economy if it is additional to a regular daily job and/or the activity is in a family business.
Source: Time Budget Changes in the Way of Life of Hungarian Society according to the time-budget surveys 1976/77 and 1986/87, KSH, (Budapest, 1990).

The marked shift from the formal towards the informal economy in the 1980s provided a successful survival strategy for the majority of society. The decline in real wages of the formal economy could be balanced by expanding activity in the parallel economy. By building their lives on two complementary bases, most households could gain some protection against the gradual erosion of the formal economy. In addition, earnings (and thus spending) came further under individual control and could more flexibly adjust to the changing needs of families.

The informal economy has thus played an important role in mitigating the negative economic and social consequences of the gradual economic transformation that took place in the 1980s. However, it also means that incomes and living standards have been strongly influenced by opportunities to increase participation in this informal economy. This has contributed to the sizeable income differentials characteristic of Hungarian society during the transition. In 1982 the average income of the top decile was 3.8 times that of the lowest decile, while in 1987 it was 4.6 times as large. The relative dispersion of incomes increased from 40 to 48 per cent over this period.[32] In 1990, the income of the top decile was an estimated 4.8 times that of the lowest decile.

This survival strategy may have reached its limits. The parallel economy itself is now shrinking, partly due to the transformation of informal activities into legalised private businesses, and partly to overall economic recession. Accelerating inflation makes it increasingly difficult for most people to fight against the deterioration in living standards.

Industrial relations

Hungary's transformation process in industrial relations started many years ago, but progress was slow and halting. Developments have accelerated since the fundamental political changes of 1989-90, and a market-type industrial relations system is gaining ground.

Industrial relations partners

The collapse and transformation of the previous monolithic trade union structure, and the development of new forms of worker representation, began in 1988. Today there are seven national trade union federations, which differ considerably in their membership and orientation (table 4.22).

Table 4.22. **Trade union national federations, Hungary**

Trade unions	Membership[1] (000s)	Orientation[2] Blue-collar	White-collar	Number of member organisations[3]
National Federation of Hungarian Trade Unions (MSZOSZ)	2 683	xx	x	71
Trade unions which existed before 1987 and did not join MSZOSZ:				
Rally of Trade Unions for Intellectual Workers (ÉSZT)	63		xxx	3
Confederation of Autonomous Trade Unions	351	xx	x	22
Reconciliation Forum of Trade Unions (SZEF)	557		xxx	19
Trade unions emerging after 1987:				
Democratic League of Independent Trade Unions (LIGA)	130	x	xx	84
Solidarity Workers' Alliance	75	xxx		n.a.
Workers' Councils	106	xxx		160
Other independent groupings	24	x	xx	6

Notes:
1. Latest figures from a survey carried out by the CRI, also published in Heti Világgazdaság (Babus Endre: Megállt az ido, 1991. April 20, p. 16.)
2. xxx: heavily oriented, x: slightly oriented.
3. Data refer to different dates as follows:
    MSZOSZ: March 1991
    ÉSZT: October 1991
    Autonomous Trade Unions: October 1990
    SZEF: October 1990
    LIGA: September 1990
    Workers' Councils: April 1991
    Independent groupings: October 1990.
n.a. not available.

In May 1988 the first independent union, the Democratic Trade Union of Scientific Workers (TDDSZ), was created, followed in December 1988 by the first national organisation of independent alternative unions, the Democratic League of Independent Trade Unions (LIGA). The National Council of Hungarian Trade Unions (SZOT), which had previously been the only union, declared its independence from the Communist Party in September 1989 but was dissolved in March the following year. The majority of its member groups established a new national organisation, the National Federation of Hungarian Trade Unions (MSZOSZ). Other ex-members of SZOT, which did not join MSZOSZ, later formed various groups: the Confederation of Autonomous Trade Unions, the Rally of Trade Unions for Intellectual Workers (ÉSZT), and the Reconciliation Forum of Trade Unions (SZEF). In July 1990 the National Federation of Workers' Councils (MOSZ) was established. The coalition government has recognised all registered trade unions and workers' representation groups and has deliberately avoided partiality.

The duality characteristic of the trade union movement at the end of the 1980s — the "official" and single federation of trade unions (SZOT) versus the first "opposition" trade union grouping (LIGA) — has been replaced by a more diverse and complex arrangement. A quarter of all trade union members belong to three formations which have emerged in the "grey zone" between these two extremes: the Confederation of Autonomous Trade Unions, ÉSZT and SZEF. However, MSZOSZ, the successor of SZOT, has remained dominant, with two-thirds of all trade union members. Some 8.4 per cent have joined the most important rivals of MSZOSZ, the new grass-roots workers' organisations.

After initial hostilities between the old and new trade unions, when each aimed at defeating and displacing the other, there was a short "cease-fire" from mid-1990 to February 1991. In August 1990, a trade union round-table was founded to monitor the privatisation process and develop a joint strategy on changes in property rights.[33] The unions also wanted to create an institutional framework to settle conflicts among themselves. However, disagreement over SZOT's assets and the legitimacy of its successors caused major conflicts and the collapse of the round-table in 1991.

The questions at the heart of these conflicts were: Should there be a general renewal of trade union membership in which every employee declares his commitment to a given union? Can this provide the basis for the division of SZOT's assets, or should the allocation take place prior to, and separate from, membership renewal? As the trade unions could not reach a consensus, parliament passed its own legislation in 1991. Under the new law all trade unions must declare their assets, financial resources, and so on, and the total wealth of the trade union movement will be divided among the unions according to each union's membership. The new law has been strongly opposed by some trade unions and by the Socialist Party, as has the involvement of parliament in trade unions' internal affairs. This could delay implementation and thus final settlement of the long debate on trade union assets.

These inter-union quarrels have diverted attention from the trade unions' original objective — the representation of workers' interests — and risk leaving employees without proper protection in the midst of economic crisis and at the start of extensive privatisation.

The renewal of membership is likely to lead to a steep drop in membership for all trade unions, owing to the general disillusionment and passivity of workers, the difficulties of everyday life, and growing unemployment. So far, unionisation has been to a large extent maintained. In 1986, SZOT, the only federation of trade unions at that time, had 4.4 million members, while the various unions today have a total membership of 4 million.

The level of trade unionism is expected to decline further as a consequence of privatisation and the dismemberment of large enterprises into smaller firms. In joint ventures, foreign partners normally accept existing union organisations but in Hungary, the majority have no workers' organisations. Workers do not see the need to set up a trade union, since their pay is much better than in Hungarian companies and they receive a wider range of benefits. Foreign employers profit from this situation: as there is no unified trade union movement workers' loyalty can be "bought" quite cheaply.

While there have been considerable changes in the representation of workers over the past three to four years, the same does not apply to the representation of employers. Parts of the Chamber of Economy, which was previously the only employers' organisation, have split off — for example, the National Association of Entrepreneurs (VOSZ). New organisations have also appeared, such as the Association of Hungarian Manufacturers (GYOSZ) which claims the name and mantle of the most important pre-war employers' association. However, it is still difficult to identify the real owners and employers because the Hungarian economy remains dominated by the state sector. It is even more complicated to decide whether the representative organisations of the different co-operatives (agricultural, industrial and commercial co-operatives such as MTSZOSZ, OKISZ, AFEOSZ) represent the interests of employers or employees. There are also organisations of the self-employed (e.g. IPOSZ, KISOSZ), and it is doubtful whether they represent employer interests.

A third partner, the Government, has traditionally played a decisive role in industrial relations in Hungary. For several reasons this is unlikely to change in the near future: privatisation is slow; the state-owned and co-operative sectors remain dominant; and employer and worker organisations do not represent a force strong enough to restrict the role of the State in industrial relations.

The current Government is trying to develop new industrial relations based on tripartism and has already taken several initiatives. Laws have been submitted to parliament, and institutions established such as the CRI, to resolve problems. Nevertheless, the Government has been subjected to severe criticism on the grounds that these initiatives are reminiscent of former practices when all regulations were dictated by the "centre": the government is again determining the basic mechanisms and institutions, and the roles and rights of the social partners have been defined almost exclusively by legislation. To counter these accusations, the Government has had to take steps to develop and clarify the rules under which all parties operate as it is of common interest to everyone that a new and smoothly functioning system of industrial relations be created.

Industrial relations institutions

Comparing Hungarian industrial relations institutions with those in market economies, we find major differences in three respects: first, the Hungarian institutional system is incomplete and unbalanced. For example, branch-level collective agreements are rare and there are no procedures for the settlement of industrial disputes. Bargaining is centralised at the national level, which implies a predominance of tripartism over bipartite agreements.

Second, current industrial relations regulations were adopted at various times and under different conditions. For example, the right of workers to participate in enterprise management, and how these rights are to be exercised, were included in legislation in the mid-1980s. The Act on Strikes was adopted in 1989, while a new Labour Code is currently being prepared. The "old" and the "new" institutions exist at the same time and do not always complement each other. So far, though, a model of future industrial relations has not been promulgated.

Third, industrial relations in Hungary are burdened by problems associated with the lack of legitimacy and credibility of the social partners and with their own conflicts as to their roles. These problems hinder both the development of a new system of industrial relations and the functioning of the existing one. Any significant progress towards genuine industrial relations seems blocked until the parties "mature".

Collective bargaining versus consultation

When the NCRI was established in October 1988, its purpose was to provide a forum for agreements on wage increases and exceptions to wage regulation. However, the NCRI was soon expected to deal with other issues, such as prices, profit taxation and personal income taxation. The conflict of national wage bargaining with general economic and social consultation (or even co-determination concerning general social and economic issues) remains a fundamental issue for the NCRI's replacement body, the CRI.

The mixture of functions, and the problems of separating them, arise from three main factors. First, other consultative organs have not yet been developed to give other representatives, not only those of employers and workers, the opportunity to influence national decision-making. Second, wage-related issues are difficult to discuss when taken out of the context of prices, inflation and the overall transformation of the economy. Third, the CRI, as the only national tripartite institution, is understandably trying to maximise its decision-making powers.

These factors have led to an expansion of the CRI, which has established several — tripartite — committees. There is a clear danger that the CRI could become a "multi-actor central power". It will be necessary to set up industrial relations institutions to counteract this tendency.

Bipartism versus tripartism

The NCRI served as an example of tripartism. The Employment Law of March 1991 prescribes the establishment of country-level tripartite Labour Market Boards. These boards will be responsible for easing labour market tensions arising from either the decline or the restructuring of the economy. They have the right to decide how to use central funds (allocated to the different counties by one of the CRI committees) and the programmes to assist the unemployed, as well as the right to create new jobs and retrain redundant workers, etc.

The labour market is not the only area where the State is retreating from its previous dominant role and sharing responsibilities with employers' and workers' organisations. There is now a large number of tripartite bodies, and consequently industrial relations are often regarded as being intrinsically tripartite. This simplification could impede bipartite negotiations which are badly needed for further economic development.

Participation versus representation of interests

Currently, the most controversial industrial relations issue is worker participation in enterprise management. This is partly because property reform has not been completed, so that companies are in a state of flux over ownership, structure, management, etc. Additionally, participation in the management of state-owned companies has been exercised both by shop-steward bodies and the Enterprise Councils.[34] This dual model of participation means that the division between participation in management and the representation of workers' interests has been blurred.[35]

Shop-steward bodies have a significant influence on the way enterprises are run, and were the organisations which exercised the participatory rights of workers in management. Until recently, workers' interests were represented by a single trade union. It will therefore be a difficult process to separate the rights of participation from the defence of workers' interests.

Enterprise councils (assemblies of workers or of workers' delegates at smaller companies) were introduced in 1984-86, based on the concept of the worker as co-owner. Current problems stem from the fact that enterprise councils (and other new collective forms of enterprise management) infringe upon the rights that in market economies are generally regarded as belonging to owners and employers. The disbanding of these institutions seems inevitable, although it will be hard to implement. They have been recently acknowledged as legitimate institutions.[36] Moreover, employees are understandably sensitive because certain rights (however formal) will be taken away from them.

At the end of the 1980s, supervisory boards became the means of participation in limited liability and joint stock companies employing more than 200 people. They have a more restricted say in decision-making than enterprise councils: only one-third of board members are elected from among the workers, and the board itself has limited control over company operations. Questions remain over the future of these boards, such as their relationship with the different trade unions, the "sharing" of participatory rights with the trade unions, and their emerging relationship with works councils.

In the preparatory work for the new Labour Code, a proposal was made to form works councils, similar to the Betriebsräte in Germany. This idea is still being debated. Trade unions fear that their role could be undermined as the Government intends to give some of their participatory rights to works councils. However, experts in favour of works councils argue that they could solve the confusion over participation and stop the rivalry of different trade unions at enterprise level.

Strikes

The right to strike was legalised in March 1989. There have been fewer than two strikes a month over the two years to 1991 and these were quite limited in terms of the number of workers involved. Most of the strikes have been warning strikes, only lasting two hours.

The recent strikes and the way they were settled reflect the peculiarities and contradictions of the transition period. Typically, strikes have been organised in four situations: (a) where a large state-owned enterprise and its employees have lost their privileges due to the decrease or total withdrawal of central support; (b) when civil servants and other groups of workers have been in an unfavourable situation for a long time (such as teachers, train drivers and those employed in public transport); (c) in smaller enterprises intending to break away from their parent organisation; (d) where workers have protested against government decisions (in this case, strikes have been often organised by the "traditional" trade unions). Whatever the actual reason for a strike, protesting against the general deterioration of living standards has been a strong motivating factor.

In most strikes it is difficult to recognise the adversarial interests of employers and workers. Employers and workers often jointly protest against government decisions, while strikes originating from unsettled labour conflicts may easily turn into political demonstrations that are likely to be resolved by political measures.

To date, there has not been any strike originating from a deadlock in local or branch-level collective bargaining. Workers have not used the strike as a weapon during negotiations. This indicates that collective bargaining is still far from playing the role it has in market economies.

Notes :

1. This section draws on the following surveys and statistical sources: *Iránytü a gazdasághoz - 1990* [Guide to the Economy - 1990], KSH (Központi Statisztikai Hivatal: Central Statistical Office) és Gazdaságkutató Intézet (Economic Research Institute), Budapest, 1991; *Azanyagi ágak munaügyi jellemzöi 1990* (Employment in the field of material production in 1990). *I-IV. negyedév* (Labour Data of Material Branches). KSH, Feb. 1991 *Föbb nemzetgazdasági folyamatok 1989* [Main Economic Trends, 1989]. KSH, Budapest, 1990; *Foglalkoztatottsag és kereseti aranyok 1988* [Employment and Earnings, 1988], KSH, Budapest, 1989; *Foglalkoztatottság és kereseti arányok 1989* [Employment and Earnings, 1989]. (Budapest, KSH, 1990); *Foglalkoztatottság és kereseti arányok, 1990* (Employment and Earnings, 1990), KSH, Budapest, 1991; *Jövedelemeoszlás Magyarországon* [Income Distribution in Hungary], (Budapest, KSH, 1990).

2. For details, see "Mar tiz éve eredményesebbek voltak" (They were more profitable even ten years ago), in *Figyelö*, 4 July 1991, p.17.

3. *Iráytü a gazdasághoz, 1990* [Guide to the Economy]. (Budapest, KSH és Gazdaságkutato Intézet, 1991).

4. This analysis is based on official statistics, which need to be treated with caution. They underestimate the level of employment and give a distorted picture of its structure, with a bias towards industry. In addition, large segments of the parallel economy are outside the scope of statistically monitored areas. These limitations must be recognised when analysing labour market developments. See J. Timar: "Economic reform and new employment problems in Hungary", in J. Adam (ed.): *Economic reforms and welfare system in the Soviet Union, Poland and Hungary*, (London, Macmillan, 1991).

5. See G. Sziraczki: "Redundancy and regional unemployment: a case study in Ozd", in C. Hann (ed), *Market economy and civil society in Hungary*, (London, Frank Cass, 1990).

6. Source of data: A társadalmi-gazdasági helyzet néhány jellemzöje 1990-ben (Some characteristics of the social and economic situation in 1990), KSH, unpublished report, 1990.

7. Source of data: *As anyagi ágak munkaügyi jellemzöi 1990-ben* (Employment in the field of material production in 1990), KSH, Budapest, 1991.

8. For details on the growth of employment in the private sector, see T. Laki: "Privatizáció és munkanélküliség" (Privatisation and unemployment), in *Figyelö*, 6 June, 1991, p. 19.

9. These data include the estimated number working privately without licence (moonlighting), those illegally employed in the legal private sector, and participants in small-scale agricultural production. See G. Sziraczki: "Employment policy and labour market in transition", in *Soviet Studies*, 1990, No.4. On trends in participation in the second economy, see table 8 in the third section of this chapter on wages, incomes policy and industrial relations.

10. See J. Timar, *Idö es Munkaidö* [Time and working time], KJK Budapest, 1988.

11. See J. Köllö and K. Fezekas.: "Patterns in unemployment in Hungary — a case study", in Structural Change and Economic Dynamics, 1990, No.1.

12. See A. Hárs, G. Kövári and G. Nagy: "Hungary faces unemployment", in *International Labour Review,* 1991, No.2 (Geneva ILO), pp. 165-175.

13. See A. Hárs, G. Kövári and G. Nagy: "Hungary faces unemployment", in *International Labour Review*, 1991, No. 2 (Geneva ILO), pp. 165-175; G. Nagy and G. Sziraczki: *Labour market in transition: Employment, lay-offs, unemployment and policy responses in Hungary*, paper presented at the Conference on Restructuring Labour Markets in Eastern Europe, Milan, June 11-13, 1991.

14. See A. Hárs and G. Nagy: *Changes in unemployment and the composition of the unemployed in the light of statistics*, Research report, (Budapest, Labour Research Institute, 1990).

15. An earlier draft of this section is included in G. Nagy and G. Sziraczki: *Labour market in transition: Employment, lay-offs, unemployment and policy responses in Hungary,* paper presented at the Conference on Restructuring Labour Markets in Eastern Europe, Milan, June, 11-13, 1991.

16. See G. Kovacs and K. Nagy: *A munkahelytermtö beruházásokrol Borsod-Abaúj-Zemplén megyében* [Job-creating investment in the Borsod-Abaúj-Zemplén County], Research report, (Budapest, Labour Research Institute, 1989).

17. See M. Frey: *Preconditions and means towards labour market rationalisation in Hungary,* Labour Research Institute, Budapest, 1991 (manuscript).

18. Hungarian florints.

19. See *Statisztikai Évkönyv, 1989* [Statistical Yearbook, 1989] (Budapest, Központi Statisztikai Hivatal 1990). According to some experts, only one-third of entitled families receive assistance.

20. For more examples of how social security schemes have been misused, see J. Szalai: *Transition and social security*, paper for the Workshop on Participation and Changes in Poverty Relations in East-Central Europe and the Soviet Union. UNDRISD and ISS, The Hague, Netherlands, May 22-25, 1991.

21. This is a popular argument among the "new" entrepreneurs, and it is widely propagated by their chambers of commerce, associations and the Party of Entrepreneurs.

22. This idea has been put forward by the new free trade unions and it has also been outlined in the programmes of some of the new parties. For a detailed version, see the programme of the Alliance of Free Democrats.

23. See for details: E. Cukor: "Kereseti különbségek a fizikai dolgozók körében" [Earnings differentials among blue-collar workers], in *Kösgazdasági Szemle*, 1989, No. 3; E. Cukor: "A szellemi dolgozók keresti viszonyainak alakulasa az elmúlt é vtizedekben" [Trends in earnings of white-collar workers in the past decades], Ibid., 1990, No. 12; G. Sziraczki: *Economic adjustment, pay structure and the problem of incentives in Eastern European countries*, WEP research working paper No. 46, (Geneva, ILO, 1990).

24. See studies referred to in note 1.

25. See L. Aradi et al.: *Kisvállalkozások — kereseti arányok* [Small enterprises — Earnings differentials], (1987; manuscript).

26. The first joint ventures were established in 1974, but there were still fewer than 50 in 1985. Their number later grew rapidly from 179 in 1988 to 1,590 in 1989, and an estimated 5,000 by the end of 1990. Joint ventures accounted for 11 per cent of all enterprises at the beginning of 1990, and almost 20 per cent of external trade.

Information has been drawn from the following studies: S. Kukcsár and J. Bagó: "Ipari tevékenység külföldi müködötökével" [Industrial activity with foreign capital], in *Közgazdasági Szemle*, 1991, No.2; E. Viszt et al.: "A vegyes vállalatok munkaügyi és személyzeti politikájának sajátossagai" (Joint ventures and their human resource policy), *Munkaügyi Szemle*, 1990, No. 3; A külföldi részvételü ipari gazdálkodó szervezetek 1989. évi tevékenysége [Industrial joint ventures in 1989], KSH, 1990 (manuscript); H. C. Pfohl, V. Shultz and S. Freichel: "Joint ventures Magyarországon. [Joint ventures in Hungary], *Ipar-Gazdaság*, 1990, No.10; K. Nagy: "Mit tanuljunk egymástól? — Egy vegyesvállalat munkaerö-polotikájának tanulságai" [What can we learn from each other? — Lessons from a joint Venture], 1990, (manuscript).

27. On the NCRI as part of the industrial relations system see: L. Hethy and V. I. Csuhaj: *Labour Relations in Hungary*, Budapest, Institute of Labour Research, 1990.

28. On the missing "middle level" of collective bargaining, see: V. I. Csuhaj: "Bértarifaegállapodások" [Agreements on job classification], *Figyelö* 1989, April 20; V. I. Csuhaj, "A kollektiv tárgyalásokról — Lehetöségek és kérdö jelek" [Collective Bargaining — Opportunities and Question Marks]. *Munkaügy Szemle,* 1989, No. 6.

29. Workers' councils (which differ from works councils) are grass-roots worker organisations formed in some state-owned enterprises. Three types of workers' councils can be distinguished: those assuming trade union functions, those acting as forums for participation in management, and those interested in gaining ownership of a given enterprise. For details, see: V. I. Csuhaj, and T. Németh: "Munkástanácsok és dilemmák" [Workers Councils and Dilemmas], *Jelzö*, 1989, No. 12; V. I. Csuhaj and T. Németh: "A munkástanácsokról" [On workers' councils], *Mozgó Világ,* 1990, No. 7.

30. Idömérleg [Time-Budget: Changes in the Way of Life of Hungarian Society According to the Time-Budget Surveys of Spring 1977 and Spring 1986]. (Budapest, KSH) 1987. The report of the first findings was written by Istvan Harcsa and Béla Falussy.

31. According to the nation-wide survey on social stratification and living conditions in 1981 and 1982, 59 per cent of all households had a garden or a small farm for agricultural production. After covering their own needs, 55 per cent of these households had produce for sale. See: *Társadalmi rétegzödés* [Social Stratification, Living Conditions. Way of Life II]. (Budapest, KSH) 1986. As to construction activity, 882,000 new privately owned flats (75 per cent of all new flats) were built exclusively by family efforts between 1971 and 1985. See: J. Farkas and A. Vajda,: "Második gazdaság a lakásépitésben" [The second economy of home-building], in *Arat a magyar* [The Hungarian Harvest]. (Budapest, Magyar Tudományos Akadémia, Szociológiai Kutatóintézete, 1988); see also P. Galasi and G. Sziraczki (eds). *Labour Market and Second Economy in Hungary,* Campus Verlag, Frankfurt/New York, 1985.

32. *Jövedelemeloszlás Magyarországon* [Income distribution in Hungary], (Budapest, KSH) 1990.

33. Privatisation represents a challenge for the entire industrial relations system, but especially for trade unions. See L. Neumann: *Labour conflicts of privatisation (Government vs. trade union approach).* Paper presented at the conference on Changes in labour markets and industrial relations in Europe, Aalborg, Denmark, May 25-27, 1991.

34. Enterprise councils consist of worker representatives (50 per cent) elected by all workers in the enterprise (50 per cent) and management representatives (50 per cent). Councils are authorised to make decisions on strategic issues, including marketing and production policy, and the election of the director. In practice, they have had only a formal say in decisions. The councils have served the interests of management, and have never been regarded by workers as "their" institutions. At the same time, enterprise councils have increased the autonomy of companies, and thus made them more independent of central directives and/or governmental bodies.

35. For details see: L. Héthy: "Az új vállalatirányitási formák" [New Forms of Enterprise Management], *Valóság,* 1987, No. 3; L. Lengyel: *Végkifejlet* [Final Outcome], (Budapest, Közgazdasági és jogi Kiadó) 1989.

36. In September 1990, the coalition Government initiated the re-election of members of enterprise councils, intending to ensure legitimate collective management. The re-elected enterprise councils were supposed to replace or confirm directors by balloting within 15 days of their formation. Four out of five directors were confirmed. See A. Havas; "Öszi nagytakaritás? — Vállalati tanácsok újraválasztása" [Re-election of enterprise councils] *Heti Világgazdaság,* Sep. 15, 1990.

Chapter 5

Poland: labour market trends and policies

by
Marek Gora*, Irena Kotowska, Tomasz Panek, Jaroslav Podgorski

Labour demand and structural change

Employment

The year 1990, though crucial for the transition process, should not be regarded as the beginning of the path from a "classical" command economy towards a market economy. The Polish economy probably ceased to be a classical command economy in the mid-1970s. Although attempts to reform the command economy at that time were unsuccessful, they destroyed some basic elements of the previous system. Hence, the transition observed in 1990 and early 1991 was an attempt to replace a partially reformed command economy with a market system.

In market economies, employment is usually determined by labour demand. In the Polish economy, as in other central and east European economies, labour supply has frequently fallen short of labour demand, as shown by the large numbers of unfilled vacancies — almost half a million in 1988. Open unemployment did not exist, and there was labour hoarding on a massive scale. Thus the employment structure reflected labour supply rather than labour demand.

Data on employment are presented in two ways in Polish statistics.[1] Stock figures at 31 December each year are presented without recalculation into full-time equivalents, while the yearly average is recalculated. Some information is given in one form, some in the other. In addition, the definition of some subcategories of employment has changed so that data are not always comparable. Basic information on the structure of employment by sector and ownership is presented in table 5.1.

---

* Warsaw School of Economics. We are grateful to the Division of Employment and Wages of the Central Statistical Office in Warsaw and to the Institute of Labour and Social Policy for help in gathering data for this report. We are also grateful to Tito Boeri and Hartmut Lehmann for comments made on an earlier draft.

Table 5.1. **Employment by economic sectors[1], Poland**

Sector	1980 (000s)	(%)	1989 (000s)	(%)	1990 (000s)	(%)	Employment change 1989	% 1980-1990
National economy								
Total[2]	17 333.7	100.0	17 129.8	100.0	16 501.3	100.0	-3.7	-4.8
of which:								
Industry[3]	6 581.5	38.0	6 212.6	36.3	5 852.6	35.5	-5.8	-11.1
Agriculture[4]	5 307.1	30.6	4 671.6	27.3	4 558.8	27.6	-2.4	-14.1
Services[5]	5 091.3	29.4	5 555.5	32.4	5 719.9	34.7	3.0	12.3
Socialised sector								
Total[2]	12 717.9	100.0	12 054.6	100.0	10 927.9	100.0	-9.3	-14.1
of which:								
Industry[3]	6 206.9	48.8	5 140.7	42.6	4 585.3	42.0	-10.8	-26.1
Agriculture[4]	1 294.0	10.2	1 103.1	9.2	981.0	9.0	-11.1	-24.2
Services[5]	4 855.5	38.2	5 148.0	42.7	5 172.0	47.3	0.5	6.5
Private sector								
Total[2]	4 615.8	100.0	5 075.2	100.0	5 573.4	100.0	9.8	20.7
of which:								
Industry[3]	374.1	8.1	1 071.9	21.1	1 267.3	22.7	18.2	238.8
Agriculture[4]	4 013.1	86.9	3 568.5	70.3	3 577.8	64.2	0.3	-10.8
Services[5]	235.8	5.1	407.5	8.0	547.9	9.8	34.5	132.4

Notes:
1. Annual average.
2. Figures do not add up to 100 per cent of the total, as a category "Other" is not shown.
3. Industry comprise mining, manufacturing and construction.
4. Agriculture comprises agriculture and forestry.
5. Services comprise transport, communications, trade, public utilities, housing, research and development, education, culture and arts, health care and social welfare, sport, tourism and recreation, public administration and justice, finance and insurance.
Sources: Central Statistical Office (CSO) *Rocznik Statystyczny 1990*, (Warsaw). Unpublished data provided by the Central Statistical Office. Author's own calculations.

Employment in the national economy fell by 4.8 per cent in 1980-90 (3.7 per cent in 1989-90). However, it declined only in the socialised sector, where it dropped by 14.1 per cent in 1980-90 (9.3 per cent in 1989-90). Employment in the private sector substantially increased, by 20.7 per cent in 1980-90 (9.8 per cent in 1989-90) though this was not sufficient to offset job losses in the socialised sector. The share of the latter fell from 73.4 per cent at the start of the decade to 66.2 per cent in 1990, and this change was evident in almost all industries and services.

Employment in the non-agricultural private sector more than trebled in 1980-90, to just over 2 million. Between 1989 and 1990, non-agricultural private employment increased by 32.2 per cent, partly due to the expansion of private firms, but also to the fact that numerous firms changed their ownership status, particularly shops, restaurants and other small businesses. So-called small privatisation began in November 1989 and was quite effectively pursued throughout 1990.

Table 5.1 suggests that the structural change in ownership started some time before the "big bang" of 1990. The economic changes of 1990 accelerated this process and made it more straightforward — especially from the legal point of view. In the past, private enterprises were discriminated against to some extent, through regulations on credit, taxes, limits to enterprise size, foreign trade and so on.

In many cases state enterprises were formally discouraged from co-operating with the private sector. However, by the end of 1991 most, if not all, restrictions had been abolished. On the other hand, the changed economic situation itself partly discouraged the expansion of private firms. A kind of "parasitic" relationship was established under the command economy, as private firms took advantage of the wasteful operation of state enterprises. Since 1990, socialised enterprises have been forced to account for their financial situation, and an easy source of profits for private enterprises has vanished.

Structural change in the 1980s did not only concern ownership; the sectoral structure of the economy changed as well, with a big decline in the employment share of mining, manufacturing and agriculture. Within mining and manufacturing, the state sector declined while the private sector increased. In agriculture (excluding forestry), traditionally dominated by private ownership (83.3 per cent in 1980), private employment also declined by 10.9 per cent from 1980 to 1990, and the share of agriculture in total employment fell from just over 30 per cent to around 27 per cent. Employment in services increased in the 1980s but its share remained at 34.7 per cent in 1990, relatively small in comparison with many other countries. This share would be higher if employment in the parallel economy were included.

Structural change in the private sector was more significant than structural change in the economy as a whole. For instance, the share of industry in total private employment increased from 8.1 per cent in 1980 to 22.7 per cent in 1990, while the share of agriculture (including forestry) declined from 86.9 per cent to 64.2 per cent. For the first time in many years, Polish agricultural output is today in substantial surplus and peasants have problems selling their production. This and demographic processes (in particular, the ageing of the rural population) mean employment in agriculture is likely to decrease further in the short term.

Services represented only 9.8 per cent of employment in the private sector in 1990, having increased only moderately during the 1980s. This was mainly because the State covered most areas of possible expansion, especially education, finance and insurance, communications and foreign trade. Moreover, official data have limited coverage of private activities, and thus probably underestimate employment in private services.

Non-agricultural private sector employment in 1989 (table 5.2) was highly concentrated in "Crafts and services", which accounted for 80.5 per cent of the total, mainly in very small firms often comprising only the owner and his family. In 1989, owners and their families represented 51.9 per cent of total employment in the non-agricultural private sector (table 5.3).

Table 5.2. **Employment in the private non-agriculture sector, Poland, 1989 (thousands)[1]**

	Total, of which: mining and manufacturing		Construction	Transport	Trade	Public
Total						
of which:	1 780.1	824.6	409.1	51.1	140.6	119.2
Crafts and services	1 432.2	674.3	354.3	50.1	129.5	118.2
Commercial companies	134.7	39.3	43.6	0.7	10.5	0.8
Foundations	2.4	0.3	-	-	-	-
Joint ventures	29.9	22.3	0.5	0.1	0.5	0.1
Foreign enterprises (small)	100.2	87.6	11.1	0.1	-	0.1
International companies	0.3	0.2	-	-	-	-

1. As at 31 December.
Source: CSO: *Rocznik Statystyczny 1990,* (Warsaw).

Table 5.3. **Female employment, Poland, 1980 and 1989[1]**

		1980	1989	1980	1989
		(000s)		Percentage of women in sector	
Total	Total	17 768.9	17 558.0		
	Women	8 222.2	8 031.9	46.3	45.7
State sector	Total	12 797.9	11 709.4		
	Women	5 689.9	5 501.4	44.5	47.0
Agriculture	Total	951.3	745.4		
	Women	265.3	206.9	27.9	27.8
Private sector	Total	4 971.0	5 848.6		
	Women	2 532.3	2 530.5	50.9	43.3
Non-agriculture	Total	621.9	1 780.1		
	Women	170.3	439.0	27.4	24.7
Owners and families	Total	386.3	923.4		
	Women	96.7	189.0	25.0	20.5
Employees	Total	213.2	829.6		
	Women	73.6	250.0	34.5	30.1
Agriculture	Total	4 349.1	4 068.5		
	Women	2 362.0	2 091.5	54.3	51.4

1. As at 31 December.
Source: CSO: *Rocznik Statystyczny 1990,* (Warsaw), and author's own calculations.

In 1989, women accounted for 45.7 per cent of employment (table 5.3.). This percentage declined throughout the 1980s, but only in the private sector (especially agriculture); in the state sector female employment increased. This phenomenon is probably connected with changes in employment by ownership. The share of women employed in the non-agricultural private sector was low in 1989 at 24.7 per cent. More men than women probably started their own businesses or exchanged lower paid but safe jobs in state enterprises for better paid but less secure employment in private firms. In addition, many young women moved from rural to urban areas, generally involving flows from the private sector to the socialised sector.

Little information is available on the structure of employment by age. Nevertheless, in the absence of unemployment (before 1990), this structure was very close to that of the labour force.

Labour hoarding

Though labour hoarding is not directly measurable, there have been several attempts to estimate its level in the Polish economy. Nowicki (1986), based on an analysis of overstaffing within different groups of employees, estimated that 56 per cent of the labour force may be disguised unemployed.[2] Gora and Rutkowski (1990) tried to gauge the level of labour hoarding in the Polish economy by using international comparisons to estimate the implicit demand for labour that would have prevailed under market conditions.[3] They calculated that labour demand would have been 25 per cent lower than its actual level if firms had been fully responsive to changes in input prices, and as much as 75 per cent lower if they had also been fully responsive to wage costs. Finally, Rutkowski (1990) estimated labour hoarding in Polish industry using a Cobb-Douglas aggregate production function. This analysis suggested that in the late 1980s labour hoarding rose to up to 25 per cent of employment in industry.

There are at least four main categories of hoarded labour in the transition period:

(a) Employees who turn up for work but who have done very little for a long time;

(b) Employees who work, but less than if they worked in a competitive enterprise;

(c) Employees who have been laid off by recession;

(d) Employees who have been laid off by changes in input prices.

The second category, inherited from the past, would seem to be the most important in the long run, and may be seriously affected by the restructuring of the economy [Gora (1990)].

Labour hoarding is unlikely to have decreased in 1990. It may have increased as [more workers were laid off categories (c) and (d)]. Relatively few workers in categories (a) and (b) were dismissed, perhaps because managers of state enterprises still believed it was possible to avoid real market adjustment, or because the price of labour was still low. Hence, dismissing workers scarcely affected the financial position of the enterprise.

In 1990, employment in the whole economy fell by 3.7 per cent, while GDP fell by 12.0 per cent. The difference between these numbers may serve as a rough estimate of the increase in labour hoarding. Even in the socialised mining and manufacturing sectors, the fall in employment (10.1 per cent) was considerably lower than the fall in output (20.0 per cent).

The parallel economy

Unofficial or "parallel" activities flourished throughout the many years of the command economy system, and especially in the 1980s.[4] The term "parallel economy" is commonly used instead of "black economy" because these kinds of activities were not actually illegal, but simply unofficial and were, to some extent, tolerated by the authorities.

Since no data on unofficial activities were collected, and since the banking system was underdeveloped (i.e., money flows were under-recorded), the size of the parallel economy can only be estimated indirectly. According to Bednarski and Kokoszczynski (1990), if the parallel economy had been taken into account, GNP in 1988 would have been 9 to 12 per cent higher than that reported by official statistics.

The parallel economy was based primarily on the household, as its main purpose was to supplement family budgets. However, many official enterprises also conducted unofficial activities, taking advantage of high prices for goods and services in short supply and wasteful operations in socialised firms.

It is very difficult to analyse employment in the parallel economy. In Poland, as in all other Central and east European countries, it was important to be attached to the official economy because this was a condition of entitlement for key benefits such as free health care. Thus most of those working in the parallel economy were employed in the official economy.

Some groups receiving social security, such as retired people, women on maternity leave and the slightly disabled served as the main sources of employees for the parallel economy (Bednarski, 1991).

The parallel economy is likely to be affected in the years ahead by the elimination (or substantial reduction) of shortages of goods, lower demand for goods produced in the parallel economy, and the worsening financial condition of large state enterprises that were once a source of easy profit. As a consequence, activities in the parallel economy could virtually disappear, or at any rate become an insignificant element of the economy. They could become part of the official private sector or of the ordinary "black" economy (so as to avoid taxes and regulations such as those on working conditions).

Labour supply and unemployment

Structure of the working-age population

From 1975 until 1988 the rate of growth of the working-age population declined steadily. Demographic projections (Kotowska, 1991a) suggest that this tendency will be altered in the 1990s, when a stable annual rise of about 0.8 per cent is expected. This will lead to a working-age population about 4 per cent higher in 1995 than in 1990 (table 5.4). The urban share rose steadily from 56 per cent in 1975 to 61 per cent in 1988, and is predicted to reach 64 per cent in the year 2000. The rural population ceased to decline in 1988 and should now stabilise at about 8.5 million.

Table 5.4. **Working-age population by age and sex: Poland, 1980-2000**

Year	Age	Total	Males (000s)	Females
1980	Total			
	of which:	35 734.9	17 410.6	18 324.3
	15-60/64	22 800.8	11 577.4	11 223.4
	15-24	6 016.3	3 085.3	2 931.0
	25-44	10 192.8	5 116.6	5 076.2
	45-60/64	6 591.7	3 375.5	3 216.2
1985	Total			
	of which:	37 340.5	18 211.0	19 129.5
	15-60/64	23 297.2	11 997.0	11 300.2
	15-24	5 213.4	2 668.3	2 545.1
	25-44	11 255.4	5 680.2	5 575.2
	45-60/64	6 827.9	3 648.3	3 179.6
1990[1]	Total			
	of which:	38 791.0	18 930.7	19 860.3
	15-60/64	23 942.1	12 398.7	11 543.4
	15-24	5 400.2	2 755.4	2 644.9
	25-44	12 032.0	6 083.5	5 948.5
	45-60/64	6 509.9	3 559.8	2 950.0
1995[1]	Total			
	of which:	40 102.5	19 578.8	20 523.8
	15-60/64	24 838.8	12 853.0	11 985.8
	15-24	6 116.3	3 120.3	2 996.1
	25-44	11 603.2	5 867.1	5 736.0
	45-60/64	7 119.2	3 865.6	3 253.6
2000[1]	Total			
	of which:	41 425.8	20 226.1	21 199.7
	15-60/64	25 883.4	13 356.6	12 526.8
	15-24	6 568.7	3 353.1	3 215.6
	25-44	11 127.0	5 629.0	5 498.0
	45-60/64	8 187.7	4 374.4	3 813.3

1. Forecast.
Source: CSO: National census 1978 and 1988, and author's own calculations.

The transition process began at a time of rapid growth of the working-age population in 1989 and 1990, as more young people entered the labour market. According to population projections, the youth population will continue to grow, at 2.5 per cent a year between 1990 and 1995 and 1.4 per cent from 1995 to 2000 (Kotowska, 1991b).

The population of working-age in Poland is generally relatively young, especially in urban areas: about 72 per cent are in the mobile (18-44) age group, although this percentage will significantly decrease by the year 2000. However, the ageing of the population is much more pronounced in rural than in urban areas. In 1989 the share of people aged 60 and over was about 17 per cent, while in urban areas it was 13 per cent. The usual retirement age is 65 for men and 60 for women.

Labour force participation rates

Trends in labour force participation rates (LFPR) can be analysed from data provided by the two national censuses of 1978 and 1988. The LFPR declined from 67.3 to 65.3 per cent between these years, falling from 63.2 to 61.2 per cent in urban areas and from 73.2 to 71.8 per cent in rural areas. Table 5.5 provides detailed information on LFPRs by age and sex in urban and rural areas. Two urban trends are worth noting:

Table 5.5. **Labour force participation rates by age, sex and location, Poland, 1978 and 1988**

Age	Nation-wide				Urban areas				Rural areas			
	Males		Females		Males		Females		Males		Females	
	1978	1988	1978	1988	1978	1988	1978	1988	1978	1988	1978	1988
Total[1]	76.6	74.3	58.7	57.0	73.4	66.3	54.1	53.2	81.0	80.4	65.6	63.5
15-17	7.5	3.9	5.2	2.4	4.1	2.2	2.4	1.2	12.1	6.9	8.9	4.3
18-19	58.3	52.6	43.2	41.7	50.0	41.9	35.1	32.8	70.1	67.7	54.8	54.6
20-24	82.7	79.0	68.4	64.0	78.1	70.5	65.2	58.5	89.0	90.3	73.6	72.5
25-29	96.2	94.3	75.1	70.0	95.6	92.4	76.2	69.5	97.2	96.9	73.2	70.7
30-34	97.1	96.1	79.5	76.7	97.1	95.7	79.4	76.3	97.2	96.9	79.7	77.4
35-39	96.2	95.6	81.9	83.0	96.1	95.2	80.5	82.1	96.4	96.2	84.3	85.0
40-44	94.8	94.1	82.7	85.5	94.2	93.4	80.4	84.0	95.7	95.4	86.5	89.0
45-49	92.1	89.6	78.5	81.2	90.5	87.6	73.2	78.1	94.5	93.4	86.0	87.4
50-54	87.1	82.4	71.6	71.1	83.1	77.6	62.7	65.1	92.3	90.1	83.2	81.5
55-59	81.5	72.0	57.9	50.6	74.8	63.1	42.6	36.6	89.3	85.0	76.4	71.5
60-64	62.4	53.6	37.4	34.3	45.6	37.8	15.0	17.5	79.2	74.4	63.3	57.2
65-69	43.0	40.4	27.8	26.8	18.8	22.3	7.8	10.9	65.7	61.2	50.9	46.8
70 and over	29.3	27.1	14.7	15.0	9.7	11.9	3.5	5.0	46.5	41.9	27.8	27.4

1. Percentage of economically active people in the total population aged 15 and over.
Source: CSO: Nantional census 1978 and 1988.

- First, LFPRs fell in all male age groups (excluding the over 65s). For younger groups this may be partly explained by emigration and employment in the parallel economy; for older groups it may be the result of a growing proportion categorised as disabled.
- Second, LFPRs fell for young women (under 35), the result of a baby boom in the early 1980s, and rose for older groups.

LFPRs for the rural population were higher and more stable over this period.

Labour force by age, sex, sector, location and education

Table 5.6 gives information on the labour force by age, sex and sector for 1988. There is a distinct difference in the age composition of the agricultural and non-agricultural labour force. About 76 per cent of the non-agricultural labour force was aged 15-44, compared with 45 per cent in the agricultural sector. The agricultural labour force is also less skilled than the non-agricultural one. Only 22 per cent of the non-agricultural labour force comprises unskilled workers; the proportion is 67 per cent for the agricultural sector.

Table 5.6. **Labour force by sector, age and sex, Poland, 1988**

Age	Total			Males			Females		
	Total	Non-agr.	Agric.	Total	Non-agr.	Agric.	Total	Non-agr.	Agric.
	(000s)			(000s)			(000s)		
Total[1]	18 452	13 449	5 003	10 070	7 403	2 667	8 382	6 045	2 337
15-17	53	27	27	34	17	17	19	10	9
18-44	12 397	10 154	2 243	6 865	5 548	1 318	5 532	4 607	925
45-59/64	4 740	3 050	1 690	2 706	1 756	950	2 034	1 294	740
60/65 and over	1 243	204	1 040	456	76	380	788	128	660
	Per cent			Per cent			Per cent		
Total	100	72.88	27.12	100	73.52	26.48	100	72.12	27.88
15-17	100	50.30	49.70	100	49.78	50.22	100	51.23	48.77
18-44	100	81.91	18.09	100	80.81	19.19	100	83.27	16.73
45-59/64	100	64.34	35.66	100	64.89	35.11	100	63.61	36.39
60/65 and over	100	16.40	83.60	100	16.63	83.37	100	16.26	83.74

1. Total may not add up owing to the nature of the data.
Source: CSO: National Census 1988, and author's own calculations.

Labour turnover

Turnover data are available only for the socialised sector and for certain years. The fairly high levels of turnover, shown in table 5.7, coexisted with near-zero unemployment as a large part of frictional unemployment was not registered.

Table 5.7. **Turnover rates in the Polish economy (socialised sector), 1985-1989**

Sector	1985		1988		1989	
	Resignations %	Hirings %	Resignations %	Hirings %	Resignations %	Hirings %
Total	17.9	19.0	18.0	17.3	19.8	16.2
Manufacturing & mining	17.2	17.7	17.2	16.1	19.3	15.8
Construction	26.2	27.1	30.7	27.5	31.8	22.0
Agriculture	16.6	16.1	15.2	14.5	17.6	13.5
Forestry	17.8	19.4	17.1	14.9	18.0	11.8
Transport	18.0	16.6	18.0	15.1	19.5	14.1
Communications	16.6	18.3	16.6	18.1	21.8	23.2
Trade	17.3	19.5	18.3	17.9	22.3	15.9
Public utilities	24.1	24.2	23.9	22.7	25.5	19.8
Housing	21.8	24.3	23.2	21.6	23.8	20.2
Research & development	13.8	15.0	13.9	12.9	18.7	10.7
Education	13.8	16.5	12.2	14.2	11.3	13.1
Culture & arts	20.7	24.2	19.5	18.7	22.2	19.6
Health care & social welfare	15.2	19.3	14.1	16.7	14.1	15.5
Sport, tourism & recreation	26.4	29.0	26.4	24.7	30.3	24.8
Public administration & justice	12.4	16.3	13.4	13.2	14.2	13.5
Finance & insurance	12.1	14.7	14.4	18.7	15.4	23.6
Material sphere	18.6	19.1	19.1	17.7	21.2	16.4
Non-material sphere	15.4	18.6	14.7	16.3	15.3	15.7

Source: CSO: Rocznik Statystyczny 1990, (Warsaw).

The limited information available on turnover rates in 1990 shows that voluntary resignations fell sharply as jobs ceased to be automatically assured; recruitment fell, as enterprises became more careful in hiring new employees; and lay-offs started to affect turnover rates. However, lay-offs in 1990 were not very significant and turnover rates decreased mainly because of lower resignation and hiring rates.

There is little micro-economic evidence on the nature of employment termination: according to Spoleczne *aspekty bezrobocia w Polsce* (1991), from those interviewed 9.8 per cent of people who had left their last job had done so voluntarily, and this percentage was higher for males than for females.

In the vast majority of cases laid-off workers simply become unemployed. However, since inflows to unemployment were not recorded in 1990, it is not possible to establish how many laid-off workers became unemployed.

Labour

Economic policy in the years 1970-80 caused migration inflows to urban areas comparable with the large-scale migration of the period 1950-55, especially among people aged 20-29. This process continued in the 1980s, but slowed down markedly at the end of the decade (see table 5.8).

Table 5.8. **Internal migrations, Poland, 1976-1989 (thousands)**

	1976-1980[1]	1988	1989
Total	932.4	639.5	596.5
Men	446.2	313.2	292.9
Women	486.2	326.3	308.6
From urban areas	385.7	261.2	248.5
Men	184.5	127.5	119.6
Women	201.2	133.7	123.9
From rural areas	546.7	378.8	353.0
Men	261.7	185.7	177.3
Women	285.0	192.6	179.7

1. Annual average.
Source: CSO: Rocznik Statystyczny 1990, (Warsaw), and author's own calculations.

Recent information on migration by age and sex is provided in table 5.9. The most remarkable fact is that about half of migrating women were aged 20-24. Young women "escape" from rural areas because of relatively poor standards of living and lack of employment opportunities. This results in a lack of potential wives for peasants and pressure on men, particularly those whose land yields little profit, to move to urban areas. However, internal migration in Poland is sharply limited by the shortage of housing.

Table 5.9. **Internal migration by age and sex, Poland, 1989**

Age group	Total	Migration per 1,000	
	Total 15.7	Male 15.8	Female 15.6
15 - 19	11.7	8.7	14.8
20 - 24	41.2	32.7	50.0
25 - 29	37.2	39.4	34.9
30 - 34	20.5	22.7	18.3
35 - 39	11.6	13.1	10.1
40 - 44	7.4	8.5	6.4
45 - 49	5.4	6.1	4.8
50 - 54	4.5	4.9	4.2
55 - 59	4.2	4.2	4.2
60 and over	6.3	5.2	7.3

Source: CSO: Rocznik Statystyczny 1990, (Warsaw).

Another factor strongly affecting the labour force structure in Poland has been emigration, which became very significant in the 1980s. Unfortunately, official data are not fully reliable. Recent attempts to estimate emigration indicate that between 1981 and 1988 about 830,200 people, mainly of working age, left Poland and stayed abroad. In addition, thousands of young people went abroad for temporary work.

Emigration and temporary departures were linked strongly with the economic and political situation in Poland, and work abroad is today less appealing than it used to be. Average monthly pay in Poland was equal to about US$20 throughout the 1980s (at the exchange rate prevailing in the black market) whereas at the end of 1990 it was worth about US$150. Moreover, Polish currency may now be easily and legally changed into foreign currencies. All this may imply lower labour outflows from Poland in the future. Wage differentials, however, are not the only determinant of migration decisions. Other factors, including political factors, play an important role.

The Polish labour market has become more attractive for citizens of some other countries, and the supply of labour may therefore increase. Up to 50,000 Russians are working in Poland today, in addition to a few Romanians and Vietnamese.

Unemployment

Unemployment started to rise at the beginning of 1990. The initial unemployment rate, at the end of December 1989, was 0.05 per cent of the total labour force. At the end of 1990 it was 1,124,000, (6.1 per cent) and in June 1991 it reached 1,574,099 (8.4 per cent). Monthly unemployment figures for 1990 are shown in table 5.10 (see also figure 5.1). The rise so far closely resembles a straight line.[5]

Figure 5.1. **Unemployment and vacancies, Poland, 1990-91**

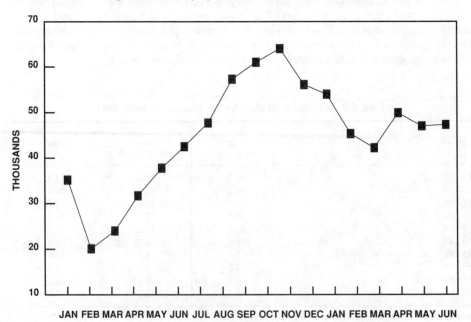

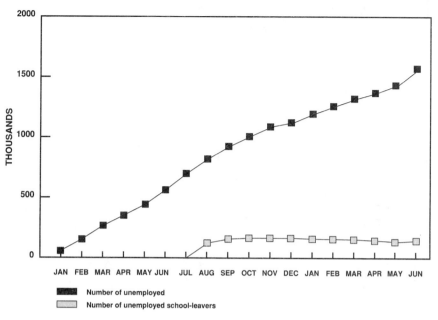

Figure 5.2. **Unemployment (Jan. 1990 - June 1991)**

■■■ Number of unemployed

▢ Number of unemployed school-leavers

Table 5.10. **Unemployment, vacancies and unemployment to vacancies ratio[1], Poland, 1990 and 1991**

Month	Unemployment (000s)	Rate (%)	Vacancies (000s)	Rate (%)	U/V[2] ratio	U/V ratio (Males)	U/V ratio (Females)	School leavers[3] (000s)
1990								
January	55.8	0.3	35.2	0.19	2	1	3	.
February	152.2	0.8	20.1	0.11	8	6	14	.
March	266.6	1.5	24.1	0.13	11	8	24	.
April	351.1	1.9	31.7	0.17	11	8	23	.
May	443.2	2.4	37.8	0.21	12	8	23	.
June	568.2	3.1	42.5	0.23	13	9	30	.
July	699.3	3.8	47.7	0.26	15	9	36	.
August	820.3	4.5	57.3	0.31	14	9	33	124.2
September	926.4	5.0	61.0	0.33	15	9	37	157.4
October	1 008.0	5.5	64.0	0.35	16	9	45	164.9
November	1 089.0	5.9	56.1	0.31	19	13	41	164.8
December	1 124.0	6.1	54.0	0.29	21	14	40	164.3
1991								
January	1 195.7	6.6	45.3	0.25	26	18	46	158.4
February	1 258.9	6.8	42.2	0.23	30	20	53	156.1
March	1 322.1	7.1	45.8	0.25	29	19	56	153.4
April	1 370.1	7.3	49.9	0.27	27	18	57	145.2
May	1 434.5	7.7	47.0	0.25	31	19	66	134.5
June	1 574.1	8.4	47.3	0.25	33	21	74	144.2

1. Unemployment and vacancies are month-end figures.
2. U/V Unemployment to vacancies.
3. Data first published in August 1990.
Source: CSO: *Informacja Sygnalna, Informacja Statystyczna* and *Biuletyn Statystyczny*, (Warsaw).

Table 5.11. **Composition of unemployment¹, Poland, December, 1990 - June 1991**

	December			January			June		
	Total	Males	Females	Total	Males	Females	Total	Males	Females
Total	1 126 140	552 454	573 686	1 195 656	584 319	611 337	1 574 099	754 377	819 722
Manual		·	·	810 363	440 265	370 098	1 044 596	561 161	483 435
Non-manual		·	·	385 293	144 054	241 239	529 503	193 216	336 287
Youth		·	·	14 105	7 505	6 600	22 573	11 307	11 266
School-leavers	164 254	69 052	95 202	158 357	6 6314	92 043	144 226	63 515	80 711
of which:									
Tertiary	8 906	4 323	4 583	8 419	4 056	4 363	6 038	2 508	3 530
Secondary	70 980	20 510	50 470	65 825	17 765	48 060	80 976	29 165	51 211
Vocational	84 368	44 219	40 149	84 013	44 393	39 620	57 812	31 842	25 970
Disabled				13 363	7 752	5 611	16 545	9 576	6 969
Receiving benefits	891 651	445 059	446 592	9 661 56	477 634	488 522	1 238 235	601 479	636 756
In mass lay-offs	183 113	800 070	103 043	218 719	93 754	124 965	315 304	134 662	80 642
New employment found for²		·	·	35 101	19 809	15 292	38 465	22 988	15 477
Intervention works for²		·	·	41 347	24 699	16 648	24 557	14 749	9 808

1. Data at the end of each month.
2. In the month.
Source: CSO: *Informacja Statystyczna* and *Biuletyn Statystyczny*, (Warsaw).

Information on flows into and out of unemployment is not available. In terms of outflows, we know only that 274,400 unemployed people found new jobs, while another 106,900 took part in community public works. New businesses were started by 27,900 of the unemployed, including both new labour force entrants and redundant workers.

Data on the length of jobless spells are also not available, but rough calculations and anecdotal evidence suggest that the vast majority of people who became unemployed in 1990 were still unemployed in 1991. This implies lengthy average spells. Since the country's economic performance is not expected to improve in the near term, a large number of those without work will become long-term unemployed.

There is also little information on the characteristics of the unemployed (tables 5.11 and 5.12). Displaced workers account for 68 per cent of the unemployed, 75.9 per cent of males and 60.4 per cent of females (*Spoleczne, 1991*).

Table 5.12. **Some characteristics of the unemployed, Poland, 1991**

Age group	% of unemployed	Education	% of unemployed
15-17	1.4	Below secondary	70.0
18-34	60.0	Secondary	26.7
35-54	35.0	Tertiary	3.3
55 and over	2.4		

Source: CSO (recent data quoted in weekly economic newspaper).

Additional information

Age	% of unemployed	Sex	% of unemployed
18-44	87.6	Males	52.7
45-59	12.4	Females	46.7
Educational level		Working experience	
Tertiary	8.5	Under 1 year	24.8
Secondary	41.9	1 to 10 years	58.6
Vocational	33.5	more than 10 years	16.6
Unskilled	16.4		

Source: Spoleczne aspekty bezrobocia w Polsce, 1991 Warsaw, Institute of Labour and Social Studies.

School-leavers entered the labour market in the middle of 1990.[6] At the end of June 1991, they accounted for 9.2 per cent of the unemployed. The number of school-leavers registered as unemployed declined slightly over time, largely due to a much smaller inflow of new unemployed school-leavers at the end of the year.

Unemployment rates differ substantially between regions (voivodships). At the end of February 1991, they varied from 3.1 per cent (unemployment to vacancy ratio 4) in Warsaw to 15.8 per cent in Torun (unemployment to vacancy ratio 89.1). In 22 of the 49 regions unemployment rates exceeded 10 per cent, while in four regions they were below 5 per cent. The largest numbers of unemployed were in the highly industrialised regions of Katowice (79,685) and Lodz (74,882). However, the labour force in these regions is large, so that unemployment rates were relatively modest.

147

At the end of 1990 the monthly growth rate of unemployment declined, probably as a result of the introduction of stricter eligibility criteria for unemployment benefits. Until September 1990, all unemployed people, even those who had never worked before, were entitled to benefits. After December 1990, those who were not entitled stopped receiving benefits, so that some in this position did not bother to register. Others who used to receive benefits, but did not fulfil their obligations (such as looking for a job) were removed from the register. It should be stressed that unemployed people do not expect to find a job through labour offices. In many cases they register simply to receive benefits. As a consequence, some outflows from unemployment were caused by legal regulations rather than by job availability.

Data on unemployment by occupation are available only for June 1990. At that time unskilled workers represented some 25 per cent of the unemployed, that is, a relatively minor component of unemployment. Administrative employees accounted for about 7 per cent. Some unemployed people were former housewives and were among the unemployed not entitled to benefit (21.3 per cent in June 1991). In some cases these housewives were not in fact unemployed. However, in perhaps the majority of cases, the registration of housewives as unemployed reflected a serious change in the position of many households. This is part of the wider problem related to the large expansion in unemployment drawn from outside the labour force.

Unemployment also influences attitudes towards new economic developments. People were used to being employed as unemployment had not been part of the Polish experience for decades. Workers were used to regarding employment as an obligation of the State, and people still tend to feel "insiders" even if they have lost their jobs. However, even if typical forms of behaviour of "insiders" and "outsiders" have not yet been established in Poland, people's attitudes towards the new phenomenon are changing (Gora, 1991).

Vacancies

In the 1980s the number of vacancies was high owing to widespread shortages typical of command economies. Excess labour demand (roughly measured by unfilled vacancies) started to decrease in 1989, from 430,000 to 254,500 over the year. At the beginning of 1990, vacancies almost vanished, falling to 20,100 in February, as labour shortages disappeared or shrank. Since enterprises were no longer obliged to register their vacancies with labour offices, the most recent figures are likely to understate the actual number of vacancies (table 5.10 and figure 5.11). Neither the upward trend from February to October 1990 nor the rapid downturn from November 1990 can easily be explained by the performance of the economy. Flow analysis of the labour market could perhaps shed some light on this matter, but unfortunately data on flows are not available.[7]

The distribution of vacancies varies among regions, with rural areas particularly disadvantaged. The largest numbers of vacancies were registered in the Warsaw and Katowice voivodships. These two highly industrialised regions also had high vacancy rates.

The number of vacancies listed as suitable for women was smaller than that for men. In June 1991 there were nine men and 45 women for every unfilled job. Women especially are likely to suffer from the absence of employment opportunities in the transition phase. Over decades of very high demand for labour, women were absorbed into many activities where men are usually preferred by managers, but rising male unemployment could change this situation, leading to the dismissal of women and their replacement by men in enterprises.

148

Labour market policies

Legal environment

Before 1990 there was legal definition of unemployment and, nor was there an unemployment benefit system in place. Those "searching for a job" were registered but received no benefits and accounted for less than 0.1 per cent of the labour force. Open unemployment became a legal and economic reality only in 1990. Unemployment legislation (the Acts on Employment and on Group Lay-offs) was issued in December 1989. The Employment Act was amended in July 1990, just a few months after its introduction, and will be revised again in the near future.

The official definition of an unemployed person, contained in the Employment Act, is "a person able and ready to start a job, who does not have another job, who is registered with the appropriate regional labour office, and: is not drawing an old-age pension; is not the owner or co-owner of a farm; does not run his/her own business; and is not covered by social security for any other reason."

The Act on Group Lay-offs applies to firms that shed at least 10 per cent of their staff or at least 100 employees (firms when they employ more than 1,000 persons), go bankrupt or are liquidated. Enterprises are not legally obliged to give a detailed justification of mass lay-offs, and managers can simply cite economic reasons. For lay-offs in general, Blaszkiewicz (1990) found that employees were dismissed for economic reasons in 41.6 per cent of enterprises, for organisational reasons in 37.7 per cent, and for disciplinary reasons in 36.4 per cent. (These categories are not mutually exclusive.) In only 2.6 per cent of enterprises were employees dismissed solely because of privatisation.

Enterprises are legally obliged to inform the employment service in advance about mass lay-offs, though this requirement is often not fulfilled. In many cases, enterprises advise on expected redundancies simply to dissuade their workers from demanding higher wages or to reduce the pressure from financial authorities. However, many enterprises which have not informed the employment service of planned redundancies do lay off workers. Hence, the information on expected mass lay-offs provided in labour market statistics is often misleading.

Employment services

In 1990 there were 390 employment offices in Poland, of which 341 regional offices were dealing directly with the unemployed. These regional offices employed about 4,000 people. Thus in December 1990, there were on average 3,300 unemployed people per regional employment office and 280 unemployed people for each staff member.

The labour exchange structure is not equipped to cope with the new problems arising from transition, and funds available in 1990 to combat unemployment were limited. As a consequence, the activity of employment offices was concentrated mainly on the registration of the unemployed and the payment of benefits.

The offices do not have the necessary equipment, especially computers and communication systems, and there is little circulation of information between them. Also, the staff at employment offices lack experience in helping the unemployed find jobs. Their previous role was to find workers for unfilled vacancies. The scale of unemployment too has exceeded all forecasts, while the new legal system turned out to be unclear not only for the unemployed but also for some staff.

The number of unemployed involved in various kinds of training aimed at acquiring or improving new skills was only 10,300 in 1990, though the situation improved slightly in 1991. One problem arises from the legislation which requires new employment after training. Most enterprises are way of engaging new employees months in advance.

As mentioned above, the unemployed do not believe that labour offices can help them to find work. In *Spoleczne* (1991) only 20.7 per cent of respondents expressed such a hope. Labour offices are regarded primarily as a source of benefits.

Labour market policies

The Employment Act established the Labour Fund to finance labour market policies. There are four sources of revenue for the Fund:

(a) mandatory contributions by enterprises (2 per cent of the wage fund);

(b) subsidies from the central budget;

(c) income from businesses owned by the Fund; and

(d) credits.

The Fund's expenditure in 1990 is presented in table 5.13. Over half the total was spent on unemployment benefits. This reflects the fact that open unemployment proved to be higher than expected. Active labour market policy measures were less important, as indicated by the meagre 16 billion zloty spent on training. (Official forecasts published at the end of 1989 predicted that "only" 400,000 people would lose their jobs in 1990).

Overall, in 1990 and 1991, labour market policies were relatively weak, due to the limited funds available and lack of experience in this field. Active labour market policies were particularly penalised and did not have a significant impact on the adjustment of labour markets.

Job losses, lay-offs and job creation

For several decades before 1990, job losses were insignificant. Employment in the economy decreased mainly as a result of reductions in labour supply. In 1990, the situation changed dramatically. Some 900,000 jobs were lost — about 5 per cent of total employment at the end of 1989.[8]

No data are available on the distribution of job losses between the socialised and private sector, but there is little doubt that most of these losses concerned the socialised sector. However, despite the relatively poor financial condition of state enterprises, there were no bankruptcies among them in 1990 and jobs were not destroyed on a large scale. Overall, private employment increased, but about 154,000 private (mainly small craft) firms went out of business during 1990 (table 5.14). All this seems to indicate that job destruction observed in 1990 and 1991 had little to do with economic restructuring.

150

Table 5.13. **Labour fund expenditure, Poland, 1990**

	billion zloty
Total	3 702.3
Unemployment and social security benefits	1 890.9
Unemployment	1 349.1
Social security	541.8
Training of unemployed	16
Benefits	5.3
For social security	2
Costs of courses	8.7
Loans for unemployed	5 17.8
Loans for enterprises (for hiring unemployed)	444
Public (intervention) works	2 09.2
Compensation	1 47.6
For social security	61.6
Additional payments for those dismissed in group lay-offs	2.2
Costs of new jobs for disabled	13.4
Refunds for enterprises employing disabled people	2.6
Compensation	1.9
For social security	0.7
Youth training in vocational schools	69.1
Compensation	67
For social security	2.1
Young workers	434.7
Compensation	305.6
For social security	129.1
Special support for mentally handicapped	58.2
Computer facilities	11.5
Other expenditure	32.7

Source: Ministry of Labour and Social Policy.

Table 5.14. **Non-agricultural private sector, Poland, 1990**

Number of firms		(000s)
Total	created	516.2
	shut down	154.0
Craft	created	140.6
	shut down	75.0
Trade	created	300.7
	shut down	41.9
Services	created	74.8
	shut down	37.0

Source: CSO: *Komunikat,* (Warsaw).

In spite of the recession, there were new job openings in 1990 in both socialised and private enterprises. Thus 80 per cent of enterprises located in the Warsaw voivodship hired new employees in 1990 (Blaszkiewicz, 1990): 42.7 per cent hired up to 10 new employees, 26.7 per cent hired from 11 to 50 new employees and 10.4 per cent hired more than 100 new employees. In the country as a whole, 516,200 new private enterprises were created (table 5.14). Moreover, existing firms hired some new workers in 1990. Among owners of a sample of over 300 small private firms (Tulski and

Wozniakowski, 1990) 26.4 per cent planned to increase employment and 36.1 per cent were keen to employ additional workers if costs were refunded by the Labour Fund. (On the other hand, 33.3 per cent answered that they did not intend to use this opportunity and 28.4 per cent of respondents did not know about the Labour Fund.) Enterprises can obtain special credits — equal to 20 times the official average monthly wage — to create jobs for the unemployed. In 1990 loans were also given to unemployed people who wanted to start their own businesses. (These amounts can be halved after two years if the job or business activity still exists). In both cases the cost of the credits was quite low.

Temporary jobs for unemployed people were also created through government schemes for community public works. These jobs may last up to 6 months. In 1990, about 106,900 unemployed people took part in various kinds of public works.

There is a general lack of information on employment by size of enterprise. However, due to the shift towards private firms and services (where firms are generally smaller than in manufacturing), we can guess that the average size of expanding enterprises has been smaller than the size of declining enterprises.

Hiring and dismissal policies

For many years the hiring policy of state enterprises consisted largely of finding new employees. Private non-agricultural enterprises hired very few employees and private agricultural enterprises were mainly family-based.

In 1990, the labour shortage vanished or substantially decreased, so that enterprises were no longer under pressure to hire new employees quickly. Moreover, the costs of labour, though still very low, began to impinge on the budgets of socialised enterprises, which consequently became more selective in recruitment. In Oleksyn's sample of 100 state industrial enterprises (1991), 60 per cent thoroughly interviewed job applicants, 9 per cent required some practical proof of skills, and 2 per cent applied formal tests. From the same investigation we know that part-time employees were most likely to be laid off and 49 per cent of enterprises intended to dismiss some part-time workers. In 17 per cent of enterprises decisions for dismissals had already been taken. Discrimination against part-time employees was also found in the 99 enterprises in the Warsaw area studied by Blaszkiewicz (1990). Working pensioners, most of whom are part-timers, are also vulnerable to redundancy.

Polish legislation distinguishes between individual and mass lay-offs. The proportion of the latter may be used as a rough indicator of the stage of transition. If it is low, this suggests that enterprises are still in a strong position because if they were forced to restructure, they would need to lay off more workers and mass lay-offs — which are more costly for enterprises — would be unavoidable. According to a survey carried out in July 1990 by Oleksyn (1991), only 19 per cent of state enterprises had already made mass lay-offs, while 69 per cent had no plans to do so.

In December 1990, 16.3 per cent of the total of registered unemployed people had suffered mass lay-offs. This figure rose to 18.9 per cent (237,924 people) in February 1991.

Other methods of reducing redundancies are rarely used. The law does not encourage early retirement which in 1990 was applied to only about 40,000 people. Short-time working is used in very few enterprises. Some enterprises have resorted to forced holidays for a proportion of their staff, a phenomenon that has become quite frequent.

While in the socialised sector permanent full-time contracts dominate, the private sector does not provide the same kind of job security and employment may be temporary. There is little information on the type of labour contract used for new employment.

Policies for income support

Living standards

Indices of real personal incomes serve as statistical indicators of living standards (table 5.15). Consumer prices in 1990 were about 58 times higher than in 1985, rising moderately in the period 1985-88 but accelerating in 1989 with the start of the transition to a market economy. Nominal per capita incomes also soared over this period. Real incomes were stable in the years 1985-87 and even rose in 1988 as a by-product of policies aimed at stopping the wave of strikes. The situation was reversed in 1990 with a drop in real wages in the socialised sector. As the state sector is still the largest employer in Poland, changes in real wages in state enterprises feed through to changes in real household incomes.

Table 5.15. **Changes in prices and incomes, Poland, 1985-1990**

	1985	1986	1987	1988	1989	1990
	1985 = 100					
Consumer prices	100.0	117.3	147.2	234.1	841.5	5 764.3
Personal incomes per capita						
Nominal	100.0	119.3	150.9	271.6	1 036.7	.
Real	100.0	101.7	102.5	116.0	123.2	.
Average wage (socialised economy)						
Nominal	100.0	120.4	145.8	265.2	1 039.1	5 174.61
Real	100.0	102.6	99.0	113.3	123.5	89.81
Average pension/wage (%)	51.4	52.4	57.2	51.2	47.9	56.8

Source: CSO: *Studia i Analizy Statystyczne*, (Warsaw).

Old-age and invalidity pensioners were the groups most seriously affected by price increases. Changes in their position can be assessed using the ratio of the average pension to the average wage in the state sector. This ratio improved in 1986 and 1987 but then deteriorated, falling below 50 per cent in 1989. The ratio improved again in 1990, though mainly due to a steep drop in real wages.

Household incomes directly determine the living conditions of households. Nominal household incomes have shown a steady upward trend for all socio-economic groups over the last decade (table 5.16), especially in 1988 and 1989. However, a rise in nominal incomes is often only a consequence of a previous increase in the cost of living.

Table 5.16. Nominal incomes, cost of living and real income of households, Poland, 1981-1990

Households	1981	1982	1983	1984	1985	1986	1987	1988	1989	1990
Nominal incomes										
Employees	126	160.1	123.4	119.6	118.2	118.7	120.4	174.5	397.3	379.6
Peasant-workers	136.4	173.1	119.2	118.9	117.6	119.5	122.5	185.1	394.6	384.4
Farmers	150.5	163.1	115.4	114.7	119.4	121.4	120.7	191.1	390.9	353.4
Pensioners	123.4	169.0	117.2	118.0	116.9	123.7	131.3	162.1	375.5	443.2
Cost of living										
Employees	124	201.4	122.9	115.8	114.3	117.2	125.6	158.7	360.4	617.4
Peasant-workers	119.5	202.0	124.7	115.0	115.0	117.7	124.8	160.8	354.2	575.8
Farmers	127.8	203.3	125.3	114.7	114.8	117.9	125.3	162.2	348.8	642.8
Pensioners	119	211.5	118.1	116.3	116.2	117.1	126.6	159.3	363.1	653.1
Real incomes										
Employees	101.6	79.5	100.4	103.4	103.1	101.4	95.9	110	110.2	61.5
Peasant-workers	107	83.8	99.7	104.0	103.4	102.8	97.5	115.7	112.2	66.8
Farmers	117.5	79.0	97.1	100.4	105.4	104.5	95.6	118.1	113.1	55.5
Pensioners	103.3	79.9	99.2	101.5	101.0	105.8	103.7	101.8	103.4	67.8

Source: CSO: *Studia i Analizy Statystyczne*, (Warsaw), and authors' own calculations.

154

The cost of living rose most sharply in 1982, 1989 and in the first quarter of 1990 when real household incomes fell steeply — by 32.3 per cent from 1989 levels for pensioner households and 54.3 per cent for peasant households. However, real incomes increased in the second and third quarters.

The official cost of living indices, based on price changes of a representative basket of consumer goods and services, take no account of changes in the structure of household consumption. An investigation (Panek, 1990) of changes in food consumption in the first half of 1990 suggested that real incomes may have fallen by about one-third less than indicated by official statistics.

Measures of economic affluence[9] can be used to estimate relative income changes for one group of households compared with others, but they do not define the hierarchy of household types in overall income distribution. Thus, in the period 1980-89 the income difference between pensioners' households — consistently the poorest group — and others was smallest in 1987 (table 5.17), with the widest gap in 1989 and 1990. Nominal incomes were deflated using the household cost of living indices published by the Central Statistical Office. The biggest changes in relative prosperity over the period occurred in peasant-workers' and farmers' households (table 5.18). Pensioner households experienced smaller changes. In 1988 and 1989, employees' incomes rose despite strong inflationary pressures, but high inflation in 1990, which was not fully compensated by wage increases, worsened their situation. (Somewhat similar changes occurred for farmers and peasant-workers.)

Table 5.17. **Relative economic distance between groups of households, Poland, 1980-1990**

Year	Employees	Farmers	Peasant-workers	Pensioners
1980	0.521	0.279	0.163	#[1]
1981	0.558	0.484	0.347	#
1982	0.510	0.475	0.406	#
1984	0.541	0.082	0.233	#
1985	0.509	0.476	0.479	#
1986	0.431	0.475	0.466	#
1987	0.242	0.367	0.320	#
1988	0.443	0.589	0.562	#
1989	0.606	0.907	0.828	#
1990	0.601	0.648	0.912	#

1. # denotes the household group with the lowest per capita monthly income.
Source: T. Panek: "Changes of income distribution of households in Poland, Diagnoses 1980-89. Projections 1990-92", in *Polish Population Review*, 1991.

Real income changes in the 1980s also varied within groups of households. Inequality of income distribution within groups may be measured by the maximum compensation coefficient: this shows what proportion of total income must be transferred from more to less affluent households to equalise income distribution. As table 5.19 shows, peasant-workers and farmers had the greatest income inequalities.

Table 5.18. **Relative economic distance between years for groups of households, Poland, 1980-1990**

Year	Employees	Farmers	Peasant-workers	Pensioner
1980	0.488	0.467	0.389	0.421
1981	0.505	0.563	0.488	0.512
1982	#[1]	0.34	0.233	0.066
1984	0.048	#	#	#
1985	0.183	0.395	0.363	0.161
1986	0.188	0.44	0.419	0.282
1987	0.1	0.423	0.394	0.372
1988	0.376	0.612	0.608	0.425
1989	0.519	0.855	0.811	0.316
1990[2]	0.239	0.22	0.646	0.529

2. Forecast based on the first 11 months.
1. (#) denotes the year in which given group of households has the lowest monthly income per capita.
Source: As table 5.17.

Table 5.19. **Maximum compensation coefficients (per cent)[1], Poland, 1980-1989**

Households	1980	1981	1982	1983	1984	1985	1986	1987	1988	1989
Employees	16.1	16.1	13.2	15.9	16.8	17.2	16.9	17.0	16.2	17.0
Peasant-workers	17.5	17.5	16.6	16.9	17.9	17.2	16.9	16.8	17.0	17.7
Farmers	22.7	22.7	20.5	25.3	25.6	23.9	22.9	22.6	23.4	24.2
Pensioners	16.5	16.5	11.5	15.2	17.0	15.8	14.9	15.2	15.2	16.4

1. Proportion of total income of group that must be translated from more to less affluent households to equalise income distribution.
Source: CSO: *Studia i Analizy Statystyczne*, (Warsaw).

The proportion of people with low real incomes increased sharply in 1990 as real household incomes fell overall. The share of those on low incomes in the second quarter of 1990, compared to 1985, jumped by 26 per cent for employees and by 16 per cent for pensioners (table 5.20).

Table 5.20. **Proportion of people with law incomes in groups of households (per cent), Poland, 1984-1990**

Households	1984	1985	1986	1987	1988	1989	1990 Q1	Q2	Q3
Employees	19.5	18.5	17.9	24.0	17.9	13.7	37.0	44.0	40.0
Peasant-workers	27.7	21.2	20.6	24.0	16.6	12.3	.	.	.
Farmers	32.8	30.3	29.8	32.0	24.9	22.3	.	.	.
Pensioners	37.4	34.9	28.9	27.0	28.4	26.4	41.0	51.0	39.0

Source: CSO: *Studia i Analizy Statystyczne,* (Warsaw).

Income versus needs

The lack of any significant improvement of real wages in the period 1985-88 and the subsequent deterioration in household incomes are strongly associated with changes in consumption patterns, notably the share of family expenditure on food. We present here the data for employee and pensioner households, and for the two lowest income groups, to highlight the plight of the poorest. Table 5.21 shows a tendency for the share of spending on food in total expenditure to decrease in both types of household between 1985 and 1988. Since real incomes made no progress over that period, lower spending on food was probably the result of changes in relative prices, with non-food prices rising faster than those for food. In pensioner households, spending on food takes a far higher share of incomes — 59 per cent in 1989 compared with 46 per cent for employee households. This is due not to the different age structure of pensioner households but to poverty. The share of food expenditure in the poorest employee households is also much higher than the average for that group.

Table 5.21. **Food spending as percentage of total expenditure: Poland, 1985-1989**

	1985	1986	1987	1988	1989	1990		
						Q1	Q2	Q3
	Employee households					Employee households		
All households	46.6	45.6	44.2	40.9	45.8	52.0	53.0	50.0
Lowest income group	55.4	53.3	50.7	46.4	51.1	64.0	64.0	60.0
Second lowest income group	60.3	56.0	53.7	46.0	0.0	75.0	67.0	64.0
	Pensioner households					Pensioner households		
All households	55.0	54.1	51.1	49.8	58.7	61.0	62.0	60.0
Lowest income group	59.8	59.6	57.2	54.1	58.5	72.0	69.0	65.0
Second lowest income group	58.8	60.4	56.9	55.0	6.0	62.0	65.0	66.0

Source: CSO: *Studia i Analizy Statystyczne*, (Warsaw).

The most dramatic changes in consumption patterns occurred in 1990 when the average share of food expenditure exceeded 50 per cent for employee households, and 60 per cent for pensioner households. In the lowest income groups the share of food expenditure ranges from 60 to 70 per cent, leaving little over to pay for other necessities such as housing and clothing. Housing, once cheap, has become increasingly expensive.

Subjective assessments of household living standards have been collected in three large-scale surveys, the results of which are summarised in table 5.22. They show that a decreasing number of people regard their economic situation as good and a rising number regard it as bad: these latter can be considered as living below the poverty line. The very high incidence of households in poverty among pensioners (about 35 per cent in 1990) is striking. Data for other groups of households for 1990 (table 5.23) show only a moderate difference between households of those employed in the state and private sectors. Business owners and professionals, and to a lesser extent farmers, rated the material situation of their families much better than did employees. Thus the largest proportion of households with incomes insufficient to satisfy basic needs was among pensioners.

Table 5.22. **Answers to the "Income evaluation question"[1], Poland, 1985-1990**

Answer No. (%)	Employee households			Pensioner households		
	1985	1989	1990	1985	1989	1990
1	1.5	1.4	1.3	0.9	0.8	0.7
2	21.3	17.8	16.3	14.8	11.3	10.0
3	48.9	52.8	38.5	33.1	35.0	22.3
4	21.4	21.4	28.2	32.7	33.1	31.4
5 or 6	6.9	6.6	15.7	18.5	19.8	35.5

Note :
1. The following "income evaluation question" was asked: "Which answer best reflects the income situation of your family?"
   1. Our income is sufficient for all our necessities.
   2. Our income is sufficient if we economise to some extent.
   3. We have to economise greatly to save for greater expenditures.
   4. We can buy only the cheapest food and clothing.
   5. Our income is just enough for the cheapest food but not enough for clothing.
   6. Our income is not enough even for the cheapest food.
Source: Unpublished data.

Table 5.23. **Answers to the "Income evaluation question"[1], Poland, 1990**

Answer No. (%)	Farmers' households	Peasant-workers' households	Private sector employees' households	Private owners' professional households
1	1.3	0.9	2.7	7.3
2	16.8	17.5	18.2	36.2
3	50.3	49.9	37.6	38.0
4	23.5	23.9	25.9	13.5
5 or 6	8.2	7.8	15.6	4.9

1. See table 5.22. for the "income evaluation question".
Source: Unpublished data.

Benefits and compensation for price increases

Under the command economy the State provided some free services (schools, health care) and subsidised certain products (transport, food, energy, housing) to keep prices low. However, many years of inefficient economic performance was detrimental to the quality of the services. Subsidies became inadequate and prices began to rise steeply, so that people had to pay more without the possibility of earning more. In the new situation of a partially reformed command economy, prices were too high for consumers and too low for producers. The Government tried in various ways to compensate incomes for price increases, but as such compensation consisted of frequently changing elements, people could not often say what their real incomes were.

Unemployment benefits

Unemployment benefits are paid to people who are registered as unemployed, with no offer of an appropriate local job (commensurate with education and skills), nor of a training place, nor of a place on a community public works scheme, and who have worked at least 180 days in the 12 months preceding registration.

In practice, the last restriction was the most significant in 1991. It denied benefits to some groups of people requiring work to supplement household income, such as women who had not previously worked because their husband's income was sufficient.

However, the 180-day rule has many exceptions. It does not apply to unemployed people who: have been dismissed in a mass lay-off; are under 18; are school-leavers; are the only bread-winner in the family; have registered within three months of finishing military service; have registered within three months of leaving prison; have returned to the labour force after raising children; have lost the right to draw a pension; have been employed for at least 20 years (male) or 15 years (female); or have a spouse drawing unemployment benefits.

Before the new Employment Act was introduced in December 1991 (limiting benefits to a maximum of 12 months) benefits were paid for an indefinite period unless the person was subject to some form of restriction. The most important related to refusal, without good reason, of two appropriate job offers within 30 days, or offers of a place on a community public works scheme. From 1991, benefit was set at 70 per cent of the previous wage for the first three months, it was 50 per cent for the next six months, and 40 per cent thereafter. The benefit was reduced to 50 per cent of the previous wage if the unemployed person searching for full-time work had started a part-time job. These are general rules. In many individual cases, benefits were paid under special regulations. Unemployed school-leavers received benefits for the first six months, based on 125 per cent of the minimum wage (graduates from higher education), and 110 per cent of the minimum wage (others). After six months the benefit was set at 95 per cent of the minimum wage for all school-leavers and other unemployed young people. In any event, benefits could not be lower than 95 per cent of the minimum wage or higher than the average wage.

There is some anecdotal evidence that a substantial number of those who receive benefits also work. Estimates vary from 30 to 60 per cent, but these may be influenced by negative views of the unemployed.

At the end of 1991, unemployment benefits legislation was changed to limit benefit payments to one year. This was intended to create an incentive for unemployed people to look for work. However, the effectiveness of these activities depends not only on the efforts of the unemployed, but also on the level of labour demand — and this is not going to recover quickly. Hence, some efforts to create (or stimulate the creation of) new jobs should be made by the State.

Unfortunately no information is available on the duration of unemployment. This means, inter alia, that it is not possible to calculate replacement ratios.

Social welfare system

Until the end of 1990, the social welfare system was still based on regulations dating from the 1950s. The Social Welfare Act of November 1990 sets out a basic framework for the new system.

The implementation of social assistance is the responsibility of municipalities and regional state administrations (voivodships), though the system of social welfare is funded mainly from the state budget. Local financial contributions are relatively small. In 1990 responsibility for social welfare was transferred from the Ministry of Health Care to the Ministry of Labour and Social Policy.

There were about 43,000 social workers in Poland at the end of 1990, of whom about 15,000 worked at the community level. There were also 510 social assistance offices with 52,800 employees. Grants for social welfare amounted to 4,989 billion zloty (plus 140 billion zloty for new investment).

In 1990, 1,534,000 people were covered by social assistance. In general, assistance reached the groups targeted, though the situation was worse in rural areas. It is probable that no more than 10 per cent of those receiving these benefits have any other, informal, sources of maintenance. In 1990, as a result of the new legislation, some 150,000 people left the register.[10]

Permanent or temporary social assistance benefit is set at 90 per cent of the minimum pension. It can be 30 per cent higher for people over the age of 75, disabled people, and pregnant women.

It must not be forgotten that the state system of social assistance is supported by voluntary associations (e.g., religious and charity organisations). The point to be emphasized, though, is that poverty on a large scale is a new phenomenon in Poland; in the past, basic needs at least were satisfied.

Minimum wage

The main function of the minimum wage has been in the calculation of benefits. Consequently, its level has been important not just for the lowest income group but for the majority of the whole population. It also plays an important role in incomes policy, and is subject to bargaining between the Government and trade unions. The minimum wage rose significantly throughout the 1980s, from 2,000 zloty a month in 1980 to 120,000 zloty a month in January 1990 and 555,000 zloty a month at the beginning of 1991.

Economically inactive population

In 1988 the inactive working-age population was almost 10 million, of whom some 56 per cent received various social benefits. The greater proportion (69 per cent) lived in urban areas, 35 per cent were elderly and 64 per cent were women. Of the inactive population aged 18-44, 56 per cent were women maintained by others. Including children, about 51 per cent of the Polish population is inactive, and the growth of official unemployment in 1990 has increased the burden on those in work.

The 18-44 age range constituted about 28 per cent of the total inactive population, the 18-59/64 age group 47 per cent. About 4,300,000 of inactive people, or 44 per cent, were not receiving social benefits. However, the proportion without any official source of maintenance was markedly different in the two broad working-age groups. In the 18-44 age group 76 per cent of the inactive population had no source of maintenance, about a quarter of them men. Only about 15 per cent of the inactive population aged 44 to 59/64 were without any source of social income.

Women outnumber men in all age groups of the inactive population except 15-17 year olds, a feature which is more marked among those without any official source of maintenance, a group considerably less qualified than average.

Wages, income policy and industrial relations

Wages and income policy

Prices and earnings

In the late 1970s the State lost a large measure of control over prices which rose rapidly in the 1980s. At the end of the decade the economy entered a period of hyper-inflation (figure 5.3).

In 1990 a stabilisation programme was introduced to check inflation. Although prices rose by 249.4 per cent over the year, the rate of inflation decreased (figure 5.4). The beginning of 1991 brought a new price shock, but one which was much less severe than in the previous year.

Figure 5.3. **Consumer price inflation, Poland, 1980-90**

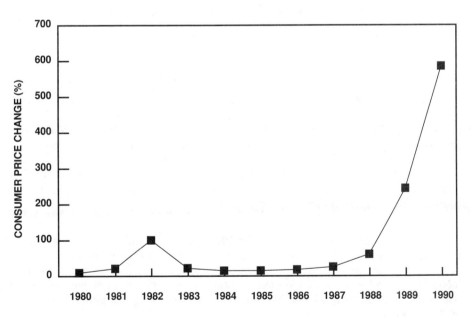

Figure 5.4. **Consumer price inflation, Poland, Janv. 1990-June 1991**

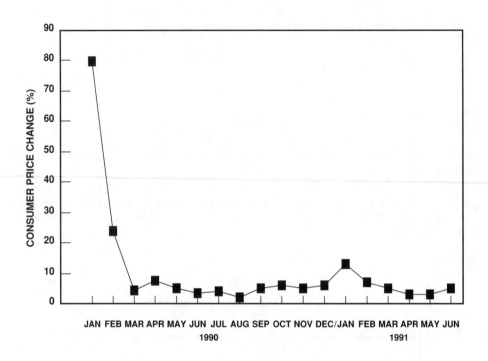

Information on employees' earnings is limited to the socialised sector. It is not possible to isolate the "tariff wage" within total pay in Polish statistics, but other wage elements and fringe benefits play an important role in family budgets. Virtually all groups of employees have some privileges, such as free transport, free coal and subsidised recreation. Bonuses play little incentive role as they are regarded as an "obligation" owed by the State. Also, their value is low, averaging 4 per cent of total remuneration in December 1990 in five economic sectors (mining and manufacturing, construction, transport, communications, and trade).

Nominal earnings rose steeply in the 1980s, but rapid inflation ensured that their real value grew by only 1.7 per cent over the period 1981-89. Wage setting was subject to an incomes policy.[11] However, enforcement measures were weak and inconsistent, and were not supported by other macro-and micro-economic policies. Although nominal earnings rose by 143 per cent in 1990, in real terms they declined by 30.4 per cent.

Earnings distribution

During the 1980s, the average real wage fell by 0.1 per cent in material production and rose by 14.2 per cent in non-material production (table 5.24).

Table 5.24. **Growth of nominal and real wages by sector (socialised economy), Poland, 1981-1989**

		1981-89 %	1988 %	1989 %
Total	N[1]	3 344.0	81.9	291.8
	R[2]	1.7	14.4	10.7
Manufacturing & mining	N	3 472.0	83.9	282.8
	R	5.6	15.7	8.1
Construction	N	2 870.0	77.4	251.0
	R	-12.3	11.6	-0.8
Agriculture	N	319.0	86.7	296.5
	R	1.0	17.4	12.0
Forestry	N	3 322.0	79.0	283.1
	R	1.1	12.6	8.2
Transport	N	2 915.0	86.9	260.7
	R	-13.9	17.5	1.9
Communications	N	2 979.0	106.1	228.6
	R	-9.0	29.6	-7.2
Trade	N	2 426.0	90.6	275.4
	R	4.2	19.9	6.0
Public utilities	N	2 953.0	77.1	287.2
	R	-8.8	11.4	9.3
Housing	N	3 263.0	69.7	288.7
	R	-0.6	6.7	9.8
Research & Development	N	3 136.0	84.1	233.6
	R	-4.4	15.8	-8.6
Education	N	3 941.0	64.2	419.4
	R	19.4	3.3	46.7
Culture & arts	N	3 692.0	80.3	318.4
	R	12.0	13.3	18.2
Health care & Social welfare	N	3 901.0	81.7	368.8
	R	18.2	14.3	32.4
Sports tourism & recreation	N	3 549.0	80.9	279.6
	R	7.8	13.8	7.2
Public administration & justice	N	3 885.0	71.7	346.5
	R	17.7	8.0	26.1
Finance & insurance	N	5 085.0	75.9	418.4
	R	53.2	10.6	46.4
Material sphere	N	3 281.0	84.4	276.8
	R	-0.1	16.0	6.4
Non-material sphere	N	3 767.0	72.9	355.7
	R	14.2	8.7	28.7

1. N : nominal wages.
2. R : real wages.
Source: Socha, 1990.

Traditionally, earnings in mining are particularly high (63.3 per cent above the average in the socialised sector in 1989), whereas in non-material production they are below average (10.6 per cent in 1989). These have been stable elements of the earnings structure over many years. However, this situation is slowly changing.

Within the socialised sector (with the exception of mining), the earnings distribution curve is flat and more employees receive below-average than above-average pay.

Tables 5.25 to 5.28 provide information on the earnings structure in the economy in May 1990, by sector, age, sex, length of employment in one job and level of education. Four facts stand out:

— average pay remained the highest in mining;

— the average pay of women was much lower than that of men in the whole economy and in all sectors. This difference was slightly smaller for women with higher education, where the differential was 18.6 per cent;

— men over 40 (and especially over 60) were the highest earners;

— average pay displayed a positive correlation with educational attainment.

Table 5.25. **Average monthly earnings by sector, Poland, May 1990**

Sector	Total	Male	Female	F/M(%[1])
Manufacturing	811.0	899.3	680.6	75.7
Mining	1 242.0	1 320.2	741.3	56.2
Construction	837.4	865.8	710.3	82.0
Agriculture	764.5	790.7	690.4	87.3
Forestry	754.6	790.9	625.5	79.1
Transport	750.0	779.0	651.5	83.6
Communication	675.1	731.7	635.3	86.8
Trade	647.0	729.8	608.9	83.4
Other material sphere	878.6	1 007.3	721.5	71.6
Public utilities	812.8	869.6	660.7	76.0
Housing	704.9	762.7	626.9	82.2
Research & development	817.2	900.6	722.3	80.2
Education	812.6	949.8	773.4	81.4
Culture & arts	755.9	809.1	726.1	89.7
Health	712.3	853.5	680.8	79.8
Sports, tourism & recreation	759.5	901.3	648.3	71.9
Other non-material sphere	605.3	690.5	561.6	81.3
Public Administration	819.0	955.0	753.1	78.9
Finance & insurance	936.9	1 003.9	921.2	91.8
Five main industries[2]	809.0	904.8	660.6	73.0
Socialised sector	777.9	909.1	738.0	81.2
Material production	803.8	886.6	663.5	74.8
Non-material production	775.6	886.0	735.8	83.0

1. Female earnings as a percentage of male earnings.
2. Of the socialised sector, namely mining & manufacturing, construction, transport, communications and trade.
Source: CSO: *Badanie plac, maj 1990,* (Warsaw).

Table 5.26. Average monthly earnings by age[1], Poland, May 1990

Age	Total	Male	Female	F/M(%)[2]
Under 20	534.6	574.2	475.7	82.8
20-24	611.3	665.2	559.3	84.1
25-29	721.6	787.8	628.1	79.7
30-34	766.6	860.2	652.9	75.9
35-39	801.3	911.6	683.1	74.9
40-49	842.3	946.8	739.9	78.1
50-59	873.2	949.2	767.3	80.8
60-64	+ 954.9	999.3	797.2	79.8
65 and over	945.2	991.5	752.1	75.9

1. In the five main industries of the socialised sector, namely mining & manufacturing, construction, transport, communications and trade.
2. Female earnings as a percentage of male earnings.
Source: CSO: *Badanie plac, maj 1990*, (Warsaw).

Table 5.27. Average montlhy earnings by period in employment[1], Poland, May 1990

Period (years)	Total	Male	Female	F/M(%)[2]
Below [1]	578.8	635.7	541.9	85.2
1-2	601.0	651.5	563.1	86.4
3-5	644.4	708.7	577.1	81.4
6-10	719.0	797.2	600.3	75.3
11-15	768.9	870.5	631.6	72.6
16-20	808.6	916.0	698.4	76.2
20 & over	911.7	981.0	806.4	82.2

1. In the five mains industries of the socialised sector, namely mining & manufacturing, construction, transport, communications and trade.
2. Female earnings as a percentage of male earnings.
Source: CSO: *Badanie plac, maj 1990*, (Warsaw).

Table 5.28. Average monthly earnings by level of education[1], Poland, May 1990

Education	Total	Male	Female	F/M (%)	Male	Female
					highest = 100	
Tertiary	1 089.9	1 200.6	977.4	81.4	100.0	100.0
Secondary	803.7	905.8	732.2	80.8	77.9	74.9
Secondary, technical	806.0	918.7	711.6	77.5	76.5	72.8
Secondary general	750.2	837.9	663.5	79.2	69.8	67.9
Lower technical	761.1	842.1	603.9	71.7	70.1	61.8
Elementary	726.3	818.2	605.2	74.0	68.2	61.9

1. In the five main industries of the socialised sector, namely mining & manufacturing, construction, transport, communications and trade.
Source: CSO: *Badanie plac, maj 1990*, (Warsaw).

Wage policy

Several forms of wage policiy were introduced in the 1980s. However, their effects were limited because of lax financial discipline, exemptions and the politically powerful position of workers' councils.

Wage policy in Poland is based on a monthly indexation scheme, using an indexation coefficient determined by the Government. The indexation coefficient determines the ceiling on wage increases which are not liable to a punitive tax *(popiwek)*. This tax amounts to 500 per cent of the excess increase.

Actual and forecast changes in the retail price level are given by the Ministry of Finance. The difference between the two figures for a given month is the basis on which the wage ceiling for the following months is calculated.

In 1990, the punitive tax was related to overall wage costs. In 1991 it became a tax on the wage per worker. Only socialised enterprises are subject to wage policy.

In the first two quarters of 1990 actual wage increases were significantly below the ceiling. In the third quarter wage growth exceeded monthly targets but enterprises were able to avoid the tax by taking advantage of the unused wage increase from the first two quarters. Some possible explanations for the remarkable wage moderation of early 1990 are offered in Coricelli and Revenga (1991), Rutkowski (1991), and Schaffer (1991). The authors stress the uncertainty concerning the future of enterprises, and hence jobs. However, there is no indication that the introduction of the new market-based economic policy led to plant closures and mass unemployment. There is also no indication, as confirmed by many successful strikes that workers lost their strong position. Hence, other factors may have played an important role in inducing wage moderation, including the time it took workers to become accustomed to rising indexes and political factors. One trade union (Solidarity) was heavily involved in the new Government, while another (Ogolnopolskie Porozumienie Zwiazkow Zawodowych or OPZZ) was restricted politically owing to connections with the previous regime.

In the second half of 1990 and in 1991, wage increases significantly exceeded norms in many areas of the economy. Incomes policy has become one of the most important political issues in the country. In 1991, certain regulations on wage increases were modified and a new wage norm established, independent of enterprises' 1990 wage levels. In addition, wage ceilings were linked to firms' profitability: enterprises with rising profits were allowed to pay higher wages without incurring tax penalties.

Productivity

Data on productivity are published in Polish statistics for mining, manufacturing and construction only. This is because productivity is calculated using net production instead of value added. Data on productivity growth in mining and manufacturing over the 1980s are provided in table 5.29. It will be seen that earnings growth bore little relation to productivity growth. Productivity fell dramatically in 1990. In mining and manufacturing it fell 21.1 per cent in the first three quarters of the year.

Table 5.29. **Productivity growth mining and manufacturing, Poland, 1980-1989**

	Average nominal wages	% Change 1980-1989 in:	
		Earnings	Productivity
Sector			
Total	3 476	4	12.9
Coal	3 296	-1.2	-70.6
Fuel	4 308	28.2	-40.1
Power	3 729	11.4	-70.1
Basic metals	3 108	-6.7	-30.2
Non-ferrous metals	3 588	7.3	-2.7
Metal products	3 267	-2.1	77.2
Engineering	3 246	2.7	138.3
Precision instruments and apparatus	3 479	1.2	173
Transport equipment	3 194	-4.2	27.2
Electrical engineering and electronics	3 492	4.5	97.4
Chemicals	3 585	7.2	39.7
Building materials	3 149	-5.2	23.2
Glass products	3 278	-1.7	30
Pottery and china	3 411	2.1	76.6
Wood	3 508	4.9	112.6
Paper	3 708	10.8	46
Textiles	3 548	6.1	63.5
Clothing	3 405	1.9	81.1
Leather	3 428	2.6	15.7
Food	3 861	15.2	44.1

Source: Socha, 1990.

In the vast majority of enterprises (84.3 per cent) employment fell in this period. However, in only 38.8 per cent of enterprises was the fall in employment greater than 10 per cent (in 8.1 per cent the drop in employment was above 25 per cent). A moderate reduction of employment (from 2 to 10 per cent) had a positive effect on average earnings in enterprises, because workers could be paid more while avoiding the restrictive wage tax. However, in those enterprises which laid off more than 10 per cent of their workers, average compensation fell simultaneously with employment.

Industrial relations

Industrial relations in Poland have been strongly dominated by state and Communist Party structures. The development of modern industrial relations requires the removal of the old structures, and time. Ownership of the bulk of the national economy accords the State the role of super-entrepreneur. This is awkward for the authorities and distorts industrial relations.

Trade unions had to fight for their independent existence for many years, and throughout that time they developed their political power rather than acquiring experience in solving workers' economic problems.

There were no entrepreneurs' organisations under the old system. An organisation has recently emerged but remains rather weak, as the private sector is still only a small part of the economy and there are relatively few private firms which employ hired workers in addition to the owner and his or her family. However, within private firms entrepreneurs are in a strong position to deter union activity.

Workers' councils are very powerful in state enterprises and not only because they lack any effective opposition. Workers have been fighting for their rights for a long time. In 1980 and 1981, they tried to establish new workplace relations, a struggle that was interrupted by martial law. Afterwards, some rights were granted to workers but remained on paper, as the authorities felt strong enough to block any attempt to use these rights in practice. Since the end of 1989 the State's power has waned and these rights have become real. Nowadays, workers' councils have a predominant role in state enterprises, and through them workers can put strong pressure on management. This includes securing the dismissal of directors, a practice which has become increasingly common.

Workers' councils became a leading force in enterprise decision-making after the collapse of the command system, and now a worker-managed firm is often a state enterprise at which directors and workers are on the same side against the state economic administration.

Unionisation

Information on unionisation is based mainly on anecdotal evidence and is limited and often inconsistent. There were 155 nation-wide trade unions legally registered in Poland at the end of 1990, the largest being Solidarity and OPZZ. According to OPZZ, it had 126 associated unions. Anecdotal sources suggest that some 30-40 of these trade unions were nation-wide organisations.

Estimates of membership vary. OPZZ leaders claimed to have about 5.2 million members in June 1990, but this number has since declined. Solidarity leaders claimed to have about 2.3 million members in July 1991, and this number is increasing. Data provided by unions, particularly small ones, tend to exaggerate numbers. Membership data of some smaller unions sometimes suggested that the total number of union members in a sector exceeded the numbers employed. Union data are inconsistent with data collected by the Central Statistical Office, which suggest that members of all unions totalled 5,064,000 at the end of 1990, of which 2,294,000 were women.[12]

According to the Spoleczne inquiry, (1991), 8.6 per cent of dismissed employees claimed they were members of Solidarity, and 4.9 per cent members of OPZZ.

Trade unions, especially Solidarity, have ceased to represent a political opposition and consequently many people are less interested in membership. (Solidarity claimed to have 10 million members in 1981.)

As of 1991, a new law regulating trade union activity is expected. Under the present regulations, many strikes are illegal, but strikes are not the only problem under the present industrial relations system. For example, workers remain members of trade unions after retirement. New legislation is also planned for collective agreements.

Notes

1. It has been common to use the concept of employment in relation only to the socialised sector. For others receiving wages, salaries or incomes from work the term "working population" has been used. This report, however, treats "employment" as equivalent to "working population".

2. These groups overlap to some extent, which may lead to an overestimation of hidden unemployment.

3. Two models have been compared: one for a market economy (the British economy in the 1960s), and the other for a command economy (the Polish economy in the 1980s).

4. See Bednarski (1991) for detailed information on the parallel economy in Poland.

5. The fitted line trend is as follows:

$$U = -45.34 + 103.18t$$
$$(32.11) \quad (2.68) \quad R^2 = 0.99$$

where U stands for the number of unemployed and t for months. Standard errors of the coefficients are reported in parentheses.

6. Data are available only since August 1990.

7. See Gora and Lehmann (1991).

8. This rough estimate is based on data on the fall in employment and on changes in the number of vacancies.

9. See Dagum (1980).

10. According to information provided by the Ministry of Labour and Social Policy.

11. See Socha (1990) for a more detailed analysis of wage policies in the 1980s.

12. Unpublished data.

References

BEDNARSKI, M. 1991. *Drugi obieg gospodarczy.* (Warsaw, Przeslanki, mechanizmy i skutki w Polsce lat osiemdziesiatych).

BEDNARSKI, M. and KOKOSZCZYNSKI, R. 1990. "Drugi obieg a dochod narodowy", in *Gospodarka nieoficjalna.* (Rzeszow, Uwarunkowania lokalne i systemowe).

BLASZKIEWICZ, A. 1990, *Zatrudnienie — ruch kadrowy — zwolnienia — przyjecia*, (Warsaw, Solidarnosc; mimeo).

GORA, M. (1990), *The Post-CPE Market Economy in Poland: Remarks on the Labour Market,* Conference of the European Association of Labour Economists (papers), Lund.

GORA, M. (1991), "Labour Market in Transition: Poland 1990", in *International Labour Review* (Geneva, ILO), No 2, 1991.

GORA, M. and LEHMANN, H. (1991), *Flow and Stock Analysis of Polish Unemployment: January 1990-May 1991*, Working Paper No. 129, Centre for Economic Performance, London School of Economics.

GORA, M. and RUTKOWSKI, M. (1990), "The demand for Labour and the Disguised Unemployment in Poland in the 1980s", *in Communist Economies* 2, No. 3, pp. 325-335.

KOTOWSKA, I. (1991a), *Application of the LIPRO model for Poland's population projection till 2050* (in Polish), Warsaw, Monografie i Opracowania 16/331, Instytut Statystyki i Demografii SGPiS.

KOTOWSKA, I. (1991b), "Demographic determinants of the labour market in Poland", in *Polish Population Review.*

NOWICKI, J. (1986), *On Disguised Unemployment in the Centrally-Planned Economy,* Working Paper 86-09, Warsaw, World Economy Research Institute, Central School of Planning and Statistics.

OLEKSYN, T. (1991), *Polityka zatrudnienia i plac w przedsiebiorstwach przemyslowych,* Warsaw, Institute of Labour and Social Studies; mimeo.

RUTKOWSKI, M. (1990), *Labour Hoarding and Future Open Unemployment in Eastern Europe: The Case of Polish Industry,* Discussion Paper No. 6, Centre for Economic Performance, London School of Economics.

SPOLECZNE, (1991), *Aspekty bezrobocia w Polsce,* Warsaw, Institute of Labour and Social Studies; mimeo.

TULSKI, J. and WOZNIAKOWSKI, A. (1990), *Miejsce i rola sektora prywatnego w polityce wzrostu zatrudnienia,* Warsaw, Institute of Labour and Social Studies; mimeo.

DAGUM, C. (1980), "Inequality Measures Between Income Distribution with Applications", in *Econometrica,* 48, 7.

PANEK, T. (1990) *Living Conditions of the Population in Poland in 1989 and in the First Half of 1990* (in Polish); Research Centre for Statistical and Economic Analyses of the Central Statistical Office and Polish Academy of Sciences, Warsaw.

PANEK, T. (1991), "Changes of Income Distribution of Households in Poland. Diagnoses 1980-89. Projections 1990-92", in *Polish Population Review.*

CORICELLI AND REVENGA (1991), *Wages and unemployment in Poland: Recent developments and policy issues,* Washington D.C., World Bank; mimeo.

RUTKOWSKI, M. (1991), *Is the labour market adjustment in Poland surprising?* Washington D.C., World Bank; mimeo.

SCHAFFER, M.E. (1991), *A Note on the Polish State-owned Enterprise Sector in 1990,* Working Paper No. 106, Centre for Economic Performance, London School of Economics.

SOCHA, M. (1990), "Wynagrodzenia", in Z. Morecka, (ed.), *Podzial w latach osiemdziesiatych.* Kontynuacja czy zmiana, Wydzial Nauk Ekonomicznych, Warsaw University.

SPOLECZNE, (1991), *Aspekty bezrobocia w Polsce,* Warsaw, Institute of Labour and Social Studies, Warsaw; mimeo.

Chapter 6

Romania: labour market trends and policies

by Georghe Raboaca
Labour and Social Protection Research Institute
Bucharest

Introduction

Romania's transition to a market economy that began in December 1989 has seen the beginnings of a fundamental reorganisation of the country's labour market, social policies and system of industrial relations. This reorganisation is leading Romania away from authoritarian control to a decentralised and democratic-based form of government. While transition has proved difficult, Romania has taken the first steps towards transforming its economy and social support system. The framework for a comprehensive restructuring process is now in place.

At the beginning of 1990, a broad range of measures designed to facilitate transition was introduced, including price liberalisation, introduction of wage policies, and the creation of new institutions and policies to encourage tripartism and ensure social protection in changing economic conditions. Meanwhile, the old order was being dismantled and the seriousness of the economic crisis facing the nation became increasingly apparent.

Economic and social action since December 1989 has concentrated on four broad areas of concern:

1. *Legislation.* New laws have been adopted and old laws modified or repealed on a host of issues dealing with protecting the disadvantaged, facilitating economic transition and introducing the right to free association and collective bargaining.

2. *Establishment of a new institutional framework.* The Government has embarked on a complete restructuring of social institutions. District-level labour and social protection agencies have been reorganised. The role and responsibilities of trade unions and employer associations have been recast. The training and job placement services provided by employment offices are being overhauled and information-gathering techniques refined.

3. *Development of a policy framework to facilitate economic transition.* Movement from a command system to one based on market principles requires a co-ordinated policy to promote labour flexibility, privatisation and economic efficiency. To this end, the Government has abolished the system of state-subsidised enterprises and implemented a concerted programme to privatise agriculture, industry and services. Efforts to encourage labour mobility have accelerated. Policies governing wage increases and price liberalisation have been introduced.

4. *Development of an effective system of social protection.* A broad range of social protection measures has been implemented including the establishment of a minimum wage, provision of unemployment benefit and family allowances, assistance in retraining, and exemption from taxation for those with low incomes.

Responding to these policy challenges is difficult because people lack experience in market practices, many are resistant to change and the economic system is riddled with inefficiency. Furthermore, economic conditions have deteriorated rapidly because of poor economic planning and the collapse of trade relations with the Council for Mutual Economic Assistance (CMEA).

Table 6.1 shows the dramatic decline of the main economic indicators in 1990, a trend which continued in 1991. During the first five months of 1991, industrial production declined 26.8 per cent from the same period in 1990, exports were down 29.8 per cent and investment fell by 29.5 per cent.[1] Clearly, economic expansion is needed in Romania to increase the supply of goods and services. However, if adequate social protection measures are not implemented, economic transition will fail. Economic development must be accompanied by a just and effective system of social support.

Table 6.1. **Main economic indicators, Romania, 1990**

Indicator	Index 1990 (1989=100) (estimate)
Industrial production	80.2
Agricultural production	97.1
New construction	62.0
Investments	61.7
Exports	58.3
Imports	114.4
Employed population	101.5
Labour productivity (per employed person)	90.8
Nominal wage	110.5
Real wage	104.6

Source: National Statistics Commission: *1990 Statistical Annual.*

172

Labour market developments

The labour market in Romania is undergoing significant change. However, it has been somewhat insulated from the effects of restructuring and a declining economy by Government policy. The Government has sought to soften the blow of transition labour market with a series of protective measures. Although exports, productivity and investment declined dramatically in 1990-91, wages and employment levels have increased.

Labour demand

Employment steadily increased during the 1980s, a trend which accelerated between 1988 and 1990. From 1980 to 1988 the number of employed rose on average by 0.6 per cent per year. In 1989, the employed population grew by 1.3 per cent and in 1990 by 1.5 per cent for a total employed population of over 11 million. Tables 6.2 and 6.3 present data on employment by sector from 1980 to 1990.

Table 6.2. **Change in employment by economic sector, Romania, 1980-89**

Economic sector	Annual change in employment (%)		Sector share of total employment (%)		
	1980-88	1989	1980	1989	1990
Industry	1.5	8.5	45.3	47.5	50.9
Construction	-0.9	-33.3	10.7	8.9	5.9
Agriculture/forestry	1.0	1.7	8.2	8.2	8.3
Transport and communications	0.6	1.9	8.9	8.7	8.8
Trade	0.3	-10.6	8.5	8.7	7.1
Household services	3.9	-59.5	4.6	5.7	2.3
Education/culture/art	-1.4	13.3	5.7	4.5	5.1
Health	0.4	6.3	3.7	3.6	3.8
Administration	-1.9	11.3	0.8	0.6	0.7
Other branches	4.0	84.4	3.2	3.9	7.1
Total economy	1.0	1.3	100	100	100

Note : Totals may not add up to 100 owing to rounding.
Source: National Statistics Commission: *Statistical Annual* (various years).

Table 6.3. **Increase in employment in industry and agriculture, Romania, 1980-90**

	Annual average increase (%)		Proportion of total employment (%)		
	1980-89	1989-90	1980	1989	1990
Employed population	0.62	1.5	100	100	100
of which:					
- Industry	1.13	0.8	35.5	38.1	37.8
- Agriculture	-0.01	-0.4	29.4	27.5	27.0

Source: National Statistics Commission: *Statistical Annual* (Various years).

The large increase in the number of employed in 1990 is due to a variety of factors. These include a reduction of the working week from 46 to 40 hours, less stringent application of employment standards, an increased number of people taking job leave, and the granting of maternity leave to those with children less than a year old.

The rise in employment was accompanied by a decline in labour productivity of 7.2 per cent by the end of 1990 (see table 6.4). A high degree of labour hoarding and the inefficient use of resources were to blame.[2] Regardless of economic considerations, enterprises hired additional labour to ensure that production goals were met. For example, the high employment growth recorded in the industrial sector in 1989 of 8.5 per cent was unjustified in economic terms; in 1991 many of these enterprises will have failed.

Table 6.4. **Growth of labour productivity, Romania, 1980-90 (1980=100)**

	1980	1985	1986	1987	1988	1989	1990
Labour productivity[1]	100	111.5	112.8	112.6	110.6	102.6	92.8

1. Calculations based on total employed population.
Source: National Statistics Commission: *Statistical Annual* (various years).

It is difficult to estimate the degree of privatisation in Romania. At the beginning of 1991, 93 per cent of those employed worked in the state sector.[3] Growing private sector activity contributed to the decline in jobs in the trade and household services sectors (see table 6.2). The impact of privatisation is most marked in agriculture. Approximately 70 per cent of all agricultural workers were previously employed in state co-operatives, which are now disbanded. This raised private activity in agriculture from 15.4 per cent in 1989 to 60-65 per cent in 1991. According to data released in May 1991, the number of people involved in private, non-agricultural activities was 142,713, up from 97,499 at the beginning of the year. Table 6.5 gives a breakdown of private sector employment by type of enterprise.

The structure of employment by company size is also changing. In industry, larger firms now account for a greater share of total employment than in the past (table 6.6).

Table 6.5. **Growth in private enterprise employment by type of enterprise (non-agricultural sectors), Romania, December 1990 - May 1991**

	Number of employed				
	Small enterprises	Work associations	Family associations	Independent persons	Total
December 1990	23 026	3 996	20 045	50 432	97 499
May 1991	25 481	3 993	35 777	77 462	142 713
% change	10.7	-0.1	78.5	53.6	46.4

Source: National Statistics Commission: *Statistical Annual* (Various years).

Table 6.6. **Distribution of enterprises and employees in industry by enterprise size, Romania, 1980-89**

	Enterprises		Employees	
	1980	1989	1980	1989
Total industry (number)	1 752	2 102	3 198 100	3 690 200
Percentage share				
Up to 200	8.5	6.7	0.7	0.5
201-500	19.5	18.8	4.1	3.6
501-1 000	23.0	23.4	10.2	9.3
1,001-2,000	23.3	22.4	20.2	17.0
2,001-3,000	11.5	12.5	17.1	16.7
3,001-5,000	8.5	9.4	19.5	20.1
Over 5,000	5.7	6.9	28.2	32.9

Note : Percentages may not add up exactly owing to rounding.
Source: National Statistics Commission: *Statistical Annual* (various years).

Labour supply

Romania's population at the beginning of 1991 was 23,190,000, down by about 20,000 over the previous year. The natural growth rate of 2.9 per 1,000 inhabitants in 1990 was insufficient to offset the number leaving the country (3.3 persons per 1000 inhabitants). Some 80,250 Romanians emigrated that year, a third of them skilled workers.[4]

The natural rate of growth fell from 5.3 per cent in 1989 to 2.9 per cent in 1990. This is a direct result of a decreasing birth rate and a high infant mortality rate. Romania had a very low birth rate, with only 13.6 live births per 1,000 inhabitants, the result of lifting sanctions on abortion and wider availability of contraception. In 1990 there were 992,000 abortions compared to 185,000 in 1989. Although the adult mortality rate of 10.7 per 1,000 inhabitants is close to that in developed countries, the infant mortality rate of 26.9 per 1,000 live births is one of the highest in Europe.

The age structure of employment changed in the period 1980 to 1990 (table 6.7), notably with a decline in employment among the 16-19 and 50-plus age groups. For young people, this resulted primarily from the falling birth rate. For older workers, it was due to more early retirement, for health and other reasons.

The labour force participation rate for the decade 1980-90 was about 81 per cent. The participation rate for women increased from 74 per cent in 1980 to 76.8 per cent in 1990, offsetting a decline for men (table 6.8).

The proportion of women in the total labour force rose from 43.9 per cent in 1980 to 45.2 per cent in 1989. This was due primarily to a greater need for two incomes per family and the expansion of certain sectors where large numbers of women are employed.[5] Table 6.9 gives data on the proportion of women in the labour force by occupational group.

Table 6.7. **Structure of employment by age group, Romania, 1979 and 1990 (percentages)**

Age group (years)	Total		Of which: women	
	1979	1990	1979	1990
Total	100	100	100	100
- Under 16	0.2	0.2	0.2	0.2
- 16-19	4.3	3.7	5.1	4.0
- 20-24	13.6	12.3	16.8	13.8
- 25-29	16.6	12.9	18.9	14.1
- 30-34	14.2	15.8	15.0	17.2
- 35-39	13.1	16.5	12.9	17.6
- 40-44	13.1	14.2	12.4	14.1
- 45-49	11.0	10.8	9.6	10.2
- 50-54	8.0	8.1	6.4	6.1
- 55-59	5.1	4.7	2.5	2.3
- over 50	0.9	0.8	0.2	0.1

Note : Percentages may not add up exactly owing to rounding.
Source: National Statistics Commission: *Statistical Annual* (various years).

Table 6.8. **Employment in Romania: Romania, 1980-89**

	1980	1985	1987	1988	1989	1990
Labour force (000s)						
Total[1]	12 770.5	13 217.6	13 376.0	13 430.6	13 482.0	...
Women	6 141.5	6 326.5	6 404.3	6 435.9	6 444.4	...
Employment (000s)						
Total	10 350.1	10 586.1	10 718.6	10 805.4	10 945.7	...
Women	4 546.8	4 757.8	4 853.2	4 889.5	4 942.6	...
Employment rate (%)						
Total	81.0	80.1	80.1	80.5	81.2	81.0
Women	74.0	75.2	75.8	76.0	76.7	76.8

1. Labour resources include pupils and working-age students on day courses or in secondary and higher education. If they were not included in labour resources, employment rates would be greater. These would be swollen further if members of the armed forces and of public organisations were included in the employed population. Data for 1990 are provisional.
Source: National Statistics Commission: *Statistical Annual* (various years).

Table 6.9. **Proportion of women in the labour force by occupational group, Romania, 1989 and 1990**

	Women as percentage of labour force				TESA[1]	
	Non manual Non-TESA[1]		Manual			
	1989	1990	1989	1990	1989	1990
Total economy	40.4	41.4	37.7	38.6	51.0	51.7

1. Technical, economic, specialised and administration personnel.
Source: National Statistics Commission. *Statistical Annual* (various years).

However, the number of women in the labour force grew more slowly than men, by 0.5 per cent in 1989 compared to 1.3 per cent for all workers and by 0.1 per cent in 1990 compared to 1.5 per cent for all workers.

Table 6.10 presents data on the educational level of Romania's workforce. Some 78.5 per cent of workers are classified as blue-collar and 21.5 per cent as white-collar. This proportion varies, however, from sector to sector. Blue-collar workers make up a greater proportion in the production sphere of the economy. White-collar workers predominate in sectors such as scientific research (59.9 per cent), education, culture and arts (88.1 per cent) and health (85.3 per cent). Table 6.11 gives information on employment levels by sector and occupation.

Table 6.10. **Employed population by educational level, Romania, 1990**

	Total	Higher education	Secondary	Professional schools	Other courses
Thousands	7 905.7	691.9	1 900.3	2 486.3	2 827.2
Percentage	100	8.7	24.0	31.4	35.7

Note: Percentages do not add up exactly owing to rounding.
Source: National Statistics Commission: 1990 *Statistical Annual.*

Table 6.11. **Average annual change in employment by sector and occupation, Romania, 1980-89**

Sector	Annual average increase (%) 1980-89	% within sector 1989
Industry	1.5	100
Employees	1.51	95.3
Co-operative craftsmen	0.31	3.3
Associated craftsmen	10.81	0.4
Private craftsmen	1.43	1.0
Construction	-1.18	100
Employees	0.86	92.6
Co-operative craftsmen	-5.11	4.9
Associated craftsmen	1.43	0.4
Private craftsmen	-0.11	2.1
Agriculture	-0.11	100
Employees	1.02	16.0
Co-operative craftsmen	-0.41	67.2
Co-operative associates	1.57	1.4
Private agriculture	-0.07	15.4
Transport	0.80	100
Employees	0.42	92.4
Private transporters	8.86	7.6
Trade	0.52	100
Employees	0.48	99.1
Associates	7.73	0.6
Private businessmen	4.77	0.3
Household services: *of which:*	4.02	88.0
Building administration staff	11.59	6.2
Private craftsmen	-1.14	1.9
Home-working employees	-5.31	3.6
Associates	-	0.2

Source: National Statistics Commission: *Statistical Annual* (various years).

Labour mobility

The move to a market economy has revealed the need to promote greater labour mobility in Romania. Districts in the north-eastern part of the country have an excess supply of workers while many others have labour shortages. The command economy resulted in an inefficient distribution of workers among enterprises; if productivity is to be raised nationally, workers need to move jobs. Rural areas also need workers because the population there is ageing more rapidly than elsewhere.

Regional, urban and rural economic structures must be redesigned to promote labour mobility. The Government's policies to reform agriculture and liberalise prices should help working people to relocate. In addition, the Government will need to provide more training, especially for the young, to facilitate labour market mobility. Job creation efforts and the provision of social support systems will also help this process. Without a strong economy and improved mobility, Romania runs the risk of losing greater numbers of workers, especially the well-qualified, through emigration.

Unemployment

Although economic reorganisation has just started, unemployment has grown in Romania. In April 1991 the number of unemployed people receiving benefits was 42,583; by June this figure had reached 104,436. Predictions of future unemployment rates are difficult to make but, considering that unprofitable businesses are just beginning to go bankrupt, unemployment should increase substantially.

The above figures are based on the number of people who are eligible to receive unemployment compensation. There is a second category of unemployed: those not eligible for benefits but registered at an employment office. There were 69,088 people in this category in April 1991 and 65,503 in June. While it is encouraging that the number in this group has declined, this could be attributed to the fact that fewer people see the need to register.

Tables 6.12 and 6.13 present data on those eligible to receive unemployment compensation and those registered at an employment office. The unemployment rate, based on both groups of unemployed, was 1.0 per cent in April 1991 and 1.5 per cent in June. Table 6.14 gives the unemployment rate by labour force group in 1991.[6]

Certain groups are more affected by joblessness than others, notably women: they accounted for 54 per cent of the unemployed against roughly 45 per cent of the total workforce. Higher unemployment rates for women run across professional and educational groups. Among registered unemployed who are not eligible for benefits, women made up 74 per cent.

Manual workers are also more likely to be unemployed than non-manual workers. Of those receiving benefits, 86 per cent were manual workers. This is because manual workers predominate in those sectors where inefficiency was highest and where the first major job cuts occurred.

Redundancies account for 88 per cent of the unemployed, with the remaining 12 per cent jobless for a variety of reasons including disciplinary dismissals and entrance to the labour market.

Table 6.12. **Number receiving unemployment benefits, Romania, 1991**

Group	April 1991		June 1991	
	Number	%	Number	%
Number receiving benefits	42 583	100.0	104 436	100.0
of whom: women	22 732	53.4	56 215	53.8
Manual workers	36 466	85.6	89 803	86.0
of whom: women	19 126	44.9	47 337	45.3
Other professional categories				
Advanced secondary education	4 525	10.6	10 699	10.2
of whom: women	2 766	6.5	6 773	6.5
Basic secondary education	1 592	3.7	3 934	3.8
of whom: women	840	2.0	2 105	2.0
Number unemployed through reduced enterprise activity	33 523	78.7	91 744	87.8

Source: National Statistics Commission.

Table 6.13. **Unemployed registered but not receiving benefits, Romania, 1991**

	April		June	
	Number	%	Number	%
Persons registered	69 335	100	65 503	100
of whom:				
- Women	49 088	70.8	47 141	72.0
- Qualified workers	36 644	52.9	33 191	50.7
- High-school graduates	22 864	33.0	19 247	29.4
- TESA[1]	1 778	2.6	1 483	2.3
- Unqualified persons	30 913	44.6	30 829	47.1
of whom:				
- Without secondary-school education	6 782	9.8	6 556	10.0

1. Technical, economic, specialised and administrative personnel.
Source: National Statistics Commission.

Table 6.14. **Unemployment rate, Romania, 1991**

	April 1991	June 1991
Unemployed as % of employed population[1]	1.0	1.53
Unemployed as % of number of employees	1.4	2.1

1. Includes those employed in agriculture.
Source: National Statistics Commission.

There is no reliable information on the total number of vacancies in Romania. The number of vacancies in June 1991 listed by employment offices was 6,480, although this figure probably understated the true number. The districts with most vacancies were Bucharest, Braila, Gorj, Timis and Oimbovita. Skilled manual workers were most in demand — bricklayers, carpenters, welders, etc. These jobs are the least desirable because of the heavy work involved. Table 6.15 gives the numbers of workers leaving their job from 1980 to 1990 by reason.

Table 6.15. **Labour mobility in industry, Romania, 1980-90**

	1980	1981	1982	1983	1984	1985	1986	1987	1989	1990
Total of turnover	602.8	562.8	481.5	507.8	438.3	436.8	441.7	474.3	410.5	399.5
of which:										
- Voluntary	315.5	282.1	250.3	273.5	237.3	233.2	243.2	279.5	229.3	229.6
of which:										
- Due to activity reduction or completion of work	62.6	59.9	43.4	46.3	46.0	35.8	43.1	44.9	31.3	20.7
- Dismissals	287.2	280.7	231.2	234.2	201.1	203.6	198.4	194.8	181.2	169.9

Note: Totals may not add up exactly owing to rounding.
Source: National Statistics Commission: *Statistical annual* (various years).

Labour market policies

Labour market policies are a corner-stone of the Government's economic transition programme. These policies are designed to prevent a sudden explosion of unemployment by providing temporary work for the jobless and establishing institutions to assist those seeking work. Achievement of these goals has required an extensive review of existing laws and the introduction of new legislation.

The right to work and the new unemployment law

The new constitution being considered by Parliament includes an article on the right to work, and the new Labour Code will define the parameters for its implementation. However, a number of related laws were introduced at the beginning of 1991: the Social Protection and Re-employment of the Unemployed Law, the Wage Law, the Collective Labour Contract Law and the Resolution of Collective Labour Conflicts Law.

Article 1 of the Resolution of Collective Labour Conflicts Law states clearly that the right to work and its associated social rights cannot be restricted. The Collective Labour Contract Law establishes rules and regulations on agreements between employers and employees and the payment of wages. Like the Wage Law, this law is based on the principle of negotiation and states that "the parties of the collective labour contract are equal and free in negotiating its clauses".

The Social Protection Law and Re-employment of the Unemployed Law introduced the concept of unemployment in Romania for the first time in 40 years. The law defines an unemployed person as someone able to work but who cannot be employed because of a lack of jobs which match his or her training and skills. It codifies the following:

- the eligibility requirements for receiving unemployment compensation;

- the amount of benefit and other protection for the unemployed;

- the sources from which unemployment benefits will be paid;

- the establishment of a specialised body within the Ministry of Labour and Social Protection whose task is to supervise activities such as setting the amount of unemployment compensation and the payment of benefits.

Those eligible to receive unemployment benefits are: a) graduates of educational institutions who are at least 18 years old, do not have their own source of income equivalent to half the minimum indexed wage, and have been unable to find a job within the past 60 days which corresponds to their professional training; b) youths who were not employed prior to military service and have been unable to find a job within 30 days of its completion; c) people whose labour contract was cancelled according to article 130, paragraph 1)a-f; d) people unjustifiably dismissed whose re-employment by the company is no longer possible; and e) people whose employment contract has expired, are unable to find work, and have worked for at least 6 months during the year prior to applying for unemployment benefit.

In addition, the Social Protection and Re-employment of the Unemployed Law requires enterprises to inform employment offices about vacancies within three days of their availability, and obliges employment offices to announce this information.

Employment services

The restructuring of the system of employment offices has focused on two objectives: providing the necessary staff and increasing their number; and defining the tasks and responsibilities of the employment offices.

Regarding the first objective:

1. The number of employment offices has increased from 90 to 162.

2. Staffing for these offices increased rapidly, from 500 to over 1,200 people. The new employees were usually well educated, and included economists, psychologists, lawyers and statisticians.

3. All staff were trained in the understanding of labour legislation to deal effectively with labour issues.

4. Managers of employment offices were given a 30-day training course in labour force management. These courses were organised by the Romanian Institute for Management.

5. Each employment office was assigned a sociologist and psychologist to deal with problems of re-employment.

Concerning the second objective:

1. Each employment office is responsible for keeping records on the number of jobless and the disbursement of benefits.

2. Each employment office is responsible for collecting information about vacancies and notifying job applicants of their availability, although one problem has been that many enterprises, especially large ones, do not advise of vacancies.

3. Each employment office is assigned the task of training and reorientation of the unemployed.

4. All employment offices have been equipped with computers and an information database has been established.

In addition to the expansion of the employment office system, the Government has established a nation-wide network of training centres for the unemployed which began operation in May 1991. Each of these centres is expected to train upwards of 500 people annually in courses lasting approximately 17 weeks. To date, they have trained some 2,500 people.

Labour market restructuring

The Government's transition programme includes a series of policy measures to restructure the labour market and encourage labour mobility across sectors and professional groups. Some of the main measures are:

1. *Application of the land law*. This law grants the right to own land and is expected to encourage about 70,000 people to move from non-agricultural to agricultural work. The first titles to ownership made possible through this law will have been granted by the end of 1991.

2. *Development of private enterprise in non-agricultural sectors*. A number of laws related to non-agricultural private ownership have been passed. Law No. 31 of December 1990, for example, approved the establishment of joint venture trading companies. Privatisation occurred first in the services and commerce sectors, followed by small industries. By late 1991 there were 142,000 private companies, a number expected to rise to 250,000 by the end of the year.

3. *Encouraging small enterprise activity*. To promote growth in small enterprises the Government has proposed a loan programme with an expected interest rate of 3 per cent and a pay-back period of five years. In addition, employment offices have introduced short-term training courses for people who wish to start a small business; they also offer consultancy services free of charge for one year.

4. *Job creation for secondary and higher education graduates*. To encourage the hiring of graduates, the Government has introduced a programme designed to give graduates on-the-job experience. The Government offers each graduate enrolled in a nine-month training course at an enterprise a subsidy equivalent to 70 per cent of the wage for that job. This programme includes an assistance component to help graduates find a job following training.

Policies to reduce labour supply

The Government has introduced measures to reduce labour supply, primarily to avoid chronic unemployment. The main labour supply reduction measures to date include:

1. *Allowing people to retire at an earlier age*. Beginning in March 1990, all working people were eligible to retire before the retirement age of 60 for men and 55 for women depending on length of employment service. About 393,000 people have taken advantage of this programme.

2. *Reduction of the work-week.* A standard work-week of 40 hours was introduced nation-wide (down from 46 hours). In addition, other reductions in hours were introduced in jobs with special working conditions such as mining, gas and oil exploration. This policy has generated an additional demand for labour of approximately 230,000 people.

3. *Encouragement of temporary leave and retention of workers subject to retrenchment.* Many enterprises were faced in 1990 and 1991 with severe declines in production caused by power rationing and a lack of raw materials. Rather than implement mass lay-offs, many of these enterprises decided to pay workers only 50 per cent of their regular wage. In some cases, workers took unpaid leave in rotating shifts. These measures were first applied at the beginning of 1990 and involved roughly 300,000 people. In February and March 1991, following the Government's decision to ration power supplies, about 240,000 workers went on employment leave with a tax-free allowance equivalent to 60 per cent of the monthly net base wage.

4. *Extension of paid maternity leave.* After childbirth, mothers are allowed 112 days of paid maternity leave from work. When maternity leave is over, mothers are allowed additional leave until the child is 1 year old and are given an allowance from the social insurance fund equivalent to 65 per cent of the monthly base wage. In 1990 approximately 100,000 women took advantage of this programme. The primary goal of extended maternity leave, a programme which continued in 1991, is not to reduce the supply of labour but to allow greater early care of children.

5. *Measures to promote employment among disadvantaged groups.* The Government has initiated action to help disadvantaged groups gain the skills necessary to succeed in the labour market. In particular, the Government has conducted talks with Gypsies, a minority group with a low level of education and job skills when compared to the regular population. These talks resulted in the creation of special job training centres to assist the integration of Gypsies into the labour market.

Institutional restructuring

Tripartism was not the basis for co-ordinating labour market activities immediately following the upheaval of December 1989, but has gradually become the focus for formulating transition policies. A dialogue between employers, trade unions and the State has now begun, although the trade unions and employers play only an advisory role.

Labour market budget and programme participants

A complex employment programme was being finalised in 1991. Very few such programmes had until then been officially funded. The budget for retraining programmes was established and, for 1991, is estimated at 6 billion lei. Some of the financing issues reviewed include:

1. The state budget will cover the financing of training programmes and, in the case of pension and unemployment funds, will contribute to other funds which do not have adequate resources to cover costs.

2. The social insurance fund will finance retirement benefits and the maternity leave programme. In 1990 approximately 500,000 people received benefits from this fund and expenditure was approximately 6,400 million lei.

3. The unemployment fund, which stood at 10,524 million lei in May 1991, will finance unemployment benefits, payments for short-time working, training for the unemployed and information gathering concerning the unemployed. Certain designated workers on employment leave receive a tax-free allowance equal to 60 per cent of the monthly net tariff wage and price compensation. Beginning in February 1991, after the social protection law was issued, this fund was constituted as follows: i) a 4 per cent levy on the monthly wage fund; ii) a 1 per cent contribution from the monthly wage of employees; iii) a 1 per cent contribution from the monthly income of craft co-operative members; and iv) a state budget subsidy to the fund in case items (i), (ii) and (iii) do not cover payment obligations.

Policies for income support

A major concern of the transition programme is to ensure an adequate system of social support to protect those disadvantaged by economic reform, involving measures on unemployment compensation, pensions, wages, family allowances and working conditions.

Nominal income and family expenditure

In 1990, the National Statistics Commission carried out a nation wide study of household budgets based on 2,700 farming households, 5,900 non-farming households and 400 pensioners. The survey found that over the previous 12 months total nominal incomes increased more than expenditure for all three household categories (table 6.16). For non-farming households, wages represented almost three-quarters of total nominal income (wages increased 17.9 per cent between 1989 and 1990). Income from agricultural work (payment in cash and in kind) and from other work rose significantly for all three household groups. For farming households, income from agricultural work accounted for four-fifths of nominal income. For pensioner households income from pensions and other social assistance programmes provided 70 per cent of nominal income.

Table 6.16. **Monthly family incomes and expenditure, Romania, 1989 and 1990**

	Average incomes (lei)			Average expenditure (lei)		
	1989	1990	Index 1990 (1989=100)	1989	1990	Index 1990 (1989=100)
Employees[1]	6 315	7 800	123.6	5 658	6 858	121.2
Peasants[2]	3 456	5 828	168.7	3 468	4 713	135.2
Pensioners[3]	2 741	3 478	126.8	2 445	2 979	121.8

1. With an average of 3.7 members, of whom 1.7 were employees.
2. With an average of 2.6 members.
3. With an average of 1.7 members, of whom 1.3 were receiving pensions and social assistance.
Source: National Statistics Commission: *Statistical Annual* (various years).

Expenditure increases were highest for non-food items, primarily electrical appliances, furniture and petrol. Farming households had to spend more to purchase animals and fodder. Expenditure on services accounted for a relatively small share of household costs: 6.7 per cent for farming households, 12.6 per cent for non-farming households and 16.8 per cent for pensioner households.

Purchasing power of incomes

In 1990, the real wage rose by 4.6 per cent over 1989 (nominal wages rose 10.5 per cent and retail prices rose 5.4 per cent for non-farming, non-pensioner households). However, in November 1990 retail prices increased 23.2 per cent over prices in October, and in December they jumped an additional 38.0 per cent from October' levels. Nominal wages increased 2.8 per cent between October and November but decreased 5.7 per cent between October and December.

The real value of social security pensions increased 6.1 per cent in 1990. Pension payments increased 10.9 per cent while retail prices for pensioners rose by 4.6 per cent. However, there is significant variation among pension categories. Pensions for those receiving survivor benefits are only two-fifths (859 lei per month) of those for workers retiring at normal pensionable age with the required years of service. Pensions for the disabled are only 45 per cent of this level. The lowest pensions had the biggest increases in 1990: 29.9 per cent for the disabled and 25.0 per cent for survivors. Maximum pensions in 1989 were 66.1 per cent of the average nominal wage but in 1990 declined to only 63.1 per cent.

Compared to October 1990, retail prices for pensioners rose by 23.6 per cent in November 1990 and 35.2 per cent in December, resulting in a drop in purchasing power of 8.7 per cent and 10.3 per cent respectively. For the 387,000 pensioners receiving survivor benefits, over four-fifths had an income below 1,000 lei per month (not including the additional compensation of 400 lei granted in November and December 1990).

Indexation policy and compensation

From November 1990, the mean price ratio has been calculated quarterly and used for the indexation of wages and pensions. The mean price ratio is based on the cost of a defined basket of goods and services, and households are compensated according to the price increase for this basket of goods in relation to family incomes and a typical family budget. (A fixed net sum of 750 lei for employees and 400 lei for pensioners was given regardless of family income.) The following groups have been compensated monthly from the second quarter of 1991:

1. The unemployed (compensated according to the amount of their unemployment benefit).

2. The disabled (compensation between 225 and 375 lei).

3. Those receiving social security pensions, the military and the I.O.V.R (L,470 lei).

4. Wives of those in military service (300 lei).

5. Those receiving special family allowances (500 lei).

6. School-children and students on state-funded scholarships (800 lei for school-children and 960 lei for students).

7. Children receiving state allowances (220 lei).

8. Children over 16 years of age enrolled in day-time education courses but not on a scholarship, provided that parental monthly net income does not exceed 20,000 lei (550 lei for school-children and 730 lei for students).

9. Women on paid maternity leave.

10. Employees in the state sector (2,825 lei). From May 1991, the standard compensation of 2,825 lei was included in the base wage, because separate compensation had led to some workers neglecting their work.

Other indexing measures include a programme of temporary compensation for higher energy costs, rents and transport charges. Pensioners are reimbursed half the cost of medical prescriptions. The minimum wage (5,975 lei per month in mid-1991) will be increased according to price and productivity changes.

Unemployment benefits and other forms of social protection

Unemployment benefit is based on the length of an individual's employment record and the minimum indexed wage, as follows:

1. Graduates of non-higher education and vocational schools who are under 18 years of age but have at least one year of employment receive 60 per cent of the minimum indexed wage.

2. Higher education graduates receive 70 per cent of the minimum indexed wage.

3. Those who have between one and five years service receive 50 per cent of their last monthly wage provided that it is not less than 75 per cent of the minimum indexed wage.

4. Those who have between 5 and 15 years of service receive 55 per cent of their previous wage provided that it is not less than 80 per cent of the indexed wage.

5. Those who have over 15 years of service receive 60 per cent of their previous wage provided that it is not less than 85 per cent of the minimum wage.

People are ineligible for unemployment benefits if they: own more than 10,000 square metres of flat land or 20,000 square metres of mountain land; have private sources of income greater than 50 per cent of the minimum indexed wage; have unjustifiably refused a job or training course; are eligible to retire; or are members of co-operatives.

Conclusions

During the short time that transition policies have been in effect, the Government has implemented a broad range of measures to ensure an adequate level of social protection for the active and non-active population. Working people and pensioners are well protected against price hikes by the compensation indexing measures. However, farmers are not similarly protected. Also, although young people enjoy a high level of protection, young families with children remain at risk.

The Government is attempting to improve social protection measures through improved information gathering. Efforts are under way to examine different levels of poverty and what the minimum acceptable wage should be.

Wages, incomes policy and industrial relations

Introduction

The wage system in effect prior to 1990 was characterised by a high degree of centralisation with policy being determined solely at the national level. The old wage system favoured maintaining the interests of enterprise management rather than improving productivity. Higher wages led to inflation. Wage policy led to labour hoarding and generally misdirected labour resources. Redistribution of labour reserves through a co-ordinated wage policy is one of the most difficult challenges facing Romania today and has important economic, social and political implications. Table 6.17 presents data on wage growth by economic sector.

Table 6.17. **Wage and employment growth by sector, Romania, 1989 and 1990**

Sector	Wages 1990 (1989=100)	Employees[1] 1990 (1989=100)
Total economy	110.5	98.9
Agriculture	122.3	103.5
Transport	118.3	100.6[2]
Research and development	112.6	62.9
Health protection, social assistance and sport	111.2	104.0
Household, buildings and other services	110.8	40.1
Trade (tourism included)	110.8	97.0
Education	109.7	111.6[3]
Industry	108.5	105.9
Culture and art	108.1	n.a.
Administration	108.0	n.a.
Construction	105.8	65.3
Telecommunications	105.5	n.a.

1. Employee data refer to September 1990.
2. Includes telecommunications.
3. Includes culture and art.
Source: National Statistics Commission.

Nominal wage trends

Beginning in January 1990, measures were taken to change certain aspects of the wage system. They included giving up the "accord global" wage form as the sole method of relating wages to results, and introducing new wage increments for those working under special conditions. For example, night-workers saw their wage increments increase from 15 to 25 per cent.

These and other measures taken in 1990 fuelled growth in the nominal wage, which rose 10.5 per cent (3,062 lei on average) over 1989. This compares with an annual average rise of 4.1 per cent in 1980-89. Reduction of the work-week also led to excessive wage increases in 1990, with the hourly wage, for example, increasing by 15 per cent. In addition, the link between wages and results weakened considerably because work norms were relaxed and the "accord global" system eliminated without a better replacement.

During the first stage of price liberalisation, real wages dropped sharply (table 6.18). The second stage saw an extremely high rise in nominal wages in trading companies of 20 to 60 per cent. This counteracted the rise in prices and led to a recovery in the real wage. However, wage increases were negotiated on the basis of price increases rather than the enterprise's financial well-being. This has increased the likelihood that unprofitable enterprises will go bankrupt, further damaging employment prospects.

Table 6.18. **Nominal and real wages during the two stages of price liberalisation, Romania, 1991**

	Stage I					Stage II	
	Nov. 1990	Dec. 1990	Jan. 1991	Feb. 1991	Mar. 1991	Apr. 1991	May 1991
Net nominal wage	120.6	121.5	115.4	113.4[1]	119.3	184.2[1]	225.0[1]
Consumer price index	128.0	137.8	158.2	169.6	180.7	227.4	239.2
Real wage	94.2	88.1	72.9	66.8	66.0	81.0	94.0

1. Inquiry data.
Source: National Statistics Commission.

Wage differentials

Under Communism wage differentials narrowed across branches and occupations, and wages did not promote the efficient use of labour resources or labour mobility.

Tables 6.19 to 6.21 show wage differentials between economic sectors and forms of property, while table 6.22 gives a breakdown by sector of the elements making up the average wage. Although wage differentials are already significant in Romania, differentiation is expected to increase across occupations and economic sectors as the economy moves towards market principles. Wage differentials are not, however, hard to accept if they are honestly based on labour which benefits the individual and society.

189

Table 6.19. **Net wage by economic branch, Romania, 1989-90**

Branch	1989	1990	Index 1990 (1989=100)
Total economy	3 063	3 384	110.5
Industry	3 037	3 295	108.5
Construction	3 697	3 912	105.8
Agriculture	2 983	3 647	122.3
Transport	3 195	3 780	118.3
Telecommunications	2 826	2 970	105.5
Trade (tourism included)	2 629	2 913	110.8
Household, buildings & other services	2 945	3 262	110.8
Education	2 980	3 269	109.7
Culture and art	2 904	3 138	108.1
Health protection, social assistance and sport	2 870	3 191	112.2
Research development	3 253	3 663	112.6
Administration	3 732	4 029	108.0

Source: National Statistics Commission.

Table 6.20. **Net wage by economic branch: Romania, 1990-91**

	First quarter		Percentage increase (%)
	1990 (lei)	1991[1] (lei)	
Total economy	3 091	3 978	28.7
Industry	2 984	3 977	33.3
Construction	3 718	3 881	4.4
Agriculture	3 651	3 822	4.7
Forestry	2 708	3 470	28.1
Transport	3 194	4 530	41.8
Telecommunications	2 744	4 311	57.1
Trade	2 707	3 627	34.0
Household services	2 709	3 730	37.7
Research & development	3 490	4 310	23.5
Education	3 043	3 988	31.0
Culture and art	3 044	3 725	22.4
Health protection	2 859	4 027	40.8
Social assistance and insurance	2 569	3 382	31.6

1. Compensation added to wages is included.
Source: National Statistics Commission

Table 6.21. **Net wage by form of property, Romania, 1991**

	First quarter 1991 (lei)
Total economy[1]	4 814
State property	4 877
of which :	
- Self-managing enterprises	5 877
- Trading companies with state capital	4 661
- Other state economic units	4 435
- Public institutions	4 837
Mixed property	5 013
Co-operatives	3 949
Public property	4 546

1. Wages would be even more unequal if private enterprises were included.
Source: National Statistics Commission.

Table 6.22. **Wage structure by economic branch, Romania, 1989-90 (in percentages)**

	Industry		Construction		State agriculture				Railways		Road transport	
					IAS		SMA					
		Q1		Q1		Q1		Q1		Q1		Q1
	1989	1990	1989	1990	1989	1990	1989	1990	1989	1990	1989	1990
Mean wage	100	100	100	100	100	100	100	100	100	100	100	100
of which:												
- Tariff wage	85.5	85.1	78.4	84.1	94.9	95.3	93.5	94.3	77.5	72.6	82.9	86.7
- Variable part-total	14.5	14.9	21.6	15.9	5.1	4.7	6.5	5.7	22.5	27.4	17.1	13.3
of which:												
- Accord difference (+/-)	-0.3	+1.6	+10.6	+3.1	-1.5	-2.8	-5.1	-2.0	+4.5	-	-	-
- Service increments	6.3	6.4	4.5	4.7	4.2	6.2	7.4	6.9	8.8	10.2	6.8	6.7
- Total increments and other parts	2.2	5.0	1.4	4.0	1.0	1.0	0.1	0.4	3.0	15.8	3.1	5.4
- Awards	1.7	1.5	1.0	1.1	0.2	0.2	0.4	0.2	1.2	1.3	1.3	1.0
- Profit participation	1.3	0.4	0.8	3.0	0.3	0.1	0.1	0.2	1.0	0.1	1.1	0.2
- Compensation	3.3	-	3.3	-	1.6	-	3.6	-	4.0	-	4.8	-

Source: National Statistics Commission.

Until December 1989, remuneration was established at the central state level. Since 1990, remuneration decisions have been made at enterprise level through collective bargaining. Thus the system to make decisions on pay based on market principles is already in place.

Wages and incomes policies

High inflation has made price curbs a major concern of the Government. In the past, neither employers nor trade unions have tried to prevent inflationary wage increases. Although the Government has established a minimum wage, it has not set a cap on wage increases to slow inflationary trends. However, it has introduced a system of double taxation — a progressive tax on individual wages and a similar tax on wages across wage groups — which is intended to dampen wages growth. For the future, the Government, employers and trade unions must make a concerted effort to ensure that wage growth accurately reflects economic factors such as productivity. Employers who disregard this will eventually go bankrupt.

Industrial relations

Development of institutions

Industrial relations in Romania, previously dominated by the State, are now moving towards a fully-fledged tripartite system. The Government is gradually handing over industrial relations issues to other social and economic groups.

Privatisation marks the first step in developing tripartite relations. In 1991 Parliament adopted the Collective Labour Contract Law, which promotes negotiations between workers and employers at the enterprise, sector and national levels. At the enterprise level, labour contracts are concluded between employers and workers. Workers are represented by trade unions or, if not all employees are members of the same union, by representatives chosen by secret ballot.

Bipartite and tripartite discussions have been conducted principally at relatively high organisational levels. For example, a commission of government and trade union members was established to discuss national issues of labour and social protection, based on a government study of labour issues which focused on current legislative problems including the introduction of a minimum wage and wage indexing. The commission also formed government/trade union organisations at sectoral level. In addition, the Government is to submit to Parliament a law on social partnership in Romania which will propose the creation of a non-governmental council for social policy. This council will identify possible approaches to creating a better system of industrial relations and open channels for discussion.

Employer associations have been established at both the district and national levels. Dispute settlement procedures are being developed and their objectives defined. However, the functioning of employer associations hinges on the full implementation of privatisation.

Trade union organisation

The trade union movement in Romania has undergone a complex restructuring process. Along with efforts to develop new forms of trade union organisation, attempts have been made to define better the goals of trade unions and how to achieve them.

Many disparate trade unions have been formed, howing to the absence of a legal framework for their development. Organisationally, the lowest level comprises trade unions at enterprises, followed by federations, leagues and other coalitions at sectoral level, and groupings of several federations, unions and leagues to represent workers in national affairs. Individual trade unions at the enterprise level have been created by aggregating an array of worker groups.

There are currently 40 unions, leagues and confederations organised primarily along occupational lines, and 100 federations organised mainly according to type of activity. Several groups within a given branch of activity may represent the rights of workers. Although many of the unions are stable and were well organised at their inception, most are still in the process of defining their roles.

At the beginning of May 1990, there were only four sectoral confederations, but their number had grown to 13 by mid-1991.

Trade union membership levels were initially high but then declined steadily to about 60 per cent in mid-1991. The move towards privatisation has led to reduced interest in union activity and more emphasis on the role of the individual as an independent player in the labour market. In addition, the pre-revolution experience of trade unions led many people to retreat from union activity or join newly created unions. Finally, the legal framework for new forms of trade union activity took time to put into place.

An analysis of 35 enterprises by the Labour and Social Protection Research Unit, Bucharest, found that trade union activity varied by size of enterprise. In small enterprises there was usually only one trade union with membership covering 40 to 60 per cent of the workforce. In about 60 per cent of enterprises with over 1,000 employees, there were usually between two and four worker organisations, also covering about 60 per cent of the workforce. Enterprises with unionisation rates of over 80 per cent were rare.

The organisation of trade unions influences their relationship with management, according to the survey. In enterprises with only one trade union, unions generally co-operated well with management in tackling employee problems. In enterprises with several trade unions, only two in five described union-management relations as good. In a third of these enterprises there was also considerable conflict between trade unions.

The same survey found that in 35 per cent of the enterprises, trade union members said they trusted their leaders, but in over 35 per cent they did not, and in 25 per cent they were indifferent to them. Distrust was often based on the belief that the trade union representatives took advantage of their union position to achieve personal goals rather than those of union members.

Following adoption of the wage payment and collective labour contract laws in February 1991, trade unions and management began to negotiate wages and establish mutual obligations on working conditions, social protection and settlement of disputes. Disputes over pay, labour protection, leave, holidays and other working conditions have been settled.

193

Although collective bargaining in Romania is in its infancy, two general remarks are in order. First, all parties in the negotiating process are seen as equal partners. The importance of this cannot be overemphasised in the light of past history. Second, although negotiations have resulted in excessive wage increases with adverse consequences for all social partners, the Government has learned much from the process, and this augurs well for the future.

Notes

1. All statistics, except where otherwise stated, are drawn from the Romanian National Statistics Commission and yearly *Statistics Annuals*.

2. Studies of various enterprises in different branches of the economy estimate the level of labour hoarding at between 20 and 25 per cent of total labour resources. This, coupled with a lack of employee motivation and discipline, contributed to enterprises' higher staffing needs.

3. Of those employed in the state sector in 1991, 63.1 per cent were in trading companies with state capital, 16.7 per cent were in self-managing companies and 14.5 per cent were in public institutions.

4. Of those emigrating, 33.6 per cent were skilled workers, 12.8 per cent were clerks or technicians with a medium level of education, 4.7 per cent had a higher education, and 48.9 per cent were from other categories (pensioners, domestic workers, children). Of those emigrating, 78.3 per cent went to Germany, 9.3 per cent to Hungary, 4.7 per cent to the United States, 1.5 per cent to Canada and 1.0 per cent to Israel.

5. Sectors with predominantly women workers include health and social assistance (75.4 per cent), education, culture and arts (67.6 per cent) and agriculture (56.4 per cent).

6. The unemployment rate was calculated on the employed population rather than the active population because active population figures were not available. The unemployment rates therefore overestimate jobless levels.

Chapter 7

The labour market, social policy and industrial relations in the USSR under transition

by
Alexander Samorodov

Introduction

Economic conditions in the former USSR continue to deteriorate. GNP is estimated to have dropped 17.9 per cent in 1991; production fell roughly 15 per cent[1]. The decline in output has been accompanied by growing inflation. The official inflation figure was about 10 per cent for 1990 but may have been as high as 25 per cent.

By the end of 1991, the rouble had been devalued six times since December 1990, declining over 80 per cent in value. Food and consumer goods remain in short supply. Currency devaluations and the disruption of economic links have plagued the economy; barter trading has become a principal means of exchange and a stumbling block to an effective market economy. External trade declined over 38.5 per cent in 1991; the dramatic fall in export revenues has made international debt obligations increasingly difficult.[2] National unrest and ethnic conflict have aggravated the situation with greater numbers of refugees and increased obstacles to economic activity.

It was against this bleak background that the former USSR began the transition to a market-oriented economy with the adoption by the Supreme Soviet of the "Main Guidelines for Stabilisation of the Economy and Transition to the Market" on October 19th, 1990. The measure called for demonopolisation, an open economy and the guarantee of basic social rights. It sought to spur economic growth by freeing prices and removing government from direct involvement in most areas of microeconomic activity. A principal goal was to establish the producer as a social player able to respond to the changing demands of a market economy.

The collapse of the Soviet political system and the foundation of the Commonwealth of Independent States opened the gate for rapid and radical economic reforms. This paper does not assess in detail the economic and political developments since that time, but focuses on events and issues prior to 1992.

The anti-crisis programme

In April 1991, the Soviet Cabinet of Ministers introduced a set of proposals designed to combat the crisis. These included:

i) revitalizing economic links between enterprises;

ii) selling new, unused factory equipment;

iii) re-establishing severed economic ties with enterprises in central and eastern European countries (the former COMECON trading area);

iv) giving "most favoured nation" status in internal trade to republics wishing to sign a union treaty among themselves while trade with republics not belonging to the new union would be conducted on the basis of world prices;

v) hiring enterprise managers and experts on a contract basis;

vi) banning strikes during the entire anti-crisis programme;

vii) in order to provide incentives to workers and employees, removing the limits on personal income and increasing the level of income exempt from taxation;

viii) encouraging privatisation, especially in small establishments, two-thirds of which would belong to work collectives, families or private owners, whereas with larger state enterprises, priority was to be given to transforming them into joint-stock companies.

The break-up of the USSR has changed the situation and now each republic pursues its own anti-crisis programme. Their common elements include privatisation, price liberalisation and lifting limits on personal income. The task of re-establishing economic ties with enterprises in central and eastern European countries (CEEs) has been made more difficult by the need to re-establish links between enterprises in different Commonwealth republics. Trade at world prices with the breakaway republics was resisted by them, and a compromise of "agreed" prices was found. Trade at world prices would have been equivalent to an "oil shock" to republics other than Russia, which produced most of the energy in the former USSR.

Recently enacted market-oriented legislation

A range of new laws has been promulgated and enacted in the past three years in the USSR. These were designed to encourage the move towards a market economy. This legislation included: "Fundamentals of the Legislation of the USSR and its Constituent Republics on Employment" (1990), "On Enterprises in the USSR" (1990), "On Trade Unions, Rights and Guarantees of Their Activities" (1990), "Fundamentals of the Legislation on Investment Activities in the USSR" (1990), "On Monetary Regulation in the USSR" (1991), "On General Principles of Entrepreneurship by Citizens in the USSR" (1991), and "On Resolving Collective Industrial Disputes (Conflicts)" (1991). After the dissolution of the USSR, the individual republics, in becoming independent States, began to adopt their own legislation.

Together with the earlier legislation on co-operatives, self-employment and property, these new laws are expected to accelerate the move towards a market-oriented economy and to create the necessary legal framework. Current efforts include support for entrepreneurship and privatisation. The Law on Entrepreneurship, for example, was adopted in April 1991. The governments in the republics consider privatisation a popular measure and hope for public support. In the USSR, the Law on Entrepreneurship was adopted in April 1991. Legal issues such as taxation and business law only began to be introduced in 1990. Despite all these measures, the necessary legal framework for a market economy had not been put into place by late 1991.

Foreign businesses will benefit from new legislation which allows the repatriation of profit, the formation of wholly foreign-owned companies and the unhindered sale of their products abroad. Companies are also allowed to import most goods without licences from the authorities.[3]

Legislation on investment, adopted in 1990, was designed to create the same conditions for foreign businesses as for their Soviet counterparts, equalising rights and thus attracting investment. Many believed that the success of transition depended on the success of efforts to attract foreign capital. In short, the success of these efforts depended to a large extent on the stability of the political situation, public support and a clear delimitation of responsibilities between different authorities.

Private ownership of land has been allowed and is intended to boost the development of private commercial farming. Families starting private farms will be exempt from taxes and land rent for two to three years from the beginning of commercial operations. As rural areas lack farmworkers, migrants willing to go there will be offered financial assistance for moving and refurnishing their homes. The authorities are drawing on Western experience of private farming by setting up model farms based on the experience of countries such as the Netherlands and France, and by attracting technical assistance from other countries.

Labour market developments

Recent changes in employment and labour supply

If we look at labour supply trends in the ex-Soviet Union, we see that they were affected by several factors. First, population growth rates declined everywhere except in the Central Asian republics, while urbanisation continued, with two-thirds of the population urban dwellers, as compared to 48% in 1959. Total employment fell, from 139.3 million in 1989 to 138.4 million in 1990. However, while public sector employment declined, new employment and production forms have appeared such as co-operatives, self-employment, and joint-stock companies (table 7.1).

Table 7.1. **The Soviet workforce, by employment forms, March 1991 (in millions)**

Public sector	114.8
Co-operative sector, including	16.7
Collective farming sector	10.4
Consumer societies	3.5
Co-operatives in consumer goods and services	2.8
Private sector, including	
Subsidiary farming	3.5
Private business	0.3

Source: Ekonomika i Zhizn (Moscow), Apr. 1991, No. 17, p.16.

In 1991 the expected employment crisis of mass lay-offs did not materialise: open unemployment did not surge. However, in the first half of 1991 hidden unemployment, part-time work, a reduced number of working weeks and seasonal unemployment became widespread. Some 20 million people were estimated to be in these categories.[4]

Experts estimated that the worst time for redundancies would come after March — April 1992 when the disruption of economic links between enterprises would be most felt. Before this, managers of most enterprises apparently tried to pursue a soft line towards workers, trying not to lay them off if possible.

The present stage of employment restructuring is characterised by an accumulation of difficulties related to the transition to a market-oriented economy. *Imbalances between labour supply and demand* are in evidence everywhere. There were reportedly many more people looking for jobs, but only 1.5-2 million of them apparently could be considered as unemployed at the beginning of 1991, if ILO guidelines were applied.

As illustrated by table 7.2, labour turnover in the USSR fell in the 1980s in industry, agriculture, construction, transport and communications. In 1990, 64.8 per cent of all those registering with placement offices were found jobs.[5] In Moscow in late 1991, 85 per cent of the registered vacancies were for blue-collar workers, whereas 96.6 per cent of laid-off workers were former civil service employees.[6] Blue-collar skills generally are in high demand, skills which are quite different from those of most redundant workers. This situation is made even more difficult by low geographical mobility, related administrative restrictions and the lack of a housing market. Some 1.5 million people were registered as unemployed and/or were looking for jobs in 1991. The proportion of the unemployed receiving an unemployment benefit is low. For example, in November 1991 the number of registered unemployed in Moscow was 7,000, but only 600 were found eligible for a benefit due to the strict criteria applied.[7] In addition, many of the unemployed do not register with the placement offices for a number of reasons. Either they believe the offices are ineffective, or they may even feel ashamed. Unemployment is a new phenomenon and is often regarded as a sign of personal failure. As a result, many unemployed people avoid registering and look for jobs independently. In December 1991, the number of such people was estimated at about one million for the 11 republics of the former USSR.[8]

Table 7.2. **Labour turnover, by branches, USSR 1980-1989**
(**percentage of average employment**)

Branch	1980	1985	1989
Industry	16.1	12.7	13.5
Agriculture	14.4	10.6	12.1
Construction	22.6	18.1	16.5
Railway transport	10.9	10.1	10.4
Automobile transport	19.4	15.4	15.0
Communications	20.5	14.9	12.6
Trade and public catering	-	14.4	15.7
Housing, communal and consumer services	19.2	17.6	19.3

Note: Labour turnover is defined as resignation from a public sector enterprise or organisation.
Source: State statistical office, (Goskomstat), USSR, 1991.

Table 7.3. **Public sector employment in three republics of former USSR, 1990 and 1991**

	(per cent of all employment)		
	Russian Federation	Ukraine	Belarus
1990	82.6	74.4	73.3
1991	76.3	69.0	66.0

Source: Goskiomstat, Moscow, January 1992.

The transition has adversely affected young people. Two-thirds of young people (teenagers and those in their early 20s) do not possess the needed vocational training, worsening their position in the labour market. Long-term youth unemployment will be a major labour market problem.

Unemployment before transition was caused primarily by deficiencies in planning. Misjudgements were made in the allocation of productive resources, both in terms of labour availability and industrial siting in regions distant from markets. As a result, some regions have a labour surplus while others experience labour shortages.

A high level of labour release, or "shedding", is a recent development in matters of employment. Greater levels of labour release are due to increased economic accountability, the larger role played by enterprises in hiring and firing, longer periods of frictional unemployment due to difficulties in the transitional economy, and a flow of manpower from the public to the private sector. In addition to real reductions, many unfilled jobs were eliminated in 1987-1989. About 1.6 million workers and employees were released in real terms in that period.[9]

The unemployment problem has not been alleviated by the large number of vacancies. For instance, as of November 1991 there were some 1.09 million vacancies in Russia (according to data from placement offices). However, 0.9 million of them were for blue-collar workers, whereas most of the unemployed comprised white-collar workers. Most needed were metalworkers (17.7%), machine tool operators (12.1%), seamstresses (5.7%), and loaders and auxiliary workers (4.0%).[10]

There are no official data to establish whether labour is shed primarily by large or small enterprises. Most workers in industry are in enterprises of 1,000-5,000 workers (table 7.4). The authorities place much hope on employment creation in small and medium-sized enterprises.

Table 7.4. **Industrial enterprises by employment size, 1987 (percentage distribution).**

Industrial Personnel	% of enterprises	Cumulative % of employment		
		Output	Industry	All workers
Up to 100	27.2	1.8	1.7	1.7
101 - 200	19.5	3.5	3.5	2.3
201 - 500	23.8	9.4	9.7	9.7
501 - 1,000	13.1	11.4	11.7	12.0
1,001 - 5,000	13.8	38.0	36.2	36.8
5,001 - 10,000	1.7	15.7	15.6	15.2
10,000 and over	0.9	20.2	21.6	21.2

Source: USSR industry, (Moscow, Finansy i Statistika, 1988), p.14.

The mushrooming development of co-operatives and the growth of services will imply further cuts in the State sector. It is estimated that state sector employment will shrink by as much as 40 million jobs by 1995, from 120 to 80 million.[11] If the Law on Privatisation accelerates denationalisation, such declines could be even greater. Privatisation may contribute substantially to productivity growth and solve the problem of motivation. For example, lease enterprises (those leased by work collectives) were the *only production sector* that managed to increase output in 1990 (by 3.4 percent).[12]

Transition to a market system may produce another source of unemployment, namely redundancies among the 4 million workers employed by loss-making enterprises. However, with regard to the problems of unemployment caused by plant closures and industrial restructuring, much depends on the speed with which market relations are introduced.

The employment situation may get even worse if ethnic unrest intensifies, or if the Law on Emigration (adopted in May 1991) provokes a mass exodus of labour beginning in 1993 (if it is endorsed by the republics). If this scenario materialises the country will lose the youngest and most skilled workers and scientists, including those in sensitive areas. Industrialised market economies are unable to absorb large numbers of workers from the former USSR, and they are understandably selective in their immigration policy. Reportedly, the Soviet economy suffered its greatest loss of manpower in 1990 when half a million people emigrated. The loss was greatest among the young and qualified, representing a serious drain on human resources.[13]

According to estimates of the Ministry of Labour and Social Issues (now dissolved), 23.2 million people left jobs in 1990. Of those, 17 million changed jobs between enterprises; 90 per cent of them found jobs themselves, while 10 per cent were assisted by placement offices.[14]

Labour market policies

The USSR Law on Employment of Population was adopted on 15 January 1991. Although the country ceased to exist eleven months later, provisions of this legislation, wholly or partly, have been in force in the new independent States. Most of them had not yet been adopted their own employment laws at the time of finalising this paper in early 1992. Besides, where adopted, the new legislation drew heavily on the 1991 Employment Law, (e.g. Russia), and Ministries of Labour in the republics decided to co-ordinate their activities.[15]

The right to work was always enshrined in the countrys' constitution. The Soviet Law on Employment of Population of January 1991, and subsequent republican employment laws, where adopted, gave citizens the right to freely chosen employment, thereby ending the system of administrative coercion to work. Voluntary unemployment was no longer considered an offence.[16] The State made a commitment to ensure the implementation of a policy of promoting *full, productive and freely chosen employment,* "aimed at creating the conditions for citizens to exercise their right to work".[17]

The Law on Employment, representing the cornerstone in a series of market-oriented laws, consisted of the following sections: general provisions; right of the citizens to employment; regulation and organisation of employment; social guarantees in the event of loss of job; control and responsibility for law infringement. The Law allows citizens to choose productive and creative work, including unpaid activities such as raising children, housekeeping, external study, and public activities. The Law for the first time established formal definitions of, for example, employed and unemployed citizens, and what constitutes a "suitable job", etc. It superseded the compulsory nature of labour that had prevailed in the ex-USSR: "the one who does not work shall not eat".

The Law on Employment emphasised that employment services would be the backbone of the country's employment system, performing functions such as screening the unemployed, paying unemployment benefits, organising special public works and directing workers for retraining. The previous employment services were inadequate, few in number, poorly equipped and their staff inadequately trained. The labour authorities planned to increase the number of placement offices to about 7,000, to give them equipment and to train personnel. International programmes were launched to aid the ex-Soviet (then Russian) authorities in this effort, notably to set up model placement offices. As an illustration of the inadequacy of the employment services, there were three employment officers per 100,000 people, a rate many times smaller than in most industrialised countries.[18] Eventually, the Government made plans to double the strength of placement staff.

The 1991 Law stipulated the adoption and implementation of *state employment programmes* designed to facilitate employment, prevent unemployment and protect workers under changing social conditions. The programmes were to operate at the union, republic and local levels. One of the programmes' tasks was to enhance workers' mobility by providing incentives for voluntary resettlement, by improving retraining and by creating jobs.

The Law on Employment also stipulated that severance pay equal to three months of an average wage or salary must be paid to released workers, provided the person registered with the employment service within ten days of release. If workers were released due to staff reductions, liquidation or reorganisation, and were to be retrained on the job in a new place of work, they were to be paid grants equal to the average wage during the period of retraining.

The usual *grants* to workers in retraining were set at 50 per cent of the *basic* salary or wage of the former job; those with children and dependants were paid 50 per cent of the *average* wage. The grant was not to be lower than the minimum wage but was not to exceed 70 per cent of the average wage in the region (republic, large region — "krai", region — "oblast").[19]

The new law stipulated that citizens meeting benefit eligibility requirements were to be paid *unemployment benefits* from 11 days after application to a placement office until a job was found. Benefits were paid for 26 calendar weeks for those who lost their jobs or who were looking for their first job. The law provided for a minimum benefit of not less than 50 per cent of the basic wage or salary in the former job, but not less than the minimum wage. There were also special unemployment benefit rates for the long-term unemployed, demobilised military personnel and some other categories of worker such as new entrants to the labour market.[20]

An "active" labour market policy designed to combat rising unemployment must include a component to strengthen *retraining* programmes. The USSR Ministry of Labour expected that 2.0-2.5 million people would require retraining in 1991, but it was not clear how such a figure was calculated. Financing for employment policies was to come from the *Employment Fund*.

The Employment Fund was intended to finance the implementation of employment policy, programmes for the unemployed, vocational guidance, worker upgrading and retraining, special public works, employment services and various other employment programmes.[21]

Some attention has been paid to organising *public works programmes* for workers without jobs. These could be organised in social services such as health care, trade, municipal works, road construction and street cleaning.

Employment policies were also geared towards *disadvantaged groups*, such as young people, women with small children, the aged and unskilled workers. In 1991, there were 11.2 million workers of pension age and more than 43 million pensioners.[22] Their main problem was that most pensions were low, so that many of them had to work. Such pressures have become stronger with inflation and a swift transition to a market-oriented system, especially after price liberalisation in January 1992.

In 1991, there were 1.6 million *working disabled* in the ex-USSR.[23] Under a deteriorating economic situation they experienced increasing difficulties. In 1991, young people and women were the most hard hit by unemployment: about 700,000 young people were not in paid work and managers seemed to fire women first when making lay-offs. In early 1991, the Moscow City Council prohibited the mass lay-off of women with children until 1 July 1991, the date when unemployment registration began.[24] After this date, however, women with children no longer had any special status. The Moscow employment services were unprepared for mass redundancies, both among disadvantaged and non-disadvantaged groups.

The most difficult situation vis-à-vis youth employment is in Central Asia, where reportedly up to 50 per cent of the unemployed were young people in the late 1980s.[25] Their main employment problems are of a structural nature: there is a mismatch between their training and available jobs. Many young people work in jobs unsuitable for their training, in poor working conditions, and are inadequately remunerated. Even when they obtain jobs, they are often regarded by management as primary candidates for lay-offs because their work experience is considered inadequate when compared to older workers.

The Soviet authorities tried to identify and assist territories in need of special help, designated as *priority development regions*. These included labour surplus regions, the mountain regions and extreme North areas, as well as some rural areas. The economic component included lower tax rates on profits, subsidies, direct financing and other aid.

The lack of food places special importance on the need for agricultural development. Rural employment has been seriously affected by the policy of eliminating villages considered to have no future. This involved the elimination of certain villages depopulated through young people leaving the area. Rural depopulation has been acutely felt in the non-black earth area (Central Russia), the Far East, Belarus, the Volga river basin and Siberia.[26]

In view of the poor rate of agricultural resettlement, incentive schemes were being discussed by labour authorities to encourage the mobility of workers into rural areas. Such incentives might include a one-off payment to a resettling worker and family members, removal expenses, a daily allowance per day en route to a new residence, and loans.

The services sector was given special attention in the Soviet employment programme and was regarded as a principal absorber of labour released from elsewhere. However, the skills of released workers often do not match those needed in services. In addition, as wages and salaries of workers in services are lower, they have not helped to attract released workers. In the past 15 years (prior to the 1990s), wages and salaries in services dropped from 80 per cent to 70-75 per cent of those in the production sector, even though the former employ a much greater share of qualified personnel.[27] It is hoped that the market economy will improve remuneration in the services sector.

Some of the labour market programmes described above remained only on paper, while others have been implemented only partially. With the break-up of the USSR, it is likely that each new country will develop its own policies which best suit its particular circumstances.

Training and retraining

The workforce in the ex-USSR is, in general, skilled. Given the technological and employment structure, a large proportion of the workforce could be said to be "trained" in required skills. In 1991, for instance, there were 35 million specialists (skilled workers and employees with higher education) and 82 million skilled blue-collar workers. Over the last few years, there were 2.6 million new vocational training school graduates annually. Over 33 million workers and 10.5 million managers and specialists were being trained on an ongoing basis.[28]

Many new problems in training and retraining flow from the changed employment situation, as labour shortage is replaced by labour surplus. Many workers need to change jobs, and must therefore be assisted to remain competitive in the labour market. Retraining and other social support programmes are vital.[29]

The problem of structural unemployment has come to the fore, and has consequences for retraining policy. The structure of vacant jobs does not correspond to the occupational structure. Many workers have a narrow range of skills, and this impedes their chances of changing jobs.

The scale of retraining is also inadequate. On average in the late 1980s, a Soviet worker was trained less than his or her counterpart in developed market economy countries. Due to the transition to a market-oriented system, enterprises doubt whether they should invest in retraining when trained workers may have to be released. Such problems did not exist in the past because most workers remained within an enterprise for the whole of their working lives.

In 1991 the USSR pursued a policy of retuning the retraining system. One method was to establish training/retraining centres, in order to make the workforce more employable. Surveys show that the majority of released workers were prepared to undergo retraining.

One problem in such initiatives is to ensure all groups, notably women, have access to these opportunities. The share of women in retraining has, however, been low, in part because many women set a condition for retraining, such as preferring to be retrained near their homes.[30]

Social policy evolution in the period of transition

The transition to a market economy, although *initially* not "a shock therapy" as in some CEECs, has taken its toll on living standards. The situation was made more difficult because about a quarter of the population of the ex-USSR, i.e., 70-80 million people, already had incomes at the minimum wage level. About 25 per cent are workers, employees and collective farmers, and more than a third are pensioners or disabled.[31] Worse, the situation is harving children because many live in families most affected by transition. By late 1991, about 23 million children, or every third child, was living below the poverty line.[32]

The twin challenges in the transition from low paid employment in secure jobs, to better paid but less secure jobs, is to provide social protection to the poor and other vulnerable segments of the population; and to check emerging unemployment without impairing labour flexibility.[33]

The State always used to guarantee *minimum incomes* and regulated increases separately for different population groups, such as pensioners, students and children. The ceilings for non-taxable incomes were raised accordingly. However, rapidly rising inflation undermined the purchasing power of fixed minimum incomes in 1991. In the first four months, prices rose by 200 per cent, and by December 1991 had increased by about 600 per cent.[34] The subsistence level, as calculated by the USSR Ministry of Labour in early 1991, was 227 roubles. (It should be noted that the minimum wage in the country previously had been 70 roubles).[35] At the end of the year, the Russian Government set a level of 342 roubles as the minimum level of income for 1992. However, with growing inflation, an income of 342 roubles was inadequate. Following price liberalisation in January 1992, prices grew by over 500 per cent.[36] The subsistence level, as calculated by trade unions, should have been 1.070 roubles. Trade unions argued that prices had already grown 500 per cent prior to price liberalisation in January 1992.[37]

According to the USSR programme of 1991, there were three types of prices: *fixed prices* (prices fixed by the state for trading, and not to be raised above a certain level), *regulated prices* (accounting for about 15 per cent of the total) and *free* prices (about 30 per cent). However, by the end of 1991 it was decided that all prices (with a few exceptions) would be freed.[38]

At that time, the Government began to realise that it was not possible to protect *all* groups against inflation in times of hyperinflation. The idea was to protect only the poorest. Indexed payments for pensioners, students, teachers and other State employees not working in industrial enterprises, were to come from the budget. Compensation for workers in State enterprises was to come from the wage fund.[39]

In an effort to help families with children, the Government issued decrees raising allowances: up to 70 roubles for a child under 18 months of age, as well as an allowance to families with children for each child in the age group 18-24 months of 50 per cent of the minimum wage, provided that family income per head did not exceed twice the minimum wage.[40]

A Law to protect the interests of the disabled became effective on 1 January 1991. This covered the social protection of 35 to 40 million people. Now each State is pursuing its own programme to protect the disabled.

Some groups will be the focus of special programmes. Special programmes will primarily protect old people, the disabled, orphans and families with many children. However, it is difficult to determine what should be the level of guaranteed minimum income in view of inflation.

A Social Insurance Fund was established in 1991, responsible for the administration of short-term social security benefits and independent from the General Confederation of Trade Unions, which used to be responsible for such activities. The Fund had responsibility for reorganising the medical care benefit system (previously under the control of the Ministry of Health) and for the administration of social insurance programmes.[41]

Workers' remuneration issues

Labour remuneration will be a critical issue in the transition to a market economy. A rigid, centralised wage system is not compatible with market economies. The reform of 1987 added some flexibility in wage setting and gave enterprises more freedom, but did not change the system radically.[42] Moving to a market economy, however, has begun the process of radical change in remuneration, through decontroling wages.

In the USSR, workers' wages accounted for 42 per cent of national income in 1985, whereas in the United States this figure was 61.2 per cent. Adjusted for differences in calculation, the gap is wider. Incomes from personal household plots and from other sources accounted for 4.5 and 6.0 per cent respectively. Entrepreneurial revenue has recently grown as a source of income, but there are no exact data on its magnitude. About 95 per cent of workers' income in the USSR consisted of wages, the remainder including social benefits, annual bonuses, and other merit-related incentives.[43]

Table 7.5 shows that average monthly wages in the Soviet economy grew continuously in the years of *perestroika*. Some argue that this was one of the mistakes. Neglect of the budget deficit and the greater deregulation of wages when compared to prices contributed to excessive money supply, inflation and mounting social expenditure.[44] Wages continued to grow in 1991. Wage increase ceilings were removed and bargaining over wages was allowed. Immediately it was reported that wages grew as a result of bargaining, sometimes doubling.[45] Hence, wages continued to grow in spite of the decline in labour productivity and a fall in production.

Table 7.5. **Average monthly wage of workers and employees, USSR, 1985-1990**

	(bonuses included apart from the wage fund) (roubles)					
	1985	1986	1987	1988	1989	1990[1]
Total	190.1	195.6	202.9	219.8	240.4	270.0
Material production	201.1	207.5	214.7	233.8	256.9	289.0
Non-production branches	154.0	158.3	165.8	177.0	192.0	220.0

1. Estimated.
Source: Goskomstat, USSR, 1991.

Inflation accelerated because of the growth of money incomes, accompanied by a fall in production and curtailment of imports of consumer goods and food. In the early stages of the reform after 1985, the Government wanted the growth in labour productivity to exceed wage increases. This was never achieved. Moreover, considerable wage differentials developed between workers in the state sector and those outside it, notably in co-operatives. In 1990, an average wage in a co-operative was 704 roubles whereas in the state sector it was only 254 roubles.[46] This was a leading factor in labour mobility from the public to the private sector.

However, the lack of real competition, and the greater freedom given to enterprises in deciding on workers' remuneration, enabled enterprises to channel some of the surplus obtained through price increases into the wage fund (the "consumption fund"). The Government decided to correct the situation by introducing a special tax on any increment of the wage fund above 3 per cent. It was not an effective measure because exceptions to the rule were made, and enterprises found ways to circumvent the system by, for example, directing money into social development funds rather than wage funds.

Table 7.6 shows diverging directions of developments in production efficiency and incomes of the population. However, workers find rises in money incomes inadequate because of inflation. Soviet miners in 1991 demanded a two-fold increase in wages, and air traffic controllers wanted their wages increased three-fold.

Table 7.6. **Dynamics of production and incomes, USSR, 1987-1991**
(percentage change over previous year)

	1987	1988	1989	1990	1991
			First quarter		
Gross national product	2.9	5.5	3.0	-2.0	-8.0
Produced national income	1.6	4.4	2.4	4.0	-10.0
Industrial production	3.8	3.9	1.7	-1.2	-5.0
Labour productivity	1.6	4.8	2.3	-3.0	-9.0
Money incomes of the population	3.9	9.2	13.1	16.9	19.0

Source: Wages in the USSR in 1990-91. Tchetvernina, (Geneva, ILO, 1991; unpublished manuscript).

It should also be taken into account that the population has been stratified by level of income during the transition. Those with fixed incomes (grants, stipends, pensions) especially have suffered. Income differentiation has reached the point where the first millionaires have begun to appear — and these immediately set up their own trade union (with secret membership).

In 1991 the Government tried to place all enterprises under equitable conditions of competition by reducing taxes on industrial enterprises to 35 per cent. However, since enterprises were made responsible for compensating workers for price increases, the wage race might well continue.

The process of wage reform is far from finished, although under way, and minimum wages for various professional and skilled groups of workers are planned. Restrictions have been lifted on individual earnings. Enterprises have been granted the right to determine the forms and systems of wages.[47] Raising wage ceilings, however, might further fuel inflation. Thus, the need arises to combat inflationary trends and soak up excess money. An important feature of the new approach is the *negotiability* of wages and salaries.

The USSR Government's anti-crisis programme envisaged, beginning in 1992, the introduction of a system of tripartite collective labour agreements. The parties will be the Government, owners (associations of employers) and trade unions. The levels of remuneration are to be determined by the market.[48] April 1991 marked the conclusion of the first agreement between the Government and the General Confederation of Labour.[49]

At the enterprise level, the main instrument to control wages and salaries will be a *collective contract* (or agreement) between management and labour. Under the centrally planned economy, collective contracts were a formal exercise whereas under present conditions such contracts can become an effective instrument of *bargaining*. In the past, the work collective simply pledged to fulfil the enterprise's production plans.

Under conditions of shortage, some enterprises, particularly those engaged in foreign trade, could be allowed to make supplementary payments to workers in convertible currencies. Others have already started to pay in kind, an attractive method when there are shortages of goods.

In short, the new approaches towards remuneration comprise lifting restrictions on higher wages and salaries, freedom in issues of remuneration for enterprises and flexibility in choosing alternative forms of remuneration, including payments in kind. Public sector enterprises have been given a free hand to raise wages and salaries. The State retains the obligation to determine compensation for workers for conditions of work, Sunday and holiday work, night work, overtime and certain other payments.

Industrial relations, privatisation and worker participation

Privatisation and creation of institutional framework for tripartism

Privatisation is a key element of the transition to a market economy. Suggestions on possible methods of privatisation include: 1) giving citizens a certain rouble equivalent in privatisation investment shares (7,000 roubles for the Russian Federation); 2) handing over fixed funds of State enterprises to workers in these enterprises; and 3) allowing citizens to buy out enterprises, and establish joint-stock companies.

While theoretical discussions on privatisation were going on, a workable mode of privatisation was implemented in practice — i.e., establishing joint-stock companies in place of public enterprises. Employee participation schemes in the form of workers' shareholding became widespread. According to official data, at the end of 1990 there were, under a lease system, 2,400 industrial enterprises, about 180 large construction firms, 33,000 shops and public catering establishments, 400 municipal services enterprises, 400 public transport companies, and some others.[50] After the attempted coup in August 1991, the new Government of the Russian Federation accelerated privatisation efforts. In Moscow, for instance, a survey of enterprises was started. Those found unprofitable were subject to rapid privatisation. The mayor of Moscow decided to privatise retail shops at the end of 1991.

In agriculture, privatisation took the form mainly of private farming, as it struggled to replace collective and state farms. Although private farming only really began in 1989, in 1990 there were about 100,000 private farmers. It is expected that this number will have soon tripled.[51]

Measures have been taken to train employers and managers of new private enterprises, sometimes abroad. Still, concerns are expressed that it would take 10 years or more to have sufficient numbers of trained workers, partly because nobody has any experience of operating in a market environment.

The emergence of employers' organisations

In the command economy, there were no tripartite relations. They had to be created, but first, genuine partners for such relations had to be identified, and this could not be accomplished quickly. Laws forming a legal environment for a market economy have since created the legal basis for social partners to operate.

By 1991, organisations of employers had been formed. *Employers at co-operatives*, were the quickest to establish an organisation. There are also others, like the Union of Small Venture Enterprises, and the Union of Small Enterprises of the USSR.[52]

The newly established *Union of Lessees and Employers* covers more than 10 million people, working at 2,700 leased and 50 private enterprises (bought out completely). An international fund to assist entrepreneurship is being set up, as well as an institute of business.

With hundreds of members, the *Scientific Industrial Union* incorporates 1,500 of the largest enterprises and 40 associations. Enterprises linked with this union produce two- thirds of the USSR's industrial output.[53] Still, the public sector remains dominant, although employment in it shrank in 1991 by 2.6 million (see table 3 for data an three republics). Most employers are still managers of public sector enterprises; entrepreneurs with their own companies employ only about 10 per cent of the total labour force.[54]

New trade unions

Trade unions are re-emerging in a new guise. During the pre-*perestroika* period they were part of the state system, and ensured implementation of party decisions. Nowadays, independent trade unions are a feature of emerging tripartism.

Unionisation has always been very high, and de-unionisation has not touched the countries of the former Soviet Union yet. At the beginning of 1985, unions had more than 136 million members or 99 per cent of the country's industrial, office and professional workers, collective farmers, vocational school trainees and students at specialised secondary and higher educational establishments.[55] Unions have been very active in providing social and cultural services to workers, including pensions, medical insurance, recreation, food supplies. Their new position, acquired during *perestroika*, involves *independence* from political and state institutions, and *pluralism*. The major new role of trade unions is bargaining for conditions of employment. Trade unions are being formed either through the transformation of old unions or the establishment of new ones. There are several types of new union organisation, as discussed elsewhere.[56]

Independence was announced in the autumn of 1990, when the All-Union Central Council of Trade Unions (AUCCTU) was proclaimed independent from any political party as well as from the state and administrative bodies. The most notable new trade unions are the Confederation of Labour and the Association of Social Trade Unions (Sotsprof).

Pluralism in types of ownership and privatisation have led to the establishment of trade unions specifically designed for the first time to protect the interests of *workers employed in the private sector*. It has been reported that a Confederation of Trade Unions of Co-operative Workers has been established. This consists of about 10 million workers in 11 former republics of the USSR. The main task of the Confederation is the legal and social protection of co-operative workers. It should be noted that working conditions and remuneration of core and periphery workers in co-operatives in the various republics can differ substantially.

Although there are no exact data on its membership, Sotsprof is estimated to have between 20,000 and 30,000 members. This union's affiliates include the Lawyers' and Law Enforcement Agencies Employees' Union, the Local Government Employees' Union, the Directors', Managers' and Scientific Workers' Union, 13 city trade union organisations (of which 11 are in Moscow), the Journalists' Union, the White-collar Workers' Union and others.[57]

The changes were made at the state level in December 1990 when the Supreme Soviet adopted the Law on Trade Unions, their Rights and Guarantees of their Activities. This allowed for pluralistic approaches towards trade union activities. Workers and students were granted the right to set up trade unions on a voluntary basis, and to join existing unions.

All trade unions enjoy equal rights. No distinction is made between unions in the public or private sector. In terms of the Law, unions participate in negotiations over labour issues at different levels, including elaboration of labour laws, employment policies and the social protection of workers. No enterprise liquidation or reorganisation leading to poorer working conditions or staff reductions can be made without one month's notice to a trade union. The Law gives unions the right to enter into collective negotiations with management, employers or their representatives to conclude collective agreements. Unions are demanding "market salaries" for working in a market economy. In particular, they are pushing for wage indexation.

Conclusions

The economies of the successor states to the USSR are in deep crisis. These states have decided that only a market-oriented economy can achieve economic progress and reverse stagnation. At all levels of policy-making, there is consensus in favour of a market-oriented system. Transition already seems to have started in all republics. Meanwhile, unemployment, officially recognised only in July 1991, has kept growing, up from thousands to tens of thousands. Forecasts of unemployment depend, however, on the variant of economic reform (no privatisation, slow privatisation, "shock" therapy) adopted. In 1991, unemployment was still under control. Unemployment first affected Soviet women, especially in their 50s, and young people. Of course, the Soviet Government had taken preparatory measures to limit unemployment, but they were inadequate. For example, retraining centres for the unemployed in Moscow did not start to function until after the shedding of workers began.[58] For the whole of the former USSR there were, in 1991, only 30 pilot centres to retrain workers, and five centres to reintegrate former Soviet military servicemen. This, of course, meant that practically the only way to help the unemployed was to pay them benefits while trying to find jobs for those affected by redundancy. Therefore a major challenge for the governments of the Commonwealth of Independent States is to develop effective labour market policies to cope with the social consequences of the reforms.

Notes

1. These preliminary figures were provided by the State statistical office Goskomstat at a meeting in Moscow in early 1992. As only six of the former Soviet republics have agreed to maintain a common statistical gathering system, such information may become even harder to verify in the future.

2. *Izvestia* (Moscow): 20 Apr., 1991, p.2

3. *International Herald Tribune* (Paris), 30 May 1991, "Soviet bill to boost foreign investment".

4. *Moskovskie Novosti* (Moscow), 20 Oct. 1991, p.7.

5. *Vestnik Statistiki* (Moscow), No. 4, 1991, p.44.

6. *Voprosy Ekonomiki* (Moscow), No. 9, 1991, pp. 33,35.

7. Data from Goskimstat, 1992.

8. *Izvestia* (Moscow), 6 Dec. 1991, "Chto za dushoi...".

9. Ministry of Labour (Goskomtrud), USSR, 1991.

10. Goskimstat, Moscow, 1992.

11. Goskomtrud, USSR, 1991.

12. *Rabotchaya Tribuna* (Moscow), 6 Mar. 1991, p.1.

13. *Izvestia* (Moscow), 21 June 1991, "Nuzhno li...."

14. *Khozyastvo i Pravo* (Moscow), No. 8 (164), Aug. 1990, p.34.

15. *Trud* (Moscow), 6 May 1991, p.1.

16. *Fundamentals of the Legislation of the USSR and its Constituent Republics on Employment*, Moscow, 1991, Art. 1.

17. Ibid.

18. *Izvestia* (Moscow), No. 31, 5 Feb. 1991, p.3

19. *Trud* (Moscow), 25 Jan. 1990, pp.2-3.

20. Ibid.

21. *Pravda* (Moscow), 31 May 1991, p.1, "Employment Fund".

22. Goskomstat, Moscow, 1992.

23. Goskomtrud, USSR, 1991.

24. *Rabotchaya tribuna* (Moscow), 18 Apr. 1991, p.1

25. G. Standing (ed.): *In search of flexibility: the new soviet labour market*, Geneva, ILO, 1991, Ch. 7: *Labour market problems and developments in the republics*, by A. Samorodov.

26. Goskomtrud, USSR, 1991.

27. G. Standing (ed.): *In search of flexibility: the new Soviet labour market*, (Geneva, ILO, 1991), Ch. 11: *"Wage differentials: The trade union view"*, by V. Veretennikov 1990.

28. Goskomtrud, USSR, *State all-union employment programme*, 1991, (draft).

29. G. Standing, *Social Labour* (Moscow), No.2, 1991, pp 31-41.

30. Russia Labour Flexibility Survey, (Geneva, ILO, 1991-92, unpublished document).

31. *Sovetskie Profsoyuzy* (Moscow), No. 23-24, 1990.

32. *Trud* (Moscow), 25 May 1991, p. 1.

33. Standing, 1991, an interview with S*ocial Labour*, op. cit.

34. *Trud* (Moscow), 25 May, 1991, p. 1.

35. *Izvestia* (Moscow), 29 May, 1991, p. 2 *Trud* (Moscow), 25 May 1991, p. 1, Pravda (Moscow), 22 May 1991, p. 2.

36. *Literaturnaya Gazeta* (Moscow), 13 Nov., 1991, p. 1.

37. *Rabothchaya tribuna* (Moscow), 27 Dec. 1991, p. 1.

38. *Literaturnaya Gazeta* (Moscow), 13 Nov. 1991, p. 1.

39. *Financial Times* (London), 29 May, 1991, p. 2.

40. *Argumenty i Fakty* (Moscow), No. 17, 1991, p. 4.

41. ILO data, 1991.

42. See V. I. Shcherbakov, *Results-based remuneration in the USSR* (Geneva, ILO, 1988).

43. *Izvestia* (Moscow), 20 Apr., 1991, p.2.

44. Aslund, IMF Survey, 27 May 1991, p. 170.

45. I. Zaslavski, in *Voprosy Ekonomiki* (Moscow), No. 9, 1991, p. 34

46. *Sovetskie Profsoyuzu* (Moscow), No. 4, 1991, p.23.

47. *Argumenty i Fakty* (Moscow), No. 17, Apr. 1991, p.5. (FBIS-SOV-91-086, 3 May, 1991).

48. *Rabotchaya tribuna* (Moscow), 17 Apr. 1991.

49. *Trud* (Moscow), 26 April, 1991.

50. T. Tchetvernina: *Wages in the USSR in 1990-91* (Geneva, ILO, 1991; unpublished manuscript).

51. *Moskovskie Novosti* (Moscow), 20 Oct., 1991, p.1.

52. *Trud* (Moscow), 11 Jan., 1991, p.3.

53. *Izvestiya* (Moscow), 28 June 1991, (an article by A. Volsky).

54. L. Gordon and E. Klopov, *Labour Relations in the Conditions of Soviet Society Reform*, a working paper for the ILO (Moscow), 1991, p. 28.

55. Profizdat Publishers: *The Soviet trade unions* (Moscow), 1985, p.5.

56. See, e.g., Gordon and Klopov, 1991, op. cit.

57. ILO data, 1990.

58. *Izvestia*, "There are already thousands of unemployed" (Moscow), 1 Aug. 1991.

Chapter 8

Women's employment in central and eastern Europe: status and prospects

by
Sabine Hübner, Friederike Maier, Hedwig Rudolph *
Wissenschaftszentrum, Berlin

Introduction

This chapter considers how changing economic and political conditions during the transition process in central and eastern Europe affect men and women differently. Transition implies a far-reaching redistribution of work, income and opportunities. With access to paid work no longer a "natural" right, increased social inequalities would seem inevitable. The very notion of work changes once guaranteed job security, and the duty to contribute to production, are replaced by individual risks and opportunities. Thus training can no longer be regarded as a "loan" granted by society, but becomes an individual "investment in human capital".

The division of labour — paid and unpaid, productive and reproductive — within the family is also at issue in the transition countries. There is growing support for the role of the family as a social and economic unit and a renewed debate about the marketability of certain services which can be provided within the family, such as caring for children, for ill or elderly family members.

With the assistance of Silke Meyer. The authors draw heavily on four country studies for Czechoslovakia, Hungary, Poland and the former USSR, and additional information from Bulgaria. These were carried out by Alena Kroupova of the Federal Ministry of Labour and Social Affairs, Prague (Czechoslovakia), Maria Lado of the Labour Research Institute of the Ministry of Labour, Budapest (Hungary), Renata Siemienska of the Sociology Institute, University of Warsaw (Poland), Natasha Zakharova of the Vienna International Centre (USSR) and Silvia Dilova of the Sociology Institute, Bulgarian Academy of Science, Sofia (Bulgaria).

The transition process will therefore undoubtedly affect gender relations, especially since men and women in these countries enter the "new age" from unequal positions. This is clear from an analysis of women's previous employment status and living conditions. In spite of women's high labour force participation rate, men and women were concentrated in different occupations, with different career prospects and marked income differentials. Unlike men's, women's lives were characterised by their dual role as workers and mothers. The politically propagated female role model assigned responsibility for child care exclusively to the mother — witness the prolonged maternity leave provisions introduced in the 1980s.

If social differentiation is one of the main features of the transition process, there is a need to identify vulnerable groups at risk of marginalisation. Women are just one group; other vulnerable groups include older people and single parents. In order to avoid social disintegration, social and labour market policies should identify target groups of special concern. In this context, research can identify causes of vulnerability, point to factors likely to aggravate inequality of opportunities and suggest policies to help reduce segmentation. For example, taking into account the professional qualifications and experience women have acquired in the transition countries, it would not seem wise to let female labour force participation decrease — even temporarily, since qualifications are perishable goods.

Apart from problems of cross-country data comparability and availability, the most serious methodological problem of this synthesis report relates to different national patterns of transition. Hungary has had a long record of reform debate and transition to a market economy while Romania began transition only recently when virtually unprepared. Paths, programmes and priorities differ as well as timetables. So, what was supposed to serve as a common framework for the comparative analysis of women's prospects on the labour markets of central and eastern Europe turned out to be part of the question.

Women in the labour force

Participation rates

The massive mobilisation of women for the labour market was a prominent feature in all central and eastern European countries (CEECs). Based on the constitutional principle that every citizen had both a right and an obligation to work, women's participation in paid employment increased rapidly in the years following the Second World War. The process of women's integration in the labour market was supported ideologically by equating employment with emancipation, and reinforced economically by the low - productivity, labour - intensive economy. For individuals, it was buttressed by low wage levels which made it hard to support a family on one income.

In 1988, women's share in total employment ranged from 40 per cent in Romania to 50.6 per cent in the former USSR, which means that nearly half of the employed workforce were women (Kroupová, 1990).[1] Women's activity rates (defined as the economically active as a proportion of the total female population over 14 or 15 years) varied in the mid-1980s from 39 per cent in Hungary to 50 per cent in Bulgaria. Both men and women had the highest participation rates in the 30-40 age group. In 1980 in the USSR, Bulgaria and Czechoslovakia, more than 90 per cent of all women in the 25-40 age group were economically active, while the figure in Hungary, Romania and Poland was 80 per cent (see table 8.1).[2] In Hungary, the high percentage of economically active women in the lowest age bracket is due to the fact that eligibility for maternity leave benefit requires women to have completed at least one year of employment.

Table 8.1 Activity rates by age and sex, central and eastern Europe, selected years (in percentages)

Age group	Bulgaria[1]		CSFR[2]		Hungary[3]		Poland[4]		Romania[5]		USSR[6]	
	Male	Female	Male	Female	Male	Female	Male	Female	Male	Female	Male	Female
15-19	4.2	8.1	29.0	29.8	45.5	40.4	29.3	21.4	37.5	32.1	10.5	9.5
20-24	85.5	91.0	86.5	83.4	91.9	59.9	82.7	68.4	87.1	75.6)	91.5	89.1
25-29			98.2	90.7	98.2	69.8	96.2	75.1	97.0	83.1)		
30-34	97.8	96.4	98.7	92.0	98.4	81.1	97.1	79.5	97.9	83.5)	98.2	95.6
35-39	95.8	94.8	98.4	92.8	97.8	84.9	96.2	81.6	97.2	83.6)		
40-44	95.5	94.6	97.6	91.7	96.0	83.1	94.8	82.7	95.8	81.7)	97.0	94.1
45-49	94.6	91.0	96.0	88.1	92.9	77.5	92.1	78.5	93.8	77.6)		
50-54	88.1	83.6	92.7	79.9	86.2	67.4	87.1	71.6	88.8	69.7	90.0	82.0
55-59	80.9	32.0	84.2	40.8	72.2	18.8	81.5	57.9	78.7	52.5)	78.4	29.4
60-64	39.2	16.6	46.3	21.5	13.2	8.7	62.4	37.4	44.7	25.2)		
65-69	28.4	9.3	30.3	12.2	5.3	5.1	43.0	27.8	20.9	13.2)	15.5	5.3
70 and over	14.0	3.6	17.9	6.1	3.7	3.1	35.0	20.2	13.4	10.3)		
Total	55.1	49.6	56.2	46.7	55.3	39.9	57.4	45.4	55.2	45.1	55.7	48.1

1. 1985, comprises all persons aged 16 years and over who, during the reference period, were either employed or temporarily out of work (all sectors of the economy, including unpaid family workers).

2. 1980, economically active population figure *excludes* unpaid family workers; comprises all persons aged 15 years and over who, during the reference period, were employed or performed any work of value, including womens' maternity leave (all sectors of the economy).

3. 1980, comprises all persons aged 15 and over who, during the reference period, were employed, excluding students with jobs, those receiving child-care/benefits (all sectors of the economy).

4. 1978, comprises all persons aged 15 and over who, during the reference week, performed any work of economic value (including unpaid family workers, temporarily absent, all sectors of economy).

5. 1977, comprises all persons aged 14 years and over who, on the day of the census, performed work in a job, business or any economic activity, (including unpaid family workers, temporarily absent, all sectors of economy).

6. 1979, comprises all persons aged 16 years and over who, on the day of the census, were engaged in the national economy or individual subsidiary farms (including women on child-care leave, excluding unpaid family workers).

Source: ILO: *Yearbook of Labour Statistics 1949-89* and ILO: *Statistical Sources and Methods*, Vol. 5: *Total and economically active population, employment and unemployment* (Geneva)

Participation rates as defined above are influenced by population age structure and by policies on length of compulsory education, retirement age, and so on. Since 1970, all CEECs, as well as western European countries, have experienced decreasing participation rates of young people, partly due to prolongation of compulsory education. At the other end of the age spectrum, there has been an increase in participation rates of both men and women beyond official retirement age, reflecting financial incentives for pensioners to stay in the workforce and rising living costs which have not been matched by corresponding increases in pensions.

High female labour force participation rates are a relatively recent phenomenon. In the early 1950s, women accounted for much lower proportions of the labour force: 30 per cent in Hungary, 38 per cent in Czechoslovakia, 42 per cent in Bulgaria, 44 per cent in Poland and 47 per cent in the USSR (Kroupová, 1990). In the following decades the integration of women into paid work contributed significantly to the growth in the total labour force.

By the 1980s, women's economic activity rates no longer differed by marital status (married or single). In addition to a high intrinsic motivation to do paid work, this reflected the dependence of most families on two wages.

More than 90 per cent of all economically active women in CEECs have one child or more. The Western model of successive periods of child-bearing, lengthy withdrawal from and then re-entry into the labour market has not applied. Only recently has child-care leave been available in all the countries. Many young women (hardly any men) have taken advantage of this to withdraw for a short period from paid employment (for a summary of the regulations, see table 8.2). In Hungary, around 9 per cent of women workers were on maternity or child-care leave in 1988, in Poland an estimated 10 per cent in 1985, while in Czechoslovakia around 40,000 women re-entered the labour market after maternity leave each year. A temporary withdrawal from paid employment did not affect job opportunities, which had to be guaranteed, but it did impair employment status with respect to wage increases, access to training and career advancement.

The impact of these measures thus had paradoxical consequences for women's social status. The opportunity of paid leave to care for children, with a guaranteed right to return to a similar job, offered women some degree of choice: they could decide whether and when to have children, and when to return to the workforce. However, the measures also reinforced the notion that paid work should be of secondary concern for women, and buttressed the traditional division of labour within the household. Women were legally defined as workers and mothers, but there was no equivalent definition of men as workers and fathers.

Family structure

The demographic structure in central and eastern Europe differs somewhat from that in western Europe. Birth rates have fallen in most of the countries since the mid-1970s or early 1980s, but remain generally higher than in the West[3] (see table 8.3).

Over the past 20 years in central and eastern Europe, there has been a shift in fertility towards younger age groups with a sharp rise in birth rates among women under 25. Some 50 to 60 per cent of fertility occurs in women under 25, compared with only about 40 per cent in western industrialised economies. In central and eastern Europe, birth rates peak in the 20-24 age group; in the West the 25-29 age group has the highest rates (see table 8.4).

Table 8.2. **Maternity leave/child-care leave, central and eastern Europe, 1990**

	Maternity Leave	Prolonged maternal/ parental leave	Additional holidays Caring for sick family members	Dismissal regulations	Leave effects on employment/ social security
Czechoslovakia[1]	28 weeks. Maternity benefits: 90% of net wage. Obligation to keep original job open.	In the first 3 yrs. Fixed sum (allowance): fathers eligible, parents may alternate part-time or flexible working hours (2 hrs/ day).	Holidays: none. Caring leave: 7 working days for every illness if child under 10; sickness benefits to mother or father. (Single parents: 13 working days).	General: no dismissal of pregnant mothers, mothers with children under 3, but does not apply in cases of total closure.	Counts towards length of service.
Hungary[1]	24 weeks, full net wage. Job corresponding to work contract.	Until child is 2, 75% of net wage (allowance). Third year: flat-rate sum. Father eligible in second year. Part-time employment on request in second year.	Holidays: up to 3 children under 18, 2 days anually; further children, 2 days. Caring leave: child up to 3 - 84 days 3-5 - 40 days 6-10 - 14 days. Sickness benefit to mother or father	General: no dismissal of pregnant mothers, mothers on maternity leave, single mothers with children under 18, but does not apply in cases of total closure.	Counts towards length of service.
Poland[1]	First child: 16 weeks. Any further child: 18 weeks. Full net wage. Obligation to keep original job open.	First child: until 2nd birthday. Second and further: until 3rd birthday. Fixed sum (allowance)(25% of average monthly wages). Fathers eligible.	Holidays: 2 days annually for every child under 16. Caring leave: mothers of young children or in large families - 30 days annually.	General (until 1990): no dismissal of pregnant mothers, mothers on maternity leave until child is 2 (3 if single parent); since 1990, dismissal allowed when firm undergoes basic change and group dismissals occur.	Counts towards length of service.

217

Table 8.2. (cont'd)

USSR[2]	18 weeks, full net wage. Job corresponding to work contract.	Until child is 3. Fixed sum (allowance) plus compensation for increases in retail price index. Fathers eligible.	Holidays: 2 or more children under 12 years; 3 days annually + 10 days unpaid caring leave: child under 14, 7 days; over 14, 3 days. Sickness benefits.	General: no dismissal of pregnant mothers, mothers with children under 1 year (Far East: 2 years) but, does not apply in cases of total closure.	Counts towards length of service.
Bulgaria[3]	Minimum: 12 weeks; first child, 120 days; 2nd, 150 days; 3rd, 180 days; 4th, 120 days. 100% of gross wage. Job corresponding to work contract.	1st, 2nd and 3rd child: until 2nd birthday. Fixed sum (minimum wage). Unpaid: until 3rd birthday. Fathers or grandparents eligible.	Holidays: 2 days annually with 2 children under 16, 4 days with more. Caring leave: 60 days annually for children under 16; for children under 7: 100% of gross wage. For older children: depends on length of service, to mother or father.	No dismissal of pregnant mothers, mothers with children under 8 months, even in cases of closure (obliged to transfer them).	Counts towards length of service.
Romania[4]	112 days.	Until first birthday, 65% of monthly wage (as provided in job evaluation scheme).	Holidays:unknown. Caring leave: on medical advice for sick children under 3.	No dismissal of pregnant mothers, mothers on maternity leave, mothers caring for a sick child under 3.	Counts towards length of service.

Sources:
1. Country reports and Alena Kroupová: Women - employment and earnings in central and east european countries, (1990), manuscript for the Tripartite Symposium on Equality of Opportunity and Treatment for Men and Women.
2. Polina Maeva: National mechanisms for affairs of women in the Union of Soviet Socialist Republics, their structure, functions and role in perestroika processes, (1991), paper prepared for the Regional Seminar on the Impact of Economic and Political Reform on the Status of Women in Eastern Europe and the USSR, Vienna, 8-12 April 1991.
3. "Women Workers: Protection or equality?", Conditions of Work Digest (Geneva, ILO), Vol. 6, 2/1987; V. Bodrova and R. Anker (eds.), Working women in socialist countries: The fertility connection, (Geneva, ILO, 1985); Dumitra Popescu: Present situation and trends affecting women in Romania, paper to the Regional Seminar on the Impact of Economic and Political Reform on the Status of Women in Eastern Europe and the USSR, Vienna, 8-12 April 1991.

Table 8.3 **Selected countries/areas: Live birth rates, per 1,000 inhabitants**

	1985	1987/88
Bulgaria	13.3	12.9
Czechoslovakia	14.6	13.8
Hungary	12.2	11.9
Poland	18.2	15.5
Romania	15.8	15.5
USSR	19.4	19.8
Belarus	16.5	16.1
Ukraine	15.6	14.8
Denmark	10.5	11.5
Sweden	11.8	13.3
Ireland	17.6	16.6
Fed. Rep. of Germany	9.6	11.0
United Kingdom	13.3	13.8
United States	15.5	15.9
Japan	11.8	11.0

Source: United Nations: *Demographic Yearbook 1988*, table 9, (New-York).

Table 8.4. **Selected countries: Live birth rates by age of mother[1]**

	Age of mother (in years)					
	Up to 20	20-24	25-29	30-34	35-39	All age groups
Bulgaria (1986)	81.1	186.1	94.4	34.4	10.0	57.1
Czechoslovakia (1986)	50.6	187.7	108.9	41.7	12.8	58.8
Hungary (1987)	47.6	145.4	107.1	44.3	14.7	49.2
Poland (1987)	32.2	171.6	129.5	63.1	27.2	65.8
USSR (1986)	43.9	192.2	146.4	79.2	33.8	79.8
Romania (1985)	57.8	191.4	121.1	55.2	21.4	65.2
Denmark (1987)	9.5	70.7	122.3	71.3	21.5	43.5
Sweden (1987)	11.0	83.6	139.0	95.2	33.2	52.2
Ireland (1985)	16.8	87.1	160.3	136.2	74.5	75.0
Fed.Rep. of Germany (1986)	8.6	57.7	108.2	70.0	23.8	40.1
United Kingdom (1987)	30.9	93.9	125.5	81.3	26.6	55.3
United States (1986)	51.7	108.2	109.2	69.3	24.3	59.1
Japan (1986)	3.8	59.6	169.7	86.8	17.2	44.7

1. Rates are the number of live births by age of mother per 1,000 corresponding female population.
Source: United Nations: *Demographic Yearbook 1988* (New-York), table 11.

219

The overall decrease in fertility rates has influenced family size in CEECs. Only 6 to 10 per cent of women have no children,[4] but the average number of children per economically active married woman of child-bearing age was, at the beginning of the 1980s, 1.6 in Hungary, 1.8 in Bulgaria, 1.8 in Estonia and 3.9 in Uzbekistan (Bodrova and Anker, 1985). In all countries examined here, the majority of children are growing up in families with one or two children.

While in a number of western European countries the propensity to marry has decreased, marriage rates in CEECs have remained relatively high. However, the number of single-parent families is rising, partly as a result of increasing divorce rates. In Hungary the proportion of single-parent families (80 per cent of them headed by mothers) reached 10 per cent of all families at the end of the 1980s. In Czechoslovakia, there were 179,000 single-parent families, 97 per cent of them headed by mothers, in 1989. In the former USSR, an estimated 17 per cent of families were headed by single parents in 1990. Bulgaria also has reported an increase in the number of single mothers.

Changing family structure and falling birth rates, as well as economic and political instability, have influenced public opinion and policy measures towards population issues. From the 1960s to the later 1980s, most of the countries examined tried to stimulate population growth through various social policy measures and pro-natalist programmes. While economic activity was still regarded as a necessary precondition for women's equal status, the programmes were designed to reduce the conflict between women's roles as mothers and workers.

More recently, public opinion concerning working mothers has shifted. In Hungary, for example, it has been quite common to blame women and their unwillingness to have more children for the "dying-out of the Hungarian nation" (Lado). The threat of depopulation has become an argument for excluding women from the labour market in order to give them the opportunity to be full-time mothers. In the USSR in 1987, Mikhail Gorbachev promised measures to ensure that women could handle both work and family responsibilities. However, he also attributed severe social problems to the fact that women were not sufficiently fulfilling their "natural role as mothers" (Gorbachev, 1987). In Poland there is strong pressure, largely influenced by the Roman Catholic Church, for women to stay at home and take care of the children. This pressure is motivated not only by a falling birth rate but by rising employment problems and a growing public emphasis on women's family role.

Gender relations

This section deals with the relationship between women and men within the family, though of course gender relations are also influenced by work relationships as seen in methods of co-operation and hierarchical structures.

Attitudes towards marriage differ from country to country. In the former Soviet Union, the dissolubility of marriage seems to prevail, with a high propensity to remarry, decreasing age of first marriage, high divorce rate (3.3 per 1,000 population in 1988) and many children born out of wedlock (Bütow, 1988). The institution of marriage is much more stable in Poland, which had a divorce rate of 1.3 per 1,000 population in 1983. In republics of the ex-Soviet Union with Islamic cultures, traditional family structures prevail, women's social position is weak and violence in marriage is common. Though separations occur, remarriage is not possible (Bystydzienski, 1989,

p. 677). In Romania, marriages can be dissolved only "in exceptional cases" and the divorce rate is relatively low at 1.6 per 1,000 population (Popescu, 1991, p. 25). The traditional attitude in Czechoslovakia manifests itself in a small number of children born out of wedlock and a high number of pregnant brides, whereas the divorce rate is moderate (Kroupová, 1990).

Combining demands of work and the family puts a heavy burden on women. In none of the countries under review have men assumed an equal share of household and child-raising duties. Time-budget studies show that male attitudes towards housework have barely changed. The differences in leisure time between the sexes tend to be more marked in eastern Europe than in the West (Ziemska, 1988, p.21). Grandmothers too are often involved in care of children, as in the ex-USSR, Bulgaria and Czechoslovakia (Kroupová, 1990; Dobrianov et al., 1985, p. 78).

Women in the different countries do not react in the same way to the unequal division of household chores. Russian women were reported to file for divorce for reasons of alcoholism, physical cruelty and infidelity, but also because husbands were not willing to share household and child-care duties. In Poland, with its more traditional attitudes towards the family, conflicts about gender roles and the private division of labour were of minor importance (Bystydzienski, 1989, p. 677).

All these factors are linked to women's attitudes towards employment. For most women in central and eastern Europe it was quite natural to be economically active. Studies in the former USSR on women's propensity for paid work showed that only a small proportion would give up their jobs if their husbands' income was high enough (Kobzeva, 1990). In Poland, however, more than a third of women favoured the housewife model (Holzer and Wasilawska-Trenkner, 1985, p.162), though in practice Polish women normally returned to work after job leave (Kotowska, 1991, p. 3).

Structure and conditions of women's employment

Female employment

Women's access to paid work in central and eastern Europe was accompanied by processes of gender-based labour market segmentation and stratification, which were also reproduced by the educational system and, especially, vocational training. Skilled occupations in heavy industry — men's jobs — were among the most highly esteemed and best paid jobs in socialist countries, whereas clerical, administrative and service jobs — women's jobs — were ranked at the bottom.

Women's employment by sector varies among the different countries. For instance, in 1985, the share of agriculture in women's employment ranged from roughly 12 per cent in Czechoslovakia to 43 per cent in Romania (Kroupová, 1990).

Meanwhile, as table 8.5 shows, services (defined as sectors 6 to 9) attracted ever increasing numbers and percentages of working women; in Czechoslovakia and Hungary, about 50 per cent of all economically active women are employed in services. This reflects a global trend, although the markets for services in central and eastern Europe are less developed than in the West.

Table 8.5. **Economically active women by sector, central and eastern Europe (in per cent)**

	Bulgaria (1985)		Czechoslovakia (1988)		Hungary (1988)		Poland (1978)		Romania (1977)	
	(1)	(2)	(1)	(2)	(1)	(2)	(1)	(2)	(1)	(2)
1) Agriculture, fishing	49.1	17.0	40.4	9.9	39.8	15.5	49.1	32.6	62.3	50.3
2) Mining			17.6	0.9			11.5	0.6	10.1	0.5
3) Manufacturing	46.6	37.0	46.4	32.7	43.8	25.8	41.7	24.7	36.5	23.6
4) Electricity, gas, water			28.7	0.8			22.4	0.3	17.6	0.7
5) Construction	19.3	3.5	14.8	2.6	19.6	2.7	17.0	3.1	11.1	1.6
6) Trade, restaurants, hotels	69.4	12.4	75.7	18.3	65.4	13.9	72.0	12.1	56.2	6.9
7) Transport and communications	25.4	3.6	35.1	4.6	28.5	4.7	23.9	3.6	17.7	2.2
8) Finance, insurance	78.6	0.9	52.0	3.8						
9) Community, social and personal services	57.7	25.6	67.9	25.9	59.2	27.8	60.4	22.9	55.0	13.8
10) Other	-	-	- -	-	97%	9.6%				
Total (000s)	2235.0	100	3925.0	100	2452.9	100	8155.9	100	4926.7	100
(%)	47.6		49.0		48.5		45.4		45.6	

1. Women as percentage of total of economically active people in sector.
2. Sector share of economically active women.
Source: Bulgaria, Poland and Romania: Census data.
Czechoslovakia: Establishment data, excluding armed forces.
Hungary: Official estimates, persons in receipt of child-care allowance included in category 10.
ILO:Yearbook of Labour Statistics 1945-1989 for Bulgaria, Poland, Romania (table 2a); ILO: Yearbook of Labour Statistics 1989-90 for Czechoslovakia, Hungary (table 3b).

Roughly one-half to one-third of the female labour force is employed in industry. Women's share of the total of economically active people in industry (groups 2 to 4) is between 40 and 50 per cent. However, light industry is almost exclusively female territory, whereas women are under-represented in heavy industry (Siemienska). Throughout the industrial sector, women have mainly semi-skilled or unskilled jobs.

Looking at occupations, women's access to the labour market in ever increasing numbers has been accompanied both by their integration into a wider range of occupations and by increased "feminisation" in their traditional fields. The most detrimental consequence of feminisation is the social devaluation of these occupations affecting not only wages but skill levels.

Feminisation has advanced furthest in services. All service occupations (clerical, sales and service workers) consisted of at least 60 per cent women, and some — especially clerical jobs — were more than 80 per cent female (see table 8.6). Accountants, clerks, finance and insurance workers and social welfare workers were almost exclusively female. Women also formed the majority in public administration. Equally, a high degree of feminisation characterised jobs requiring a university degree, such as teachers, economists and doctors. Poland even set higher entry qualifications for women to study medicine, arguing the risk of over-feminisation (Plakwicz, 1991).

Moreover, there is abundant empirical evidence that in all CEECs, women's place has been mainly at the bottom of the labour hierarchy. The percentage of women holding top posts has also been substantially lower than would be merited by their qualifications and experience (Kroupová, 1990, p. 19).

Wages

In the countries studied, central wage policy was supposed to improve labour productivity as well as balance labour supply and demand according to the political aims of the state plan. From the early 1950s heavy industry — a male domain — was always at the top of the wage schedule, and light industry and services — female domains — at the bottom (table 8.7).

Gender-specific wage differentials are found in all the countries, irrespective of the legal standard stipulating "equal pay for equal work". The differentials, which range from 20 to 35 per cent, have decreased only slightly in recent years (Kroupová, 1990, p. 23) (table 8.8). In Poland, where the wage differential averages around 25 per cent, research has confirmed that, with the exception of specialists, "gender influenced wages more than education, post, age or length of service" (Siemienska).

Income discrimination experienced by economically active women is to some extent continued during retirement, as old-age pensions in CEECs depend on the previous wage level and length of service. In all the countries, pensions were quite low at about 50 per cent of previous earnings (Kroupová, 1990, p. 8). Low pensions have to be considered in the context of low retirement ages (55 for women and 60 for men in Bulgaria, Czechoslovakia, Romania and the former Soviet Union, and 60 for women and 65 for men in Poland, though the number of children a woman has borne and raised can lower the retirement age). Low pensions can (and in many cases have to) be supplemented by paid employment beyond retirement age (see table 8.1).

Table 8.6. Occupations/sectors with high female employment shares, selected, mid-to late 1980s (women as % of all employees)

USSR (1989)		Hungary (mid-1980s)		Poland (1989)		Czechoslovakia (1986/87)	
Credit/state insurance	87	**Industry**		Finance/insurance	84.5	Clothing industry	89.3
Trade/public catering	82	Weaving		Health service	81.4	Textile industry	74.7
Health care, social security	81	Spinning		Education	76.5	Leather industry	67.5
Information/computing sector	81	Sewing	at least 66	Trade	69.7	Food industry	52.4
Public education	75	Garment		Public administration	64.4	Social welfare	90.1
Culture	72	Shoe making				Health service	85.9
Clothing industry	89	Leather				Banking/insurance	75.2
Textile industry	70	Food				Trade, public catering	76.2
Bakery	72	**Occupation**				Education/culture	74.9
Librarians	91	Shop assistant					
Book-keepers	89	Hairdresser	at least 66				
Economists	87	Cosmetician					
Teachers	70	Typist					
Doctors	67	Accountant					
Engineers	58	Clerk	over 90				
		Cashier					
		Ticket-office clerk					
		Child-care					
		Teaching	over 90				
		Nurse/assistant					
		Librarian					
		Chemist					
		Programme designer	predom. female				
		Chief accountant					
		Financial controller					

Sources: Reports of national experts.

Table 8.7. **Wage differentials among industrial sectors, selected CEECS 1980**
(average industrial wage = 100)

	Czechoslovakia[1]	Hungary[2]	Poland[3]
Fuel and energy			153
Coalmining		148[4]	170
Fuels	137		104
Electricity production	112	103	103
Basic metal industries		112	131
Iron and steel	119		128
Engineering	101	95	96
Metal products	91[5]	90	90
Machinery	105	97	100
Chemicals and rubber	101		
Chemicals		104	93
Construction materials	102	94	93
Wood products	90	87	84
Textiles	82	88	87
Clothing	77	78	80
Food	91	98	86

1. Gross wages in industry.
2. Earnings in state industry.
3. Net wages in socialist industry.
4. Mining.
5. Including electrical engineering.
Source: G. Kertesi and G. Kövári: Real wages in Eastern Europe (Budapest, 1986; mimeographed), pp. 52, 60.

Table 8.8. **Earnings differentials by occupation and sex, CEECS 1980**
(male professional earnings = 100)

	Bulgaria	Czechoslovakia	Poland	Hungary
Men				
Professionals	100	100	100	100
Administrative and clerical workers	83	93	86	80
Skilled workers	90	85	82	78
Unskilled workers	80	82	77	69
Women				
Professionals	78	73	79	77
Administrative and clerical workers	62	60	65	59
Skilled workers	73	56	57	61
Unskilled workers	66	50	57	53

Source: As for table 10.7.

Working conditions

Time is the most serious constraint for women because they — and only they — have to combine paid work with family duties. So it was especially burdensome for women that the normal working week in CEECs was over 40 hours, longer than in the West (Kroupová, 1990, p. 10).

In all the CEECs, part-time work was included in the Labour Code and social security regulations (ILO, 1989). However, legal provisions allowing shorter working hours or more flexible time schedules for mothers were of little practical relevance due to the reluctance of employers to use them. The supply of part-time jobs was far lower than women's demand for them (Kroupová, 1990, p. 10). In 1987, the proportion of part-timers in the labour force was 6 per cent in Poland, 3 per cent in Hungary and 11.6 per cent in Czechoslovakia. In the ex-USSR, it was just 1 per cent in 1988.

Shift working is another critical time aspect of women's employment; in CEECs it was much more widespread in traditional female industries than in men's. Apart from the many women who accept shift work for lack of alternatives, quite a number choose it to gain higher wages, additional paid leave and early retirement. In Hungary, the proportion of working women in two — or three — shift patterns was 46.2 per cent in 1984 (Pulay, 1989, p. 101). Night shifts have been widespread among female workers in Bulgaria (Staikova-Alexandrova, 1991, p. 9). In the former USSR as many as 38 per cent of working women do night shifts. In Poland political initiatives to ban night work for women were stopped by the resistance of women (Plakwicz, 1991). Similarly, overtime work was reported by almost half of all women employed in industry in Czechoslovakia in 1986 (Kroupová, 1990, p. 16).

All the countries had laws that prohibited or restricted the employment of women in certain activities or occupations.[5] Even so, many women's jobs — especially in industry — were characterised by hard physical and low-skilled labour. The so-called light industries were not exempted from difficult and hazardous working conditions.

Working women were often exposed to health risks. In Hungary, 56 per cent of female manual workers were employed in jobs with health hazards in 1984 (Lado). Married women in particular took these jobs for the better pay (Pulay, 1989, p. 102). In the former Soviet Union, 44 per cent of women in industry — especially in manual jobs — were estimated to work in hazardous conditions (Zakharova). In Bulgaria, women with family problems or single mothers chose this type of work (Staikova-Alexandrova, 1991, p. 9).

Women in the agricultural sector were no better off. In the ex-USSR in 1989, twice as many women as men working on collective farms were in low-skilled, hard manual jobs (Zakharova). In Poland, a high percentage of private farms were managed by women, either widows or women whose husbands had taken industrial jobs in the cities. This was both hard and inefficient work because the farms were rarely equipped with modern machinery (Siemienska).

While official reports from CEECs on working conditions are quite detailed, they are also biased and therefore misleading. Those aspects that are typical of female work — such as monotony, stress, standing while working — are for the most part disregarded. "Thus women's working conditions are described by male standards and therefore the outcome is not realistic" (Lado).

Qualifications and Skills

Women have taken advantage of the expansionist educational policies of the socialist countries over recent decades (Kolankiewicz and Lewis, 1988). In all CEECs, young women have higher levels of schooling than their male peers. However, there is much empirical evidence which points to mismatches between women's qualifications and their career opportunities (Lapidus, 1988, p. 97). The problem is the *type* of qualification. "The labour market acknowledged only skills and not the level of schooling" (Lado). In Czechoslovakia, since employment opportunities for secondary-school leavers were inadequate, for many young people — mainly girls — this branch of the educational system turned out to be a "detour" on the way to the labour market (Hörner, Kuebart and Himmel, 1989). Many girls continued their education in general secondary schools both through choice and because of channelling by the planning authorities. Conversely, girls were heavily under-represented in training programmes for skilled technical jobs.

The vocational training systems in the CEECs had certain features in common: vocational training took place predominantly in schools; and a certain level of access to higher education was created by offering training courses that combined vocational training with general secondary education. Table 10.9, however, shows that the systems differed widely in their efficiency. The former Soviet Union had the lowest training ratio of all the countries (with the exception of Romania), that is, the lowest number of students at vocational schools as a proportion of the total labour force (Bütow, 1988, p. 97f).

Table 8.9. **Qualification levels of young people[1] (16 -30 years), selected CEECS (in per cent)**

	Bulgaria	Czechoslovakia	Hungary	USSR
Unskilled/semi-skilled	53.4	10.0	28.5	57.7
Skilled workers	17.2	34.0	34.5	24.5
Employees without specialised training	4.8	3.7	10.0	1.9
Employees with specialised training (technical)	16.1	42.5	15.0	8.6
Employees with higher education	7.9	4.7	7.0	7.2
Other	0.6	5.1	5.0	0.1
Total	100	100	100	100

1. Data refer to the end of the 1970s.
Source: H. Bütow, (ed.): *Länderbericht Sowjetunion* (Country Report USSR), Vol. 263
of the *Schriftenreihe zur Geschichte und Politik*, (Bonn, Bundeszentrale für politische Bildung, 1988), p.97.

The inadequacies of the vocational training system did not affect the various economic branches equally. Since the prevailing objective was to provide skills needed in heavy industry, schools training for skills needed in light and food industries, commerce and public catering faced capacity limits which constrained the qualification opportunities of women, at least in the ex-USSR. Thus, in 1988, women constituted only about 30 per cent of students attending Soviet vocational training schools (Rimachevskaya and Zakharova, 1989, p. 9). In Hungary, where a higher proportion of young people attended vocational training (because it was one stream of compulsory schooling), training for "female" occupations such as nursing, typing and secretarial work was given at the least prestigious vocational schools offering mainly two-year courses (Koncz, 1989).

Experts from central and eastern Europe all refer to inadequate methods and institutions for vocational guidance (e.g., Kaszor, 1990; Schapkin, 1990). The deficiencies of vocational guidance (and of employment prospects) are manifested in high drop-out rates from vocational training schools in Hungary and Poland (Héthy and Héthy, 1990; Kaszor, 1990). The drop-out rate seems to be correlated with the degree of feminisation of an occupation. Even if students successfully finished vocational training, they often looked for jobs other than those for which they had been trained. The vicious circle of poorer career perspectives and lower career motivation meant that women made up a high proportion of those who switched.

Women had to accept limited opportunities for further training, upgrading and occupational mobility (Lado; Zakharova). Responsibilities for child-care were said to be the main obstacle to women's participation in further training, a prerequisite for professional advancement. However, because women were deemed unreliable workers, they had less opportunity to gain adequate rewards for more training. Having "survived" the family phase, they were regarded as too old for upgrading in view of their earlier retirement age.

Various reasons may induce or force women to change their job: married women who follow their husband, whose job has been relocated, may have to take any job they can find. In addition, women have tried to cope with the concurrent demands of job and family by looking for employment in the service sector that offers more flexible time schedules and sympathetic female colleagues. Conversely, with decreasing family responsibilities as children grow up, jobs in "male" sectors can become attractive because of their higher wages. Taking all these factors into account, it is not surprising that women's qualifications are not always fully used. In Czechoslovakia, only two out of three women reported a match between their job and skills (Kroupová, 1990, p. 18).

Social policy

In the countries considered, social policy consisted of two elements: cash benefits such as pensions, student grants, paid holidays and assistance to families; and public services such as health care, education, housing, child-care facilities, homes for the elderly and cultural activities. Unemployment benefits did not exist; the right to work was coupled with an obligation to work and therefore participation in the labour market was the main source of income.

A minimum wage existed in all the countries under review. This had an important social and political signalling function both for the wage structure and for social benefits. Minimum pensions were (e.g., in Poland) calculated as a percentage of the minimum wage and maternity/parental leave allowances were often based on the minimum wage.

All citizens of the CEECs were covered by social security schemes, traditionally administered by the public authorities or by the trade unions. In Poland, there is a Social Insurance Institute; Bulgaria and Hungary transferred the administration of social insurance from the trade unions to the State in 1984.

The most notable trend in the development of social security in CEECs during the 1980s was the emphasis put on measures to assist families. Additional cash benefits were introduced and existing benefits improved. Two benefits were expressly intended to help women reconcile their maternal and job obligations: paid leave to care for children (extended maternity or parental leave) and the assistance allowance for workers who had to care for a sick child at home. Both types of leave were targeted at working mothers.[6] The political process leading to the introduction of maternity leave regulations is described most clearly for Hungary (Szalai, 1991, p. 23ff.): the growing demand for public child-care in the 1950s and 1960s was not met by appropriate investment in facilities and personnel. The number of children registered for child-care increased and the quality of care deteriorated. The growing uneasiness of parents to put (especially small) children into crèches was not met by higher investment in public child-care, but by allowing working mothers to stay at home for the child's first three years.

In addition to paid maternity leave, which at mid-1991 ranged from 28 weeks in Czechoslovakia to 18 or 20 weeks in the ex-USSR, mothers (and recently fathers and grandparents) can take extended periods of child-care leave up to a child's third birthday (Czechoslovakia and ex-USSR). Allowances paid to mothers were introduced in nearly all countries (table 8.2). It is important to note that, while on leave, women usually continue to accumulate their entitlement to social benefits (such as pensions) as well as additional years of seniority. Pregnant women and mothers on maternity leave have the right to return to a job corresponding to their job contract and are protected against dismissal. These measures were intended not only to lower the demand for public child-care, but also reduce conflict between women's roles as mothers and workers.

For mothers who return to work, several other regulations were introduced:

- additional holidays (in Hungary, Poland and the ex-USSR; Kroupová, 1990);
- legal entitlement to part-time work or more flexible working hours, if mothers apply for it;
- time off from work in case of sickness of the child (or another family member), in all the countries (see table 8.2).

Family allowances accounted for a considerable part of family income in CEECs (table 8.10). The regulations concerning family allowances were shaped progressively or regressively according to the "ideal" family size. In Hungary, which has had the most generous and progressive allowances, the family allowance in the mid-1980s covered "about 25 per cent of the average costs spent on family from the personal income of the family, and in the case of families with three or more children, it covered about 30 per cent" (Barta et al., 1985, p.43).

In Bulgaria and Czechoslovakia, allowances were progressive up to the third child. For the fourth and further children only the basic amount was paid. The allowance for two children amounted to 40 per cent of the minimum wage. In Czechoslovakia in 1990, a family with two children received allowances equivalent to one-third of the minimum wage.

The share of pensions, allowances and grants in total social consumption increased between 1975 and 1984, whereas the share of public services decreased. Within public services, employment in public administration dropped whereas employment in social and cultural services increased between 1980 and 1986 (with the exception of Poland and the former USSR).

Table 8.10. **Cumulative family allowances by number of children as a percentage of the average wage, central and eastern Europe 1978-80**

Country	Number of children					
	1	2	3	4	5	6
Hungary (1980)	12[1]	24	48	64	77	89
Czechoslovakia (1979)	5	21	40	57	67	80
Poland[2] (1978)	3	9	16	23	_[3]	_[3]
Romania[4] (1979)	8	16	26	35	45	55
Bulgaria (1978)	3	13	35	38	41	45

1. Only for single (unmarried, widowed, divorced) mothers.
2. Payable where income per person is less than 1,400 zlotys.
3. Not calculated.
4. Lowest income group in urban areas.
Source: Valentina Bodrova and Richard Anker (eds.):
Working women in socialist countries: The fertility connection (Geneva, ILO, 1985), p.43.

For women, and more generally for families, the provision of child-care facilities has been crucial. The supply of public child-care varies widely. The demand for crèche places dropped considerably during the 1980s due to the introduction of paid maternity leave. Available information suggests that the supply of crèche places for children 0-3 years old seems to meet or even exceed present demand. From Romania, an excess supply of at least 50 per cent is reported (Popescu, 1991). The situation in kindergartens, however, looks different, with crowding in Hungary and Poland and broad balance between supply and demand in Czechoslovakia. In the former USSR, places are provided for about two-thirds of children of the relevant age, which probably does not meet the demand, while in Bulgaria the proportion is about three-quarters. Very little information is available about the demand for and supply of day-care centres for children of primary school age. In Hungary, 40 per cent of pupils can be looked after at school. In the former USSR, only 23 per cent of primary schools are fulltime, so that there must be a big demand for day-care places. Parental fees for child-care places were low: in the ex-USSR, they amounted to 20 per cent of the costs, and in Hungary between 20 and 40 per cent.

Additional services provided for working mothers and working women in general were school meals, summer and winter camps for children, and canteen meals organised by enterprises. Roughly 55 per cent of workers in Czechoslovakia, about 33 per cent in Poland, 40 to 50 per cent in Hungary, and roughly 60 per cent in Bulgaria and the ex-USSR took these meals (Kroupová, 1990, p.16). Quite neglected, in number, quality, location, opening times and — above all — affordable prices, were services to aid household activities, such as laundries, shops and repair services. Domestic duties have never been "socialised" at an acceptable level. Since the mid-1980s even fewer families have been able to afford household services because of price increases. In Hungary at the beginning of the 1980s, two-thirds to four-fifths of all families did not make any use of such services (Lado).

Transformation process and women's employment prospects

Employment restructuring

In the process of restructuring employment by industry and sector, and within industries, the relative weight of the agricultural, manufacturing and services sectors will change, while the introduction of a market-oriented economy will alter the nature of work and the skills required. Restructuring will be accompanied by the introduction of new technologies and more flexible use of labour (including part-time work, more flexible working hours, and better matching of time paid and time worked).

The transition to a market economy inevitably involves large-scale displacement of the workforce, through:

- The reduction of over staffing: large-scale lay-offs will occur when enterprises are confronted with hard budget constraints. The propensity to lay off excess labour has already been influenced by the introduction of unemployment benefits.

- The closure of non-competitive firms: the ending of subsidies paid to different sectors is leading to plant closures and large job losses. Industries hit hardest by these developments are heavy industry, the textile and food processing industries and (part of) the agricultural industry.

- Structural change: job losses are occurring both in capital and consumer goods industries due to heightened competition in world markets. Whereas the share of manufacturing in total employment will decrease, service sector employment will increase but will need restructuring. Production-related services, financial and counselling services, and retail and wholesale trade are likely to grow. There will be a shift from public to private provision of personal services.

- De-bureaucratisation of central government and enterprise administration will lead to job losses.

Women will be affected by the loss of jobs in all sectors of the economy. Women are more often employed in agriculture and manufacturing than in western industrialised countries. They are concentrated in the overstaffed administrative units of these industries and they constitute the majority of workers in light industry and in agriculture, mostly in unskilled or semi-skilled jobs.

The expansion of the service sector may create new opportunities for women's employment. A market-oriented economy requires different types of managerial, financial and institutional knowledge and skills. Most CEEs lack the necessary experience and expertise, particularly in the areas of accountancy, finance, insurance and counselling. Women have a long tradition in employment as bookkeepers, accountants and other administrative workers, but these occupations often involved very little skill beyond bookkeeping and did not have a high status. With the move towards a market economy, such jobs will become more prestigious. If given access to training, women will have the opportunity to maintain their position in this key area.

Other fields of employment, such as personnel management, manpower planning and marketing, will become even more significant. The crucial factor behind employers' decisions to recruit women to skilled managerial or administrative jobs seems to be the overall labour supply; if, and only if, male workers are scarce, women get their chance. Thus jobs previously defined as "women's jobs" in the service and administrative sector will gain social status and better pay. Whether these jobs go to women will, however, depend on the access men have to other equally attractive jobs.

Given women's high educational levels, it would seem important that Governments maintain or improve women's labour market position in the transition in order to utilise effectively the human resources that these countries desperately need.

CEECs are undergoing a restructuring of enterprise ownership. The decentralisation of state enterprises, one of the most radical changes under way, is leading to privatisation and the creation of smaller-scale firms. The tradition of small business has, despite the bureaucracy of a centrally planned economy, survived among small-scale rural entrepreneurs and urban street vendors. A "parallel economy", unregulated but economically necessary, has emerged and could be the basis for self-employment and small firms.

Recent developments, however, enjoin scepticism as to whether women, although engaged in informal business activities, will be numerous amongst the self-employed. In Czechoslovakia, Hungary and Poland, most people starting a business now run their firms as a second job in addition to being employed in "socialist" enterprises. Most of these second or third jobs are a specific feature of male employment. Moreover, most of the newly founded or privatised firms are run by former managers of the state-owned enterprises. In all the countries under review, women seem only to be the flexibly used "new" staff of these enterprises at the bottom of the job ladder, even in the service sector where they have comprised the majority of skilled employees. Without financial and technical assistance to give women access to training in accounting, financial skills and personnel management, the opportunities for women to move from informal business activities to viable and legal small business will not be realised. Special efforts at national and international level will be needed to make use of women's existing entrepreneurial skills, demonstrated in managing daily family life and in combining first, second and third jobs.

Employment reduction

The overall reduction of employment will not, in the short term, be matched by expanded employment in the service sector or in newly founded small enterprises. Displaced workers will therefore face the choice of leaving the labour force, emigrating or becoming unemployed.

The extent to which leaving the labour force is a viable option will depend on the generosity of retirement pensions and severance payments. Older workers close to retirement age and pensioners have, until now, often stayed in the labour market because of low pensions. Women's pensions especially have tended to be poor. In most CEECs, retirement pensions rose in 1990-91 but by less than prices of food, clothing and rent.

It seems unlikely that younger women will voluntarily opt to leave the labour force. The current social transformation process will nevertheless weaken the notion of labour force participation as the norm for women, and the return to the family as their exclusive sphere of responsibility will have profound repercussions. Not only will it undermine women's economic independence, it will also affect their confidence, self-esteem and social role. Voluntary temporary exits, especially to have children, recently combined with the right to return to work after a period chosen by the mother, may end up as involuntary permanent exits from the labour force.

In western industrialised countries women tend to form a majority among "discouraged workers" who no longer actively apply for jobs after a certain period of unemployment or after unsuccessful attempts to find paid work. This involuntary withdrawal from the labour market may be forced on them by social policies which lead to a reduction in child-care facilities, publicly provided meals and other services that in the past have enabled women to combine full-time work and family responsibilities.

There is some anecdotal evidence that a proportion of women in CEECs are accepting redundancy, looking forward to the opportunity to spend more time with their children. However, a few years off could turn into long-term unemployment with all its negative material and psychological consequences.

The return of women to the labour market will depend on the development of overall employment opportunities and, to some extent, on the existence of part-time work. The growing service sector, with more flexible working but also with lower social and employment security, will presumably absorb many women and act as a kind of flexibility reserve.

Migration from CEECs to western industrialised countries will increase, especially among highly-skilled, young, male workers. Intranational migration caused by regional imbalances in job prospects also seems to play a substantial role. However, whereas women are less numerous among migrants in the former Soviet Union, Poland and Bulgaria report a high proportion of women migrating from rural to urban areas.

The process of restructuring national economies is causing growing unemployment, with a tendency for women to be disproportionately represented. However, it is difficult to get gender-specific data. The information gathered by national experts gives the following picture.

In *Hungary* the data on people receiving unemployment benefits show that in 1989 women accounted for 25 per cent of all benefit recipients; the proportion increased to 40 per cent in 1990. In 1989 16.5 per cent of all male benefit recipients had been out of work for over six months, compared with 17.1 per cent of women. In 1990 the proportions were 4.2 per cent for men and 4.3 per cent for women, the fall being due to the rapid increase in unemployment. The average monthly benefit for unemployed women was only 70 to 75 per cent of men's benefits in both years, reflecting the existing wage gap between men's and women's earnings. Comparing women's qualification levels in general and amongst the unemployed, skilled women (previously working in industry) were more than proportionally represented amongst the unemployed at the end of 1989.

The under-representation of women amongst unemployment benefit recipients can be explained mainly by the fact that in 1989 and 1990 closures and cut-backs were concentrated in male-dominated heavy industries.

In *Czechoslovakia* there were in mid-1991 no gender-specific data available on unemployment, vacancies, jobseekers or recipients of unemployment benefits. Predictions for 1991 and 1992 show a sharp rise in unemployment, with women likely to represent two-thirds of those unemployed (Mitter, 1991).

In *Poland* women accounted for 50 per cent of the unemployed in December 1990, when there was one job vacancy for 20 unemployed people. Data on vacancies and unemployed by sex show that it was more difficult for women to find a new job than for men: there were 40 unemployed women for each vacancy for women and 13.9 unemployed men for each vacancy for men in 1990.[7] This general picture varied between the regions, being even worse in rural areas. The majority of vacancies (85 per cent) were manual jobs. Among the unemployed, women with non-manual skills and higher education (university degrees, vocational and general secondary school) were more than proportionately represented.

In the former *USSR* no gender-specific data on unemployment, jobseekers, vacancies or discouraged workers were available at mid-1991. According to some estimates, women made up about 60 per cent of those who had lost their jobs in 1989 and 1990. The restructuring of the economy resulting in plant closures and sectoral adjustment seemed to be most evident in industries where women predominated. The reduction in administrative and management jobs from 1985 to 1987 hit women hardest; they represented more than 80 per cent of those dismissed. There are considerable regional differences in the level of unemployment in the former USSR. Unemployment among Uzbek women was estimated to be above average — despite the fact that their labour force participation rate is quite low — accounting for 66.5 per cent of all the unemployed in Uzbekistan in 1988 (Zakharova).

In *Bulgaria* women accounted for 60 per cent of the unemployed in May 1991. Youth unemployment was a growing problem, and two-thirds of the young unemployed were women, particularly skilled women such as engineers, economists and teachers.

The lack of gender-specific data reflects partly the underdevelopment of the labour market information system as a whole, and partly the fact that women's position in the labour market seems of minor interest to policy-makers. As in western countries, the methods and definitions used are crucial in determining the extent to which women's situation is reflected in the data. Thus if unemployment is only registered when a person receives benefits or comes regularly to the employment service, unemployed women disappear from the statistics. The criteria for registration and benefit eligibility influences the "visibility" of women's unemployment in the paid economy (OECD, 1988). With respect to the CEECs, it is too early to say, as at mid-1991, to what extent definitions of unemployment and criteria for receiving unemployment benefits will discriminate directly or indirectly against women.

Labour market policies and social policies

Labour market policies, in addition to training and social policies, will play an important role during the transition period. Labour offices or employment services in central and eastern Europe were used primarily to search for and activate labour reserves (for the ex-USSR, see Gramatzki, 1988; for Poland, see Kortan, 1988). Economic restructuring means that many employed and unemployed workers are looking for new jobs, and enterprises are looking for suitable personnel. More developed labour market services such as vocational counselling, retraining, provision of work experience and job creation programmes would improve the efficiency of the matching processes.

All the countries examined are starting to restructure their employment services or, like Hungary, have already gained some experience in that field. However, labour offices still have too few staff to meet the different needs of job creation, job counselling and assisting the unemployed. To meet these needs, labour offices need to increase the number of their employees — and this could provide job opportunities for women.

Eligibility for unemployment and related benefits depends on both the definition of unemployment and the conditions for receiving assistance. As most women in CEECs have been employed, most will fulfil the eligibility criteria in the first instance. However, they will be in a less favourable position than their male colleagues as benefits will be calculated on the basis of their (generally lower) previous earnings. The "discouraged worker" effect will also be stronger for women, unless employment offices make special efforts to get women back into jobs. In most CEECs job vacancies are offered to men and women separately; this may help women to find new jobs in female-dominated spheres. However, nobody knows to what extent the "gendered" labour market will be transformed in the sense that hitherto "female" jobs become attractive for men.

In all the countries under consideration, active labour market policies put most emphasis on training and retraining programmes to give employees the opportunity to gain new professional skills. Experience from western countries shows that women's participation in labour market programmes is in general lower than the proportion of registered unemployed women. The main reason for this is the individual entitlement criteria, which women in the West often do not fulfil, and the selective recruitment policies of the employment services or training institutions. Sometimes it seems to be a result of direct discrimination against mothers with young children.[8] As recent developments in eastern Germany show, even women who meet the individual entitlement criteria are not equally represented among the participants in labour market programmes. Special programmes and a general regulation that women should constitute a proportion equal to their rate among the unemployed were recently introduced for the first time.

There is a special need for training courses in administrative, managerial and financial skills which would enable women to stay in skilled non-manual occupations. If job creation programmes were directed towards social services this would extend the existing social support system and enhance women's employment both in terms of quantity and quality.

A certain reluctance to target policies on equal opportunities for women can be expected, because the previous protective measures and "privileges" for working mothers are now criticised by women themselves on the grounds that they created dead-end jobs instead of opening up career paths. Experience from western countries suggests, however, that because the labour market is not a gender-neutral institution, there is need for positive action to ensure that men and women are treated equally.

The economic transformation will certainly have a significant impact on social policy. The share of the national product which is redistributed to families in order to "socialise" the financial burden of raising children will be renegotiated and, most likely, reduced. If family, child and parental leave allowances are not adjusted for inflation, they may become merely symbolic, because parents will no longer be able to afford to take leave. This development has already been observed in Poland. In Hungary, women who are officially on child-care leave are taking unprotected jobs in the second economy. A reduction in goods and services, which up to now have been supplied freely by the State (health, education, culture), is even more likely.

Public child-care has not always met the standards demanded by parents. A lowering of standards might induce parents to withdraw their children from public child-care facilities. So it will not be sufficient to provide enough places; the quality must also be improved. Until now, parents have contributed only a small part of the costs of public child-care. Paying market prices might be beyond the financial reach of many parents.

A substantial share of places in child-care establishments has been provided by enterprises (in Hungary, 30 per cent see Lado). In the event of plant closures or financial cut-backs, child-care as well as other social facilities will be closed, risking the creation of a vicious circle of unemployment and lack of child-care facilities. In addition, dismissal regulations do not protect pregnant women or mothers on maternity leave when plants are closed, and in Poland, they can be dismissed by firms undergoing basic structural changes. In these cases, women should be offered other jobs according to their qualifications.

Caring for and educating children has traditionally been women's work. The borderline between paid work (nurses, teachers) and unpaid work (mothers, grandmothers) has been shifting in central and eastern Europe. A collapse of the public child-care system would not only aggravate the situation, but also force many women into unemployment. The transition process and the new texture of personal and social responsibilities necessitate a new system of social services, and this could be a growing area of female employment. Different countries report a need for enhanced psychological and pedagogical assistance for families. Care for the elderly has to be organised on a different basis and training facilities for social workers will be necessary.

Conclusions

The restructuring and transformation of the socio-economic institutions in the countries of central and eastern Europe has already started. The process of transformation from a centrally planned economy to a market economy has no historical model. Seen from the perspectives of gender relations and women's future status the following points are relevant.

The institutional systems in CEECs determined women's status and, more generally, gender relations in such a way that traditional gender roles remained stable, especially in the private sphere. Women and men, although in legal terms equally treated, remained socially unequal. Traditional gender roles were reinforced, for example, by social policies, the education and training system, and employment structures. Whilst the institutional and political framework gave little room for individual choice and freedom, the transition to a market economy with its different regulatory system appears to open up a whole range of individual opportunities. However, the laws and regulations of market economies, as the experience of western countries shows, do not necessarily favour women. There is therefore a need to safeguard women's interests in the transformation process, and to acknowledge that some aspects of earlier regulations and institutions worked to women's advantage.

The goal of improving flexibility and productivity in the economy is being linked with revisions in the social security net and in regulations concerning employment protection. Deregulation of labour market institutions, social security systems and employment protection hits women harder than men. Since women's status in the labour market is already weaker than men's, the general crisis in employment will, if not faced up to politically, be solved at the expense of women's employment prospects. Women's job opportunities will lie primarily in the formal economy as paid employees. Nevertheless, government programmes to assist people starting a new business could be useful for women, too. Programmes should be targeted at women who wish to become self-employed, and should provide counselling, training and special subsidies as well as funds reserved exclusively for women.

The majority of women will need help in safeguarding their employment. Such help could be given efficiently through training and retraining programmes targeted towards women. When the education and training system is restructured it will be important to open up all professions to women. Although central and eastern European women have attained high levels of education, the various economies have neglected their skills as a human resource in modernisation. To make sure that women do not have to remain in low-skilled, poorly paid occupations, special efforts should be made to integrate women into all kinds of vocational training activities and to oblige employers to implement equal opportunity policies giving women access to skilled jobs.

Increasingly, employment in central and eastern Europe will be different from the "normal" employment schedule of full-time work. In order to avoid a "second rank" labour market all forms of employment should be covered by social security and labour law regulations. It is clear that a certain number of women would prefer part-time to full-time work. A right to part-time work, through a temporary reduction in individual working time, including the right later to return to a full-time job, would honour a person's contribution to the flexibility needed by the economy instead of marginalising him or her.

If women's interests in the transformation process are to be secured, it is crucial to create the appropriate political machinery. It would be highly desirable to have more women in politically and economically powerful bodies (rather than ever fewer, as at present). The traditional political actors (parties, governments, trade unions, employers' associations, public authorities) must be confronted with women's "issues".

In the process of transformation the balance of power between labour and capital is shifting, with a weakening of the position of trade unions. New organisational structures have to be built up, and both new and old unions will be staking out their claims. There is little evidence that the question of female employment, wages and working conditions has priority on union agendas.

An independent women's movement, institutional networks and women's offices at all levels of public administration, trade unions, political parties, etc., are prerequisites for establishing and supporting women's political influence. International institutions and existing networks could and should support the process of generating public discussion and of educating policy-makers with the aim of promoting a more equitable and efficient use of the nations' human resources — both women and men.

Notes

1. The share of women amongst workers and employees (excluding farmers) differed in the regions of the USSR, from 58 per cent in Latvia to 39 per cent in Tadjikistan (Zakharova)

2. As described in table 10.1, countries use different methods and definitions in calculating the economically active population. Some of the differences in women's status may be due to the different methods/definitions used.

3. The number of live births per 1,000 population is affected by the overall distribution of the population by age and sex. Central and eastern European countries seem to have a higher mortality rate of medium age groups and a higher proportion of women in the population, mainly in the older age groups.

4. Having no children is more common in some western European countries. For example, in the former Federal Republic of Germany approximately 26 per cent of women have no children *(Statistisches Bundesamt 1990,* p.204).

5. The following applied:

- dangerous, arduous or unhealthy work, to be specified in a list, was not allowed or only under certain conditions in all countries;

- underground work was explicitly prohibited in Czechoslovakia, Hungary, Poland and the former USSR;

- weight limits concerning the manual transport of loads existed in Hungary, Poland and the former USSR;

- work with dangerous substances or agents (especially poison, lead products, benzene and radiation) was prohibited or restricted in all countries but with different specifications.

Some restrictions and prohibitions held exclusively for pregnant women and nursing mothers. This was most evident in the ex-USSR, but did not apply in Hungary.

In Bulgaria, women had priority for jobs deemed suitable for them by a tripartite official body (ILO, 1987, pp.87-125).

6. The legal entitlement for fathers to take caring leave for sick children had hardly any relevance in practice.

7. It seems to be common in Poland and in Czechoslovakia to offer vacancies to men and women separately — a gender-neutral job offer is not required.

8. To be registered as unemployed and to be entitled to participate in labour market programmes, a mother in Germany, for example, must prove that the child is cared for. This means that one of the (rare) places in crèches or kindergartens is a necessary precondition for a job or a training offer by the employment service.

References

Barta, Barnabás et al. 1985. "Hungary", in Bodrova and Anker (1985), pp. 23-55.

Bodrova, Valentina; Anker, Richard. 1985. (eds.): *Working women in socialist countries*: The fertility connection (Geneva, ILO).

Bütow, Hellmuth G. (ed.). 1988. *Länderbericht Sowjetunion,* Vol. 263 of the *Schriftenreihe zur Geschichte und Politik*, (Bonn, Bundeszentrale für politische Bildung).

Bystydzienski, Jill M. 1989. "Women and socialism: A comparative study of women in Poland and the USSR", in *Signs,* Vol. 14, No. 3, Spring 1989, et al. p. 668-684.

Dobrianov, Velitchko. 1985. "Bulgaria", in Bodrova and Anker (1985), pp. 57-91.

Gorbachev, Mikhail. 1987. *Perestroika: New thinking for our country and the world* (New York, Harper and Row).

Gramatzki, H.E., 1988. "Employment policy in the USSR - limitations on enterprises' personnel and wage policies", in Dlugos, G. et al.; *Management under differing labour market and employment systems,* Berlin/New York, pp. 246-259.

Héthy, Annamària; Héthy, Lajos. 1990. *New technologies, work organisation, qualification, structures and vocational training in Hungary.* CEDEFOP Document. Luxembourg. (Amt für amtliche Veröffentlichungen der Europäischen Gemeinschaften/Office for Official Publications of the European Communities).

Hörner, Wolfgang et al. 1989. *Technisch-ökonomischer Wandel und Reform in der Berufs- und Allgemeinbildung sozialistischer Staaten.* Bochum (Arbeitsstelle für vergleichende Bildungsforschung der Ruhr-Universität).

Holzer, Jerzey Z.; Wasilawska-Trenkner, Halina. 1985. "Poland", in *Bodrova and Anker* (1985), pp. 129-165.

ILO. 1987. "Women workers - Protection or equality?", *Conditions of Work Digest,* (Geneva), Vol. 6, 2/1987.

ILO. 1989. "Part-time work", *Conditions of Work Digest,* (Geneva), Vol. 8, 1/1989.

Kaszor, Stanislaw. 1990. *Neue Technologien, Arbeitsorganisation, Qualifika-tionsstrukturen und Berufsbildung in der Volksrepublik Polen.* CEDEFOP Document, Luxembourg. (Amt für amtliche Veröffentlichungen der Europäischen Gemeinschaften/Office for Official Publications of the European Communities).

Kobzeva, Elena. 1990. *On the results of sociological study titled "Role played by woman in family and society".* City of Naberezhnye Tchelny (unpublished).

Kolankiewicz, George; Lewis, Paul G. 1988. "Poland", *Politics, Economics and Society.* London, New York (Pinter).

Koncz, Katalin. 1989. *Diversification of women's training and employment in Hungary.* ILO Discussion Paper No. 42, Geneva.

Kortan, J. 1988. "The Development of the Labour Market in Poland - Restrictions for Management", in Dlugos, G. et al. *Management under differing labour market and employment systems,* Berlin/New York, pp. 261-271.

Kotowska, Irena. 1991. *Labour Supply in Poland.* Warsaw School of Economics, mimeo.

Kroupová, Alena. 1990. *Women - Employment and Earnings in central and east European Countries,* Tripartite Symposium on Equality of Opportunity and Treatment for Men and Women in Employment in Industrialized Countries, manuscript, Prague.

Lapidus, Gail Warshofsky. 1988. "The Interaction of women's work and family roles in the USSR, in B.A. Gutek et al. *Women and Work.* Vol. 3. Newbury Park u.a.: Sage, pp. 87-121.

Mitter, Swasti. 1991. *A comparative analysis of women's industrial participation during the transition from centrally-planned to market economies in east central Europe.* Paper prepared for the Regional Seminar on the Impact of Economic and Political Reform on the Status of Women in Eastern Europe and the USSR, organised by the United Nations Division of the Advancement of Women, Vienna.

OECD. 1988. *Employment Outlook*, Paris.

Plakwicz, Jolanta. 1991. *The impact of restructuring in political and economic spheres on the status of women.* Paper prepared for the Regional Seminar on the Impact of Economic and Political Reform on the Status of Women in Eastern Europe and the USSR, United Nations Division of the Advancement of Women, Vienna.

Popescu, Dumitra. 1991. *Present situation and trends affecting women in Romania.* Paper prepared for the Regional Seminar on the Impact of Economic and Political Reform on the Status of Women in Eastern Europe and the USSR, organised by the United Nations Division of the Advancement of Women, Vienna.

Pulay, Gyula. 1989. "Women's labour force participation patterns: Changes in the division of labour within society and the family", in T.D. Horvath; G. Sziraczki (1989), *Flexibility and rigidity in the labour market in Hungary,* (Geneva), International Institute for Labour Studies, Research Series 90, pp. 95-104.

Rimachevskaya, Natalia; Zakharova, Natalia. 1989. *The diversification of women's training and employment: The Case of the USSR.* ILO-Training Discussion Paper No. 44. Geneva.

Schapkin, W.W. 1990. *Die berufstechnische Bildung in der USSR.* CEDEFOP Document. Luxembourg. (Amt für amtliche Veröffentlichungen der Europäischen Gemeinschaften/Office for Official Publications of the European Communities).

Staikova-Alexandrova, Raia. 1991. *The present situation of women in Bulgaria.* Paper prepared for the Regional Seminar on the Impact of Economic and Political Reform on the Status of Women in Eastern Europe and the USSR, organised by the United Nations Division of the Advancement of women, Vienna.

Statistisches Bundesamt. 1990. *Familien heute, Strukturen, Verläufe und Einstellungen.* Stuttgart.

Szalai, Julia. 1991. *Some aspects of the changing situation of women in Hungary in the process of transition.* Paper prepared for the Regional Seminar on the Impact of Economic and Political Reform on the Status of Women in Eastern Europe and the USSR, organised by the United Nations Division of the Advancement of Women, Vienna.

Ziemska, Maria. 1988. "Die Familienrolle der Frauen und Männer aus der Sicht internationaler Vergleiche", in *Informationen des wissenschaftlichen Rates "Die Frau in der sozialistischen Gesellschaft".* Heft 2/1988, pp. 19-33.

Chapter 9

Labour market developments and policies in central and eastern Europe: a comparative analysis

by
Tito Boeri and Gyorgy Sziraczki

Introduction

The country reports prepared for this conference offer a good overview of long-term demographic and labour force trends and provide a very informative description of the dynamics of labour markets in the initial phases of the transition process. The purpose of these notes is both to summarise those stylised facts described in the reports which have the most relevant implications for the design of labour market policies, and to make some cross-country comparisons of recent developments.

It should be stressed at the outset that central and eastern European countries (CEECs), while often grouped together for the sake of convenience, differ considerably in terms of structure and trends of employment, labour force growth and population growth. Such national differences should be taken into account when assessing current developments and the potential for different kinds of labour market policy. Hence before identifying common denominators among the responses of labour markets to market-oriented reforms in central and eastern Europe, it is worth highlighting those structural features that differentiate the adjustment process in the various countries.

As shown by the national reports, labour supply pressures are likely to be stronger in some countries than in others. Whilst in the most populous countries (Poland, Romania and Czechoslovakia) the working-age population is expected to rise in the next decade, Bulgaria and Hungary will soon have to face — like many OECD countries — the potential problems of a rapid rise in the number of aged persons relative to the working-age population (Figure 9.1).[1]

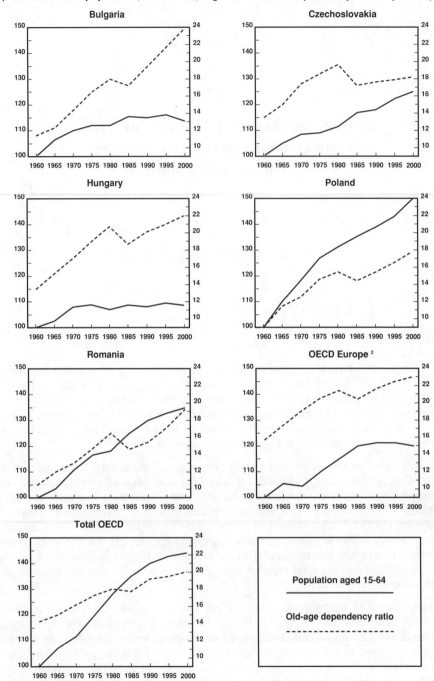

Figure 9.1. **Growth of the working age population and the old-age dependency ratio[1]**
(Left hand scale: population, 1960 = 100, Right hand scale: dependency ratio in percent)

1. The old age dependency ratio is defined as the population aged 65 and over divided by the population aged 15-64
2. Excluding Turkey.
Sources: Global estimates and projection of population by sex and age, 1988 revision, United Nations, 1989, for the central and eastern European countries and the OECD demographical data bank for the OECD countries.

It is usually stressed that CEECs have higher labour force participation rates, especially among women, than many OECD countries. However, this is more so for some countries (e.g., Bulgaria) than for others (e.g., Hungary) (table 9.1). Moreover, the gap in labour force rates between, on the one hand, CEECs, and, on the other hand, OECD countries, has narrowed considerably in the 1980s.

Another well-known feature of the planned economies of central and eastern Europe was the promotion of a strong industrial base with particular emphasis on heavy industry. Even before the start of the current wave of reforms, however, there was some shift in several countries towards promoting light industry, the production of consumer goods and the expansion of services. Some countries have proceeded faster than others in reallocating labour towards these sectors. As a result, the share of employment in the service sector varies considerably across CEECs, ranging from slightly more than 25 per cent in Romania to just over 40 per cent in Hungary, the country where the structure of employment is today more similar to that of OECD countries (figure 9.2).

Recent developments

Three major developments are common to all economies in transition, although the speed and characteristics of these events may differ across countries. First, a significant decline in employment has occurred, involving all major branches of activity, including almost all service industries. Second, employment in the private sector has increased quite dramatically, reflecting both the actual beginnings of new business activities and the privatisation of many relatively small firms previously belonging to the socialised sector. Thirdly, open unemployment has started to rise steeply whereas vacancies registered at labour offices have fallen, and sometimes almost disappeared, with a consequent explosion of U/V (unemployment to vacancy) ratios.

The distribution of job losses

Employment has declined markedly in all countries, except Romania, where, however, short-time working arrangements were quite extensive prior to the introduction in early 1991 of a new unemployment law. Large job losses have not been as great as the fall in output volumes (table 9.2), implying a decline in labour productivity. This is not surprising as productivity tends to behave pro-cyclically in Western countries also. However, elasticities of employment with respect to changes in activity levels such as those currently observed in CEECs can be observed in the OECD area only on a quarterly basis; on a yearly basis, a fall in output by one percentage point tends to be associated with a 0.7-0.8 per cent fall in employment. In the United Kingdom, for example, a fall in industrial production of 5 per cent in the first quarter of 1975 was accompanied by a fall in employment of only 0.5 per cent, but over 1975 as a whole, industrial output fell by 6 to 7 per cent and employment by 5.6 per cent, implying a 1.1 per cent fall in labour productivity. By contrast, in Poland a 23.3 per cent fall in industrial output in 1990 was associated with a 5.8 per cent decline in employment and hence a 18.6 per cent fall in labour productivity.

Of course, production declines such as those currently experienced by CEECs are not directly comparable with those occurring in OECD countries during cyclical downturns. Nevertheless, the dramatic decline of labour productivity in some CEECs seems to indicate that time lags in the adjustment of employment to changes in output are much greater in CEECs than in OECD countries. In other words, falls in employment are likely to continue well after the end of the current decline in economic activity.

Table 9.1. Participation rates in CEEs[1] and OECD Countries (in percent)

	Bulgaria				Czechoslovakia				Hungary			
	1956	1965	1975	1985	1961	1970	1980	1988	1960	1970	1980	1989
Men	98	86	81	81	89	83	87	82	98	87	84	75
Women	71	68	72	74	59	65	75	77	50	58	63	62
Total	84	77	76	77	74	74	81	80	73	72	73	69

	Poland				Romania				OECD			
	1960	1970	1978	1988	1956[2]	1966	1977	1989	1960	1970	1980	1989
Men	93	88	86	83	100	92	85	83	94	89	85	83
Women	66	72	70	68	78	73	70	68	46	47	53	59
Total	79	80	78	75	89	82	77	75	69	68	69	71

1. The participation rate is defined as the total labour force as a percentage of the population aged 15-64. For CEECs, participation rates have been derived, principally from census data. For some countries, adjustments have been made to the original source data and a number of supplementary sources have been used to derive estimates for the latest data shown.
2. Total labour force as a percentage of the population aged 14-64.

Sources: ILO: Year Book of Labour Statistics, Retrospective edition on population censuses, 1945-89, (Geneva, 1990), and, for the OECD countries, OECD Labour Force.

Figure 9.2. **Employment by sector (as a percent of total)**

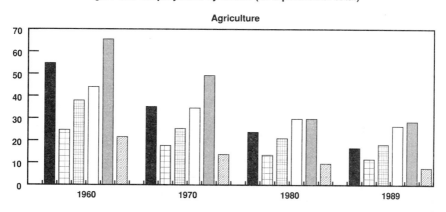

Agriculture

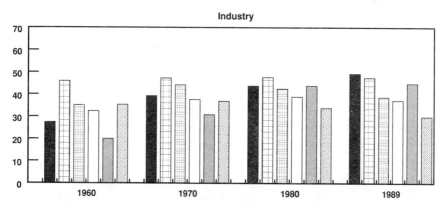

Industry

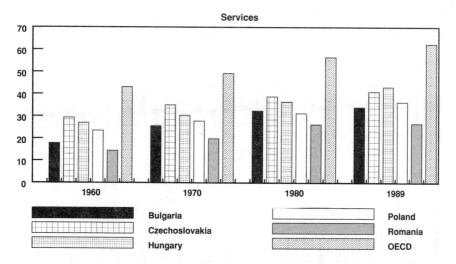

Services

■ Bulgaria	□ Poland
▦ Czechoslovakia	▨ Romania
▤ Hungary	▧ OECD

Source: See Annex for sources for the central and eastern European countries. The OECD total is taken from OECD Labour Force Statistics.

245

Table 9.2. **Change in output and productivity in CEECs (percentage annual growth rates)**

	Net material product		Total employment		Labour productivity	
	1989	1990	1989	1990	1989	1990
Bulgaria	-0.4	-11.7	-1.3	-6.2	0.9	-7.9
Czechoslovakia	1.3	-3.1	0.3	-0.8	1.0	-2.3
Hungary	-0.2	-5.0	-0.5	-1.4	0.3	-3.7
Poland	-0.2	-13.0	0.6	-3.7	-0.8	-9.7
Romania	-7.9	-10.5	1.3	1.5	-9.1	-11.8

	Industrial production		Employment in industry		Labour productivity in industry	
	1989	1990	1989	1990	1989	1990
Bulgaria	2.2	-14.1	-1.0	-7.7	3.2	-6.9
Czechoslovakia	0.8	-3.7	0.1	-3.3	0.7	-0.4
Hungary	-2.5	-4.5	-2.1	-2.2	-0.4	-2.4
Poland	-0.5	-23.3	0	-5.8	-0.5	-18.6
Romania	-2.1	-19.8	2.6	0.8	-4.6	-20.4

Sources: Data on net material product and industrial production from Economic Commission for Europe (1991) and OECD: *Economic Outlook*, No. 49, June 1991. Employment data provided by national statistical offices or taken from national statistical yearbooks.

There are several possible explanations for this. Some are based on the political economy of the liberalisation process, namely the consensus-seeking patterns followed by governments. Others are based on microeconomic legacies of the past system which have been extensively analysed in literature, e.g., the control exerted by workers on the management of firms, managers inexperienced in dismissal policies, the chronic tendency of firms to hoard labour, etc. Whatever the explanations for the delayed response of employment to changes in output in the CEECs, current trends in labour productivity are disturbing, especially when one considers the initial conditions, namely the very low labour productivity levels (by Western standards) at the beginning of the transition process.

The decline of employment in industry accounted for the bulk of job losses, although there were also marked falls of employment in agriculture and construction. Surprisingly enough, in 1989-90, employment fell in most service activities (table 9.3) in spite of the low share of services in total employment in CEECs.

This seems to indicate that major sectoral shifts have still to take place. The lack of net job creation in most service sectors is a particular reason for concern for future developments because it shows that further job losses in mining and manufacturing, and in heavy industries in particular, are unlikely to be fully compensated in the short term by job gains elsewhere.

The limited information available concerning the distribution of job losses across firms shows that they have affected a wide number of business units rather than a relatively few, large firms. As a result, there are more individual lay-offs than mass lay-offs. However, large scale lay-offs are to be expected in all CEECs as the phasing out of many industrial subsidies and a greater exposure to international competition lead to the closure of many large, inefficient plants.

The growth of the private sector and the role of small firms

The above remarks should not conceal the considerable dynamism displayed by small units, at least in some countries. For instance, as shown in the country report on Hungary, the share of units with twenty or fewer employees in the total number of private firms has jumped from 22.7 per cent in January 1989 to 59.5 per cent in December 1990. This does not necessarily mean that small firms have created new jobs: many small businesses might have originated from the decentralisation of large companies, especially in those countries where incentives for the creation of small businesses have been introduced, or they might reflect the legal registration of activities that were previously part of the parallel economy.

Whatever the significance of the development of a multitude of new small-scale activities in generating employment, it has certainly contributed to the introduction of more flexible wage systems, contracting arrangements and working-time arrangements. This by itself is an important development given the rigidity of labour allocation inherited from the past command system and the heavy concentration of labour in large plants. The centralised system of planning in central and eastern Europe was indeed reflected in a production structure organised around large state-run enterprises (figure 9. 3). In 1989-90, around 80 per cent of all employees worked in enterprises with over 500 employees, with negligible employment in small enterprises with under 100 employees. While production by the large state-run enterprises in CEECs was spread across several plants or production units, the average factory size tended to be bigger than in the West (bottom panel of figure 9. 3). In other words, not only firms, but also plants, were larger than in OECD countries. This means that the restructuring process is bound to involve not only the decentralisation of ownership, but also the decentralisation of production sites.

247

Table 9.3. **Employment losses in the initial phases of transition, selected CEECs**

Change from 1989	Bulgaria %	(000s)	Czechoslovakia %	(000s)	Hungary %	(000s)	Poland %	(000s)
Agriculture	-7.3	-59.3	-0.9	-8.0	-13.0	-124.0	-2.4	-112.6
Industry	-7.8	-128.0	-2.8	-83.0	-1.8	-29.0	-5.8	-283.7
Construction	-8.8	-31.8	4.3	30.0	-2.2	-7.7	-5.8	-76.3
Services	-3.5	-54.2	1.0	32.0	-0.8	-20.5	-2.5	-155.9
Transport	-3.7	-9.2	4.1	21.0	0.2	1.0	-6.0	-48.8
Communications	3.9	1.7					1.4	2.3
Wholesale and retail trade	-6.8	-27.0	-3.6	-30.0	4.5	27.8	-4.8	-70.2
Community services, etc.	-4.3	-4.2	2.9	18.0	-9.8	-27.4	-2.4	-15.5
Research and development	-10.7	-10.4					-12.9	-14.5
Education	0.7	1.8	2.8	13.0	-2.1	-17.2	2.1	22.9
Culture and art	-2.4	-1.1	0.4	2.0			-4.0	-5.0
Health, sport, tourism	1.5	3.3					0.9	9.5
Finance and insurance	-3.1	-0.8	14.6	28.0			5.2	8.9
Public administration	-7.9	-4.8					-0.4	-1.0
Other	-8.5	-3.5					-10.7	-44.5
Total	-6.3	-273.3	-0.4	-30.0	-3.3	-180.9	-3.7	-628.5

Sources: All data provided by national statistical offices.

248

In Bulgaria, Hungary and Poland, the fall in state sector employment (including the co-operative sector) in 1990 was partly offset by a rise in private sector employment. In Poland, in particular, employment rose by about half a million in the private sector over the year to the end of December 1990 compared with a loss of more than 1.1 million jobs in the state sector. Similarly, in Hungary, there were twice as many job losses in the public sector as job gains in the private sector, whereas in Bulgaria the growth of the private sector was very small compared to the decline of employment in public enterprises.

Unfortunately, the information available does not allow us to separate the different sources of the growth in employment in the private sector, namely the effects of privatisation of many small shops, workers who left the state sector and became self-employed, e.g., in small shops and restaurants, and the creation of new private enterprises. Such an analysis would allow an assessment of the extent to which the growth of the private sector is associated with the creation of new employment opportunities, rather than with the replacement of jobs previously provided by the state sector.

Figure 9.3. **Distribution of employees in industry by enterprise and establishment size in CEECs and OECD countries**[1]

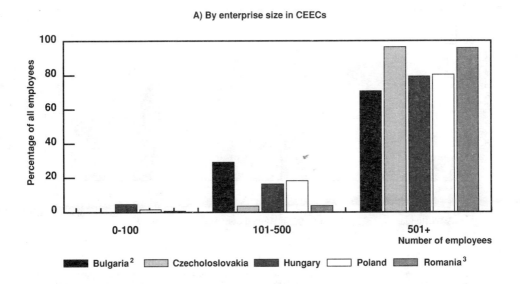

A) By enterprise size in CEECs

Notes 1, 2, 3 : voir p. 246

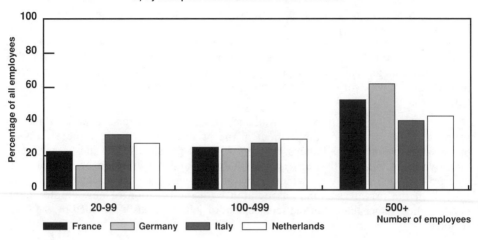

B) By enterprise size in selected OECD countries

Percentage of all employees

20-99   100-499   500+

Number of employees

■ France   ▨ Germany   ■ Italy   ▢ Netherlands

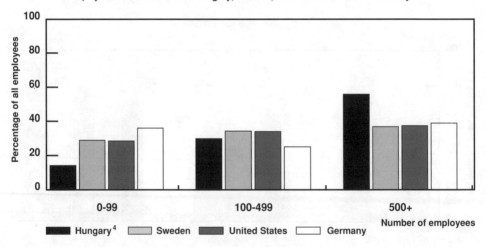

C) By establishment size in Hungary, Sweden, the United States and Germany

Percentage of all employees

0-99   100-499   500+

Number of employees

■ Hungary[4]   ▨ Sweden   ■ United States   ▢ Germany

1. Industry generally refers to mining, manufacturing and electricity, gas and water sectors. For the Netherlands, only the manufacturing sector is included and, for Sweden and the United States, the electricity, gas and water is excluded. The reference year is 1989 for Czechoslovakia. Hungary, Poland and Romania; 1988 for Bulgaria, France, the Netherlands and Sweden; 1987 for Germany and Italy; and 1986 fot the United States.

2. The category of 101-500 employees also includes the category of 0-100 employees.

3. The category of 0-100 employees refers to 0-200 employees and the category of 101-500 employees refers to 201-500 employees.

4. The establishment sizes are 20-100, 101-500 and 501 + employees.

Sources: National statistical yearbooks for the CEECs, Germany (establishment data), the Netherlands, Sweden and the United States: The Structure and Activity or industry. Data by size of enterprises - 1985, 1986, 1987 - EUROSTAT, 1990, for Italy and Germany; and La Situation de l'Industrie en 1988. French Ministry of Industry, 1989, for France.

The rise of unemployment

As part of the reform process in CEECs, unemployment has been officially recognised, and a system of unemployment benefits has been implemented in all these countries. From being virtually non-existent at the beginning of 1990, officially recognised unemployment increased in all countries throughout 1990 and in the first half of 1991. The rise in unemployment rates was particularly steep in Poland during 1990 and in Bulgaria during 1991. By June 1991 unemployment rates had reached almost 9 per cent of the labour force in Poland compared with 6 per cent in Bulgaria, 4 per cent in Czechoslovakia and 3.5 per cent in Hungary (table 9.4).

It should be stressed that available unemployment figures are drawn from registration data. Hence, they are likely to be affected by each country's eligibility criteria for receiving unemployment benefits, as well as by the scope and efficiency of the network of labour offices. Experience in the OECD countries has shown that there can be substantial differences both for the same country, and between countries, in unemployment rates derived from administrative data and from labour force surveys based on OECD-ILO definitions.

Bearing these caveats in mind, some inferences can be made on the likely direction of the bias in the administrative data on the unemployed. The rise of just over 1 million in registered unemployed during 1990 in Poland is not surprising given a similar fall in the number of people employed over the same period. However, in the first six months of 1990 the number of registered unemployed exceeded job losses, reflecting, among other things sizeable registrations of school-leavers and other new entrants to the labour force. This was probably the by-product of the fact that until September 1990 all unemployed people were entitled to benefits, irrespective of whether they had been previously employed. In fact, with the tightening of eligibility criteria, the share of school-leavers in total unemployment has decreased sharply.

In the case of Bulgaria, Czechoslovakia and Hungary the relatively low unemployment rate does seem somewhat anomalous given the large declines experienced in output and the sharp falls in employment in 1990. This may reflect both an increase in emigration and also some initial reluctance to register as unemployed on the part of displaced workers, as well as strict eligibility conditions for benefits. Nevertheless, in these three countries there appears to have been an acceleration in the rise of unemployment since the start of 1991.

So, who are the unemployed? Figure 9.4 provides a breakdown of the registered unemployed by sex, major age group, educational attainment, skill level, and entry status (i.e., whether they are school-leavers or displaced workers). The following facts are of note. First, in all countries for which data are available, displaced workers represent the vast majority of the unemployed. The proportion of school-leavers is in some countries, e.g., Hungary, relatively small because young graduates from secondary school or university have only been able to qualify for unemployment compensation since February 1991.

The fact that most of the registered unemployed were recently in employment might help to explain cross-country differences in the share of males and females among the unemployed. Such differences might simply reflect the different gender composition of those industries which have been hardest hit by economic restructuring. The possibility of receiving unemployment compensation might have also induced women to leave full-time posts in the public sector and look for jobs with more flexible working-time arrangements in the expanding private sector.

251

Other characteristics of the unemployed tend to be shared, although with varying intensity, by all CEECs. In particular, most of the unemployed belong to the prime working age group, and have a primary or vocational training level of education.

Surprisingly, skilled workers constitute the majority of the unemployed in all countries for which data are available. However, this does not necessarily mean that skilled workers face a higher risk of becoming unemployed. Rather, it might simply reflect the underlying skill structure of the labour force. Unemployment rates are, indeed, much higher for unskilled than for skilled workers. For instance, in Hungary the unemployment rate for skilled workers was 2.6 per cent in February 1991 compared with 9.9 per cent for unskilled workers.

Limited information is available on the duration of unemployment. There is some indication, however, that the rise in unemployment levels experienced by all CEECs is a by-product not only of larger inflows into the categoriy of unemployed status, but also of longer spells of joblessness. In the case of Hungary, for example, the average length of time a person received unemployment compensation between February and December 1990 increased from 3.3 to 5.1 months. Available information does not enable us to establish whether this reflects the appearance of a relatively few long-term unemployed people or an increase in the duration of unemployment for a large number of people registered at labour offices. However, we know from the report on Czechoslovakia that in the Czech Republic the distribution of registered job-seekers by duration of unemployment was highly uneven in March 1991 with a small number of people (0.5 per cent of the total) remaining unemployed for longer than 12 months.

Table 9.4. **Open unemployment in CEECs**

	Registered unemployed (000s)				Unemployment rate (% of labour force)			
	January 1990	July 1990	January 1991	July 1991	January 1990	July 1990	January 1991	July 1991
Bulgaria	n.a.[1]	22.4	74.1	247.6	n.a.	0.5	1.8	6.1
Czechoslovakia	n.a.	12.6	119.4	300.8	n.a.	0.2	1.5	4.2
Hungary	23.4	41.8	100.5	185.6	0.5	0.8	2.0	3.5
Poland	55.8	568.2	1 195.7	1 574.1	0.3	2.4	6.5	8.7
Romania	n.a.	n.a.	n.a.	104.4	n.a.	n.a.	n.a.	1.0
Total	79.2	800.0	1 489.8	2 844.7	0.2	1.7	3.3	6.4

1. Not available.
Sources: Monthly data on the number of registered unemployed were provided by national statistical offices. Unemployment rates were calculated using OECD estimates of the monthly labour force. These estimates were derived from annual data for 1989 and 1990 provided by national statistical offices or taken from national statistical yearbooks. These labour force estimates comprise all employed and unemployed persons, including apprentices and, except for Bulgaria, women on maternity leave.

Figure 9.4. **Characteristics of unemployment in CEECs**
(as percent of total unemployment

By gender

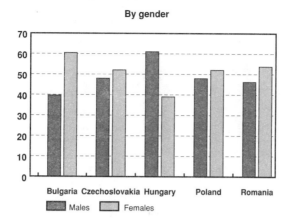

By age

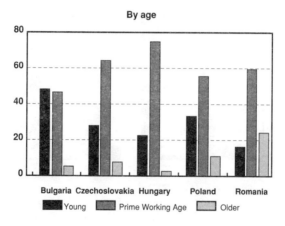

By level of education

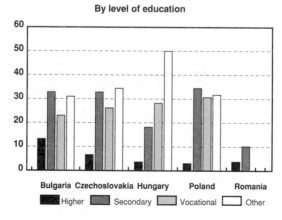

By skill level

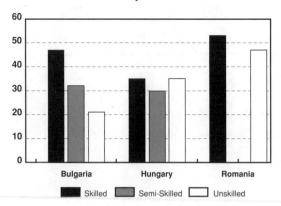

Bulgaria   Hungary   Romania

■ Skilled   ▨ Semi-Skilled   □ Unskilled

By entry status

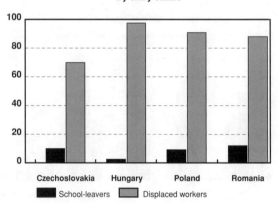

Czechoslovakia   Hungary   Poland   Romania

■ School-leavers   ▨ Displaced workers

Notes : School-leavers include order new entrance Bulgarie. All data provided by Ministry of Labour and Social Affairs. Sophia and are for July 1991. Gender and education figures include only displaced workers. Age groups rater to the following categories; young: up to 29, prime working age: 30 to 50, older: 50+, CSVR: All data provided by Ministry of labour, Prague and are for Juna 1991. Age groups refer to: up to 19, 25 to 49 and 50+ respectively. Hungary: All data provided by Centra, Statistical Office except education by National Labour Market Centre and are for June 1991. Age groups are as follows: up to 25, 26 to 55 and 56+ respectively. Poland: All data provided by the Central Statistical Office and are for June 1991. Age groups are as follows: up to 24, 25 to 44 and 46+ respectively. Romania: All data provided by the Ministry of Labour and are for June 1991 except skill level and education breakdowns which have been provided by the National Commission for Statistics (NCS) and age which is a calculation based on statistics.

Finally it should be stressed that unemployment rates vary widely from region to region within each country. Data provided in the country report on Poland suggest that unemployment is mainly a regional problem. Most of the unemployed are concentrated in certain regions or towns — e.g., the highly industrialised areas of Katowice and Lodz or the agricultural areas of the north-east — and unemployment rates are in some districts up to five times as high as the national average. There is also some evidence that the regional disparities in unemployment rates is gradually increasing, largely because of the strong geographical concentration of some of the sectors that experience large job losses as industrial restructuring proceeds.

Unfortunately, these trends in unemployment can only be expected to continue. There are no signs of a forthcoming recovery in economic activity, yet employment must still adjust fully to the large falls in output of 1990 and the first half of 1991. While waiting for future developments, many managers of firms seem to have so far confined themselves to reducing the number of shifts, introducing short-time working arrangements, and shutting production lines, without implementing large-scale lay-offs. With continuing restructuring of the larger state-run enterprises and their eventual privatisation, there will be a further wave of job losses. There is evidence that the number of bankruptcies is growing rapidly and that there could be a considerable delay before expansion in the fledgling private sector is sufficient to compensate.

It follows that the rise in unemployment is likely to become one of the — if not the — most important policy issues in central and eastern Europe in the coming months. This makes it all the more important to assess the progress made in introducing and implementing measures to combat unemployment and assessing overall labour market policies in each country.

Labour market policies in central and eastern Europe

Labour market policies have an essential role to play in the context of rapidly rising unemployment. Measures to improve the mobility of workers from shrinking to expanding sectors and give them appropriate qualifications are required in order to prevent the spread of long-term unemployment, which has proved so difficult to eradicate in OECD countries. Effective income support schemes are also needed to protect the most vulnerable groups and to avoid the erosion of social support for transition policies.

The policy response to the growth of unemployment in central and eastern Europe has been seen in the introduction of labour market policy instruments of a type that have been, although not always successfully, applied in the West. The speed with which most of the economies in transition have introduced new labour market regulations is quite striking. New laws have been enacted that took OECD countries decades to develop. The willingness to activate a full range of policy instruments indicates that policy-makers in central and eastern Europe have learnt an important lesson from Western experience, namely that to combat unemployment a diversified set of policy measures is required.

However, it must be said that at the moment CEECs lack an infrastructure and a delivery mechanism to ensure that new regulations are actually enforced. This implementation problem is made even more difficult in transition economies by the persistent large segmentation of labour markets, which calls for a highly decentralised structure of employment services and social security centres. Moreover, budgetary restraints associated with the stabilisation process have already initiated a balancing act between public expenditure on unemployment benefits and active labour market policies.

Policies to reduce labour supply

In this section we will summarise the main findings of country reports on labour market policies in CEECs that have taken place since the start of the current wave of reforms.

As a response to rising unemployment some eastern European countries have introduced measures to reduce labour supply. Efforts so far have concentrated mainly on older workers, whose participation rates, although decreasing, are still quite high by Western standards in many CEECs.[2] "Pensioner workers", i.e., those who collect both pensions and wages, represent between 8 and 12 per cent of total employment in most countries in the region. Bulgaria, for example, has pursued a vigorous policy to remove these workers from the labour market by imposing a high tax penalty on those employers who retain pensioners. Czechoslovakia is planning to introduce a policy under which workers are eligible for either wages or pensions, but not both.

Early retirement has been used in some countries, but the number of participants given this option is relatively small because it tends to be a very expensive policy tool. However, there seem to be two areas where subsidised early retirement may be advisable: in the case of large-scale lay-offs or enterprise closures (such a scheme is in operation in Hungary), and in cases where the long-term unemployed are close to retirement age (examples include Czechoslovakia and Hungary).

In addition to targeting older workers, there are several other policy options. For example, the labour supply of young workers may be reduced by increasing the age of compulsory schooling and expanding educational opportunities, especially in those countries, such as Poland, where rigid ceilings were imposed on the number of university enrolments. This could both reduce the short-term labour supply and improve its long-term quality. Furthermore, governments can discourage people from holding multiple jobs, initiate a reduction in weekly working time, or encourage part-time work (not widely used in eastern Europe).

Employment services

Major efforts are under way in all CEECs to build up and extend a network of local employment offices. This is needed for facilitating labour mobility, registering of the unemployed and paying benefits. A rough comparison with European OECD countries reveals a sizeable gap in the development of the public employment services. The total number of staff of a country's working-age population is typically about 7 to 14 officers per 10,000 working-age people in western Europe, but between 1 and 2 officers per 10,000 working-age people in eastern Europe, a level comparable with Portugal and Turkey. Even this comparison is invalid, because the staff of employment offices are less experienced in eastern Europe than their counterparts in low-income OECD countries. Another indication of the need to expand further the employment services is the small number of staff compared with the total number of jobless. At the beginning of 1991, each staff member is facing an average of 150 unemployed job-seekers in Hungary, 210 in Poland and almost 300 in Bulgaria. Great efforts are needed to accelerate the introduction of modern information technology (computerised vacancies and job-seekers' registers) and to improve the skills of employment service staff.

A major difficulty for the public employment services in eastern Europe is that it has to develop its technical and human capacities in different directions at the same time. First, in periods of structural adjustment, the primary objective should be to provide a wide range of basic placement-related services for the maximum number of clients.[3] This would facilitate structural change through a permanent reallocation of labour from declining to expanding industries. However, as discussed in previous sections, there is a danger that a high level of unemployment will be combined with long-term unemployment. Hence, the second task for the public employment services is to develop special measures tailored to the needs of the long-term unemployed and other disadvantaged groups, such as job-search courses and intensified counselling.

Third, the public employment services should operate as a delivery system for labour market policy. It is relatively easy to import an employment scheme from the West. But implementing, running, evaluating and, if necessary, adjusting a labour market programme to the changing circumstances require experience and expertise, the very things employment offices most lack. For this reason, many of the programmes CEECs imported and implemented in a rush over the past two years have proved to be inefficient or have failed. Policy-makers should give priority to easily managed schemes as they have a better chance of success than more complex programmes.

Fourth, the public employment services have to develop special services to deal with mass lay-offs, as large-scale redundancies and plant closures are expected to become more frequent in the coming months and years, (judging from the experience of those countries that first embarked on a wide-ranging liberalisation process).[4]

Training policies

In periods of economic restructuring, training programmes should be at the heart of labour market policy, because workers in declining industries are losing not only their jobs, but very often their skills as well; without training or retraining many will remain unemployed while the growth of new industries could be hampered by skill shortages. However, training efforts for the unemployed so far have been very modest. To give an example, in 1990 only 10,300 unemployed people participated in retraining programmes in Poland, i.e., less than 1 per cent of the 1.1 million registered unemployed at the end of the year. In Hungary about 7000 unemployed people participated in retraining courses, that is, 8.7 per cent of the total number of registered unemployed in December 1990. In May 1991, the proportion of the unemployed attending retraining courses was only 0.4 per cent in Czechoslovakia and 3.9 per cent in Bulgaria. The number of participants who had completed a course was probably significantly lower than the above figures. In Hungary, for example, the share of those dropping out was almost 20 per cent in 1990. Unfortunately no information is available on the proportion of ex-trainees finding jobs. Similarly, little is known about how many participants would have obtained work even without training, how long they have remained in their jobs and whether they have displaced other job-seekers in finding work.

Training to promote the employment of disadvantaged groups, such as young people, the long-term unemployed, ethnic minorities, and the disabled, is still at an experimental stage. In Romania a special programme was recently put forward to assist the reintegration of Gypsies into the labour market, while in Hungary training programmes for the long-term unemployed and unemployed refugees are going to be set up; in Poland the need to retrain the long-term unemployed and young jobless people is particularly emphasised. In general, the small number of participants in training programmes indicates that much more effort needs to be taken to develop labour market training in CEECs.

It is imperative that the problems encountered by the vocational training system also be addressed. The school-based vocational training system is rigid because specialisation is relatively strong in most countries. It seems appropriate to reorient the training system towards more broadly-based, transferable skills.

There are worrying signs that the traditional system of enterprise-based training is disintegrating in CEECs. Many large industrial enterprises, in response to financial difficulties, have cut training schemes considerably or shut down their training facilities altogether. At the same time, developing small enterprises need training for their workers but cannot afford to maintain training facilities. Assisting skills formation in small enterprises will be among the primary labour market policy challenges over the next few years.

Subsidised employment

While labour market training activity has been moderate, various forms of subsidised employment are showing a significant increase. Some countries have resorted to "bridging" policies. These measures attempt to stabilise or raise employment through subsidies. Examples include subsidised short-time working or paid leave to prevent lay-offs and subsidised public work programmes to create temporary job opportunities for the unemployed.

Subsidised short-time working and extended paid leave have been used, for example, in Hungary and Romania, (in the latter case affecting about 2.4 per cent of total employment). These measures, by delaying lay-offs, provide an opportunity for both labour market authorities and workers to be better prepared to accommodate redundancies. However, such measures should be used with caution because they tend to slow down economic adjustment and absorb a large part of limited resources.

Public works schemes were introduced in Hungary in 1987, in Poland in 1990, and in Czechoslovakia in 1991. The programmes can be regarded as useful in that they offer earning opportunities for those unemployed who are not eligible for benefits. A temporary employment opportunity may also help to reduce the risk of some long-term unemployed people becoming alienated from the life of work. However, the programmes are not effective in reintegrating unemployed people into the economic mainstream. In so far as they generally involve relatively unskilled jobs with low pay and little long-term potential, public works programmes are often stigmatised and tend to undermine rather than improve workers' chances of finding a stable job. Although more costly in the short-term, schemes that combine training with work experience may be more successful.

The largest efforts to promote regular employment for the unemployed have been taken by Hungary and Poland. The two major programmes are: financial support both to existing enterprises to create new jobs, and to unemployed people to start their own business. A programme in Hungary, which was in operation between 1988 and 1990, offered enterprises preferential loans or, in some cases, grants, tied to investments for job creation in regions with surplus of labour. According to official reports, the number of jobs created by this programme amounted to 10,463 in 1988 and 1989, and 2,694 in the first three quarters of 1990. At the end of 1990 this programme was dropped because the reliability of these data and the effectiveness of the programme itself were very doubtful. A scheme recently introduced provides recruitment subsidies to enterprises to promote employment for unemployed school leavers and the long-term unemployed. In Poland enterprises can receive special credits in order to create new jobs for the unemployed. Under this scheme 27,900 loans were granted to enterprises in 1990.

In 1990, the number of participants in programmes offering financial support for the unemployed to start their own enterprises was almost 30,000 in Hungary and 32,400 in Poland. A proper evaluation of these schemes would need detailed statistical information and careful analysis. It appears, however, that the success of the programmes depends largely on an appropriate training component and close co-operation between labour market authorities, financial institutions and the local business community. The Hungarian Government recently reshaped its programme, shifting the emphasis away from generous financial assistance towards training.

Regional policies

As shown in the previous section, there have been severe regional imbalances developing within CEECs. These trends towards greater regional differentials in unemployment rates have important policy implications. There is a growing need for a decentralisation of labour market policies to meet the needs of highly differentiated local labour markets. It is important that decentralised policies are not narrowly conceived and do not deal only with one aspect of a complex problem.[5] It seems, therefore, that more serious consideration should be given to development of local labour market adjustment strategies, consisting of a co-ordinated package of labour market, social and industrial development policies devoted to the specific needs of areas particularly affected by restructuring.

The profile of labour market budgets in CEECs: some final remarks

The development of labour market institutions and programmes, and the provision of unemployment compensation, need adequate resources. As a percentage of GDP, Hungary and Poland spent roughly 0.5 per cent of GDP on labour market policies and unemployment compensation in 1990. In 1991 the total spending for labour market measures is expected to reach between 1 and 2 per cent of GDP in Czechoslovakia, Hungary, Poland and Romania, and probably below 1 per cent in Bulgaria. In relative terms, a labour market budget which represents between 1 and 2 per cent of GDP corresponds to spending in Austria, Norway and Italy. Yet it is certainly not sufficient in CEECs because basic labour market institutions and policies need to be developed in a period of rapidly growing unemployment.

A key question is therefore: Where will additional resources for labour market policy come from? Increasing public expenditure is hardly an option in the current recession, with large external debt and public sector deficits. A movement towards self-financing is a likely development, though increasing contributions from employers and employees may meet with resistance as the share in total labour costs of social security provisions is already higher than in most OECD countries. Savings in some areas, such as subsidies to industry, might provide some further resources. In some countries privatisation gives unique short-term opportunities for innovative labour and social policy; part of the funds from privatisation could, in fact, be used to finance employment policy.

Expenditure on the main programme categories, as a percentage of the total labour market budget, reflect labour market trends and government priorities within the range of available policy options. Data reveal certain similarities and differences between the countries. A common feature, for example, is that training and retraining have played a very moderate role in labour market policy in the initial phase of transition. Money spent for training, in terms of the labour market budget, was 11 per cent in Hungary, 2.3 per cent in Poland, and less than 1 per cent in Bulgaria in 1990.

In Romania, most resources have so far been channelled to maintain the level of employment through extended paid leave. Hungary spent about 43 per cent of its employment budget on job creation, and Poland 32 per cent. Unemployment compensation accounted for 35 per cent of total expenditure in Hungary, 51 per cent in Poland and almost 83 per cent in Bulgaria. As unemployment keeps growing, expenditure tends to shift increasingly towards income maintenance. In the coming years, given the potential growth of unemployment and the constraints on state budgets, governments throughout central and eastern Europe will have to face the dilemma of how to improve labour market efficiency without cutting income maintenance provisions.

The trade-off imposed by expenditure reducing policies between active and passive labour market measures suggests that a closer co-ordination of human resource policies is required. Otherwise, increasing competition between the departments dealing with social security, unemployment and job placement for ever-scarcer resources could result in major inefficiencies and a wastage of resources.

A greater co-ordination in policy-making requires improvements in the consensus-building process. A lack or even an imperfect representation of interests of specific social groups and consequent social unrest can lead to additional pressure for policy segmentation. Another condition for improving co-ordination in decision-making is the harmonisation of the administration and delivery mechanisms for human resource policies. There is much scope, in this context, for improving horizontal links between decentralised bodies acting in different areas of human resources, and for shifting from a branch-oriented to a problem-oriented approach in preparing and implementing new legislation.

Finally, the achievement of more consistency in policy-making also involves the relation between macroeconomic stabilisation policies and human resource policies. A more careful assessment of the social implications of stabilisation packages is therefore warranted.

Notes

1. Needless to say, these projections should only be considered as broad indicators of future population trends as they were produced before the most recent wave of reforms and so, for example, make no allowance for a possible increase in migration from East to West.

2. There are remarkable differences in participation rates of older workers across CEECs. The participation rates for men and women aged 65 and over are, for example, particularly high in Poland (32.5 and 19 per cent respectively in 1988), whilst they are low in Hungary (3.9 and 3.2 per cent in 1980) even relative to OECD countries.

3. It is worth mentioning that public employment services do not have a monopoly power in CEECs as private placement agencies are tolerated. The law requires employers to inform the public employment services of vacancies in Bulgaria, Czechoslovakia and Romania, but not in Hungary and Poland.

4. In Poland, for example, the share in total unemployment of workers dismissed via group lay-offs has steadily increased reaching almost 20 per cent in June 1991 from 4 per cent in January 1991.

5. A narrowly targeted programme designed to manage local crisis situations is likely to fail. Such a negative example is analysed in detail in Nagy and Sziraczki (1991).

Labour market policies for economic restructuring

by Guy Standing

Introduction

A rapporteur can set out responsibly to reflect the views and contributions of presenters and participants of papers, or he can be slightly mischievous in presenting some of his own views and ignoring those with which he disagrees. This rapporteur hopes that the participants will be tolerant if he slips into mischievous mode.

The comments will be divided into two parts: (a) a very brief review of some stylised facts on labour market problems that were raised in the discussion and that have to be addressed in the short term, and (b) a set of propositions on labour market policies and options.

Stylised facts

There were many facts established in the papers and debates during the conference. The following does not indicate the full range of issues presented, merely some of those that were relatively prominent or that seem to complement points made in the papers themselves.

(1) Labour market restructuring in most of the countries has been considerable, yet by late 1991 it had mainly taken the form of clearing of decks, that is, a process of disemployment from state enterprises. What emerged from the country reports was that Poland had moved furthest away from the old system than the other countries in the region, but that some of the other countries were fast catching up, with massive labour shedding and a shift from state to private sector production and employment. There had been huge declines in national income that would have created an even greater labour market depression had they occurred in western Europe. Yet during 1991 labour hoarding only began to shrink, indicating the pervasive labour rigidities, in which individual lay-offs had only recently been overtaken by large group lay-offs. Employment in state enterprises has fallen, after a long time-lag, as was emphasised in the introductory paper. Above all, employment was falling while unemployment was rising very rapidly.

(2) It is a time of euphemisms in labour market analysis. Massive state enterprises throughout the region are still the main source of employment, yet they are mostly insolvent. Much of the new "self-employment" has been fictional, as in Czechoslovakia, as employers shifted forms of employment to avoid taxes. Private businesses in the dissolving USSR have been called "co-operatives", and joint-stock companies called "comradeships". Establishing an appropriate conceptual and linguistic vocabulary will take time.

(3) During 1990 and 1991, serious disequilibria emerged in almost all the countries, characterised by severe regional imbalances fostering political and ethnic polarisations. Labour force fragmentations threaten to marginalise ethnic minorities and women much more than men. Thus 70 per cent of all redundancies in the ex-USSR in 1991 were women (Samorodov), as were some 61 per cent of the unemployed in Bulgaria.

(4) Changing patterns of labour supply need further analysis. Marek Gora's point that the income effect has dominated the substitution effect in Poland may be true for some groups, but a forced substitution effect (through lower *opportunity* incomes) may lower the labour supply of older workers, minorities facing barriers to new employment and those trapped psychologically and economically in regions where there has been a demise of old state-owned enterprises, in mining, heavy manufacturing and armaments production.

(5) In 1990-91, there was a cut in employment across all sectors, but not a growth in services.

(6) So-called privatisation has been taking many forms that, it seemed, had different implications for the speed and extent of job shedding, the restructuring of employment and labour relations.

(7) Labour market policies were struggling to emerge, yet as of late 1991 their growth was in reality limited, with an emphasis on employment services, and with little retraining despite the rapid disintegration of enterprise-level training schemes.

Fourteen propositions on labour market policies

From the discussion, one might derive certain propositions about the role of labour market policies in the economic restructuring process. The following 14 points seem consistent with the discussions and papers presented at the conference.

(1) Labour market policies can make a difference in the speed and success of industrial restructuring, both in raising productivity and in reducing the short-term hardships and longer-term problems of social neglect.

(2) Labour market policies must be integral parts of industrial and macroeconomic policy. This is a message that the Conference wished to stress to ministries of finance and the international financial institutions. Without labour policies designed to help in managing the restructuring of labour markets, the risk of social discord, labour market segmentation and social marginalisation of disadvantaged groups will be considerable. In particular, labour regulations and institution-building assistance can help in limiting unemployment and the dislocation costs associated with industrial restructuring.

(3) A tripartite approach to labour market policy offers the best prospect, because adjustment based on social consensus derived from "adversarial" negotiations paradoxically offers the best prospect of being legitimised and efficient, in turn because the social costs and benefits — the externalities — are more likely to be taken into account that way.

This should include the establishment of tripartite machinery at the national level, the community level and the industrial enterprise level, whereby measures to *prepare* enterprises, communities and individual workers for the shock and opportunities of change should be developed. This set of considerations raises the issue of industrial democracy, which could be seen as an integral aspect of labour market policy.

A current difficulty in central and eastern Europe is that identifying appropriate "social partners" is complicated by the fact that in certain countries the traditional trade union body remains strong but lacks legitimacy, while the Chambers of Commerce are still monolithic, as in Hungary. According to one speaker, the national chamber there will probably decline to the point of representing about 40 per cent of all enterprises. Similarly, for tripartite labour market policy mechanisms to function effectively, an integrated national structure must exist, yet local groups have been destroyed over the past forty years. Creating such collective structures will be a major task for the national union and employer/management bodies.

(4) Labour market policy should take account of a basic point of distributive justice, which Lane Kirkland stressed in his characteristically forthright way and which one might call the *jam principle*. Policies that deliberately make people worse off today in the uncertain prospect that workers or their successors might be better off in some distant tomorrow should be treated prima facie with suspicion. This can be called the jam principle because both the old communist regimes and certain influential economic gurus now peddling their ideas seem to adhere to what the White Queen said in *Through the Looking Glass*:

"The rule is jam tomorrow, and jam yesterday — but never jam today."

As Igor Tomes said in his typically moderate tone, "No reform is good if it involves substantial social sacrifice." Of course, some policies do require some groups to sacrifice welfare for the benefit of others. Yet such policies should be questioned.

(5) The legal framework for labour market policies should be flexible, in the sense of encouraging local diversity and initiative, while meeting national standards of decency and social solidarity.

This proposition combines what seemed to be the essence of remarks made by Juhanni Lonnroth and Lane Kirkland in a floor intervention. *Decentralisation* is needed because big central government is likely to be bureaucratic, sluggish, directive and so on; *centralisation* is needed to ensure that competition does not emerge in a general lowering of standards in the long-term interest of powerful social groups.

National-level initiatives should include the establishment of labour codes, labour market policy objectives and mechanisms for integrating groups displaced or disadvantaged in the emerging labour markets. National legislation should be directed at creating public authorities and providing for the emergence of private complementary institutions. One can only agree that full employment cannot be enacted at the national level. Finally, unemployment benefit systems must be established on a national level; Lane Kirkland reminded the conference that the flaw of the United States system of unemployment insurance derived from the fact that it was left to the individual State, which competed for investment by restricting benefits and reducing employer contributions. Such problems were less likely if national structures and procedures were established.

(6) The objectives of any labour market policy should be clear and explicit, as should be the criteria for monitoring and evaluating them. Such policies should pass what one might call, somewhat whimsically, the STEP test — Simplicity, Transparency, Equity and Productivity. Are they simple enough to administer and understand? Are they transparent enough so as to be legitimised? Are they equitable in protecting employment rights in general *and* in distributive terms, protecting and enhancing the interests of special groups while allowing individual responsibility to develop.

(7) The generation of labour market information should be directly linked to policy development. There is a clear need for systematic labour market data, as Marek Gora stressed. Many policy recommendations are based on assertions backed by repetition, which may or may not be true.

Thus, for example, it is very commonly claimed that labour market training is needed on a massive scale because marketable skills are lacking. How is that known? Similarly, it is widely claimed that employment services are desperately needed to reduce frictional unemployment. However, perhaps other equally effective networks exist. This is not to state that such networks do exist or that less training is desirable, merely that such claims are usually a matter of opinion.

(8) Groups needing highest priority will vary from country to country, and the labour policy mix should reflect that. Those facing growing disadvantages as a direct result of the restructuring clearly deserve highest priority in the labour market policy mix.

Thus, in Hungary and Bulgaria ageing labour forces should incline the authorities to policies of retraining, possibly on the job to prepare for transition to other types of work, and to policies to facilitate flexible retirement and partial labour force participation, as voluntary options. In that context, one might worry about the tendency to force pension age workers to have to choose between taking a pension or a wage. As stated in the introductory paper, there is a need for policies to enable older workers to contribute through productive activities and to avoid discrimination against them as overall unemployment rises.

One of the worst fears of the restructuring is that workers with particular handicaps may be severely affected by loss of employment, income and social role. As Igor Tomes noted for Czechoslovakia, such were the problems of handicapped workers that special measures were essential, including tax breaks to encourage their employment, and some form of quota system.

(9) There should be no discrimination on the basis of gender in labour market policy. However, the principle of priority for disadvantaged groups means that in many countries women as workers deserve special priority. David Stanton was surely correct in arguing that assisting women to become or remain labour force participants is one of the most effective ways of alleviating poverty.

In this regard, labour market policy should include measures to curtail wage discrimination. Policies to facilitate work sharing, intermittent labour force participation and part-time working — the latter being particularly underutilised in central and eastern Europe — should all be encouraged, although they should not be regarded as the *only* options or as the *only* alternative to labour force withdrawal.

The paper presented by Hedwig Rudolph suggested employment quotas for women as a way of preventing their marginalisation in the process of restructuring. However, quotas run into familiar objections, which must be recognised in policy design.

More generally, for labour market policy to serve women effectively, it is essential to combine general programmes that treat men and women equally with special projects to serve the direct interests of women workers to counter discriminatory barriers. In that regard, one would like to commend the project of Liba Paukert and her colleagues in Czechoslovakia directed at helping women to set up as entrepreneurs or to take up other new economic activities.

It is also encouraging, as noted by Steven Pursey, that FRATIA, CS-KOS and SOLIDARNOSC are setting up women's sections that could lobby for more effective enterprise and government labour policies for women. In that regard, there was an interesting document circulated at the conference by the ICFTU.

Finally, it is worth drawing attention to an insidious form of discrimination that labour market policy should attempt to combat, that is, the design of job classifications for tariff or job evaluation purposes. The danger of sex bias there remains strong and could be reduced by explicit attention to the factors that tend to produce it.

(10) Labour market policy should stimulate the creation *and* the survival *and* the growth of small-scale productive enterprises. For these three complementary conditions to be met, packages of credit, training and marketing assistance must be provided. It will be vital to treat small and larger enterprises *equally* in the system, so that, as David Stanton remarked, the small-scale firms do not face barriers to market entry and do not become locked in a low-income milieu with persistently low survival probabilities.

For effective small-enterprise creation, new agencies must be set up or expanded, and should include a role for trade unions and employer organisations to advise and assist in the implementation of good practices, not just in setting up but in expanding their activities. A lesson of the 1980s from western Europe is that assistance in survival and growth is just as important as assistance in setting up new firms.

(11) Public works schemes may be useful for those unemployed or partially unemployed who are not eligible for conventional unemployment benefits, *but* they should be voluntary. They should also pay adequately, so as to minimise substitution effects.

(12) In the process of privatisation and the move to a market economy, part of the proceeds of sell-offs should be set aside for labour market policy, perhaps put into special labour market restructuring funds to be administered by a genuinely tripartite body.

It is worth recording that the issue of privatisation was raised as a labour market issue by various speakers, including Kari Tapiola in connection with the Baltic states' trade unions' fears of speculative privatisation without formal rules and regulations. In general, national standards must conform to international labour standards.

(13) In restructuring, it is crucial that due attention is given to the overall *combination* of labour market policies, so that policies are complementary to each other and that the appropriate priorities are properly addressed. One must agree with a remark made by David Fretwell when he said that identifying the *intention* of a policy is crucial. As for complementarity, if, for example, retraining policies are not consistent with job-creation schemes, then they will almost certainly fail and could create barriers to their evolution.

It may seem unremarkable, but in developing labour market policy combinations, the following objectives have to be merged:

i) Raising productivity in current jobs and sectors;

ii) Raising the labour force's potential productivity for new jobs, and for desired and anticipated forms of work;

iii) Moderating the pace of labour market restructuring, particularly important in the context of the desired shrinkage of the very large state enterprises that have occupied the industrial landscape of CEECs.

iv) Accelerating labour market restructuring, in helping to create new skills, attitudes, opportunities and information;

v) Improving distributive justice, in reducing labour market inequalities, assisting disadvantaged groups and helping in the labour market integration of groups hitherto left out of the economic mainstream.

vi) Reducing regional imbalances and helping to limit the growth of regional disparities that seriously threaten almost all the countries of the region.

14) Labour market policies must be *integrated* with forms of income support for the optimum policy approach. It is impossible to have effective labour market policies unless there is effective income support and as much labour security as feasible.

There is no evidence to support the proposition made by several speakers that income support programmes draw resources away from "active" measures. With no income support there is no possibility of integrating people into the labour market. Above all, a fundamental principle of welfare economics should be respected: a policy that permits freedom of choice is to be preferred to one that limits freedom of choice. A worker — any of us — cannot learn to be responsible unless he or she has the opportunity to develop that capacity, and any paternalistic decision by government on what is the right behaviour for individual workers should be treated with considerable reservation. Labour market policy should create opportunities and positive incentives, not rely on the threat of deprival of basic subsistence. The voluntaristic principle means relying on a combination of relatively liberal conditions for entitlement to basic income support with free and equal access to labour market policies for social and economic reintegration. In that context, a primary task of labour market and social policy in the restructuring process is surely to enable ordinary citizens to recover their sense of social and personal responsibility.

Social protection

by Georg Fischer

The first period of the transition process poses large social problems which require comprehensive policy responses. This follows from the introductory presentations by Julia Szalai and Irena Kotowska, as well as from the country reports.

The decline in economic activity has led to a corresponding decline in incomes through a fall in real wages; real benefits also fell but probably less than wages. While declining employment reduced household incomes, the effects of unemployment will become much more significant in 1992. In addition, price liberalisation and inflation have to be considered; low income workers are unlikely to obtain adequate compensation for rising inflation — therefore, this group will suffer most from inflation. Similarly, job losses and large-scale unemployment will be concentrated on households with incomes below average. In addition their consumption structure is more likely to be affected by price increases. To summarise, average incomes in the countries in transition are declining, and it is likely that households with incomes below average will be more affected by the overall decline.

This is the background against which social protection policies have to be developed. However, one should not overlook the fact that poverty related to the labour market has always existed in the former communist countries and that poverty in urban households with children was already rising throughout the 1980s, a point stressed by Julia Szalai. These trends have accelerated since 1989. Although there are differences between the countries in the groups most affected, child poverty seems to be widespread, and the position of ethnic minorities vulnerable.

While the economies in transition share fundamental social policy challenges, they differ in social and economic structures and traditions. Caution is therefore required when drawing overall conclusions on social policy design. The governments in the CEECs all see a clear need for social protection policies and the citizens of these countries seem prepared to accept that certain cuts in real incomes are inevitable during the first phase of transition. With this background, the conference examined social protection policy experiences in the economies in transition and in western industrialised countries. The following eleven points are an attempt to summarise the conclusions of a very rich and lively debate following presentations by experts and senior policy-makers from OECD and central and eastern European countries.

1. CEECs developed systems of social protection and social services which focused around the enterprise and were often administered by the official trade unions. This constituted an important difference for policy design, as observed by Louise Fox, from the situation in other countries with similar income levels. These systems have proved inadequate for certain groups in the recent past (for example, the emerging problem of child poverty in the 1980s). Fundamental reforms are now required for the transition towards a market economy and democracy. Colin Gillion's review of transition measures suggests that all the countries have now either adopted or drafted fundamental legislation on social protection. Views differed, however, among participants on the urgency of fully implementing the new systems or whether governments should concentrate on providing short-term social protection measures to cope with the immediate problems.

2. The scenario of experiences in OECD countries has to be viewed from very different levels of economic wealth than those in the CEECs. The question arises as to whether experiences with social security systems in the western industrialised countries can be helpful for policy design in economies with much lower income levels and if so, how? However, some central European participants stressed that CEECs have much in common with western Europe (cultural and educational structures, social and political traditions, in particular with regard to the labour movement) and experiences in a modified form may still be important.

3. Although OECD countries are "rich", they have not been able to establish systems which provide effective help for all those suffering from labour market or other forms of poverty. In particular, measures to protect incomes are not effective when unemployment is high and of long duration. Therefore participants from OECD countries, among them Anthony Atkinson, proposed that effective social protection to prevent and alleviate poverty cannot depend solely on the provision of income maintenance measures for those already without employment or in other precarious circumstances, but must be based on economic policies which promote employment and the creation of new employment opportunities.

4. This corresponds with a more general point which was raised in all sessions of the conference: the following quotation from one of the trade union representatives from a CEEC reflects this point quite clearly: "Not all the pressures should be on the side of social policies". Social policies must be developed as part of the overall transition strategy and not be viewed as a remedial instrument to take care of the social problems emerging from restructuring.

5. The need for linking social protection and employment promotion was seen as particularly important when discussing the situation of women. It would be unwise to hope that income protection policies alone could compensate women for the loss of employment. The high labour force participation rates provide a good chance to avoid major female poverty but only if female employment rates remain high. This is by no means certain as discrimination against women in the old employment system was strong (low incomes, no career prospects) and women are heavily affected by lay-offs resulting from restructuring. Encouraging women to stay in employment and involving them in new activities is essential for successful anti-poverty strategies. Specific mechanisms to monitor and promote women's interests were recommended for introduction into government and public administration.

6. Many years of state socialism have created a feeling of dependency on the State which makes it difficult for many individuals to take the initiative required to change their situation. This problem was emphasised by many participants from CEECs. This has a dual significance for social policy design: income protection policies need to encourage initiative and reintegration, and have to provide a framework in which the individual can take initiative and search for a solution to his or her employment problem. (Igor Tomes used the term "trampoline effect" of social policies). In this context, the provision of income security is an important precondition for job search, training or preparation for self-employment.

7. Experience in OECD countries suggests caution concerning the concept of a "Social safety net" as the main response to the transition problems, a point made by Anthony Atkinson. The existing social assistance schemes tend to have large holes and often provide insufficient levels of income protection. Therefore the meeting did not recommend putting all the emphasis on one single social protection scheme. Rather, a mix of different measures is more likely to meet the needs in the transition period, as Istvan Kakuszi, Deputy Secretary in the Ministry of Social Welfare, observed.

8. Many participants, however, for example Colin Gillion, recommended that social policy measures should not be sophisticated. Given the great demand, the underdeveloped social administrations and the rapidly changing situation, fairly simple criteria for eligibility and duration may be advisable. Some felt that this strategy should also apply for benefits and suggested flat-rate benefits; others thought that benefit levels must reflect previous earnings and work experience. On this point, it would seem that the only conclusion to be drawn from the discussion is that each country will have to find its own balance: between on the one hand providing social protection in a complex society requiring a diversified system and on the other the need for measures to support large numbers but with very limited administrative capacity.

9. An additional aspect in this discussion is the need for transparency, necessary to maintain general support for protection measures (given the experiences in the previous system).

10. Transparency is also an important feature in the development of future social administrations. Transparency for the local community and sensible implementation of policies require a decentralised system based on local administrations. However, most participants agreed on the need for general standards of social protection for each country.

11. The question of financing occupied many participants. Enterprises are already heavily burdened with social security payments, a point stressed by Peter Szirmai. Declining economic activity in the last two years makes policy design very difficult. More generally, the debate on financing reflects the dilemma of transitional social policies. While on the one hand, major redistributional measures may be opposed by those who have gained in economic restructuring and are seen as an important source for innovation and job creation, on the other, it is difficult to foresee how, without such measures, income protection and social security could be guaranteed for those who are in immediate need of support. Failure to provide social protection may lead to major social unrest and even endanger some of the achievements of the reform process so far. Two ideas for facilitating the financing problem were suggested: first, public funds could be rechannelled from subsidising state enterprises to social and labour market policies; and

second, Western assistance could contribute to easing the financing of such policies during the first period of transition.

Two proposals for direct follow-up emerged in the discussion.

1) More analytical and comparative work should be carried out on the social implications of restructuring strategies and on social protection measures. Liberalisation of housing and of rent controls is an example for such an analysis. It was agreed that this would be an urgent issue for which analytical support would be welcome. Such work would have to assess the positive effects on the supply side (more and improved housing) against the economic and fiscal effects of necessary increases in wages and benefits. Strong interest was also expressed in work on the design of social protection schemes. More specifically, co-operation on the evaluation of the newly introduced social policy measures was suggested.

2) Clearly, the financing of social security systems requires more attention and work. A crucial point must be the analysis of the various possibilities for rechannelling funds within the wider issue of external financing.

Wage formation, income policies, industrial relations and social consensus

by Peter Scherer

Introduction

This session had two main themes: wage developments and prospects, and industrial relations issues. Inevitably, these were interconnected: wage developments have evolved simultaneously with the reformation of industrial relations institutions, while the development of industrial relations has been driven, in part, by the need to accommodate the declines in aggregate output (and hence the capacity to maintain real wages) which has characterised all CEECs over the last year.

The main themes of the discussion were succinctly introduced by Marek Gora, who observed that the wage system is often expected to satisfy three, often contradictory aims: stabilise, restructure and protect the population.

However, as Jeffrey Schafer observed, it is bad practice to try to assign more than one goal to one policy instrument. It is hardly surprising that the allocation of these goals to the wage structure exposes it to contradictory pressures. Nonetheless, the three provide a useful framework for discussion.

Stabilisation

In most countries of eastern Europe, policy-makers have attempted to stabilise wage inflation by a form of tax-based incomes policy which prescribes confiscatory taxes for increases in the wage bill above a given level. These policies have been, in a sense, dependent on the state enterprise structure now being phased out. Under the former regimes, the policies were ineffective in the face of aggregate inflation pressures. They did not so much repress inflation as act as a further device for transferring real resources away from wage and salary earners, thereby reducing their real incomes (especially in the USSR). Evidence that this transfer was an implicit (hidden) aim is that these policies do not apply to the private sector nor to joint ventures with foreign enterprises. All

273

commentators at the conference regarded incomes policies of this sort as, at best, short- or medium-term expedients, although several who were concerned with macroeconomic stabilisation issues regarded them as essential for the immediate future.

It was observed that such policies, if apparently successful, may be so accidentally: for example, in Poland wage fund growth in the crucial first half of 1990 was *less* than would have been allowed under the policy. That is, for reasons which are not fully understood, enterprise managers and workers implemented or at least accepted an even sharper fall in real wage levels than the policy prescribed. However, by now (September 1991) the policy is under heavy pressure, and does not appear to be holding wage fund increases to the prescribed levels.

Several speakers, particularly some trade union spokesmen, suggested that it may be time to move from reliance on coercive measures to negotiated wage moderation policies, based on union leadership. The strongest endorsement of such an approach came from Catalin Zamfir, who argued that in Romania (and elsewhere) the unions have gained legitimacy by adopting a philosophy of tripartism and responsibility. Contact with Western unions, and specifically the seminars and training courses which ETUC/ICFTU have conducted in most CEECs (and for which support from OECD governments was urged), has been important in generating this outlook. In Hungary, the FSZDL is ready to accept short-term economic losses in return for long-term representation rights, and ETUC suggested that such union-led moderation might be a more appropriate vehicle than statutory requirements for achieving stabilisation over the next few years. This will clearly be the case if wage moderation is to extend to the private sector and to foreign enterprises, as these are currently excluded from statutory instruments. Not all participants were optimistic about the prospects for wage moderation: Robert Flanagan and Jeffrey Shafer were sceptical about the viability of contracts that imply lower real wages.

One particular issue here is the attitude of foreign enterprises. Maria Lado, in her contribution to the Hungary country paper, and Paul Forgacs of FSZDL, both claimed that some foreign investment in that country is aimed at exploiting low labour costs and inexpensive social provisions. This led to calls for the OECD/ILO guidelines on multinational enterprises to be applied by such concerns. If unions have to combat what they perceive as exploitative practice by militant campaigns, they will be less able, and perhaps less willing, to support general wage moderation. To avoid such tension, also developing in privatised undertakings, participants suggested that the privatisation process should not be confined simply to attaching value to physical assets but also to take account of the input of employees.

Most participants felt that in the long run it was only through the establishment of sound bargaining relationships that long-term stability would be achievable. However, there was disagreement on whether employers were adequately structured for bargaining. At one stage, ETUC suggested that it apparently would have to help financially in organising employer bodies! Private sector employers expressed the view that they were not sufficiently involved in the negotiating processes — particularly in Poland, where they now account for 20 per cent of employment. It was important to be flexible and to include the private sector while continuing to involve the public sector. Seminars on experience in tripartite negotiations, suggested by György Szapary of the IMF, may well be one way to help the process develop. It was pointed out in the discussion that in developing these contacts, the issue of the monopolisation of ILO representation by the successors to former "official" unions will need to be addressed.

Restructuring

Wage structures in most countries are still based on the tariff schedules established under central planning. Attempts at reform of the wage situation in isolation have often been counter-productive. In the case of the ex-USSR, Tatyana Tchetvernina's account shows that the attempts under *perestroika* to bring the wage structure more in line with contributions to production (by enhancing material incentives and returns to skills) have achieved little. These attempts have not elicited a supply response of increased output but have instead led to claims on the wage fund which have generated inflationary pressures and further demands for pay rises from unskilled workers.

There seemed to be general agreement that these inherited wage structures were unsatisfactory and should be changed. However, as the Soviet experience shows, this change needs to be guided by demand-side signals as to where the comparative advantage lies. At the moment, these are only evident in the private sector and the shadow economy where they are distorted (and hidden) by tax avoidance.

There were differences of views on the desirability of using the adjustment of the price system to reset wage ratios. Leonid Gordon suggested that the current hyperinflation had its positive aspects: it could be the occasion for a general realignment of the wage structure. Opponents of incomes policies called for the immediate freeing of the wage structure so that wage ratios could reflect relative advantage. Others considered that the need to control wage-induced price escalation precluded this. However, even those who supported the use of incomes policies as a temporary stabilisation instrument acknowledged that they preserved distortions in the wage structure.

It was generally recognised that more needed to be done to make managements responsive to relative cost pressures, so that they would start to negotiate wage structures with a view to maximising the cost effectiveness of their enterprises or their administrative units. Once this was achieved, bargaining arrangements could be put in place. Speakers on the union side argued that it was wrong to delay the implementation of collective bargaining until privatisation had been implemented.

Protection

A particular issue which evoked heated debate was the contribution which the wage structure might make to protecting the population from adverse economic impact, and in particular the role of minimum wages in this process. Reviewing Western market economies' experiences, Robert Flanagan and Jeffrey Shafer both observed that minimum wages seemed to have had little macroeconomic impact — they had not affected enough of the workforce to make a significant difference to the wage bill — and they were most significant in countries where unions were weak, such as France and the United States. However, to the extent that they were effective they tended to protect those who remained in employment at the cost of a drastic *increase* in inequality due to their effect in pushing others out of the labour market altogether.

This view was challenged on two grounds. One was empirical. Using experience in the United States, Lane Kirkland argued that, in fact, the employment impact of minimum wage increases had been minimal, and that periods during which the real value of the minimum wage had been allowed to fall had seen no employment response. The other ground was more absolute. Ray Marshall argued that wages which fall below the cost of meeting minimal living standards imply a subsidy by those workers to their employers, and on public policy grounds such employment should not be allowed.

There may have been some confusion here. As Colin Gillion's paper shows, statutory minimum wages in many CEECs are often far below average earnings, and, in fact, mainly serve as a benchmark for the social safety net. They may therefore have less employment impact — and offer less protection — than many of the protagonists in this debate realised.

In the particular case of Czechoslovakia, Igor Tomes observed that wages are important to both social and economic policy, and that, therefore, in the transition process government regulation of lower and upper limits for wage developments was needed, though this should be co-ordinated through bipartite and tripartite negotiations.

Conclusions

Two proposals were made in the discussion as to how industrial relations processes might contribute to the task of restructuring:

- Currently the framework for macro-stabilisation packages is often negotiated narrowly between the IMF and finance ministries. Several participants suggested that it would be helpful to involve the social partners in this process, especially if acquiescence in a reduction in aggregate real wages is necessary for the success of the package.

- To facilitate this process, the ILO and the OECD might envisage sponsoring seminars on tripartite negotiations and interchanges. These seminars should cover informal as well as formal methods for reaching consensus, and the ways in which the goals of anti-inflationary incomes policies might best be achieved.

A trade union perspective

by Lane Kirkland

Our task at this conference is to lay the groundwork for co-operation between the ILO and the OECD on matters affecting central and eastern Europe, so that those involved in the process of economic transition in the region will have the opportunity to draw on the expertise in labour matters of the one, and the unique analytical ability of the other.

It is important that we succeed, for the problems of work and the situation of working people are critical to that process.

Understanding and confronting those problems in a humane way is also crucial to the ultimate victory of democracy and the establishment of a decent civil society in the former totalitarian States.

Economic policies and regimens cannot be carried out in a vacuum. Real people have to live under them. And we should make it our responsibility to ensure that those who impose these economic programmes have some understanding of what the working people of central and eastern Europe have been through over the past half-century — lest everything they have accomplished in recent years fall to ruin.

They should know about the nightmarish features of totalitarianism and how the governments of these countries used employment as a means of compulsion.

They should be made to grasp the utter despair of a system designed to convert working people into nothing more than bolts in a machine — the injustice, the indignity, the lack of opportunity for self-betterment, the absence of hope.

Most important, they should be made to understand the dangers in merely replacing one misguided utopia with another.

I am talking about the proposition that the collapse of communism is the victory of capitalism and the final vindication of raw market theory.

Millions upon millions have found out, in the hardest way and in gruelling detail, exactly what is wrong with communism. It is up to those who cherish democracy to do what we can to see that they do not now proceed to discover what is wrong with the jungle of the unregulated market-place.

Both have something elemental in common. Both can atomise society by reducing humans to the level of isolated survivors. Both can be lethal to the institutions of civil society that make life tolerable to ordinary people. They are not so much opposites as mirror images.

Don't get me wrong. I have nothing against capital or markets as such — so long as they do not become the golden calves of idolatry. Trade unions emerged from them, learned to live with them and become the instruments through which they are humanised.

But they do have dangerous shortcomings. Markets have no names, no faces and they cannot be elected to or removed from office. They do not know the difference between employment and exploitation. They do not clean up after themselves, and they do not naturally promote the ideals of humanity and community.

Markets dispense many values, but not justice — except in the sense noted many years ago, on his deathbed, by an old gunfighter of the American West, Bat Masterson. He is reputed to have said :

There are those who maintain that, in this old world of ours, everybody gets about the same break in life, and that may be true. I have observed, for example, that everybody gets about the same amount of ice. The rich get it in the summertime, and the poor get it in the winter.

Yet there are those utopians out there who, from the comfort of their own regulated and semi-socialised economies, seem to relish the idea of imposing some sort of grand experiment in free market ideology on the newly emerging democracies.

In the United States, the closest thing we have had to such an experiment was the period that immediately preceded the Great Depression of the 1930s, and it seems to me that our friends in central and eastern Europe have as much to learn from this period in our history as from any other.

It was a time when markets ruled, and whatever business wanted, it got. It had command of the state, for all practical political purposes. And there was no impediment to its electrifying the countryside, or paving the highways, or reforesting the stripped and despoiled forests of our country, or providing comfort to the poor and afflicted, for that matter.

But in fact it would not do those things and had no intention of doing them. It took the New Deal to do them. And the policies that emerged from the New Deal — in which government designed a social safety net and set out to repair the damage, ameliorate the harshness, restrain the abuses, and balance the deficiencies of the market-place — are what set the stage for the greatest and most balanced period of growth and prosperity in the economic history of any nation.

These policies — which included a minimum wage, social security and the right of workers to join trade unions — were based on the proposition that everybody ought to be both a producer and a consumer, and that mass markets are what build and sustain a first-rate economy.

Most important, they helped fulfil the democratic promise that ultimate power should reside not in capital or centralised government — not in pure individualism or coercive collectivism — but rather in communities of people exercising their rights to free association in order to express their common aspirations.

This is how both States and markets are civilised. That, and not business licence, is what working people have fought and died for — in Budapest in 1956, in Gdansk in 1970, and in Tiananmen Square in 1989. And it is why workers have taken to the streets to defend democracy in the former USSR.

Clearly, in central and eastern Europe, there needs to be a major withdrawal of the State from economic management to its area of competence.

But it is equally important that it not withdraw beyond its area of competence and responsibility. The extent of that withdrawal ought to be determined not by dogmatists, as was the overwhelming extension of state power, but by democratic debate and decision.

Western institutions should see to it that this critical transition period includes the best possible co-ordination, with equal standing, between social and economic policies. Social initiatives that serve as little more than afterthoughts to the ravages of market economics will not avert the protracted chaos we must avoid.

We hear all the time the complaint that the working people of central and eastern Europe are unwilling to make the sacrifices necessary to bring them into the modern industrial era.

That brings to mind memories of the tremendous sacrifices Western European workers accepted at the time of the Marshall Plan. They did it because the Marshall Plan itself explicitly aimed, as part and parcel of economic recovery, to restore their ability to defend their own interests and because hope was kept alive by the perception of concrete improvement as the post-war reconstruction proceeded.

Had anyone tried to persuade them that things must get worse for them in order to get better eventually, they might have refused. They might have accepted the overtures of Stalin and succumbed to the lure of the workers' utopia through communist totalitarianism.

Yet this is precisely the message that the workers of the former communist dictatorships are receiving today — at home, from the Western democracies, and from the elites of international finance.

Let me point out that the message is Leninist. The idea that, for the future to be better, something must be made worse to begin with, is just another form of "revolutionary defeatism", or of Lenin's dogma that dictatorship is the necessary prelude to the universal realm of freedom. That is the doctrine that drives the relentless pursuit of utopia — whether it is undertaken by the right or left or by free-market liberals. In any case, it is a dehumanising, anti-democratic and dangerous exercise, and it is in everyone's best interest to steer clear of it.

We must certainly remind ourselves that societies and States are raised among men to serve, not the faceless market-place, but the aspirations of real people. If we do not, the end of one cold war may simply herald the dawn of another, this time between the people and the agents and instruments of another form of ruinous zealotry.

Thank you.

An employer's perspective

by Heribert Schmidt-Dorrenbach

Even before the recent changes which occurred in central and eastern Europe in early summer 1989, delegations of managers from the USSR, Hungary and Poland were travelling to western Europe to find out about the system and the functioning of a free-market economy. Our colleagues from central and eastern Europe expressed their interest in a market economy and their desire to live the way we do, with shops packed with merchandise, the possibility of choosing a profession and a job with the opportunity to negotiate the terms and conditions of employment. We, in turn, pointed out that the desired effect could not be achieved just by introducing a few changes here and there while retaining the main features of a centrally planned economy. It was clear that the entire economic system would have to be turned upside down in order to achieve the economic standards of the West. And it was equally clear that this would lead to substantial complications in the labour market and in social policies.

More than two years have elapsed and, today, we are experiencing the enormous problems associated with the transition from a centrally planned economy to a market economy. Moreover, there are many questions to which we still have not found the right answers. Obviously, our compatriots in the new German *Länder* are, in many respects, better off than our other eastern neighbours since they can directly profit from West German structures, its know-how and financial strength. But even there surmounting the weaknesses left over from forty years of socialism will be extremely difficult.

In analysing the situation, we have come to recognise that in the plants and operations of central and eastern Europe, each job was filled by at least two employees to maintain the fiction of full employment in the socialist system. We now see that this was a situation of concealed unemployment. From the point of view of economic efficiency, it is essential for the number of jobs in the plants and operations to be trimmed to an economically efficient level. This is absolutely necessary for survival in international competition and to attract foreign investment. Unfortunately, the only way out of the predicament is through the dismissal of a large number of employees. On the other hand, we can see areas of business, such as the construction industry, the craft trades, and the service industry, where the number of newly created jobs is already gradually exceeding the jobs which have been lost.

Yet we cannot simply accept a situation in which so many people are suddenly jobless and thus unable to earn their living. It is a responsibility we all must face — governments, trade unions and employers. And we do not want to escape this responsibility. BIAC is prepared to co-operate with the OECD and other organisations and bodies to find solutions to the problems facing us.

One important aspect is the introduction of a social insurance system and a properly functioning system of unemployment benefits, which requires raising corresponding funds. In the Western industrialised countries it is common practice for employers to participate in raising funds for unemployment insurance. We can only hope that the economies in central and eastern Europe will develop in such a way that employers will be in a position to contribute their share. Until then, the governments responsible — assisted by the West — must see to it that the funds for unemployment insurance are available.

It is often suggested that unemployed people should be given work which is in the public interest. Examples of such jobs would be tearing down outdated production plants no longer fit for modernisation, measures to counteract environmental pollution, modernising housing, investment designed to enhance the tourist infrastructure, and many similar projects. Irrespective of the fact that such measures would again require substantial funds, from the point of view of the employers, such jobs which are not supported by a free-market process would only be of temporary and limited benefit. Temporary for as long as the normal economic cycle is not properly functioning, and limited because it is evident that a complete economy cannot function in such a way within our market economy system.

From BIAC's point of view, a far more productive line of action would be to ensure the proper qualification of the employees, and especially of those presently unemployed. This would permit them to become re-integrated into the economy. The orientation towards new areas of employment is particularly important. It is essential that we respond to the opportunities opened up by new technologies in production and administration. We have to put special emphasis on these aspects since in the future only enterprises and employees who fulfil these prerequisites will remain competitive.

This is where the West can help, especially by providing the required know-how. It is not enough simply to hand out vast sums of money. In this case, know-how is more important than cash. There is an immense shortage of knowledge and qualifications, not only in the field of new technologies, but also as far as the basics of business management are concerned. I am thinking of marketing, sales, finance and accounting, purchasing, logistics and personnel management skills. Tens of thousands of managers are needed and we have just recently called for a major transfer of managers and experts. To co-operate in a responsible manner in moving the enterprises in the East into a free-market environment should represent a special challenge for young managers in the industrialised countries of the West.

You are all well aware that we need an efficient and independent system for freely negotiating wages and work conditions between management and labour as this is an important element of a market economy. Trade unions must therefore be free and independent of the state and be more than simple institutions administering vacation, vacancies and similar social measures — as was formerly the case in the planned economies of eastern Europe. The same applies to the employers' federations. In order to build up functioning organisations we need people who can independently negotiate work conditions based on the efficiency of the company and the social responsibilities. We certainly do not need factory directors accustomed to accepting directives from above. Clearly, experience and know-how from the West are required in order to establish constructive labour/management relations in the countries accustomed to centrally-planned economies.

List of conference participants

Adams, A. van	Senior Economist, Education and Employment Division, Population and Human Resources Department, World Bank, Washington, DC.
Alexander, T.	Directorate for Social Affairs, Manpower and Education, OECD, Paris.
Alldredge, M.	Regional Human Resource Manager, 3M Europe s.a., Brussels.
Alonso-Gamo, P.	Economics and Statistics Department, OECD, Paris.
Atkinson, A.	Suntory-Toyota, Centre for Economics and Related Disciplines, London School of Economics and Political Science, London.
Barroso, J.	Minister of Labour and Social Security, Spain.
Bartolomei, H.	Social Security Department, ILO, Geneva.
Barton, P.	AFK-CIO European Office, Paris.
Bäumer, W.	Counsellor, German Delegation to OECD.
Beattie, R.	Social Security Department, ILO, Geneva.
Becker, F.	International Economist, Bureau of European and Canadian Affairs, US Department of State, Washington, DC.
Bejenaru, C.	Director, Ministry of Labour and Social Protection, Bucharest.
Boeri, T.	Directorate for Social Affairs, Manpower and Education, OECD, Paris.
Boni, M.	Minister of Labour and Social Policy, Warsaw.
Boot, P.A.	Ministry of Social Affairs and Employment, The Hague.
Borthwick, D.	Ambassador, Australian Delegation to OECD.
Botsch, A.	Assistant Secretary-General, Trade Union Advisory Committee, Paris.
Brannen, P.	Department of Employment, London.
Brodeur, Y.	First Secretary, Canadian Delegation to OECD.
Brulard, R.	Counsellor, Delegation of Belgium to OECD.
Castillo, C.N.	Assistant Director-General of Social Security Economic Planning, Ministry of Labour and Social Security, Spain.
Chaloupek, G.	Chamber of Labour, Vienna.
Clatanoff, W.	Assistant Director of the Office for Foreign Relations, Department of Labor, Washington, DC.
Colacios, I.	Counsellor, Spanish Delegation to OECD.

Coney, N.	Confederation of British Industry (CBI), London.
Damen, C.	Bureau for Workers Activities, ILO, Geneva.
De Hullu, F.	Ministry of Social Affairs and Employment, The Hague.
De Vries Reilingh, O.	Director, Regional Office for Europe, ILO, Geneva.
Dell'Aringa, C.	Ministry of Labour and Social Welfare, Milan.
Dilova, S.	Institute of Sociology, Bulgarian Academy of Sciences, Sofia.
Elder, D.C.	Minister-Counsellor, Deputy Permanent Representative, Canadian Delegation to OECD.
Etcheverria, J.	Chargé de Mission pour les Affaires Internationales, Ministère du Travail, de l'Emploi et de la Formation Professionnelle, Paris.
Evans, J.	Secretary-General, Trade Union Advisory Committee, Paris.
Fallon, J.	Assistant Principal, Department of Labour, Dublin.
Fischer, G.	Directorate for Social Affairs, Manpower and Education, OECD, Paris.
Flanagan, R.	Graduate School of Business, University of Stanford, California.
Flemming, J.	Chief Economist, EBRD, London.
Forgacs, P.	President, Democratic League of Independent Trade Unions (FSZDL), Budapest.
Fox, L.	Senior Economist, Human Resources Operations Division, Central and East European Departments, The World Bank, Washington, DC.
Fretwell, D.	Training and Employment Specialist, Technical Department, Europe, Middle East and North Africa Regional Office, The World Bank, Washington, DC.
Friel, R.	Manpower, Education and Agricultural Affairs Advisor, American Delegation to OECD.
Fuziwara, K.	Division of International Labour Affairs, Labour Ministry, Tokyo.
Garonna, P.	Deputy Director SME, Directorate for Social Affairs, Manpower and Education, OECD, Paris.
Gaspar, M.-L.	Assistant Director-General of Council for Planning, Ministry of Labour, Portugal.
Gillion, C.	Director, Social Security Department, ILO, Geneva.
Gimpelson, V.	Institute of the International Labour Movement, USSR Academy of Sciences, Moscow.
Gommers, P.	Director, Employment, Industrial Relations and Social Affairs, European Economic Community, Brussels.
Góra, M.	Centre of Economic Performance, London School of Economics, London.
Gordon, L.	Institute of the International Labour Movement, USSR Academy of Sciences, Moscow.
Grimsmann, J.	Deputy Head, Department for International Social Policy and the European Community, Confederation of German Employers' Associations, Köln.
Grünewald, B.	Employer Expert, Brussels.

Guinet, J.	Directorate for Science, Technology and Industry, OECD, Paris.
Gundacker, F.	Federal Ministry for Labour and Social Affairs, Vienna.
Günther, H.	Parliamentary State Secretary, Federal Ministry of Labour and Social Affairs, Bonn.
Hagen, E.	Labour Market Policy Department, Federal Ministry of Labour and Social Affairs, Bonn.
Hansenne, M.	Director-General, ILO, Geneva.
Havie, H.	Deputy Director General, Ministry of Labour and Government Administration, Oslo.
Heeres, G.J.	Director, Head of Industrial Relations, Hoogovens Imuiden, Netherlands.
Hellbrunn, A.	Representative of the Vatican.
Hempel, F.	International Department, Federal Ministry of Labour and Social Affairs, Bonn.
Highland, C.	Directorate for Financial, Fiscal and Enterprise Affairs, OECD, Paris.
Hiramatsu, K.	First Secretary, Trade, Delegation of Japan to OECD.
Hoffman, J.	Conseiller Economique, Administration de l'Emploi, Luxembourg.
Hofmann, K.	General Policy Department, Federal Ministry of Labour and Social Affairs, Bonn.
Hönekopp, E.	Institute for Labour Market Research, Nürnberg.
Inal, M.A.	Labour Counsellor, Turkish Delegation to OECD.
Julien, E.	Adjoint au Directeur des Questions Sociales Européennes Internationales, Conseil National du Patronat Français, France.
Kahn, M.	CEDUCCEE, Paris.
Kakuszi, I.	Under-Secretary of State, Ministry of Welfare, Budapest.
Karoly, G.	International Department, National Confederation of Hungarian Trade Unions (MSZOSZ), Budapest.
Karpísek, Z.	Senior Officer, Employment Department, Federal Ministry of Labour and Social Affairs, Prague.
Kauppinen, T.	Manpower Service Division, Ministry of Labour, Helsinki.
Keogh, K.	Counsellor, Australian Delegation to OECD.
Kirkland, L.	President, AFL-CIO, Trade Union Advisory Committee, Washington, DC.
Kootstra, L.	Ministry of Social Affairs and Employment, The Hague.
Kosmarsky, V.	Head of Laboratory of the Institute of Problems of Employment, Moscow.
Kotowska, I.	Institute of Statistics and Demography, Central School of Planning and Statistics, Warsaw.
Kóvac, R.	President, Czech and Slovak Confederation of Trade Unions (CS-KOS), Prague.
Kreuzaler, E.	Labour Market Policy Department, Federal Ministry of Labour and Social Affairs, Bonn.

Kux, J.	Federal Statistical Office, Social Statistics Division, Prague.
Lado, M.	Institute of Labour Research, Ministry of Labour, Budapest.
Laurent, Père P.	Representative of the Vatican.
Leirpoll, A.	Adviser, Ministry of Labour and Government Administration, Oslo.
Lemke, G.	International Adviser, Danish Confederation of Trade Unions (LO-Denmark), Copenhagen.
Lönnroth, J.	Ministry of Labour, Helsinki.
Mackiejcyzyk, A.	Confederation of Polish Employers, Warsaw.
Maier, H.	Deputy Director-General, ILO, Geneva.
Manuelyan, Mme.	Services des Affaires Internationales, Union des Industries Métallurgiques et Minières (UIMM), France.
Marchandise, T.	ILO Turin Centre.
Marrese, M.	Economics and Statistics Department, OECD, Paris.
Marshall, R.	Lyndon B. Johnson School of Public Affairs, University of Texas at Austin, USA.
Martins, A.	Counsellor, Manpower and Social Affairs, Delegation of Portugal to OECD.
Matsuura, H.	First Secretary, Manpower and Social Affairs, Delegation of Japan to OECD.
McClelland, S.	Assistant Secretary-General, Trade Union Advisory Committee, Paris.
Meyer, K.	Ambassador, German Delegation to OECD. Von Kunow, P. Counsellor, German Delegation to OECD.
Michaud, Y.	Secretary General, BIAC, Paris.
Miller, P.	Federal Minister of Labour and Social Affairs, Prague.
Millich, F.	Principal Administrative Officer, Population, Employment and Migration Division, Council of Europe, Strasbourg.
Milocheva, T.	Collaboratrice, Institute of Scientific Research, Department of Employment, Sofia.
Mink, G.	CNRS, Paris.
Mitchkovsky, A.	Invited Expert, Sofia.
Molhova, S.	Expert, Department of Employment, Sofia.
Morley, J.	Chief of Unit, Employment, Industrial Relations and Social Affairs, European Economic Community, Brussels.
Murray, K.	Department of Employment, London.
Nagy, K.	Department of International Programmes, Ministry of Labour, Budapest.
Neacsu, A.	Director-General, Ministry of Labour and Social Protection, Bucharest.
Nesporova, A.	Institute for Forecasting, Academy of Sciences, Prague.
Nishizawa, H.	Saitama University, Tokyo.
Norregaard, J.	Directorate for Financial, Fiscal and Enterprise Affairs, OECD, Paris.

Paty, J.	Assistant to the Deputy Under-Secretary for International Affairs, Department of Labor, Washington, DC.
Paukert, L.	Employment and Development Department, ILO, Geneva.
Paye, J.-C.	Secretary-General, OECD, Paris.
Pearce, S.	Directorate for Social Affairs, Manpower and Education, OECD, Paris.
Pursey, S.	Head of the Economic and Social Policy Department, International Confederation of Free Trade Unions (ICFTU), Brussels.
Raboaca, G.	Director, Institute for Labour Research, Bucharest.
Rand, T.	Officer, Secretary-General's Office, EFTA, Geneva.
Retournard, J.-F.	Bureau for Employers Activities, ILO, Geneva.
Rohner, K.	Chef de Section, Office Fédérale de l'Industrie des Arts et Métiers et du Travail, Berne.
Roux, H.	Chargé de Mission pour les Affaires Internationales, Ministère du Travail, de l'Emploi et de la Formation Professionnelle, Paris.
Rudolph, H.	Director, Research Area, Labour Market and Employment, Science Centre, Berlin.
Rulewski, J.	Vice President, International Office, NSZZ Solidarnosc, Gdansk.
Rupp, K.	Senior Economist, Department of Health and Human Services, Department of Labor, Washington, DC.
Samorodov, A.	Employment and Development Department, ILO, Geneva.
Sananès, H.	Conseiller Technique, Ministère du Travail, Paris.
Sands, D.	Assistant Director-General of FAS, Department of Labour, Dublin.
Schafer, J.	Deputy Director, Economics and Statistics Department, OECD, Paris.
Scherer, P.	Head of Social Affairs and Industrial Relations Divison, Directorate for Social Affairs, Manpower and Education, OECD, Paris.
Schmidt-Dorrenbach, H.	Henkel KgaA, Langenfeld, Germany.
Schöpp-Schilling, H.B.	Director General, Federal Ministry for Women and Youth, Bonn.
Schwanse, P.	Head of Manpower Policies, Directorate for Social Affairs, Manpower and Education, OECD, Paris.
Simpson, W.	Director, Industrial Relations and Labour Administration Department, ILO, Geneva.
Sohlman, A.	Assistant Under-Secretary, Ministry of Labour, Stockholm.
Standing, G.	Coordinator of Labour Market Research, Employment and Development Department, ILO, Geneva.
Stanton, D.	Department of Employment, London.
Stechova, D.	International Secretariat, (CS-KOS), Prague.
Steinbach, G.	General Director, Federal Ministry for Labour and Social Affairs, Vienna.
Stylianou, O.	Bureau de Planification, Cyprus.
Szalai, J.	Institute of Sociology, Hungarian Academy of Sciences, Budapest.
Szapary, G.	National Bank of Hungary, Budapest.

Sziraczki, G.	Employment and Development Department, ILO, Geneva.
Szirmai, P.	Co-President, National Association of Entrepreneurs (VOSZ), Budapest.
Szurek, J.C.	CNRS, Paris.
Tapiola, K.	International Secretary, Central Organisation of Finnish Trade Unions (SAK), Helsinki.
Tarnowski, J.	International Office, NSZZ Solidarnosc, Gdansk.
Tasaka, O.	First Secretary, Social Affairs, Delegation of Japan to OECD.
Tchetvernina, T.	Institute of Economics, USSR Academy of Sciences, Moscow.
Tomes, I.	Charles University, Prague.
Välimäki, K.	Ministry of Social Affairs and Health, Finland.
Vinde, P.	Deputy Secretary-General, OECD, Paris.
Vladimirova, K.	Director, Department of Employment, Sofia.
Ward, T.	Consultant, European Economic Community, Brussels.
Watson, P.	Counsellor, UNESCO.
Wienert-Cakim, H.	Directorate for Science, Technology and Industry, OECD, Paris.
Wozniakowski, A.	International Department, Ministry of Labour and Social Security, Warsaw.
Yadlosky, B.	Human Resources Manager, Coca-Cola Eastern GmbH, Germany.
Zahlen, J.	Conseiller de Gouvernement, Ministère du Travail, Luxembourg.
Zamfir, C.	Academia Romänä, Bucharest.
Zecchini, S.	Assistant Secretary-General of OECD, Director of the Centre for Co-operation with European Economies in Transition, Paris.
Zellhoefer, J.	Representative, American Federation of Labor and Congress of Industrial Organisations (AFL-CIO).

NEW ZEALAND
NOUVELLE-ZÉLANDE
Legislation Services
P.O. Box 12418
Thorndon, Wellington   Tel. (04) 496.5652
                                Telefax: (04) 496.5698

NORWAY – NORVÈGE
Narvesen Info Center – NIC
Bertrand Narvesens vei 2
P.O. Box 6125 Etterstad
0602 Oslo 6   Tel. (022) 57.33.00
                                Telefax: (022) 68.19.01

PAKISTAN
Mirza Book Agency
65 Shahrah Quaid-E-Azam
Lahore 54000   Tel. (42) 353.601
                                Telefax: (42) 231.730

PHILIPPINE – PHILIPPINES
International Book Center
5th Floor, Filipinas Life Bldg.
Ayala Avenue
Metro Manila   Tel. 81.96.76
                                Telex 23312 RHP PH

PORTUGAL
Livraria Portugal
Rua do Carmo 70-74
Apart. 2681
1200 Lisboa   Tel.: (01) 347.49.82/5
                                Telefax: (01) 347.02.64

SINGAPORE – SINGAPOUR
Information Publications Pte. Ltd.
41, Kallang Pudding, No. 04-03
Singapore 1334   Tel. 741.5166
                                Telefax: 742.9356

SPAIN – ESPAGNE
Mundi-Prensa Libros S.A.
Castelló 37, Apartado 1223
Madrid 28001   Tel. (91) 431.33.99
                                Telefax: (91) 575.39.98

Libreria Internacional AEDOS
Consejo de Ciento 391
08009 – Barcelona   Tel. (93) 488.30.09
                                Telefax: (93) 487.76.59

Llibreria de la Generalitat
Palau Moja
Rambla dels Estudis, 118
08002 – Barcelona
                  (Subscripcions) Tel. (93) 318.80.12
                  (Publicacions) Tel. (93) 302.67.23
                                Telefax: (93) 412.18.54

SRI LANKA
Centre for Policy Research
c/o Colombo Agencies Ltd.
No. 300-304, Galle Road
Colombo 3   Tel. (1) 574240, 573551-2
                                Telefax: (1) 575394, 510711

SWEDEN – SUÈDE
Fritzes Information Center
Box 16356
Regeringsgatan 12
106 47 Stockholm   Tel. (08) 690.90.90
                                Telefax: (08) 20.50.21

Subscription Agency/Agence d'abonnements :
Wennergren-Williams Info AB
P.O. Box 1305
171 25 Solna   Tel. (08) 705.97.50
                                Téléfax : (08) 27.00.71

SWITZERLAND – SUISSE
Maditec S.A. (Books and Periodicals - Livres
et périodiques)
Chemin des Palettes 4
Case postale 266
1020 Renens   Tel. (021) 635.08.65
                                Telefax: (021) 635.07.80

Librairie Payot S.A.
4, place Pépinet
CP 3212
1002 Lausanne   Tel. (021) 341.33.48
                                Telefax: (021) 341.33.45

Librairie Unilivres
6, rue de Candolle
1205 Genève   Tel. (022) 320.26.23
                                Telefax: (022) 329.73.18

Subscription Agency/Agence d'abonnements :
Dynapresse Marketing S.A.
38 avenue Vibert
1227 Carouge   Tel.: (022) 308.07.89
                                Telefax : (022) 308.07.99

See also – Voir aussi :
OECD Publications and Information Centre
August-Bebel-Allee 6
D-53175 Bonn 2 (Germany)   Tel. (0228) 959.120
                                Telefax: (0228) 959.12.17

TAIWAN – FORMOSE
Good Faith Worldwide Int'l. Co. Ltd.
9th Floor, No. 118, Sec. 2
Chung Hsiao E. Road
Taipei   Tel. (02) 391.7396/391.7397
                                Telefax: (02) 394.9176

THAILAND – THAÏLANDE
Suksit Siam Co. Ltd.
113, 115 Fuang Nakhon Rd.
Opp. Wat Rajbopith
Bangkok 10200   Tel. (662) 225.9531/2
                                Telefax: (662) 222.5188

TURKEY – TURQUIE
Kültür Yayinlari Is-Türk Ltd. Sti.
Atatürk Bulvari No. 191/Kat 13
Kavaklidere/Ankara   Tel. 428.11.40 Ext. 2458
Dolmabahce Cad. No. 29
Besiktas/Istanbul   Tel. 260.71.88
                                Telex: 43482B

UNITED KINGDOM – ROYAUME-UNI
HMSO
Gen. enquiries   Tel. (071) 873 0011
Postal orders only:
P.O. Box 276, London SW8 5DT
Personal Callers HMSO Bookshop
49 High Holborn, London WC1V 6HB
                                Telefax: (071) 873 8200
Branches at: Belfast, Birmingham, Bristol, Edin-
burgh, Manchester

UNITED STATES – ÉTATS-UNIS
OECD Publications and Information Centre
2001 L Street N.W., Suite 700
Washington, D.C. 20036-4910 Tel. (202) 785.6323
                                Telefax: (202) 785.0350

VENEZUELA
Libreria del Este
Avda F. Miranda 52, Aptdo. 60337
Edificio Galipán
Caracas 106   Tel. 951.1705/951.2307/951.1297
                         Telegram: Libreste Caracas

Subscription to OECD periodicals may also be
placed through main subscription agencies.

Les abonnements aux publications périodiques de
l'OCDE peuvent être souscrits auprès des
principales agences d'abonnement.

Orders and inquiries from countries where Distribu-
tors have not yet been appointed should be sent to:
OECD Publications Service, 2 rue André-Pascal,
75775 Paris Cedex 16, France.

Les commandes provenant de pays où l'OCDE n'a
pas encore désigné de distributeur devraient être
adressées à : OCDE, Service des Publications,
2, rue André-Pascal, 75775 Paris Cedex 16, France.

MAIN SALES OUTLETS OF OECD PUBLICATIONS
PRINCIPAUX POINTS DE VENTE DES PUBLICATIONS DE L'OCDE

ARGENTINA – ARGENTINE
Carlos Hirsch S.R.L.
Galería Güemes, Florida 165, 4° Piso
1333 Buenos Aires   Tel. (1) 331.1787 y 331.2391
Telefax: (1) 331.1787

AUSTRALIA – AUSTRALIE
D.A. Information Services
648 Whitehorse Road, P.O.B 163
Mitcham, Victoria 3132   Tel. (03) 873.4411
Telefax: (03) 873.5679

AUSTRIA – AUTRICHE
Gerold & Co.
Graben 31
Wien I   Tel. (0222) 533.50.14

BELGIUM – BELGIQUE
Jean De Lannoy
Avenue du Roi 202
B-1060 Bruxelles   Tel. (02) 538.51.69/538.08.41
Telefax: (02) 538.08.41

CANADA
Renouf Publishing Company Ltd.
1294 Algoma Road
Ottawa, ON K1B 3W8   Tel. (613) 741.4333
Telefax: (613) 741.5439
Stores:
61 Sparks Street
Ottawa, ON K1P 5R1   Tel. (613) 238.8985
211 Yonge Street
Toronto, ON M5B 1M4   Tel. (416) 363.3171
Telefax: (416)363.59.63

Les Éditions La Liberté Inc.
3020 Chemin Sainte-Foy
Sainte-Foy, PQ G1X 3V6   Tel. (418) 658.3763
Telefax: (418) 658.3763

Federal Publications Inc.
Suite 103, 388 King Street W
Toronto, ON M5V 1K2   Tel. (416) 581.1552
Telefax: (416) 581.1743

Les Publications Fédérales
1185 Université
Montréal, QC H3B 3A7   Tel. (514) 954.1633
Telefax : (514) 954.1635

CHINA – CHINE
China National Publications Import
Export Corporation (CNPIEC)
16 Gongti E. Road, Chaoyang District
P.O. Box 88 or 50
Beijing 100704 PR   Tel. (01) 506.6688
Telefax: (01) 506.3101

DENMARK – DANEMARK
Munksgaard Book and Subscription Service
35, Nørre Søgade, P.O. Box 2148
DK-1016 København K   Tel. (33) 12.85.70
Telefax: (33) 12.93.87

FINLAND – FINLANDE
Akateeminen Kirjakauppa
Keskuskatu 1, P.O. Box 128
00100 Helsinki

Subscription Services/Agence d'abonnements :
P.O. Box 23
00371 Helsinki   Tel. (358 0) 12141
Telefax: (358 0) 121.4450

FRANCE
OECD/OCDE
Mail Orders/Commandes par correspondance:
2, rue André-Pascal
75775 Paris Cedex 16   Tel. (33-1) 45.24.82.00
Telefax: (33-1) 45.24.81.76   or (33-1) 45.24.85.00
Telex: 640048 OCDE

OECD Bookshop/Librairie de l'OCDE :
33, rue Octave-Feuillet
75016 Paris   Tel. (33-1) 45.24.81.67
(33-1) 45.24.81.81
Documentation Française
29, quai Voltaire
75007 Paris   Tel. 40.15.70.00
Gibert Jeune (Droit-Économie)
6, place Saint-Michel
75006 Paris   Tel. 43.25.91.19
Librairie du Commerce International
10, avenue d'Iéna
75016 Paris   Tel. 40.73.34.60
Librairie Dunod
Université Paris-Dauphine
Place du Maréchal de Lattre de Tassigny
75016 Paris   Tel. (1) 44.05.40.13
Librairie Lavoisier
11, rue Lavoisier
75008 Paris   Tel. 42.65.39.95
Librairie L.G.D.J. - Montchrestien
20, rue Soufflot
75005 Paris   Tel. 46.33.89.85
Librairie des Sciences Politiques
30, rue Saint-Guillaume
75007 Paris   Tel. 45.48.36.02
P.U.F.
49, boulevard Saint-Michel
75005 Paris   Tel. 43.25.83.40
Librairie de l'Université
12a, rue Nazareth
13100 Aix-en-Provence   Tel. (16) 42.26.18.08
Documentation Française
165, rue Garibaldi
69003 Lyon   Tel. (16) 78.63.32.23
Librairie Decitre
29, place Bellecour
69002 Lyon   Tel. (16) 72.40.54.54

GERMANY – ALLEMAGNE
OECD Publications and Information Centre
August-Bebel-Allee 6
D-53175 Bonn 2   Tel. (0228) 959.120
Telefax: (0228) 959.12.17

GREECE – GRÈCE
Librairie Kauffmann
Mavrokordatou 9
106 78 Athens   Tel. (01) 32.55.321
Telefax: (01) 36.33.967

HONG-KONG
Swindon Book Co. Ltd.
13–15 Lock Road
Kowloon, Hong Kong   Tel. 366.80.31
Telefax: 739.49.75

HUNGARY – HONGRIE
Euro Info Service
POB 1271
1464 Budapest   Tel. (1) 111.62.16
Telefax : (1) 111.60.61

ICELAND – ISLANDE
Mál Mog Menning
Laugavegi 18, Pósthólf 392
121 Reykjavik   Tel. 162.35.23

INDIA – INDE
Oxford Book and Stationery Co.
Scindia House
New Delhi 110001   Tel.(11) 331.5896/5308
Telefax: (11) 332.5993
17 Park Street
Calcutta 700016   Tel. 240832

INDONESIA – INDONÉSIE
Pdii-Lipi
P.O. Box 269/JKSMG/88
Jakarta 12790   Tel. 583467
Telex: 62 875

IRELAND – IRLANDE
TDC Publishers – Library Suppliers
12 North Frederick Street
Dublin 1   Tel. (01) 874.48.35
Telefax: (01) 874.84.16

ISRAEL
Electronic Publications only
Publications électroniques seulement
Sophist Systems Ltd.
71 Allenby Street
Tel-Aviv 65134   Tel. 3-29.00.21
Telefax: 3-29.92.39

ITALY – ITALIE
Libreria Commissionaria Sansoni
Via Duca di Calabria 1/1
50125 Firenze   Tel. (055) 64.54.15
Telefax: (055) 64.12.57
Via Bartolini 29
20155 Milano   Tel. (02) 36.50.83
Editrice e Libreria Herder
Piazza Montecitorio 120
00186 Roma   Tel. 679.46.28
Telefax: 678.47.51
Libreria Hoepli
Via Hoepli 5
20121 Milano   Tel. (02) 86.54.46
Telefax: (02) 805.28.86
Libreria Scientifica
Dott. Lucio de Biasio 'Aeiou'
Via Coronelli, 6
20146 Milano   Tel. (02) 48.95.45.52
Telefax: (02) 48.95.45.48

JAPAN – JAPON
OECD Publications and Information Centre
Landic Akasaka Building
2-3-4 Akasaka, Minato-ku
Tokyo 107   Tel. (81.3) 3586.2016
Telefax: (81.3) 3584.7929

KOREA – CORÉE
Kyobo Book Centre Co. Ltd.
P.O. Box 1658, Kwang Hwa Moon
Seoul   Tel. 730.78.91
Telefax: 735.00.30

MALAYSIA – MALAISIE
Co-operative Bookshop Ltd.
University of Malaya
P.O. Box 1127, Jalan Pantai Baru
59700 Kuala Lumpur
Malaysia   Tel. 756.5000/756.5425
Telefax: 757.3661

MEXICO – MEXIQUE
Revistas y Periodicos Internacionales S.A. de C.V.
Florencia 57 - 1004
Mexico, D.F. 06600   Tel. 207.81.00
Telefax: 208.39.79

NETHERLANDS – PAYS-BAS
SDU Uitgeverij
Christoffel Plantijnstraat 2
Postbus 20014
2500 EA's-Gravenhage   Tel. (070 3) 78.99.11
Voor bestellingen: Tel. (070 3) 78.98.80
Telefax: (070 3) 47.63.51

OECD PUBLICATIONS, 2 rue André-Pascal, 75775 PARIS CEDEX 16
PRINTED IN FRANCE
(14 93 07 1) ISBN 92-64-13990-7 - No. 46456 1993